# DISCOVERING SOCIOLOGY

# DISCOVERING SOCIOLOGY

**STUDY GUIDE** to accompany

IAN ROBERTSON

# SOCIOLOGY

**Third Edition**

**Carla B. Howery**

Worth Publishers, Inc.

**DISCOVERING SOCIOLOGY**
to accompany **Sociology,** Third Edition
by Ian Robertson

Copyright © 1987 by Worth Publishers, Inc.
All rights reserved.
Printed in the United States of America

ISBN: 0-87901-246-3
First printing, June 1987

**Worth Publishers, Inc.**
33 Irving Place
New York, New York 10003

# TO THE STUDENT

Your introduction to the discipline of sociology is bound to be a process of discovery: its concepts and theories will take you down paths of thinking that are likely to be quite new to you. By challenging you to "stand outside yourself" and to view your life as it connects with larger social forces, the sociological perspective encourages fresh insights into human society and behavior. This Study Guide, to be used together with *Sociology*, Third Edition, by Ian Robertson, is intended to aid you in the discovery of new ways of thinking about yourself and the social world.

Researchers have identified two keys to effective learning: it must be reinforced and it is enhanced if attained actively rather than passively. You learn as you listen attentively to a lecture or read a chapter in a book, but you will learn even more by applying this knowledge—thinking about it, analyzing it in terms of your own experience, writing about it. Completing the activities in this Guide will help to build and to reinforce your confidence and your comprehension.

*Discovering Sociology* reviews the important ideas in each chapter of the textbook and provides multiple ways of reinforcing and applying your knowledge. This will enhance and strengthen your understanding of sociology and help you to realize the value of sociology's insights and their relevance for your own life.

The chapters in *Discovering Sociology* correspond to those in Robertson: *Sociology*, Third Edition. Each chapter has three sections: Reviewing the Concepts, Testing the Concepts, and Applying the Concepts.

# REVIEWING THE CONCEPTS

*Learning Goals:*   You can identify topics for which your knowledge is spotty or incomplete by attempting to write short responses to each learning goal. When you have completed each goal in your own words, you will have a summary of the important points of the chapter and can use these as the basis for reviewing.

*Identifying Key Questions and Themes:*   The chapter material is organized according to the major headings used in the textbook. For each heading, there are key questions about the material. First read the heading and think about the subject matter included under that heading. Conduct a mental review of this part of the chapter. Next read the key questions and try to answer them in your own words. Then read the summary. Note that important terms are in bold and defined for your review.

*Defining Core Concepts:*   The most important concepts in the chapter are listed and space is provided for you to write a definition. Use your own words and give an illustration from your personal experience, where possible. Then refer back to the textbook chapter for the sociological definition provided there. You may want to work with a partner and check one another's definitions and illustrations. Sociological terminology, like the tools of any science, must be used precisely and accurately.

*Putting Ideas Together:*   In this section, the chapter material is summarized in a brief and sometimes visual way. After mastering the sociological concepts in each chapter, you can see how these ideas fit together, what generalizations can be made about them, and which ideas are most significant. You might try constructing additional diagrams to summarize the information in the chapter.

# TESTING THE CONCEPTS

*Multiple-Choice Questions:*   Twenty-five questions are provided to test your understanding of the chapter. Use a piece of paper to cover the answers at the bottom of the page. After you read the question, try to answer it aloud, either to yourself or to a study partner. Then look to see whether a similar response is among the five choices di-

rectly following the question. Once you have made your selection, check the correct answer and accompanying explanation provided at the bottom of the page. Go over each of the alternatives and think about why the other four choices are incorrect. Page references are provided so that you can reread pages from the textbook whenever you do not understand why you made an error.

*A Case Study:*   Multiple-choice questions test one kind of knowledge. Case studies, like essay questions, provide a broader test of your powers of comprehension and analysis. In this section, the situation presented requires sociological analysis. If you can supply clear and cogent answers, and if they are verified by your instructor, your learning has gone well beyond rote memorization. The result is a deeper and more enduring understanding of the topic. In addition, the type of thinking that will be required to complete these case studies will be useful long after your sociology course is over. As you read the newspaper or study another academic subject, the powers of comprehension and analysis that you have gained will add depth to your knowledge.

# APPLYING THE CONCEPTS

*Application Exercises:*   Part of the fun of sociology is discovering new things about your own life. The three application exercises ask you to look at your world from a new perspective. Your learning will be enhanced by the active participation involved in completing these assignments. You may compare notes with classmates or work in small groups.

For the Case Study and Application Exercises you can write answers directly into this Study Guide and submit the pages to your instructor. The pages are perforated for easy removal.

Your instructor may have suggestions about how to use DISCOVERING SOCIOLOGY, and you probably have your own study pattern; however, I suggest that you follow the steps listed on the next page.

**Study Checklist:** How to use the Robertson textbook and this Study Guide most effectively:

*SOCIOLOGY (Textbook)*

*DISCOVERING SOCIOLOGY (Study Guide)*

1. Read the Learning Goals

2. Read the chapter

3. Carefully read and answer the Learning Goals
4. Read Identifying Key Questions and Themes

5. Reread the chapter carefully, going over vocabulary and important points, taking notes or outlining the material as you wish.

6. Complete the Learning Goals
7. Complete the Defining Core Concepts section
8. Review Putting Ideas Together
9. Answer the Multiple-Choice Questions
10. Complete the Case Study and check it with your instructor.
11. Complete the Application Exercises; hand in exercises, as required

*Before an Exam*

1. Review text summary and list of key terms

2. Review Identifying Key Questions and Themes
3. Review Defining Core Concepts
4. Review Learning Goals
5. Practice Multiple-Choice Questions
6. Explain Putting Ideas Together in your own words

7. Review notes on the chapter

## ACKNOWLEDGMENTS

My appreciation is extended to William J. Conway, Louisiana Tech University, and Steven R. Severin, Kellogg Commnunity College, for their helpful comments and suggestions, particularly with regard to the application exercises contained in this Study Guide.

Worth Publishers is a collection of very competent, dedicated people who work together as a team with one another and with their authors. I am grateful to Linda Baron Davis for her stewardship of the supplements prior to 1987. For this edition, Patty Nankervis did an outstanding job of carefully editing the material and providing numerous suggestions that improved the final product. My thanks go to Linda and Patty and the other professionals at Worth Publishers who have helped to make my work a pleasure.

I hope this Guide will help you to discover sociology as you successfully complete your course and that the methods you have learned and the new perspectives gained will serve you well long afterwards. The author and publisher would welcome any thoughts you have about this Guide and how it might be improved.

*June 1987*                                                      Carla  Howery

# CONTENTS

# UNIT 1

# Introduction to Sociology

# CHAPTER 1

# Sociology: A New Look at a Familiar World

## Reviewing the Concepts

### LEARNING GOALS

*After studying this chapter, you should be able to:*

1. Define sociology and explain the basic insight of sociology.

2. Explain the meaning and the importance of the "sociological imagination."

3. State the assumptions of the scientific method and indicate how scientific generalizations are derived and used.

4. Compare the two branches of science — natural science and social science.

5.  Contrast social science and common sense as two ways of knowing about the social world.

6.  Briefly outline the subject matter of the five social sciences.

7.  List the historical factors that contributed to the development of sociology as a separate field of study.

8.  Describe Comte's basic vision of sociology and his contributions to the field.

9.  Contrast the views that Comte, Spencer, and Marx held regarding society and the role of the sociologist.

10. Identify two major contributions that Durkheim and Weber made to early sociology.

11. Specify key trends in sociology in the United States during the 1920s, the 1940s, and the 1960s.

12. Define theory and its place in sociology.

13. List the assumptions of functionalist theory and identify three sociologists who have used that perspective.

14. Describe the focus of conflict theory; contrast conflict theory with functionalism; and identify three sociologists who have used the conflict perspective.

15. Identify the key ideas behind interactionist theory and list three sociologists who have used that perspective; describe the basic difference between the interactionist perspective and the conflict and functionalist perspectives.

16. Explain why objectivity is a problem for sociologists and how sociologists attempt to maintain objectivity.

## IDENTIFYING KEY QUESTIONS AND THEMES

### Sociology as a Perspective

*What is sociology? What do sociologists study and how do they study it?*

*Sociology* is the scientific study of human society and social behavior. The basic insight of sociology is that human behavior is largely shaped by the groups to which people belong and by the *social interaction* that takes place within those groups. The focus of sociology, then, is on the group rather than on the individual. Much of the excitement of sociology comes from mentally stepping outside one's everyday life and looking at it as an outsider. The "sociological imagination" is C. Wright Mills's term to describe a vivid awareness of the connection between private experience and larger social forces.

### What is Science?

*Is sociology a science? What are the assumptions and goals of science?*

*Science* refers to the logical, systematic methods by

which knowledge is obtained and to the actual body of knowledge produced by these methods. Sociology is one of the *social sciences,* because its focus is on human beings and their activities rather than on biological, chemical, or physical phenomena, the subject matter of the *natural sciences.* All science assumes there are patterns in the social and natural world that are sufficiently regular for us to be able to make *generalizations*—statements that apply to most cases of the same type. Scientific disciplines seek to explain what happens in their respective domains and to make predictions about similar circumstances in the future. The use of logical and reliable methods by many scientists makes it possible to base new research on past results, so that understanding of any topic can grow over time. In some cases, the findings contradict existing assumptions or common sense, spurring further inquiry.

## Sociology as a Science

*What are the challenges sociology faces as a science? What are the goals of the scientific work done by sociologists?*

Sociologists pose questions about the social world and pursue these questions using the scientific method. Sociology is less advanced than the natural sciences for two reasons: (1) the scientific method has been used to study human behavior only in recent times; (2) human behavior is exceedingly complex and variable.

## The Social Sciences

*What are the social sciences? How are they related?*

The social sciences are a related group of disciplines that study various aspects of human behavior. The major disciplines are economics, psychology, political science, anthropology, and sociology. Each discipline has a slightly different focus, but they overlap in their commitment to the scientific method, the use of some common terms and concepts, and the relevance of their scientific data and generalizations. *Social psychology,* the study of how personality and behavior are influenced by the social context, and *cultural anthropology,* the study of the ways of life of other peoples, often through the use of an *ethnography,* may be of particular interest to sociologists.

## The Development of Sociology

*How did the discipline of sociology begin? Who were some of the important early sociologists and how did their contributions shape the field?*

It was Auguste Comte who coined the term "sociology" and argued for the scientific study of social behavior. He and other early social thinkers living in the mid-1800s were committed to the study of social life in order to gain an understanding of social processes. They observed the massive changes associated with the Industrial Revolution, the development of the natural sciences, and the increased exposure to radically different societies brought about by European colonialism. Comte's contributions to the field include the concepts of "social statics" and "social dynamics," which refer to those social forces promoting stability and those promoting change. Herbert Spencer investigated the evolution of society over time and the interrelationship of societal units. One of the most important social thinkers, Karl Marx, pointed to the social change that would occur from class conflict. He emphasized the fundamental influence that a society's economic arrangement had on virtually all other areas of the society. Emile Durkheim used statistics on suicide to show that suicide rates vary consistently from one group to another, thereby pointing up the connection between the individual and larger forces. His work demonstrated the importance of data as a basis for making reliable conclusions. The scientific methods of sociology were enhanced by the work of Max Weber, who argued for *value-freedom,* as opposed to *value judgment,* in studying society.

While early European sociologists emphasized large social forces and the problems of social order and social change, the concerns of American sociologists were somewhat different. Sociology began to flourish in the United States in the early 1900s. Until about 1940, "Chicago School" sociologists dominated the discipline, placing a great deal of importance on social reform. From the 1940s to the early 1960s, sociologists concentrated on improving research methodology and developing theories that applied to smaller, more specific problems. Currently, sociology in the United States is a very diverse field, still drawing heavily on the ideas and the commitment to science of the early founders. Many sociologists continue to work as teachers and researchers in colleges and universities. Others are employed in the public and private sectors in such fields as criminology, city planning, personnel management, and journalism.

## Theoretical Perspectives

*What is sociological theory? How is it used in sociological work?*

A *theory* is an organized set of ideas about a topic that predicts relationships. Sociologists seek to develop theories about social phenomena. In sociology, there are three major *theoretical perspectives,* or ways of thinking about the social world.

The *functionalist perspective* focuses on the processes of order and stability. It sees society as having a *structure*—a set of interrelated parts; each of these parts has a *function*—a consequence for the whole system. Functionalists look at the consequences of a given element in the social system to see how it functions. They classify these outcomes in terms of *manifest functions* (consequences that are obvious and intended), *latent functions* (consequences that are unrecognized and unintended), or *dysfunctions* (negative consequences that may disrupt the social system).

The *conflict perspective* focuses on the social processes of tension and competition, and the change that results from them. Karl Marx emphasized conflict between social classes, other conflict theorists have enlarged the perspective to include conflict among many groups and interests. Conflict may have beneficial as well as destructive results.

The *interactionist perspective* focuses on the way in which people act toward, respond to, and influence one another. As opposed to the other two perspectives, which concern themselves with large structures, the interactionist perspective views society as the product of the many encounters between human beings in everyday social activity. The most widely used interactionist approach is that of *symbolic interaction*—the interaction that takes place between people through *symbols*—anything that can meaningfully represent something else; examples include gestures, shared rules, and spoken and written language. As meanings assigned to situations and behaviors are interpreted and redefined through social interaction, social realities are constantly negotiated.

Each of these three perspectives is useful to contemporary sociologists. While their approaches to the social world differ, the viewpoints are not incompatible.

## The Problem of Objectivity

*Why is objectivity important? How do sociologists work to maintain objectivity?*

Human beings tend to see the world from a viewpoint of *subjectivity.* Consequently, *objectivity,* as a requirement of the scientific method, is crucial to reducing the confounding effects of personal *bias*—the tendency, often unconscious, to interpret facts according to one's own values. Sociologists, like anyone else, have their own feelings, opinions, and preferences. Particularly since they deal with issues of deep human and moral concern, sociologists have questioned their ability to remain objective. To ensure as much objectivity as possible, sociologists state their personal biases, try to control them, and submit their work and all their procedures to the scrutiny of their colleagues.

## DEFINING CORE CONCEPTS

*After studying the chapter, write a sociological definition in your own words for the following core concepts. Then give an example from your own experience to illustrate your definition. Refer to the chapter to check your work.*

| *Core Concept* | *Sociological Definition* | *Personal Illustration* |
|---|---|---|
| dysfunction | A negative consequence that may disrupt the social system. | |
| function | A positive consequence for a whole social system. | |
| latent function | An unrecognized and unintended consequence of some element in a social system. | |
| manifest function | An obvious an intended consequence of some element in a social system. | |
| sociology | The scientific study of human society and social behavior. | |
| symbolic interaction | The interaction between people that takes place through such symbols as signs, gestures, and language. | |
| theoretical perspective | A broad assumption about society and social behavior that provides a point-of-view for the study of specific problems. | |
| theory | A statement that organizes a set of concepts in a meaningful way by explaining the relationships among them. | |
| value-freedom | The absence of personal values or biases. | |

## PUTTING IDEAS TOGETHER

There are many sources of knowledge about society, including common sense, religious beliefs, philosophy, and social science. Sociology is the scientific study of human society and social behavior. This chapter presented the challenge of sociology as the study of a familiar world. The knowledge produced from the work of sociologists is useful in analyzing social problems, devising legislation, understanding basic social processes, and identifying important questions for future research. Sociology has always been a discipline with many different views of the social world, depending on the perspective of the sociologist. The chapter introduced the early sociologists, beginning with Auguste Comte, who defined the discipline and argued about the focus and use of sociology.

## The Development of Sociology

| The Sociologist | His View of the Social World and Sociology's Contributions to Understanding It |
| --- | --- |
| Auguste Comte (1789–1857) | The founder of sociology, Comte felt that the methods of science could be applied to the study of society. Sociologists should study how society remains stable (social statics) and how it changes (social dynamics). |
| Herbert Spencer (1820–1903) | Society evolves over time in a fashion similar to biological evolution. The parts of society are interdependent. Sociologists should not interfere with the natural progress associated with societal evolution. |
| Karl Marx (1818–1883) | Sociologists must not only describe society but change it. Social conflict is a basic dynamic of society and the source of social change. Inevitable class conflict will lead to socal revolution. Social arrangements reflect economic arrangements. |
| Emile Durkheim (1858–1917) | The parts of society are interdependent, each functioning to maintain society as a whole. Societies are held together by common beliefs and values. Those societies with lower social integration tend to have higher suicide rates. |
| Max Weber (1864–1920) | An influential sociologist, Weber expanded on the ideas of Marx, and his emphasis on the economy, to study politics and bureaucracies as important parts of social life. Sociological knowledge can be used to change society for the better, but the process of gathering information must be done in as scientific, and value-free a manner as possible. |

These early sociologists tended to take a larger view of society, studying macro social processes. Their ideas affected the work of scholars in later years and their influence will be seen in many chapters of this book.

The diverse foundations of early sociology lead modern sociologists in many directions. Sociologists, as members of the social world they study, have never completely agreed about which questions are the most important to study. Over the years various theoretical perspectives have offered different views of the social world. Some sociologists have been concerned with order and stability, while others have concentrated on social change. At the same time, some sociologists have continued to be interested in macrosociology, which focuses on large-scale social processes, and others have been drawn to microsociology, which looks at the smaller aspects of daily life. Because sociologists take different theoretical perspectives, the questions they ask about the social world are somewhat different. The diagram below presents a simplified picture of the field of sociology today and shows how the major theories are arranged in relation to one another. Sample questions are given for the three main theoretical perspectives.

## The Major Theoretical Perspectives of Sociology

|  | *Emphasis on Social Order and Stability* | *Emphasis on Social Change and Competition* |
|---|---|---|
| *Macrosociology: emphasis on large-scale social problems* | FUNCTIONALIST THEORISTS might ask: How do schools, the family, the state, and the economy fit together? How do the various social units function to maintain order? | CONFLICT THEORISTS might ask: How do societies change and evolve? Which groups are in control? Why do some groups allow themselves to be controlled and others rise in rebellion? |
| *Microsociology: emphasis on the small aspects of social life* | | INTERACTIONIST THEORISTS might ask: Why do individuals do the things they do? Do people always mean what they say? How do people reach agreement and understand one another? How important are the daily routines of unwritten rules, courtesies, and manners we take for granted? |

As you read through the book, you can assign the names of some of the prominent theorists, past and present, to the appropriate section of the diagram. For example, Karl Marx would be placed in the upper right corner, Herbert Spencer in the upper left corner, and George Herbert Mead in the bottom half. In the later chapters, when the topics of family life, education, city growth, sexuality, images of aging, social deviance, and other subjects are analyzed, you can refer back to this diagram. Consider each of the three perspectives in turn and ask what questions that viewpoint generates about the topic. You will find the three perspectives produce different but often complementary emphases.

# Testing the Concepts

## MULTIPLE-CHOICE QUESTIONS

*After studying the chapter, try to answer each of the twenty-five questions below. Mark the alternative you think is correct; then look at the correct answer and the explanation provided at the bottom of the page. Try to state why the other alternatives are incorrect, and check your understanding of the correct answer.*

1. "Dentists have higher status and pay than do grocery store clerks because they are more important to society." An advocate of which theoretical view would be most likely to agree with this explanation?
   a. interactionist theory
   b. conflict theory
   c. functionalist theory
   d. dynamic theory
   e. macrotheory

2. Emile Durkheim made several contributions to the field of sociology. One of his particularly significant ideas was that
   a. societies, like animals, are constantly adapting to their environments.
   b. social behavior can be explained by analysis of symbolic communication.
   c. people are interesting to study but so unique that no generalizations can be made.
   d. social workers need to find out which personality types are most prone to suicide, crime, and other problems.
   e. statistical methods can be used to analyze social life on the macro level.

3. The interactionist perspective
   a. is more useful for macro than for micro issues.
   b. is sometimes criticized for neglecting the importance of symbols.
   c. focuses on how people understand and interpret their lives.
   d. is often criticized as seeing all interactions as conflicts, ignoring harmonious relations.
   e. has developed from the work of Herbert Spencer.

4. As described by C. Wright Mills, the "sociological imagination" is
   a. the ability to imagine an alternative society.
   b. the awareness of the link between private experience and the wider society.
   c. sociologists' attempts to imagine why people do the things they do.
   d. the ability to imagine one is in another person's shoes and to be more sympathetic.
   e. a quality of creativity that comes with certain personalities more than others.

---

1. **c.** *Functionalist theory looks at the interrelationships among the parts of a social system. While not taking a position that the higher status of dentists is either better or necessary, functionalists would see that it rewards them for highly technical roles that must be performed. See pages 17–19.*

2. **e.** *Durkheim compared the suicide rates of different countries and showed that factors beyond the individual explained the differences in rates. The cohesion of a society, a macro factor, was crucial. See page 15.*

3. **c.** *The micro aspects of social life, the symbolic communication between people, and the meanings people assign to acts are the focus of interactionist theory. See pages 20–22.*

4. **b.** *Mills wanted people to see the connection between what went on in their lives and larger social forces. He called the ability to see this linkage between the individual and the group the "sociological imagination." See pages 5–6.*

5. If sociologists were studying dorm life, which of the following aspects of that topic would they be most likely to investigate?
   a. how much time an individual freshman spends in his or her room partying versus studying
   b. how an individual overcomes feelings of homesickness after he or she moves in
   c. which aspects of a student's personality are most related to making friends
   d. the unwritten rules of conduct that govern how much freedom students have to go into one another's rooms
   e. what techniques one housemother uses to keep the noise and vandalism problems to a minimum.

6. Max Weber's great influence on sociology comes in part from his conviction that
   a. sociology should not be concerned with political events.
   b. Marx's focus on economics was wrong.
   c. in the long run, an increase in the power of the state would be for the good of society.
   d. the work of sociologists should be as value-free as possible.
   e. the sociologist should persuasively argue for social reforms.

7. Herbert Spencer, an early sociologist, was primarily concerned with
   a. social structure.
   b. revolutionary change.
   c. social legislation as a way of solving problems.
   d. the symbolic processes people use to communicate.
   e. evolutionary change.

8. In general, functionalist theory can be said to
   a. support the status quo.
   b. encourage experimentation.
   c. be uncritical of social reform.
   d. be an increasingly popular perspective in sociology.
   e. be more testable than other social theories.

9. Karl Marx and Max Weber agreed with one another on which of the following points?
   a. Personal convictions or bias should not be a part of sociology.
   b. Capitalism is the most equitable economic system possible.
   c. Movement toward greater social equality is inevitable.
   d. Sociologists should study the factors that keep societies stable and running smoothly.
   e. Social change will occur gradually over time in an evolutionary manner.

---

5. **d.** *Sociologists look at group behavior rather than analyze a given individual. One area of interest is how people informally make up rules to keep things functioning smoothly. See pages 4–5.*

6. **d.** *Weber felt that objective, scientific analysis was the proper way to proceed to understand social life. The biases of scientists should be stated and kept to a minimum by using standard procedures. See page 15.*

7. **e.** *Spencer took a "hands off" approach to studying society, feeling that society would continue to evolve into better and better forms over time. This evolutionary*

*approach was similar to Darwin's theory in biology. See page 14.*

8. **a.** *Functionalist theory is criticized for supporting social life as it is. Functionalists seek to find the function of parts of society, and can be interpreted as justifying the status quo by finding it functional to the stability of society. See page 18.*

9. **c.** *Marx saw revolutionary change as an inevitable outcome of class struggle, resulting in a classless, equal society. Weber saw equality as coming from technological advancement and more just forms of government. See pages 14–15.*

10.  The high rates of crime in our country keep a large work force employed dealing with criminals. This employment is an example of a _____ of crime.
   a.  dysfunction
   b.  manifest function
   c.  social function
   d.  social problem
   e.  latent function

11.  The focus of the sociological perspective can best be described as falling on
   a.  social relationships and patterns of interaction.
   b.  problems of socially disadvantaged groups.
   c.  research to help social workers help their clients.
   d.  the discovery of the unique potentials of individuals.
   e.  the identification of cultural objects from civilizations of the past.

12.  The term "social statics" was used by Comte to mean
   a.  human beings caught in a stalemate.
   b.  the statistical analysis of social life.
   c.  the phenomenon of how societies hold together.
   d.  the levels of unrest in a society between competing groups.
   e.  the amount of background information needed to understand the actions of an individual.

13.  If a sociologist argued that virtually all social arrangements are influenced by the way in which goods are produced and distributed, his or her viewpoint would follow from the thinking of
   a.  Emile Durkheim.
   b.  Karl Marx.
   c.  Herbert Spencer.
   d.  Auguste Comte.
   e.  Max Weber.

14.  The chief difference between symbolic interactionism and other theoretical orientations is that symbolic interactionism
   a.  sees social order as a product of coercion and constraint.
   b.  is primarily concerned with the micro-level interactions of individuals in groups.
   c.  sees social stability as subject to disruption if enough of a population rejects society's values.
   d.  focuses on the macro-level interactions among social groups.
   e.  sees society as a set of interrelated parts.

15.  Which theorist would be *most likely* to say "Social order is maintained by shared values and beliefs"?
   a.  Emile Durkheim
   b.  August Comte
   c.  Frederick Engels
   d.  Max Weber
   e.  Karl Marx

---

10.  **e.** *No one advocates crime as a way of keeping people employed, but the many jobs created by criminal activity are a side benefit of a high crime rate. Jobs are not the purpose of crime, and thus they are latent functions. See pages 18–19.*

11.  **a.** *Sociology looks at group life and how individuals relate to one another in groups of all sizes. See pages 4–5.*

12.  **c.** *Comte looked at how societies remain stable and cohesive over time and called these forces social statics. See page 13.*

13.  **b.** *Marx thought that economic arrangements*

determined the other aspects of social life because they fixed the social class of individuals. See pages 14–15.*

14.  **b.** *Symbolic interactionism emphasizes that individuals are taught to be part of society and to communicate with other individuals by means of everyday interactions. We learn and take for granted the meanings of hundreds of gestures and words. See pages 20–22.*

15.  **a.** *Durkheim was an early functionalist who saw the interrelationship between the parts of society. His study of suicide showed the importance of shared values and beliefs — social cohesion as he called it — for the well-being of individuals and their society. See page 15.*

16. Sociologists have developed a number of distinct ways of analyzing social life called
   a. research methods.
   b. hypotheses.
   c. philosophies.
   d. theoretical perspectives.
   e. social imaginations.

17. A sociologist with a symbolic-interactionist orientation would be most likely to ask which of the following questions about family life?
   a. What functions does cohabitation serve in helping or hindering the success of a marriage?
   b. Do practices of marrying someone with a similar background make for a more stable society?
   c. What are the terms of endearment that couples develop for one another that are known only to them?
   d. What is the rate of divorce in this country, and why is it growing?
   e. What is it in American culture that makes violence a part of family life?

18. According to the text, which of the following *pairs* of items are the two major goals of the science of sociology?
   a. predicting individuals' behavior, helping them solve their problems
   b. explaining social behavior, making predictions based on evidence
   c. diagnosis of social problems, planning social changes
   d. documenting the behavior of other cultures, getting statistics on peoples' backgrounds
   e. forming legislation and government policy, studying eccentric behavior

19. The development of sociology as a separate discipline began
   a. during the Renaissance.
   b. in the mid-1800s.
   c. at the beginning of the 1900s.
   d. after World War I.
   e. after World War II.

20. The airline industry has been in flux with numerous takeovers, mergers, and price wars. In most cases, the unions representing various groups of employees have held firm to pay demands, even going out on strike rather than agreeing to management's plea for pay cuts. A dysfunction of this turmoil is
   a. lower airfare prices.
   b. a healthier economy.
   c. increased safety risks.
   d. more jobs.
   e. a decline in the power of labor unions.

---

16. **d.** *An orientation to the social world that leads to asking certain kinds of questions that can later be researched is called a theoretical perspective. See page 17.*

17. **c.** *Couples share the meaning of certain words and gestures as special communications of their feelings. The meaning attached to symbols is a central concern of symbolic interactionists. See pages 20–22.*

18. **b.** *Sociologists explain social behavior on the basis of theory and carefully conducted research. The same behavior is predicted to occur under similar conditions. Results of research can be generalized to the population studied; repeated research studies strengthen generalizations and predictions. See page 6.*

19. **b.** *The period of the Industrial Revolution changed the social conditions in Europe and the United States drastically. Many theorists wrote about the meaning of the changes, what could be done to enhance or alter them, and what lay ahead. See page 12.*

20. **c.** *A dysfunction is a negative consequence. One problem associated with the turmoil in the airline industry is the threat to safety. Less experienced people may be hired, and employees may be tempted to engage in sabotage, when management tries to cut costs. See pages 18–19.*

21.  The Gramm-Rudman bill requires cuts in government spending. Social Security increases were capped, as were Medicare payments for the elderly. Some groups called for increases in funding for day care, though it would mean even less money for senior citizens. Which theoretical perspective would be helpful in studying this political situation?
  a. functionalism
  b. symbolic interactionism
  c. social evolution
  d. ageism
  e. conflict theory

22.  The idea that human societies evolve and that evolution always means progress is typical of the thinking of
  a. Herbert Spencer.
  b. Emile Durkheim.
  c. Max Weber.
  d. Karl Marx.
  e. Robert Merton.

23.  To establish the function of some element in society, the sociologist must ask,

  a. Who benefits from the arrangement?
  b. What is the intended purpose of the element?
  c. What do the inhabitants believe is the purpose of the element?
  d. What are the consequences of the element?
  e. Who wants the element and who does not?

24.  Compared to other social scientists, sociologists are more
  a. liberal.
  b. biased.
  c. scientific.
  d. value-free.
  e. helpful as counselors.

25.  If the conflict, functionalist, and interactionist perspectives were all applied to the same problem, they
  a. would inevitably be incompatible.
  b. would not contradict one another.
  c. would yield the same results, though in different terminology.
  d. might be compatible as they deal with different aspects of reality.
  e. could not all be useful or relevant.

---

21.  **e.** *Conflict theory looks at the competition between groups over scarce resources. In this case, age groups are pitted against one another in the struggle for shrinking federal aid. See pages 19–20.*

22.  **a.** *Spencer held an evolutionary view of society and felt that over time, progress would occur on the social scene as it had in the evolution of biological species. See page 14.*

23.  **d.** *A function is determined after the fact by looking at the consequences of an element. These consequences*

*may be helpful or harmful, intended or unintended. See pages 17–18.*

24.  **a.** *The text reports findings that the political views of sociologists are more liberal than other groups. See page 23.*

25.  **d.** *The different perspectives ask different questions about the same phenomenon. The results might be complementary and give a better view of the topic under investigation. See pages 22–23.*

# A CASE STUDY

The *Brown vs. Board of Education* decision in 1954 mandated that public schools reflect racial balance. Since then, local school boards have tried a number of strategies to comply with this decision. One of the most controversial approaches has been busing schoolchildren out of their neighborhoods to other schools. Supporters argue that busing is necessary (or a necessary evil) to break through the racial barriers that have existed for so long in the United States. Opponents (of all races) state that removal of a child from the neighborhood does more harm than good.

Jackson Mitchell, a white man, Lee Campbell, a black woman, and Lu Cortinez, a Chicano man, are all members of the sociology faculty at Urban College. As parents of schoolchildren involved in the busing controversy, they decide to study the question of whether busing makes any difference in the quality of education children receive or in their attitudes toward other races. They decide on a plan to interview a representative sample of families affected by busing, asking them about their views on integration, the effectiveness of busing, and the hardships and drawbacks posed by busing. In addition, they gain legal access to school records in order to measure students' performance before and after busing at the different schools around the city. As good sociologists, these three researchers wish to draw on theory to develop their research questions.

1.    Imagine that the early sociologists you read about in this chapter were alive today. Listed below are their names and one of their contributions to the field. How might that contribution be applied to understanding the issues involved in busing?

   a.  Comte: social statics and social dynamics

   b.  Spencer: social evolution

   c.  Marx: class conflict

d. Durkheim: statistical studies

e. Weber: value-freedom

2.  What facets of the busing controversy would be the concern of each of the three major theories? On which aspect(s) of the issue would they focus?

a. functionalist theory

b. conflict theory

c. interactionist theory

3.  What pitfalls to objectivity might one have to guard against in this investigation?

4.    Other social scientists could help on this project. Write a one-sentence statement for each of the other four social sciences explaining what it might contribute to the study.

    a.  psychology

    b.  political science

    c.  anthropology

    d.  economics

5.    What is the value of the sociological perspective in looking at the busing question? Where does the "sociological imagination" come in?

# Applying the Concepts

NAME

COURSE/SECTION NUMBER

## APPLICATION EXERCISE ONE

Durkheim studied the topic of suicide as a social fact, rather than as a personal dilemma of individuals. His approach was important for sociology for two reasons: first, he saw the connection between individuals and the larger society in which they lived; second, he applied scientific principles of evidence collection to this topic and based his conclusions on that evidence.

1.   How would Durkheim approach the topic of divorce? Write a paragraph describing what his views might be on the high rate of divorce, especially among some segments of the population in the United States.

2.   If Weber were added to this research team, what might he offer? Write a paragraph on his views of value-freedom as they apply to the study of divorce.

3.    Now here comes Marx. He argues that social relationships are economically determined and that conflict is a built-in component in some relationships. Write a paragraph on the view he might take of the American divorce situation.

4.    The "sociological imagination" is the connection of personal biographies with larger social issues. What does the sociological imagination add to the study of divorce? Write a paragraph on the issues the sociological study of divorce would emphasize and the issues that would not be of primary concern to sociologists.

## APPLICATION EXERCISE TWO

Your experience in college so far will be the basis for reviewing the key elements of conflict and functionalist theories.

1.   Review the terminology used by functionalist theorists and recall their emphasis on the stability of a social system. Consider your present situation in school and identify some of the relationships between subgroups of people. For example, think about the connections between

> teachers and students
> students and administrators
> students and cafeteria workers
> teachers and administrators
> underclassmen (freshmen and sophomores) and upperclassmen

Choose one of these relationships for further study.

a.  What makes the relationship you have selected for study a functional one?

b.  Identify consequences of this relationship that promote the stability of the college system.

c.  Are there latent functions and/or dysfunctions in this relationship?

2.   Most rules or policies that affect college life have a specific goal of keeping things stable and orderly. Think of a policy at your college. Some examples might include

> intensive recruitment plan for athletics
> coed housing within the dormitories
> limits on drinking and drug use
> rules on the activities of sororities and fraternities
> allocation of fellowship money primarily to minority students
> requirement that underclassmen must all spend a semester living on campus
> off-campus courses offered around the community

(If you are not familiar with any college policies, choose one from high school or work.)

a.  What is the explicit goal of this policy? How does the goal promote stability within the college system?

b.  What latent functions or dysfunctions have occurred, or can you anticipate occurring, as a result of this policy?

3.    Using the relationship you analyzed in question one, take a conflict point of view. Conflict theorists argue that scarce resources, including power, make for strained social relationships between positions in society. Remember, the focus is not on troublesome personalities of individuals, but rather the way positions or roles relate to one another.

a.  What are the goals of each interest group?

b.  How does conflict show itself in this relationship?

c.  How intense is the conflict?

d.  Is the conflict destructive, or does it have positive effects as well?

e.  How might the conflict be resolved?

## APPLICATION EXERCISE THREE

The interactionist perspective is concerned with the meanings human beings assign certain social situations and a variety of social behaviors. Consider three interactions you have recently participated in. Pick one that involved a close friend, a date, a spouse, or someone you know well. A second situation should involve a more formal encounter, such as a job or admissions interview. The third situation selected should be one in which you had contact with strangers, but little or no conversation with them, such as the first day of school, a ride on the bus, or a transaction in a store.

NAME

COURSE/SECTION NUMBER

1.  Situation One: interaction with a person close to you

    a.  Describe the situation.

    b.  What are some of the topics of conversation permissible in this situation that are not allowed in other situations?

    c.  What language or phrases do you share that an outsider would not completely understand?

    d.  What was your dress and demeanor in this situation?

2. Situation Two: a formal interaction

   a. Describe the situation.

   b. What are some of the topics of conversation that occurred here? Could you have discussed topics you pursued in Situation One?

   c. What language or phrases did you use in this interaction? Were they interpreted by the other person in the way you intended? What language did you choose that might not have been part of your normal speech?

   d. What was your dress and demeanor in this situation?

3.  Situation Three: nonverbal contact with strangers

    a. Describe the situation.

    b. What kinds of assumptions did you make about these persons and what
       they might do?

    c. List five gestures used by you or the other persons to communicate a
       message.

    d. What was your dress or demeanor in this situation?

4.  Sociology has been called the painful elaboration of the obvious. Does the
study of micro social life by interactionists support this accusation, or does it
provide evidence to the contrary?

# CHAPTER 2

# Doing Sociology: The Methods of Research

## Reviewing the Concepts

### LEARNING GOALS

*After studying this chapter, you should be able to:*

1. Identify the contributions of theory and research to sociological knowledge.

2. Contrast sociological methodology to other ways of learning about the social world.

3. Describe the logic of cause and effect between variables; state the conditions necessary for correlation and for causation.

4. Indicate how controls are used to detect spurious or causal relationships among variables.

5. Define "variable," "control," and *Verstehen* and explain their importance to sociological research.

6. List five difficulties social scientists face in their research; give your own example of each problem.

7. Identify the advantages and disadvantages of laboratory and field experiments.

8. Explain the research concern called the "Hawthorne effect."

9. Distinguish between a population and a sample and explain the connection between them; specify ways to ensure that a sample is representative.

10. Contrast the uses of questionnaires, structured interviews, and unstructured interviews; identify three errors to avoid making when wording questions.

11. Describe the research uses of case studies and participant versus detached observation.

12. State the advantages and possible pitfalls of observational research.

13. Specify the contributions of Durkheim's study of suicide to the research tradition of sociology.

14. List and explain the seven steps of the ideal research model.

15. Describe five types of ethical dilemmas sociologists frequently face in their research.

16. Select an example of a social research topic that would be appropriate for each of the major methodologies: experiment, survey, observational study, and use of existing sources.

## IDENTIFYING KEY QUESTIONS AND THEMES

The accumulation of sociological knowledge is based on the interplay of theory and research. In sociology, research is where the real action takes place. Sociologists use research *methodology*, a system of rules, procedures, and principles that guides scientific investigation. Because the subject matter of sociology is human beings, sociologists are challenged to measure carefully, treat their subjects ethically, and interpret their results responsibly.

## The Logic of Cause and Effect

*Does every social event have a cause? How can we be confident that we have correctly identified a cause? What are variables, correlations, and controls?*

All events have causes; the challenge of science is to correctly identify the causes and avoid misinterpretation. The process begins when two *variables* are found to be related to one another in a regular, recurrent fashion; these variables are said to have a *correlation* with one another. A variable is considered *independent* if it seems to produce a change in a *dependent variable*. For example, the yearly salary of a group of persons might be a dependent variable, influenced by the amount of education each person has completed (independent variable). To further determine whether a cause-and-effect relationship is present, *controls* are applied to exclude the possibility that other variables are influencing the relationship, making the relationship a *spurious correlation.* In this example, the influence of other variables, such as race and gender, would have to be controlled. Finally, it may be necessary to analyze the logic of the relationship in question, particularly the time order involved, to firmly establish a causal relationship.

## Difficulties in Sociological Research

*What are the problems a researcher faces in studying human subjects? What strategies can be used to adhere to the scientific method as much as possible?*

A sociologist's subject matter, human beings, poses several potential problems: (1) people are quite different from one another and often behave in unpredictable ways for extremely complex reasons; (2) sometimes it is difficult to isolate and identify single factors that explain a particular phenomenon; (3) if people know they are being studied, they may not behave as they normally would — the researcher may change the behavior she or he is trying to investigate simply by examining it; (4) the researcher's personal feelings or involvement with the subjects or topics being investigated may intrude on his or her research; (5) finally, some scientifically worthwhile studies cannot be performed on human beings — professional codes of ethics guide researchers and protect subjects.

It is important to continue social science research in spite of these difficulties. The use of the scientific method helps ensure objectivity and greatly reduces the possibility of bias. In some cases, however, subjectivity may enhance the interpretation of results and the meaning of the human behavior sociologists observe. Weber called this subjective interpretation *Verstehen* and felt that it added insight to the scientific evidence collected.

## Basic Research Methods

*What research methods do sociologists use? What are the strengths and weaknesses of the various methods?*

There are four basic reasearch methods in sociology: experiments, surveys, observation, and the use of existing sources.

The *experiment* is useful for testing specific hypotheses regarding narrowly defined issues. Experiments can be conducted either in the laboratory or in the field. At least two matched groups, the *experimental group* and the *control group,* are measured before and after the treatment, which only the experimental group receives. A change in the experimental group without a change in the control group indicates that the treatment has made a difference. The use of the control group helps to ensure that it is not some unknown and unmeasured variable, rather than the researcher's treatment, that is producing the change. Sometimes subjects conform to researcher's expectations, a phenomenon called the *"Hawthorne effect."*

*Surveys* can take the form of questionnaires or interviews or a combination of the two. All three types are useful for systematically gaining information about the attitudes, behavior, or other characteristics of a large number of people. In any survey, the population is the total group of people that the sociologist is interested in. If the *sample,* a small number of individuals drawn from the larger population, accurately represents the population, the results of the sample can be generalized to that population; if it does not, then the results are valid only for the *respondents,* the people who actually participated in the survey. The use of a *random sample* — one chosen in such a way that every member of the population in question has the same chance of being selected — ensures representativeness. To be effective, survey questions must be clearly worded. Some sociologists use a fixed response format, which makes questions easy to answer and tabulate. Open-ended questions allow more in-depth and varied answers, but are more difficult to summarize.

In-depth analysis of social processes is the strength of an *observational study,* which may be conducted either in the laboratory or in the field. *Case studies* are the most common form of field observation, providing a detailed record of an event, group, or social process. *Participant observation* and *detached observation* are two approaches. Observational studies offer insights into real-life situations, but the method relies heavily on the skills of the observer, and the findings cannot be generalized to similar cases.

Existing sources are the published or unpublished data or documents that a researcher collects and analyzes. Sometimes materials gathered for one purpose can be used or reanalyzed to answer other questions. Durkheim's research on suicide is one such example.

## A Research Model

*What are the steps of an ideal research model?*

Researchers begin with a definition of the problem to be studied, a review of the relevant literature, formulation of a *hypothesis* to be tested, and the establishment of *operational definitions* that specify how concepts will be measured. The sociologist then selects an appropriate *research design,* collects the data, analyzes and interprets the results, and ultimately draws conclusions about the original hypothesis. When completed, the research becomes the common property of the scientific community

whose members may attempt to replicate the study, that is, repeat the research to verify the findings. At the final stage, new questions may be posed and a new angle on the topic may begin another cycle through the research model.

## Research Ethics

*What guidelines do sociologists use to address the ethical dilemmas they commonly face?*

Professional codes of ethics exist to guide the research process. Sociologists must: avoid harm to participants; protect the privacy of respondents; adhere to the principle of informed consent; take care that research results are used wisely, whether by themselves or by the clients or sponsors of research; and avoid deceiving their research subjects. Research projects such as Project Camelot and the Tearoom Trade reveal both the ambiguity and importance of ethical conduct.

## DEFINING CORE CONCEPTS

*After studying the chapter, write a sociological definition in your own words for the following core concepts. Then give an example from your own experience to illustrate your definition. Refer to the chapter to check your work.*

| *Core Concept* | *Sociological Definition* | *Personal Illustration* |
|---|---|---|
| case study | | |
| controls | | |
| correlation | | |

| Core Concept | Sociological Definition | Personal Illustration |
|---|---|---|
| dependent variable | | |
| experimental group | | |
| Hawthorne effect | | |
| hypothesis | | |
| independent variable | | |
| methodology | | |
| observational study | | |

| *Core Concept* | *Sociological Definition* | *Personal Illustration* |
|---|---|---|
| operational definition | | |
| research design | | |
| respondent | | |
| sample | | |
| spurious correlation | | |
| survey | | |
| *Verstehen* | | |

## PUTTING IDEAS TOGETHER

Sociology is a social science using objective methods to investigate social phenomena. The textbook outlines a step-by-step procedure for conducting a research project. At different points in the process, the researcher may be challenged by potential ethical problems, imprecise measurement, or confusion about how to interpret what is observed. In some cases, a researcher's personal interests may guide the selection of a research topic. In other cases, topics are presented to a researcher because evidence is needed for social planning and policy making. Once a topic has been identified, the research process begins.

### Possible Pitfalls in the Research Process

| | Ethical violation? | Proper measurement? | Correct interpretation? | |
|---|---|---|---|---|
| *Define the Problem* | | | | |
| *Review the Literature* | | | X | Use the work of other researchers to select a worthy topic. |
| *Formulate a Hypothesis* | | | | |
|   Operationalize the concepts | | X | | Do procedures really measure the concept? |
| *Choose a Research Design* | | X | | |
|   Experiments | X | | | Harm to subjects? Misrepresentation of research(er)? Lack of informed consent? Privacy guarantees? |
|   Surveys | X | | | |
|   Observational Studies | X | | | |
|   Existing Sources | X | | | |
| *Collect the Data* | | | | |
|   Select a sample, if any | X | X | | Representativeness? Guarantees of confidentiality and anonymity? |
| *Analyze the Results* | | | X | Spuriousness? |
| *Draw a Conclusion* | X | | X | Conclusions formed carefully on available evidence? Results used responsibly? |

Puzzling findings or newly formed questions will lead to replication and/or modification of the research process.

# Testing the Concepts

## MULTIPLE-CHOICE QUESTIONS

*After studying the chapter, try to answer each of the twenty-five questions below. Mark the alternative you think is correct; then look at the correct answer and the explanation provided at the bottom of the page. Try to state why the other alternatives are incorrect, and check your understanding of the correct answer.*

1.  Careful use of the survey method has which of the following advantages over the experimental method?
     a.  isolation of causal relationships
     b.  more truthful responses from subjects
     c.  less chance of spurious relationships
     d.  generalizability of findings
     e.  no problems with ethics

2.  Which of the following procedures constitutes ethically sound research?
     a.  placing a study group in a high-stress situation in a laboratory to see at what point mental breakdowns occur
     b.  asking adults intimate questions about their personal sexual behavior through anonymous questionnaires
     c.  offering unwed mothers-to-be free abortions in return for an in-depth interview about their reactions to their pregnancy
     d.  paying teenagers to associate with prostitutes as a way to establish a control group in an experiment on socialization and crime
     e.  going door-to-door with a survey on political attitudes, telling respondents you work for city government in order to get more objective responses

3.  Sally Sociologist hypothesizes that the later one marries, the fewer children one is likely to have. After interviewing people, Sally finds the variables of age and education affect each variable in her original hypothesis. The relationship between late marriage and few children is therefore a(n) _____ correlation.
     a.  dependent
     b.  spurious
     c.  causal
     d.  independent
     e.  sexual

4.  Which part of an experimental design is vulnerable to the "Hawthorne effect"?
     a.  the selection of the sample respondents
     b.  the impact of the treatment on the control group
     c.  the isolation of the effects of the independent variable
     d.  the generalizability of results
     e.  the operationalization of the dependent variable

---

1.  **d.** *The survey method, using random sampling, produces results generalizable to the population studied. Experimental results cannot be generalized past the group of subjects who took part. See page 39.*

2.  **b.** *In a, c, and d, the subjects could be harmed as a result of the study and may not have given consent or known what was involved. In e, the reseacher is misrepresenting him- or herself. Asking sexual questions can be handled ethically by guarding anonymity. See pages 47–48.*

3.  **b.** *When a third variable is found to affect both the independent and dependent variable in a hypothesis, the correlation is spurious, that is, not actually a relationship at all. See page 31.*

4.  **c.** *The Hawthorne effect refers to the contamination of the independent variable by the subjects' assumptions about what the researcher is trying to do. If the independent variable is contaminated, its effects cannot be clearly measured. See page 37.*

5. An advantage of a mailed questionnaire over an unstructured interview is that
   a. questions are flexible.
   b. problems in wording can be clarified.
   c. the response rate is faster.
   d. the results are easier to tabulate and summarize.
   e. the amount of insight into the respondents' answers is greater.

6. The most important quality of a sample, as shown by Gallup's 1936 election polls, is its
   a. size.
   b. accessibility by telephone.
   c. willingness to respond to questions of interviewers.
   d. representativeness.
   e. consistent voting pattern over a number of elections.

7. The research process called replication involves
   a. forming an original hypothesis.
   b. repeating the research procedures of another study to verify the results.
   c. thinking of operational definitions for the variables.
   d. drawing conclusions and reporting the results to others.
   e. drawing a stratified sample.

8. Research done in the Western Electric plant led to the discovery of the "Hawthorne effect." You are asked to observe a group of nursery-school children from "disadvantaged" homes who are in a special class to prepare them for school. The Hawthorne effect might be a problem in your research, because
   a. it is unethical to study children without telling them why.
   b. friendship groups might form in the class and children might imitate their friends, rather than act as individuals.
   c. if children get extra help now, they will be bored when they get to regular school.
   d. just observing the children might make them feel important and motivate them to work harder.
   e. the nursery-school teachers may force the children to do more work on the days the observers are there.

9. Weber's idea of *Verstehen* as a part of sociological research is probably most relevant to which method of sociological investigation?
   a. experimental designs
   b. longitudinal studies
   c. observational studies
   d. mailed questionnaires
   e. structured interviews

---

5. **d.** *Questions with fixed answers can be easily tabulated, and the anonymity of the mailed questionnaire might encourage responses to all questions. Unstructured interviews generate more information and more insight, but generalizations are difficult to form. See page 39.*

6. **d.** *Gallup's sample was more representative and thus more accurate because he took a random sample of voters, rather than using telephone and automobile records favoring the richer voter. See pages 38–39.*

7. **b.** *Published results are scrutinized by other social scientists who may choose to repeat the work of the researcher to verify the findings. If several replications*

*produce very similar results, then we consider the findings and generalizations to be very reliable. See page 46.*

8. **d.** *The presence of the observers contaminates the experiment, in that the subjects respond to the attention they are getting and the experimenter's expectations rather than to the instructional program. See pages 37–38.*

9. **c.** *Weber encouraged researchers to try to understand what the behavior of the research subjects means to the subjects themselves. Observational work tries to keep behavior in context and understand it in that light. See pages 35–36.*

10. Many ethical issues that face sociologists center on
    a. the unwillingness of people to talk about their lives.
    b. research designs that attempt to measure change over time.
    c. the issue of whether it is ethical to study human behavior.
    d. the way they treat their research subjects.
    e. the pressure the researcher feels to come up with socially relevant results.

11. The social research study Project Camelot illustrates that
    a. some sociologists knowingly use research for spying on people.
    b. theatrical plays can be used as sources of sociological information.
    c. sociologists use research to help the poor.
    d. participant observation studies always include an element of bias.
    e. government sponsorship of research can have hidden political motives.

12. A research methodology is
    a. the random selection of research subjects.
    b. a system of rules, principles, and procedures.
    c. the identification of an independent variable.

    d. the steps taken to complete a study from beginning to end.
    e. the use of statistics to make results more scientific.

13. To establish whether a correlation between variables is a causal one, a researcher must make use of
    a. informed opinions of experts.
    b. replication.
    c. controls.
    d. *Verstehen.*
    e. an experiment.

14. A hypothesis should be formulated in such a way that the variables can be scientifically measured. This requires the use of
    a. a research design.
    b. a correlation.
    c. operational definitions.
    d. generalizations.
    e. an experiment.

15. The work of George Gallup in the 1930s on opinion polls showed the strength of which aspect of sociological research?
    a. representative sampling
    b. phone surveys
    c. observational studies
    d. *Verstehen*
    e. operational definitions

---

10. **d.** *Since human beings are the subject of sociological research, care must be taken not to harm them unintentionally in the course of the research. Identifying the nature of the project, getting consent, and guaranteeing confidentiality are ways to protect subjects. See pages 47–48.*

11. **e.** *The funding source for research can make demands on the researchers. Some of these demands may be unethical according to the researcher's code. Carefully and ethically collected data may be used unethically by others. See page 48.*

12. **b.** *Scientific investigation must proceed according to a system that ensures objectivity. A methodology consists of these rules and procedures, whether a survey, an*

*experiment, or an observational study is being conducted. See page 29.*

13. **c.** *The use of controls tests the original relationship and removes the possibility that it might be spurious. See pages 32–34.*

14. **c.** *Operational definitions are the precise wordings of variables that make possible their measurement. Different researchers can come up with different operational definitions. See page 45.*

15. **a.** *Using careful sampling procedures, Gallup was able to get a representative sample of the American voting public and correctly predict election results. The representativeness of a sample is more crucial than the size of the sample. See page 39.*

16. Janice wants to know whether she will be one of the older students in law school this fall. She knows there are a few students over 50, but she wants the number that is exactly midway, with half of the students above and half of the students below. She should ask the law school for the _____ age.
   a. modal
   b. average
   c. mean
   d. middle
   e. median

17. A Soviet sociologist rushed to the scene of the Chernobyl nuclear accident to find out exactly what happened and how groups respond to disaster. He talked with all of the people from one of the towns that was evacuated. This research can be criticized on all *but one* of the following grounds:
   a. lack of a random sample
   b. response bias by the citizens who may be hurt by the fallout
   c. results cannot be generalized to other crisis situations
   d. use of survey methods when an experiment should have been used
   e. hastily constructed research design

18. If a research project were conducted to study Americans' views of epilepsy, including the views of those who have the disease, the researchers would use
   a. an experiment.

   b. a want ad in the newspaper to get interested respondents.
   c. an epileptic interviewer.
   d. a random sample of the nonepileptic population.
   e. a questionnaire to a random sample of the entire population.

19. Your professor asks you to test the hypothesis that whites earn more than blacks in similar jobs. Your data source is the 1980 U.S. Census, which gives the median incomes for jobs, divided by racial categories. This is an example of research
   a. using existing sources.
   b. with unethical treatment of the subjects.
   c. with poor operationalizations of variables.
   d. with two independent variables in the hypothesis.
   e. using stratified sampling.

20. A researcher finds a high correlation between listening to rock music and promiscuous sexual behavior. This finding indicates
   a. that all teenagers listen to rock music.
   b. that rock music causes promiscuity.
   c. that just about any variable can be correlated with any other.
   d. that the dependent variable of listening to rock music is hard to operationalize.
   e. nothing: control variables are needed to test causality or spuriousness.

---

16. **e.** *The median is the value that falls halfway in a range of numbers. The few older students in the class will pull up the mean age, so the median is a more accurate reading of the central tendency of this group. See page 33.*

17. **d.** *The study of responses to natural disasters is difficult, since the events usually are not predictable. Through survey research, conducted on a random sample, the sociologist can gather people's reactions to the disaster in a scientific way. There is no particular advantage to an experimental design, even if it were feasible. See pages 38–40.*

18. **e.** *To measure attitudes, a questionnaire is often*

*useful. The random sample would ensure proportional representation of people with epilepsy. See pages 39–40.*

19. **a.** *The census is an existing source of information to which researchers can turn to answer certain questions. The variables in this hypothesis, race and income, are measured and reported in the census. Use of existing sources is efficient because it saves additional data collection. See pages 43–44.*

20. **e.** *A high correlation does not indicate a cause-and-effect relationship. There may be a connection between these variables, but it may be spurious. Other variables, such as age, need to be controlled in the analysis. See pages 30–31.*

21. An observational study
    a. cannot be done in a laboratory.
    b. is inappropriate when an in-depth study of some event is required.
    c. is better suited for structured rather than unstructured interviews.
    d. cannot be generalized to cases that appear similar.
    e. has no scientific value.

22. In a research project, which of the following steps would precede all the others?
    a. formulate a hypothesis
    b. establish operational definitions
    c. review the literature
    d. choose a research design
    e. write questions for a questionnaire

23. A tentative statement that predicts the relationship between variables is called
    a. a hypothesis.
    b. a research model.
    c. a probability sample.
    d. a generalization.
    e. an operationalization.

24. People may behave differently in an artificial situation than they would in the "real" world. This poses a particular difficulty for research using
    a. a laboratory experiment.
    b. detached observation.
    c. existing sources.
    d. a field experiment.
    e. a stratified sample.

25. A sociologist finds a causal connection between high family income and good student grades. In this case, the student grades are
    a. the controls.
    b. the dependent variable.
    c. the independent variable.
    d. the correlation.
    e. the hypothesis.

---

21. **d.** *Observational studies produce useful data, but they cannot be generalized beyond the group actually studied. See page 43.*

22. **c.** *A review of the literature places the research idea in the context of what has been done before. A researcher can replicate work or identify what still needs to be done. See page 45.*

23. **a.** *The hypothesis makes the prediction about variables that the research study will test. See page 45.*

24. **a.** *The laboratory is an artificial setting in which research is conducted. Sometimes the setting changes the behavior of the subjects by making them feel awkward or more self-conscious about what they do. See page 38.*

25. **b.** *According to the hypothesis that was researched, grades were thought to depend on family income, that is, grades were affected by the income. See pages 30–31.*

NAME

COURSE/SECTION  NUMBER

## A CASE STUDY

The fear of being sent to prison is supposed to be a deterrent to crime, yet people are being sentenced for serious crimes faster than prison space is built to accommodate them. In 1986, nearly 529,000 Americans were in prison, a record high. You have been awarded a grant to study the problem of prisons as ineffective deterrents. In the next three months, you need to come up with some information that will educate government officials about effective deterrence: does it occur? under what conditions? for what kinds of people? You have an interest in this topic because your spouse is a criminal lawyer; perhaps you can arrange to get more cases for his or her practice.

1.    How would you set up a research project to evaluate prisons as deterrents to crime using the following methods of research?

a.  a field experiment

b.  a survey

c.  an observational study

d.  use of existing records

2.   What is your population and what is your sample? How would the sample be drawn?

3.   Formulate a hypothesis, indicating the independent variable(s) and the dependent variable(s).

4.   Assume that in the course of your research you interviewed some inmates. If you gave out your spouse's business card at the prison and suggested that inmates might consider a retrial or file a suit about their living conditions, would it be a helpful gesture or an ethical violation?

5.   If you found a medium-to-high correlation (.6, for example) between knowing someone who has been caught and imprisoned for a crime *and* avoiding illegal activities, would you consider this relationship to be spurious? How would you know?

# Applying the Concepts

NAME
_____

COURSE/SECTION  NUMBER

## APPLICATION EXERCISE ONE

Operational definitions allow researchers to measure a concept or idea they are interested in studying. For example, a sociologist might be interested in whether a fear of crime keeps elderly people from going out at night. The researcher would have to devise a way to specify what is meant by "fear," "crime," and "going out at night." The operational definition of going out at night might be: leaving your home alone after sunset.

1.   There are many ways to write an operational definition for any single concept or idea; that is where the sociologist's creativity comes into play. Suppose you are conducting an experiment to study one of the topics below, write an operational definition for one of the concepts.

|                        |                          |
|------------------------|--------------------------|
| poverty                | religiosity              |
| marital happiness      | friendship               |
| mental illness         | political conservatism   |
| abusiveness of parents | quality of life in a city |

2.   Find an article in a sociological journal that also uses this term (or studies the general topic). Give the complete citation for the article. Comment on the author's definition.

3.   Write five questions for a structured interview that would help you study the topic you selected.

## APPLICATION EXERCISE TWO

NAME

COURSE/SECTION NUMBER

Select *one* of the following topics and study it using observation as your research design:

> the amount of jaywalking that occurs in town: when, where, by whom?
> fan behavior at different kinds of sporting events
> the type of people who use various forms of transportation
> the variety and quality of goods in different stores in the city
> the decor, music, and other features of a bar that draw certain types of patrons
> the variety of sexual hustles that occur in different settings.

1.   Formulate a hypothesis to study this topic.

2.   Go to two different settings and spend ten minutes observing in each. Record field notes and organize them to test your hypothesis. (If possible, work with other students who observe the same variables in other settings.)

3.   Suppose you were using a questionnaire instead: list three questions you might ask and discuss the possible advantages and disadvantages of the survey method, as compared to the observational method, in studying this topic.

## APPLICATION EXERCISE THREE

NAME

_____

COURSE/SECTION NUMBER

From a popular magazine, select an article citing research. Examples include the "sex surveys" in *Redbook* or *Cosmopolitan* or the claims made in the tabloids like *National Enquirer*. You will critique the strengths and weaknesses of the research methodology in your example.

1.  Attach the article to which you refer or give its complete citation.

2.  What sample did it use? Comment on the representativeness of the sample.

3.  What is the main hypothesis? Identify the independent variable(s) and the dependent variable(s). (These will not be stated explicitly; you will have to figure them out.)

4.   What method was used to test the hypothesis? Was it an appropriate method?

5.   How would you improve the research study done by this magazine? Which research procedures were followed in accordance with the scientific method?

# The Individual, Culture, and Society

# CHAPTER 3

# Culture

## Reviewing the Concepts

### LEARNING GOALS

*After studying this chapter, you should be able to:*

1. Define material and nonmaterial culture; describe the relationship between culture and society.

2. Briefly summarize the process of evolution; compare the evolution of primates and their capacities with those of humans.

3. State the significance of culture for human survival and functioning.

4. Distinguish between instincts, reflexes, drives, and culturally learned behavior.

5. Discuss norms, how they relate to values, and their importance to society.

6. Compare the four types of norms—folkways, mores, laws, and taboos; give an example of each.

7. Define social control and explain how it works.

8. List several core American values and explain the significance of the "new value" that appears to have emerged.

9. State the importance of the ecological approach to understanding culture.

10. Contrast the functionalist and conflict analyses of the components of culture.

11. Illustrate the idea of cultural universals and explain why they exist.

12. Define ethnocentrism and discuss its consequences for a culture.

13. Describe cultural relativism and its appropriate use.

14. Identify factors contributing to cultural integration.

15. Contrast ideal and real culture, and high and popular culture, as sources of cultural variation.

16. Indicate how subcultures and countercultures relate to the dominant culture.

17. Describe the importance of language as a symbolic activity and a vital element of culture.

18. Summarize the linguistic-relativity hypothesis and state its implications for culture.

19. Explain how artistic production is a social process.

20. Describe the three processes that lead to cultural change.

21. Summarize the ways in which culture affects human interaction and the ways humans change culture.

## IDENTIFYING KEY QUESTIONS AND THEMES

*Culture* consists of the shared products of human society: *material culture* consists of all the artifacts, or physical objects, human beings create and give meaning to; *non-material culture* consists of abstract human creations such as language, beliefs, and customs. The objects and ideas that make up culture differ from one society to another, but all societies have culture.

### The Human Species: What Kind of Animal?

*How has the human species evolved? Why is culture important to the human species?*

In the 1850s, Charles Darwin argued that all life forms are shaped by physical evolution. His ideas stimulated other researchers in the biological and social sciences to study the changes in the human animal over time. Sociologist Herbert Spencer expanded on Darwin's theory, speaking of the "survival of the fittest"—the tendency for species to adapt and advance with succeeding generations. Using fossils and other evidence, scientists continue to trace the origins of the human race. The link between humans and higher primates is supported by the following shared characteristics: sociability; intelligence; sensitive hands; vocality; acute eyesight; upright posture; year-round mating; and the offspring's long period of dependence on adults.

It is culture that accounts for the unprecedented success of the human species. Culture provides human beings with a design for living. Humans learn better ways to adapt to changing conditions, and these lessons can be passed on, with additions and modifications, from one generation to the next.

The question of what is meant by "human nature" is still being debated. The subfield of sociobiology argues that social behavior in all species is bred into the genes through the same evolutionary pressures that shape physical characteristics, but this idea is not widely accepted. Most psychologists today agree that human beings are not born with any "instincts"—behavior patterns that are complex, unlearned, and present in all normal members of the species under identical conditions. We do have some genetically determined types of behavior, but these are simple reflexes—involuntary muscular responses. We also have a few inborn, basic drives—organic urges that need satisfaction. As the most advanced member of the primates, our biological abilities shape much of our behavior. However, even given these common biological potentials, human life shows an astounding degree of variety. Much of this variation is directly attributable to our learning experiences within our society and culture. In large part, then, "human nature" is what we make of it.

### Norms

*What are social norms? How do norms affect human behavior?*

Every culture has its own *norms,* or shared rules or guidelines for appropriate behavior. *Folkways* are the rules for everyday life. When folkways are violated, the reaction is relatively minimal. *Mores* are much stronger norms to which people attach a moral significance. Violations of mores elicit harsh reactions, punishment, or incarceration. *Taboos*—powerful social beliefs that some specific acts are utterly loathsome—make violations of certain mores almost unthinkable. Because norms are socially created, they shift with history. Preferences for long or short hair, for example, often change, and may range from a taboo to a folkway in terms of the importance of the norm to society. Norms that are part of a formal code enacted by a legislative body are called **laws** and carry specific punishments for violations. To be effective, laws must be consistent with important norms that already operate in the culture.

Norms are part of a system of **social control** through which society makes sure basic rules are obeyed and order is maintained. Positive and negative **sanctions** reinforce group norms. Pressure to behave in socially acceptable ways may come from others in the society or from formal agents of social control such as the police. The most effective form of social control comes from within the individual: as a member of the society, the individual **internalizes** its norms and values and usually complies with them.

## Values

*What are social values? How do social values affect human behavior?*

Norms are based on society's **values**—shared ideas about what is good or desirable. Because the value systems of various societies differ, the norms within those societies prohibit, allow, or encourage different behavior. By observing the normative behavior in a culture, we can infer the values behind that behavior. Within any culture, particularly a heterogeneous one, there are contradictions in values. Values, and the norms that reflect them, eventually change over time.

Sociologist Robin Williams identified fifteen basic American values. The recent trend toward **self-fulfillment** may be yet another American value, one that is at odds with existing values and may or may not endure.

## Variation Among Cultures

*Why is there so much cultural variation? Are there common elements among cultures? How do sociologists study cultural variations?*

Observation of cultures around the world shows an immense variation in norms and values. Since people create culture as a means of adapting to the environment, differences in the environment may lead to cultural variation. The **ecological approach** analyzes culture in terms of the total environment (natural and social) in which a society exists.

If the environment provides the general context in which culture develops, one way to analyze specific components of culture is by looking at the functions they perform in maintaining the social order. Cultural practices and objects provide common meanings and rituals to members of a society and help preserve it.

Culture can also be seen as the product of social tension. Conflict theorists focus on the cultural change that results from competition among different groups. One striking example is the current crisis in South Africa.

Humans' common biological heritage results in some general **cultural universals.** However, the specific norms, practices, beliefs, and behaviors that support these universals vary widely, and no specific cultural traits are found in every society.

To one degree or another, people in every society internalize their own culture and regard its ways of living as correct. The same pride that produces important feelings of cohesiveness within the group can also result in a tendency to judge other cultures by one's own standards. When encountering a foreign culture, people may be amused, upset, critical, or horrified about what they see. This position of **ethnocentrism** results in unfounded value judgments and a lack of understanding about the ways of others.

Sociologists study cultural variations and their meanings most effectively by adopting a position of **cultural relativism,** in which the elements of a culture are understood in the context of that culture's particular norms and values.

## Variation Within Cultures

*What is cultural integration? What accounts for variations in cultural integration?*

When the parts of culture, the values and norms, fit together in a consistent fashion, there is a high degree of **cultural integration.** Traditional, preindustrial societies tend to have more integrated cultures (less variation) in which cultural change takes place relatively slowly. In modern, industrialized societies, such as the United States, the frequent addition of new material and nonmaterial cultural elements that must be absorbed in some way leads to greater variation and more rapid and uneven cultural change. Often parts of a society change more quickly than others, producing a strain between the elements, and threatening cultural disintegration. This was the fate of the Plains Indians whose societies collapsed with the white settlers' slaughter of the buffalo on which their culture was based.

Another source of variation results from the discrepancy between *ideal culture* and *real culture.* Actual practices (real culture) may not be in line with the norms and values a society adheres to in principle (ideal culture). If the gap is large, the resulting tensions diminish cultural integration.

Cultural variation within a society may correspond to class differences. *High culture* consists of the prized creations of a society, primarily appealing to and supported by the elite, and establishing the standards of esthetic judgment. *Pop culture,* however, has a wider audience more typical of the tastes of mass society.

A modern, heterogeneous society contains *subcultures* and *countercultures,* groups with norms and values that differ from or contradict the dominant culture. Subcultures vary somewhat from the dominant culture but share its important values. Countercultures actually oppose the values of the dominant culture and may undermine cultural integration. The more extensive the strain from subcultures and countercultures, the more difficult it is to maintain cultural integration.

## Language

*What part does language play in culture? How important is language?*

Language, both spoken and written, is a distinctively human creation, essential for culture to exist and persist. While animals for the most part communicate instinctively through fixed signals, humans have developed systems of meaningful *symbols* that are learned by all members of a culture. Through language, humans enhance their culture, interpret their social reality, think logically about the past and future, and transmit their culture from one generation to the next.

The *linguistic-relativity hypothesis* argues that the language one speaks predisposes one to view the world in certain ways. Our words, as symbols, may provide the structure we use to interpret the world around us. Differences in language imply differences in interpretations and often reflect that which is important to a culture.

## The Arts

*How is artistic production a social process? How do the arts reflect or contribute to cultural change?*

The *arts* are important cultural products intended to inspire or entertain. They are represented in both high culture and popular culture. Artistic styles tend to correspond to the historical period and societal conditions in which the artists work. Although we often think of art as the accomplishments of specific individuals, its creation depends on more than the artist alone—the art found in any society reflects its social and cultural values as well as its level of technological development.

The social process of artistic production is well illustrated by the rock music that emerged and continues to flourish in the United States and Britain, youth-oriented cultures that tolerate themes of rebellion and personal freedom. Similarly, abstract painting, like the painting that preceded it, bears the influence of history and culture in terms of which artists, styles, etc., manifest themselves. In short, the arts are creative, cultural products that have meaning and value within a particular cultural context and evolve and change with other social conditions.

## Cultural Change

*How do cultures change?*

Changing circumstances challenge cultures and make change inevitable. Cultures that are isolated, simple, and integrated tend to change slowly. The three major processes by which culture changes are *discovery, invention,* and *diffusion.*

## Prisoners of Culture?

*How strongly are we influenced by culture?*

The culture we learn shapes our lives and provides our basic design for living. But culture is constantly changing, and humans contribute to those changes. Rather than acting as the passive recipient of the culture it is born into, each generation collectively acts on and modifies the culture it inherits.

# DEFINING CORE CONCEPTS

*After studying the chapter, write a sociological definition in your own words for the following core concepts. Then give an example from your own experience to illustrate your definition. Refer to the chapter to check your work.*

| *Core Concept* | *Sociological Definition* | *Personal Illustration* |
| --- | --- | --- |
| counterculture | | |
| cultural integration | | |
| cultural relativism | | |
| diffusion | | |
| ecological approach | | |
| ethnocentrism | | |
| folkways | | |

| *Core Concept* | *Sociological Definition* | *Personal Illustration* |
| --- | --- | --- |
| high culture | | |
| mores | | |
| norms | | |
| popular culture | | |
| sanctions | | |
| social control | | |
| subculture | | |
| values | | |

## PUTTING IDEAS TOGETHER

Culture is defined as all the shared products of human society. Some of these products are material objects and others are the ideas and values important to a society. Material culture and nonmaterial culture are very much related. Material objects such as telephones, teacups, and tomahawks have to be used in appropriate ways.

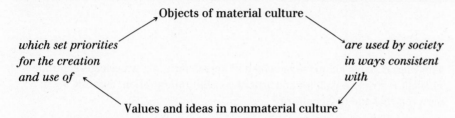

For example, the technological development of the laser beam has many implications for modern life. In the United States this technology (or material culture) is being used primarily for industrial development and medical science, two values of importance to American culture. These values (nonmaterial culture) set priorities for the kinds of material culture we want created. The same object, whether it is a laser beam, a wooden bowl, or a cross, is used in different ways in different societies because of cultural values.

An essential part of culture is the system of norms, which are rules and guidelines for acceptable behavior. Norms are based on social values and ensure that stable and predictable behavior will occur within the society. A system of social control reinforces the importance of these norms. Members of a culture also internalize important norms and control their own behavior. We can think of a range of social norms as follows.

### Types of Norms

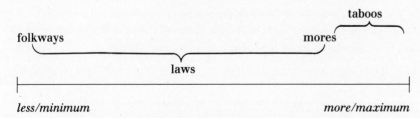

Severity of Punishment Based on Importance to Society

Obedience to parking rules is an example of a folkway and a law with little importance to society and thus a minimum penalty. Some laws, such as the prohibition of murder, are based on more serious norms, or mores, and carry a maximum penalty. Taboos are the most serious violations of all.

The range of cultural variation is immense, one indication of the adaptability of humans to their social and physical environment. As cultures change, new elements are added to existing ideas and objects, and the culture shifts, to some degree, to keep the parts integrated and compatible. Culture should be seen as a dynamic product, always changing to adapt to the circumstances of society. The chart below summarizes the ways cultures vary.

## Cultural Variation

| *Cultures Vary Due to* | *Example* |
| --- | --- |
| *The degree of cultural integration* shown in the gap between real and ideal culture | The United States claims to be a land of opportunity, yet Americans continue to adopt restrictive policies and attitudes about immigration, creating a gap between real and ideal culture |
| shown in the number of subcultures and countercultures | The arrival of Cuban, Haitian, and Asian refugees is producing additional ethnic/racial subcultures in the United States and in Western Europe. |
| *The speed of cultural change* due in part to contact with other cultures | Rapid cultural change has occurred in China as a result of reestablished relations for trade and visitation. |
| *The type of change occurring most often* discovery, invention, diffusion | Diffusion results in slower and more subtle social change than does discovery or invention. Material culture such as Coca-Cola, autos, and televisions diffuses more readily than nonmaterial culture. |
| *The physical environment* shown in their isolation from others | Aboriginal tribes in Australia have rather uniform and "simple" cultures due to lack of contact with others. Isolated groups in the United States, like Appalachian residents and Native Americans living on reservations, also have more homogeneous and "simple" cultures. |
| shown in the challenges for survival | Much cultural variation arises from the range of constraints imposed by climate and environment and the means different cultures devise to cope with them (e.g., snowmobiles or landrovers, dogsleds or camels). |
| *Basic cultural values* | The revolutionary government of Iran emphasizes Muslim values of devotion to Allah and self-sacrifice. Economic development through free enterprise will probably not occur given the importance of these values at this time. |

# Testing the Concepts

## MULTIPLE-CHOICE QUESTIONS

*After studying the chapter, try to answer each of the twenty-five questions below. Mark the alternative you think is correct; then look at the correct answer and explanation provided at the bottom of the page. Try to state why the other alternatives are incorrect, and check your understanding of the correct answer.*

1. Sociologists use the term "cultural relativism" to mean that
   a. some aspects of culture are more important than others.
   b. cultures change with time.
   c. each culture must be judged within its own context.
   d. some countries have more culture than others.
   e. culture helps people relate to one another.

2. The tendency of a group to regard its own ways as superior and to look down upon the ways of all others is called
   a. cultural relativity.
   b. cultural variability.
   c. group pride.
   d. ethnocentrism.
   e. cultural integration.

3. In the contemporary world, most cultural change comes from the process of
   a. diffusion.
   b. borrowing.
   c. invention.
   d. discovery.
   e. imitation.

4. If a society is low in cultural integration, we would expect to observe
   a. a lack of cultural universals.
   b. high ethnocentrism.
   c. a decline in moral values.
   d. conflicting values.
   e. symbolic language.

5. Which of the following actions violates the "mores" of U.S. society?
   a. whispering a comment during a movie
   b. sexually abusing a child
   c. wearing blue jeans to a symphony concert
   d. marrying someone with a different religion
   e. getting a parking ticket

6. An example of a negative informal sanction is
   a. a diploma.
   b. a handshake.
   c. a prison sentence.
   d. a dirty look.
   e. a nickname.

---

1. **c.** *The meaning of cultural elements can be understood only in the context of the culture in which they are used. Since sociologists want to understand the meaning of social life, they must adopt a position of cultural relativism. See page 74.*

2. **d.** *This is the definition of ethnocentrism, a word whose root connotes putting one's own group in the center. Ethnocentrism can build group pride but it can also be detrimental to understanding the ways of other people. See page 72.*

3. **a.** *Most cultural change results from diffusion, the slow process of absorbing elements from other cultures. We borrow the foods, words, customs, and ideas of other cultures in the subtle process of social change. See page 84.*

4. **d.** *A culture that is integrated displays a consistency among its basic values. A culture low in integration may have conflicting values. In the United States, for example, a belief in equality conflicts with a belief in the ability of an individual to rise above others. See page 74.*

5. **b.** *A mos (the singular form of mores) is an important societal rule. Sexual abuse of children is a serious offense against the values of American society and as such is proscribed by law. See page 62.*

6. **d.** *A negative sanction discourages undesirable behavior. Giving someone a dirty look communicates disapproval in everyday, informal interaction. See page 64.*

7. The distinction between folkways and mores rests on
   a. the importance of the norm to societal values.
   b. whether they are tied to cultural universals.
   c. whether the folkway is also a law.
   d. whether the norm is part of a subculture or held by a counterculture.
   e. the likelihood that people will be ethnocentric and expect other people to follow the norm.

8. The textbook's answer to the question "Are we prisoners of culture?" is
   a. no, because individuals have an opportunity to modify culture and do so.
   b. no, because culture is modified by the collective acts of human beings, as shown in many examples of cultural change.
   c. yes, because we are socialized to a particular culture and behave according to what we have learned.
   d. yes, because of ethnocentrism found in every group.
   e. no generalization can be made; individuals respond in very different ways to the culture in which they live.

9. The word "chick" is sometimes used to describe women. Some people say that it is "just an expression" and that women should not be defensive about the

name. Which of the groups listed below would take strong issue with that position?
   a. poultry breeders
   b. life-course theorists
   c. material cultural theorists
   d. functionalist theorists
   e. linguistic-relativity advocates

10. Which of the following groups would a sociologist most likely regard as a subculture rather than a counterculture?
   a. a violent street gang in Los Angeles
   b. guerrilla forces in El Salvador
   c. members of the American Nazi party
   d. practicing surgeons who graduated from Harvard
   e. the peyote cult of northern New Mexico

11. A large number of refugees from Guatemala and El Salvador have recently arrived in this country. Sociologists might hypothesize that this sudden influx would result in
   a. increases in counterculture formation.
   b. a decrease in social integration.
   c. a decrease in cultural pluralism.
   d. a need for ethnocentrism.
   e. class conflict leading to major social changes.

---

7. **a.** *Norms based on behavior that is not essential to the values of society are called folkways; they regulate courteous interaction between people. Mores, on the other hand, are norms of greater importance. They reflect the most significant and generally held beliefs in a culture. Violation of a mos receives strong negative sanction. See page 62.*

8. **b.** *Culture is created, sustained, and changed by the collective acts of human beings. Culture provides general guidelines for behavior but is modified by human actions and interpretations. See page 84.*

9. **e.** *Linguistic-relativity theorists argue that language structures thought. If we use the word "chick," and understand its meaning as derogatory to women, we will, to some degree, think of women in negative terms.*

*Thus the symbolic meaning of words is important. See pages 78–79.*

10. **d.** *A subculture has some of its own norms and values, but it coexists with the dominant culture. Surgeons share training experiences, job stresses and rewards, and their own terminology, yet they function within the dominant culture. See pages 76–77.*

11. **b.** *The culture of the refugees is quite different from that of the United States, including differences in language and norms. Like other immigrants before them, the Central Americans will add new elements to the culture, making it more varied and less integrated. At the same time, the culture that they bring with them will also be modified. See page 74.*

12. People in different societies have very different ways of living in and coping with their environment. Sociologists would note that this shows cultural
    a. conflict.
    b. relativity.
    c. integration.
    d. variation.
    e. confusion.

13. Suppose you are an art historian and a sociologist. You are asked to look at sample pieces of art, covering a 500-year period, from a culture not known to you. You should be able to comment on *all but one* of the items below. Which one?
    a. the technological development of the society
    b. the amount of social change it has experienced
    c. whether the society was characterized by cultural integration or diversity
    d. the relative worth of the various pieces of art
    e. some of the values of the society

14. A functionalist theorist might view ethnocentrism as
    a. old-fashioned ways of thinking.
    b. disruptive within a culture.

    c. evidence of low cultural integration.
    d. a way to enhance group solidarity.
    e. evidence that a culture has inferior values.

15. Some basic cultural universals exist because human beings
    a. have a rigid and patterned nature.
    b. have many instincts.
    c. have traded ideas since the development of modern communication.
    d. are ethnocentric.
    e. face similar biological requirements and have basic needs in common.

16. Language is the keystone of culture because it
    a. allows culture to be passed on from generation to generation.
    b. is important in the fine arts.
    c. identifies us with the group of people who also speak that language.
    d. allows humans to communicate in much the same manner as animals use signals.
    e. is more efficient than acting out our messages to one another.

---

12. **d.** *Cultures show immense variation in their ways of life, material objects, and norms. The environment influences cultures and explains part of this variation. See page 67.*

13. **d.** *It is not always obvious which artistic creations are high culture and which are popular culture. Items that appeal to you may or may not be those that command the highest value in a particular society. Although the value of cultural items seems to be arbitrary, the tastes of the wealthier, better-educated elite become the standard for esthetic judgments. See page 76.*

14. **d.** *Functionalists look at the consequences of ethnocentrism. One positive result is a feeling of group pride and solidarity. The text mentions other negative consequences, or dysfunctions, of ethnocentrism. See pages 69, 72.*

15. **e.** *All human beings have certain basic needs, for example, food, shelter, clothing, and care of the very young and old. These shared needs make for a connecting similarity in all cultures. See page 72.*

16. **a.** *Animals communicate on the basis of signals, such as sounds and gestures, whose meanings are fixed and limited to the immediate situation—they cannot be combined in new ways to produce different or more complex information. When animals die, their knowledge and experience die with them. Language, on the other hand, consists of learned symbols, enabling expression of any idea of which the human mind is capable. Through language, humans build on the learning of their ancestors, give meaning to their own world, and ultimately pass this information on from individual to individual and from generation to generation. See pages 77–78.*

17. The feature of human culture that distinguishes it from animal life is
    a. group life.
    b. social organization.
    c. communication.
    d. coordinated roles.
    e. symbolic language.

18. Every society has means to ensure that its members behave in approved ways. The general term for these means is
    a. social control.
    b. values.
    c. force.
    d. taboos.
    e. fines and imprisonment.

19. In a Judeo-Christian culture, the Ten Commandments represent
    a. folkways.
    b. ideal culture.
    c. ethnocentrism.
    d. out-of-date preachings.
    e. real culture.

20. A conflict theorist might look at ethnocentrism as
    a. a way in which power divisions are maintained.

    b. an example of the pride people have in their group.
    c. evidence of prejudiced people.
    d. a way to enhance group solidarity.
    e. a way to make society more stable.

21. Culture is human beings'
    a. genetic evolutionary characteristics.
    b. invented or learned means of adapting efficiently to changing conditions.
    c. random adaptation to their environment.
    d. inborn responses.
    e. music, theater, and fine arts.

22. Although equal opportunity for men and women is a central value of American culture, the Equal Rights Amendment (ERA) was not ratified. A conflict theorist's explanation would be that
    a. ethnocentrism obscured the issue.
    b. the existing cultural arrangement suited powerful groups.
    c. women are a counterculture to men.
    d. women have equal rights now, and any law is less important than the cultural value itself.
    e. the United States needs diffusion of ERA laws from other countries.

---

17. **e.** *Humans are the only species that use symbolic communication. Animals communicate instinctively through signs, but they cannot vary or add to their repertoire. Humans have a vast number of symbols available to them for communication. See page 78.*

18. **a.** *The sanctions, positive and negative, used by members of society, coupled with an individual's own internalized sense of right and wrong, guarantee that most of us obey most of our society's important norms most of the time. Social control includes all the ways obedience is taught, encouraged, and enforced. See page 64.*

19. **b.** *The Ten Commandments are important guidelines for believers of Jewish and Christian faiths. They represent ideal standards of behavior. Most individuals cannot follow them completely, but use them as guidelines for what is desired behavior. See pages 74–75.*

20. **a.** *Conflict theorists focus on the power relationships between different social groups or classes. Having an ethnocentric view implies that you look down on the ways of others; if in a power position, you might enforce your beliefs and ways on the less powerful groups. See pages 70, 72.*

21. **b.** *Culture is socially created. It arises in response to some basic human needs and the physical environment in which people live. Culture is added to as new needs and situations arise. It is the shared design for living in a society. See page 55.*

22. **b.** *Conflict theorists argue that cultural change comes about as a result of tension between competing groups. Powerful groups shape the social arrangements for their own benefit. In this case, those in power did not want a change in the Constitution that could upset certain inequalities of benefit to them. See page 70.*

23. Which of the following statements about evolution is supported by the text?
    a. Sociologist Emile Durkheim believed society evolves in the same way animals do.
    b. Reptiles evolved from mammals.
    c. Evolution is a slow, steady process of change; change does not occur in fits and starts.
    d. Darwin's focus was on the evolution of humans from apes.
    e. The key feature of human evolution is the ability to learn from experience.

24. The values of a society are very important because they
    a. influence and help shape its norms.
    b. reflect the content of its norms.

    c. are the rules or guidelines for people in particular kinds of situations.
    d. are the most visible key to what makes a society tick.
    e. do not conflict like some norms do.

25. Rock music is an integral part of the culture in the United States and Britain, but not in the Soviet Union. Why not?
    a. Early rock stars came from the United States and Britain.
    b. There is a shortage of radios in the Soviet Union.
    c. The Soviets excel in high culture, especially ballet.
    d. It is difficult to translate the lyrics of rock songs into Russian and retain their meaning.
    e. Soviet society does not tolerate dissent and rebellion.

---

23.  **e.** *Unlike other animals, human beings can learn from other members of their species via the transmission of culture. This enables them to build on past experience and to use the accumulated knowledge of their forebears to modify or quickly adapt to their natural environment.*

24.  **a.** *Values are the basis on which norms are formed. Important values are represented in mores, laws, and even taboos. Less important values are implied in folkways, the courtesies of daily life. See page 64.*

25.  **e.** *Rock music developed out of a youth-oriented culture that expressed its dissent and rebellion against traditional customs and the older generation. Rock music has been popular in democratic societies that tolerate this dissent. The Soviet Union controls popular culture and discourages rebelliousness among its citizens. See page 81.*

## A CASE STUDY

NAME

COURSE/SECTION NUMBER

Some feminists use the term "rape culture" to explain why rape is so common in the United States and to explain why rapists, when caught, receive light sentences. They argue that American culture *supports* rape indirectly by valuing male dominance of females, by accepting violence as a means of getting what one wants, and by believing that males needs to be sexually assertive to be sexually satisfied. When one looks at popular culture (the current movies, hit songs, fashions), one finds an alarming number of images showing women in bondage, women being attacked and appearing to enjoy it, men being praised for getting what they want from "bitchy" women. Few people would ever come right out and say they are "for" rape—the social support is more subtle. It is our system of values, norms, and laws that fosters rape. How else can we explain why the United States has one of the highest rates of rape in the world?

1.   What are your comments on the notion of a "rape culture?" Can you present evidence against it?

2.   If we accept, for now, the idea of a "rape culture," what objects in material culture and what ideas in nonmaterial culture allow rape to occur and even unconsciously support it?

    a.  Material culture:

    b.  Nonmaterial culture:

3.   List as many sanctions as you can that are designed to discourage or punish rapists. Which sanctions are most effective and why? Can you think of a social control mechanism to reduce the likelihood of one person raping another?

# Applying the Concepts

NAME

COURSE/SECTION NUMBER

## APPLICATION EXERCISE ONE

In the summer of 1983, Prince Charles of England, heir to the throne, married Diana Spencer. Three years later, Charles's younger brother, Prince Andrew, married Sarah Ferguson. Both weddings were lavish, full of pomp and circumstance. Television stations around the world covered the ceremonies themselves and all the pre- and postwedding fanfare. Magazines and tabloids carried pictures of the events and provided details of the clothing, the coaches, the engagement rings, even the brides' measurements. First Lady Nancy Reagan, who attended both weddings, was briefed on what to wear, how to address the royal family, what to give for a gift, and how to curtsey.

1.   The United States has never had a monarchy. What American values make this consistent with our culture? What British values buttress the monarchy even in modern times?

2.   Give examples from the royal weddings to show

   a. high culture and popular culture

   b. folkways and mores

3.    Give an example (real or hypothetical) of a newscaster covering the weddings who shows ethnocentric thinking. Then present a position of cultural relativism and contrast the two.

4.    The splendor of the royal weddings stands in sharp contrast to Britain's high rate of unemployment. How would a conflict theorist explain this discrepancy, as well as the enthusiasm most commoners have for the weddings of their princes and princesses?

5.    How would a functionalist describe the impact of the royal weddings on British society and culture?

## APPLICATION EXERCISE TWO

NAME

COURSE/SECTION NUMBER

Violate a folkway that is neither illegal nor immoral. You might select a behavior that is inappropriate for your age, sex, or even race/ethnicity. For example, you might wear mismatched shoes for a day, wear overly formal clothes to an informal gathering, eat with your hands instead of with silverware, speak in a foreign language to a salesclerk, strike up a conversation with a stranger in an elevator, or greet your parents as Mr. and Mrs. instead of Mom and Dad. Record the reactions you elicit, answering the following questions.

1.    What did you do? Why was it a violation of a folkway? What "value" underlies the folkway you violated?

2.    How serious was this violation? How was social control evident? What sanctions did you receive?

3.   How did you feel about what you did? How important are folkways to social life? Has this folkway become more or less important (to you personally and to society in general)?

## APPLICATION EXERCISE THREE

NAME

COURSE/SECTION NUMBER

You are a member of some subculture (or maybe even a counterculture). Consider, for example, a racial/ethnic subculture, an age or gender subculture, an occupational group, a special club, or a sports team that has a special identity among its members.

1.   Describe your subculture and the reasons you think it fits the definition of a subculture.

2.    Most subcultures have special language, called "argot," which is used by its members and not fully understood by nonmembers. Give examples of your subculture's argot.

3.    Do special symbols or rituals play a part in your subculture? What functions does this symbolic activity serve?

# CHAPTER 4

# Society

## Reviewing the Concepts

### LEARNING GOALS

*After studying this chapter, you should be able to:*

1. List the key components of society.

2. Define social structure and identify its four components.

3. Give an example of each of the two ways status is acquired.

4. Explain the connection between status and roles.

5. Describe how role expectations develop and how these expectations are useful.

6. Provide an example of role expectations and role performances that do not match. Give examples of role strain and role conflict.

7. Explain how groups link individuals with the social structure.

8. Compare the features of primary and secondary groups, giving an example of each.

9. Define "institution" and list the five major institutions that are present in all societies.

10. Describe the ways institutions remain stable over time and the ways in which they change.

11. Use the example of sport as an institution and identify how sports

   a. function in society.

   b. have a social organization of roles and statuses.

   c. connect with American cultural values.

   d. reflect structured inequalities in American society.

   e. have evolved with industrialization and modernization in the United
      States.

12. Explain what is meant by sociocultural evolution.

13. Identify the key characteristics and institutions of the six types of societies.

14. Describe how industrialization has resulted in changes in statuses, roles, groups, and institutions in the postindustrial society.

15. Compare the views of Tönnies and Durkheim on preindustrial and industrialized societies and on the differences in social organization that industrialization brings about.

## IDENTIFYING KEY QUESTIONS AND THEMES

Culture and society are intertwined. If culture is the shared products of living, then society is the people who share those products. More specifically, *society* is a population that occupies a common territory, is subject to the same political authority, and interacts within a common culture. Human beings are social animals who live in astonishingly diverse societies. The mutually dependent members of a given society are organized by their social structure.

### Social Structure

*What is social structure? How does it organize society and distribute the benefits of society?*

Social life proceeds in predictable ways according to the social structure of a given society. *Social structure* is the organized framework of relationships within a society. The most important components of social structure are statuses, roles, groups, and institutions.

The terms designating these components are commonly used in everyday language but have precise meanings for sociologists. A *status* is a socially defined position in society. All of us occupy several statuses. One of them, usually an occupational status, is the most significant because it is central to our social identity: it becomes our *master status.* If the various statuses are not complementary, individuals experience *status inconsistency.* The statuses that society assigns to us on grounds over which we have little control are called *ascribed statuses.* *Achieved statuses* are positions that we earn or lose by our own efforts. The values of a society determine the importance and rank of various statuses; people of roughly equivalent status in an unequal society form a *social class.*

Every status in society carries with it a set of expected behavior patterns, obligations, and privileges, called a *role.* A single status position can involve several roles. Social norms that determine how a role should be played are called *role expectations.* The actual *role performance* may differ from what is expected. *Role strain* occurs when contradictory expectations are built into a single role, and *role conflict* occurs when two or more roles place competing demands on the individual. Even with these difficulties, most role behavior conforms to norms and ensures smooth and predictable patterns of interaction within a society.

A collection of people with related statuses and roles

who interact with one another form a social *group.* Groups range in size from two people to large bureaucracies. Small groups that interact over a fairly long period on an intimate basis are called ***primary groups. Secondary groups*** have more temporary relationships, are more goal oriented, and tend to be anonymous and/or impersonal. Large secondary groups, such as government bureaucracies, are not found in the simplest societies, but they are increasingly important in modern societies.

All societies have certain basic needs in common. ***Institutions*** are the stable cluster of norms, values, statuses, roles, and groups that develop around these basic social needs. For example, all societies have a need to regulate sexual behavior and take care of children. The social institution of the family exists to fulfill these needs. Of course, the values and norms of any given culture shape the actual types of families found in a society and influence how they carry out their duties.

The institutions of any society tend to have several features in common: (1) institutions are stable, taken-for-granted patterns of behavior that provide continuity, and they therefore tend to be resistant to change; (2) the various institutions in a society tend to be interdependent and to share common features; (3) because they are so interdependent, institutions tend to change together—a change in one institution results in adjustment in the others; (4) institutions tend to be the site of major social problems, which arise when the institutions fail to satisfy the social needs on which they are centered. Such problems often develop because the institution in question responds slowly to social change. Functionalists look at the ways institutions maintain the social system, whereas conflict theorists look at who benefits or loses as a result of the prevailing system.

*Sport*—competitive physical activity guided by established rules—is an example of a social institution. Like other institutions, it serves as a microcosm of the society as a whole. In the United States, sport, in one form or another, meets the needs of a large part of society. Among its various functions are physical exercise, support of basic values, and entertainment for spectators. The type of sport that is popular in any society reflects and reinforces its values. As with other institutions, people's interest in and access to particular roles in sport are influenced by their social class, sex, and race.

## Types of Societies

*How can societies be classified? What is sociocultural evolution? What challenges do postindustrial societies face?*

The history of life on this planet has shown a general trend of ***sociocultural evolution***—the tendency for societies' social structures and cultures to grow more complex over time. By applying the ***ecological approach*** to this evolutionary process, we can account for much of the variation in a society's rate and level of advancement. Sociologists classify societies on the basis of their subsistence strategies—that is, their methods of meeting basic human needs within the context of the environment. The most efficient subsistence strategies are characterized by a greater amount of ***surplus wealth***—more food and other goods than is necessary to meet their producers' basic needs—and a significant increase in the ***division of labor***—the specialization by individuals or groups in particular economic activities.

***Hunting and gathering societies*** consist of small groups of nomadic people whose survival is based on the hunting of wild animals and the gathering of vegetation. The family is almost the only distinct institution in these societies. The domestication of animals in ***pastoral societies*** provides a more stable food supply and permits the ownership of property, including land and possessions. Status differences result. Pastoral peoples tend to develop a belief in a god or gods who take an active interest in human affairs—Judaism, Christianity, and Islam originated in pastoral societies. At the next level of complexity, ***horticultural societies*** raise edible plants, become territorially based, and possess richer material artifacts. Larger horticultural societies have well-developed political and economic systems. Since there is greater surplus wealth, status differences are more pronounced. Roles become more specialized as evidenced by an increase in the division of labor. With the invention of the plow in ***agricultural societies,*** large, permanent settlements become possible. A substantial minority no longer has to be involved in food production and can take on other occupational roles. Cities begin to form around commercial activities. As the economic institution becomes more complex, so, too, does the political institution that handles the need for governance of increasingly diverse groups. This growing complexity manifests itself in differentiation into social classes, the development of systems of writing and monetary exchange, improved transportation and communication systems, attention to the arts, and a permanent military. *Industrial societies* use mechanization as the means to produce goods. Science emerges as a new and important social institution fueling technological development. Social change occurs at a very rapid rate, and culture becomes more heterogeneous. Population and urbanization rise. Social relations become more complex, with a greater emphasis on secondary groups and bureaucracies. As achieved statuses become more important, social and economic inequality is reduced. However, the improved standard of living associated with industrialism has ecological consequences, such as environmental damage and depletion of natural resources, as well as social consequences, such as impersonalized relationships and rapid social change that constantly threatens to disrupt the existing social structure. The industrial type of subsistence is rapidly becoming the dominant form in the modern world. In the *postindustrial society,* production of services and information, especially technology, dominates the economy. Societies of this type are globally interdependent, looking to other nations for raw materials, cheap labor, and markets for products and technological skills. Education and science are important social institutions, providing support for an economy built on a belief in technology and a demand for highly skilled workers. Citizens in postindustrial societies have high standards of living, a larger number of occupational choices, more leisure, and greater opportunity for self-fulfillment. The evolution of this new type of society hinges on respect for the ecosystem and global peace and prosperity.

## Preindustrial and Industrialized Societies: A Comparison

*How have sociologists viewed the effects of industrialization?*

Modern, industrialized societies are radically unlike preindustrial societies. The difference between preindustrial and industrial societies has been studied by many sociologists. Tönnies distinguished between the *Gemeinschaft,* a "community," and the *Gesellschaft,* an "association." Durkheim described societies in terms of *mechanical organic* and *solidarity*—the former held together by the similarity of the members' roles and values, the latter held together by the fact that members play highly specialized roles and are therefore dependent on one another.

Modernization, as a result of industrialization, has profoundly affected the components of social organization and thus has changed society as a whole. Statuses are more achieved than ascribed. The number of roles has increased. Secondary groups and secondary relationships are numerous. Social institutions have become more complex and heterogeneous as far as how basic social needs are fulfilled. Indeed, the various functions of institutions have been altered. Sociologists are just beginning to grasp the significance of these changes.

## DEFINING CORE CONCEPTS

*After studying the chapter, write a sociological definition in your own words for the following core concepts. Then give an example from your own experience to illustrate your definition. Refer to the chapter to check your work.*

| Core Concept | Sociological Definition | Personal Illustration |
|---|---|---|
| achieved status | | |

| Core Concept | Sociological Definition | Personal Illustration |
|---|---|---|
| ascribed status | | |
| division of labor | | |
| Gemeinschaft | | |
| Gesellschaft | | |
| institution | | |
| master status | | |
| mechanical solidarity | | |

| Core Concept | Sociological Definition | Personal Illustration |
|---|---|---|
| organic solidarity | | |
| postindustrial society | | |
| role | | |
| social class | | |
| sociocultural evolution | | |
| social structure | | |
| society | | |
| status | | |

## PUTTING IDEAS TOGETHER

Human society consists of structured social interaction. To say that society is structured means that it has an underlying pattern of organization that makes human activity relatively orderly and predictable. The dynamic process of humans interacting with one another results in continual adaptation to social change.

## Social Structure

| | |
|---|---|
| *Institutions* | are stable clusters of values, norms, statuses, roles, and groups that develop around a basic social need. |
| *Groups* | are people interacting together in an orderly way on the basis of shared expectations about each other's behavior. |
| *Roles* | are the sets of expected behavior patterns, obligations, and privileges associated with a particular status. |
| *Ascribed and Achieved Statuses* | are socially defined positions in the society, given arbitrarily at birth (ascribed) or through an individual's efforts (achieved). |

Although every society has certain major institutions, for example, the family, the form the family takes and the accompanying roles, statuses, and values differ greatly. Fill in this pictoral example of the institution of the family as you know it in your culture.

**Institution: The Family**

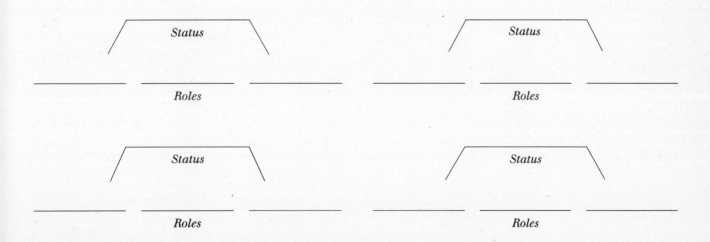

The second part of this chapter examines six types of societies and how they are organized. Sociocultural evolution describes the tendency for social structures and cultures to grow more complex over time, beginning with hunting and gathering societies, and progressing through pastoral societies, horticultural societies, agricultural societies, and industrial societies to postindustrial societies. All the components of social organization change as the process of evolution proceeds.

The shift from preindustrial societies to industrialized societies is particularly significant. Sociologists are still attempting to understand fully the implications of this change. Complete the following table, listing some of the key distinctions between preindustrial and industrialized societies.

## Preindustrial vs. Industrialized Societies

|  | Preindustrial Societies | Industrialized Societies |
| --- | --- | --- |
| Subsistence strategy |  | industrialism; postindustrialism |
| Social groups | mostly primary (longer-term, intimate interaction) |  |
| Statuses; roles |  | many achieved statuses, diverse, complex roles |
| Community | Gemeinschaft; mechanical solidarity |  |
| Division of labor |  | highly specialized occupations |
| Technology | primitive, based on human and animal muscle power |  |
| Social control |  | often formal, based on a system of laws, police, and courts |
| Values | tradition-oriented |  |
| Culture |  | elaborate, diversified; many subcultures with different rituals, beliefs, etc. |

# Testing the Concepts

## MULTIPLE-CHOICE QUESTIONS

*After studying the chapter, try to answer each of the twenty-five questions below. Mark the alternative you think is correct; then look at the correct answer and the explanation provided at the bottom of the page. Try to state why the other alternatives are incorrect, and check your understanding of the correct answer.*

1. In sociology, institutions refer to
   a. group quarters, such as prisons and asylums.
   b. long-standing organizations.
   c. ways in which a society meets the basic needs of its people.
   d. groups requiring formal membership, such as the Rotary Club or Boy Scouts.
   e. a well-known person, such as Frank Sinatra, a Hollywood institution.

2. Organic solidarity, Durkheim would argue, would be most characteristic of
   a. hunting and gathering societies.
   b. agricultural societies.
   c. pastoral societies.
   d. *Gemeinschaft* communities.
   e. industrial societies.

3. One aspect of social structure that sociologists see as functional is that it
   a. excludes outsiders.
   b. acts as a constraint on social change and preserves old traditions.
   c. enables people to undertake daily life with some degree of efficiency and predictability.
   d. gives more deserving people power over those who have not contributed to society.
   e. makes ascribed statuses more important than achieved statuses.

4. The major world religions of Christianity, Judaism, and Islam originated among
   a. pastoral societies.
   b. agricultural societies.
   c. hunting and gathering societies.
   d. nomadic societies.
   e. horticultural societies.

5. Role conflict occurs most often when
   a. a person must violate one role in order to perform another.
   b. a role is ascribed to a person.
   c. a role is not desired by an individual.
   d. a role has low social prestige.
   e. a person does not perform his or her role successfully.

---

1. **c.** *An institution is the cluster of values, norms, statuses, roles, and expectations that develop around the basic needs of a society. These stable patterns of life help to ensure that needs will be met. See page 93.*

2. **e.** *In industrial societies, people relate to one another in secondary groups. Their interrelated roles and division of labor make for a dependence on one another. Durkheim called this type of social arrangement organic solidarity. It is most common in industrial societies that are large, heterogeneous, and interconnected via secondary groups. See page 110.*

3. **c.** *Social structure consists of organized relationships in society. Because there are expectations associated with our statuses and roles, we know how to act and we can anticipate what others will do. Even during periods of change, this predictability makes for smooth social life. See page 90.*

4. **a.** *Pastoral societies were organized around the tending of herds of animals for subsistence. People developed a view of a god with an interest in human affairs, much like their own interest in guarding their herds. See page 103.*

5. **a.** *The demands of roles can be incompatible with one another. This is particularly likely in a modern society where individuals have many roles to play. See page 92.*

6. The distinctive characteristics of any society depend largely on its
    a. roles.
    b. social values.
    c. statuses.
    d. groups.
    e. level of industrialization.

7. Preindustrial society could be characterized in such terms as
    a. *Gesellschaft*, organic solidarity.
    b. *Gemeinschaft*, mechanical solidarity.
    c. mostly secondary group relationships, mostly achieved statuses.
    d. pastoral society, mostly secondary group relationships.
    e. *Gesellschaft*, heterogeneous.

8. Hunting and gathering societies
    a. live on the brink of starvation.
    b. no longer exist in the modern world.
    c. use the slash and burn method for rotating their crops.
    d. are more socially complex than horticultural societies.

    e. are generally leisured, with their members doing little work.

9. Sex, race, and age are examples of _____ statuses.
    a. social class
    b. occupational
    c. achieved
    d. ascribed
    e. negative

10. A status is
    a. an important position in society that others aspire to.
    b. a secure position of power within a community.
    c. a specific position in the social structure.
    d. a set of expectations about your behavior.
    e. a well-defined role with little conflict.

11. The term social structure refers to
    a. norms that govern the behavior of individuals.
    b. social classes of people grouped on the basis of their income.
    c. the role set attached to any single status.
    d. the hierarchy of power in a community.
    e. the orderly or patterned way people relate to one another.

---

6. **d.** *Groups are the intermediary level between the roles and statuses held by individuals and the society as a whole. Human beings spend a great deal of time in groups of all kinds and sizes, forming a complex network of interrelationships. See page 92.*

7. **b.** *Preindustrial societies have a simple structure, mostly primary group relationships, and interrelationships among people who share similar roles and values. Tönnies's term to describe this type of society is* Gemeinschaft; *Durkheim used the term "mechanical solidarity." See pages 109–110.*

8. **e.** *The simple life of the hunting and gathering society revolves around hunting game for food. The fact that there are no permanent settlements frees the people*

*from many tasks. There are few roles and more leisure time than in more complex societies. See page 102.*

9. **d.** *An ascribed status, like sex, race, and age, is one that is assigned to individuals on grounds over which they have little control.*

10. **c.** *A status is a position. Our statuses are based on ascribed and achieved characteristics, and we are expected to play the roles attached to each status. See pages 90–91.*

11. **e.** *Social relationships are organized through statuses, roles, groups, and institutions. These components of a social system give it structure and make social life orderly. See page 90.*

12. A doctor relates somewhat differently to his or her patients and their families than to nurses and other doctors. The doctor's behavior constitutes his/her
    a. master status.
    b. role performance.
    c. role conflict.
    d. ascribed position.
    e. social institution.

13. Which pair of groups listed below consists of two primary groups?
    a. the Rotary Club, the night shift at Schlitz brewery
    b. three roommates in college, two couples playing bridge each Tuesday
    c. the primary grades in Oakton school, a large high school class reunion
    d. the Democratic party in Georgia, all women named Georgia
    e. the Johanssen's nuclear family, the Association of Nuclear Engineers

14. Lydia's resumé notes that she is a twenty-four-year-old female, with a B.A. from Smith College, a membership in an honorary society, and three years of job experience. Her ascribed status is her
    a. college degree.
    b. work experience.
    c. honor society membership.
    d. female gender.
    e. name.

15. Each of us occupies several statuses. A master status is
    a. the role of an official or an authority figure.
    b. the most important socially defined position.
    c. the role in which we display the most talent or expertise.
    d. the elite class of society and the roles they play.
    e. the role that wins out in cases of role conflict.

16. Within a society, a social class consists of people with similar
    a. religious backgrounds.
    b. community boundaries.
    c. educational achievements.
    d. material possessions.
    e. status.

17. The social improvements associated with industrialization come largely as a result of
    a. bureaucratic organizations.
    b. a decline in the power of religions to restrict activities.
    c. a smaller proportion of the population needed for food production.
    d. a lower death rate due to improved medical care.
    e. elected, democratic government.

---

12. **b.** *The position of doctor involves many roles, such as dispenser of medicine, counselor to families, team member with nurses. All of these constitute a role performance. See page 92.*

13. **b.** *Primary groups are small and involve continued face-to-face intimate interaction among individuals. See pages 92–93.*

14. **d.** *Gender is an ascribed characteristic, which gives Lydia a social position. She has certain role expectations based on being female. See pages 90–91.*

15. **b.** *Our most important position is our master status. In the United States, this is often our occupational status, which determines many of our other roles. See page 90.*

16. **e.** *A status is a position in society, and those people with roughly equivalent positions form a class. See page 91.*

17. **c.** *Efficient food production, aided by technology, frees a large part of the population for other specialized roles, including the arts, manufacturing, educational pursuits, and scientific discovery. See page 106.*

18. Cities *first* appear when subsistence is based on
    a. hunting and gathering.
    b. horticulture.
    c. agriculture.
    d. pastoral herding.
    e. industrialization.

19. Sports serve many purposes in American society. Which purpose would the conflict theorists emphasize?
    a. the importance of the American value of team play and cooperation
    b. reinforcement of American class, sex, and race privileges
    c. opportunity for physical exercise and use of leisure time
    d. the number of formal organizations that have grown around sports
    e. the amount of violence that occurs in sports such as hockey and boxing

20. The distinctly American value that is most reinforced through the social institution of sport is
    a. physical exercise.
    b. supporting the home team.
    c. relaxation after work.
    d. teamwork.
    e. winning.

21. Which of the following features is *not* necessary for a society to exist?
    a. common territory
    b. a formal police agency
    c. interaction
    d. shared group membership and commitment
    e. a culture

22. In contrast to other types of societies, in postindustrial societies
    a. the majority of workers provide services.
    b. the key social institutions are sports and religion.
    c. there are few master statuses.
    d. the economy is self-sufficient, less globally dependent.
    e. adults specialize in one technical work role for most of their lives.

23. The development of an organized military is characteristic of which kind of society?
    a. horticultural
    b. agricultural
    c. preindustrial
    d. pastoral
    e. totalitarian

---

18. **c.** *Agriculture allows the formation of stable settlements and enough surplus so people can take on nonfarm roles. See page 105.*

19. **b.** *The rewards of participation in sports are not equally distributed throughout American society. The inequalities and privileges reflect society in general, e.g., exclusion of women. The number of minorities who succeed in sports is small compared to those who attempt to rise in status through this institution. See pages 97–99.*

20. **e.** *Americans value the victories that come from competition. In other societies, sports are organized so that winning is not as important as teamwork, the pleasure of playing the game, or the value of leisure activities. See page 97.*

21. **b.** *A society is a group of interacting individuals sharing the same territory and a common culture. Some method of social control will exist, but it does not have to be a formal police force as we know it. See page 89.*

22. **a.** *The economy of a postindustrial society is a service economy where knowledge, as opposed to manufactured goods, is produced. Agriculture and manufacturing are automated. Science and technology are the key institutions. See pages 107–108.*

23. **b.** *Agricultural societies tend to be almost constantly at war and to have a formal military system, which they use to protect themselves as well as to take over other groups. See page 106.*

24. The ecological approach to sociocultural evolution
    a. views human societies in the context of their environment and their strategies for exploiting that environment.
    b. focuses on the pollution and resource depletion found in modern industrial societies.
    c. cannot explain why some societies have a more complex social structure than others.
    d. is more useful for the analysis of secondary than primary relationships.
    e. is no longer applicable to studies of human populations.

25. Which institution would tend to be weaker in industrial than in preindustrial societies?
    a. the economy
    b. the state
    c. the family
    d. education
    e. sports

---

24. **a.** *Human societies work within their environments to develop a method of subsistence. The ecological approach recognizes the advantage of an environment rich in natural resources in the evolutionary process toward increasing complexity. See page 101.*

25. **c.** *Many of the functions handled by the family in preindustrial societies are handled by other social institutions in industrial societies. Examples include education and care of children, and care of the elderly and sick. See pages 109–110.*

## A CASE STUDY

Lauren completed law school, graduating third in her large, Ivy League school class. She landed a high-paying position in a prestigious firm in the downtown financial district as a beginning lawyer with thirty-two other lawyers, all but one of whom were male. After a week or so of working at Bigwig, Bigwig, and Bigwig, Lauren approached the other female lawyer and asked her to lunch, only to receive the rather brusque reply that she was "too busy." Lauren didn't pursue the matter. She tried to befriend the secretaries, all of whom were female, but they had their own cliques; when she did socialize with them, she felt uncomfortable during their critical conversations about the lawyers. Keeping to herself was not only lonely but seemed to be counterproductive in climbing to the top. Two of the men who entered the firm when Lauren did received promotions quickly. Lauren attributed this to their buddy system with the Bigwigs (the two men and the partners often lunched together, played squash, or had cocktails after work to unwind). When Lauren had her first child, she took maternity leave and then returned to work promptly. She wanted to discuss motherhood with her co-workers, but felt the topic was out of place: she confined her conversations at work to legal cases and talked about parenting with others in her neighborhood. This compartmentalization of her life continued to be Lauren's pattern of behavior.

1.    What are Lauren's roles? Which of her statuses are ascribed, and which are achieved?

2.    What examples of primary and secondary groups are evident in this case? What do the different group relationships offer the members?

3.    What evidence of role conflict and role strain do you see? How are they handled?

4.    Although Lauren's personal qualities may be causing some of her
problems, in many ways the social structure is determining her success in the
legal world. What are some of the social-structure influences that are beyond
Lauren's control?

# Applying the Concepts

NAME

_____

COURSE/SECTION NUMBER

## APPLICATION EXERCISE ONE

Each of us has several ascribed statuses. List two of yours. Comment on two situations this week in which someone responded to you primarily in terms of one of your ascribed statuses, rather than on the basis of your personality, your abilities, or your achieved statuses. For example, restaurant personnel usually respond to the ascribed statuses of age and gender, which are often associated with power and wealth, and give the oldest-appearing male the bill.

## APPLICATION EXERCISE TWO

Select two of your statuses and diagram the roles associated with them.

NAME

COURSE/SECTION  NUMBER

1.   Now comment on examples of role strain and role conflict.

2.  Indicate where role expectations and role performance have not coincided.

3.  What happened when role expectations and role performance did not match?

4.  Do you have a master status?

## APPLICATION EXERCISE THREE

NAME

COURSE/SECTION NUMBER

Sociologists use various indicators to measure social change. For example, a change in the crime rate may indicate a change in the values of a society. Your task is to develop social indicators that serve as evidence of postindustrialization in the United States.

1.   The rate of social change is much faster in postindustrial societies. Indicator: the rate at which new words appear in the language. If you were working on a new edition of the dictionary, list five new words for ideas or objects that you think ought to be included.

2.   In postindustrial societies there is a greater diversity of rituals and beliefs. Indicator: cultural diversity. Interview a classmate about his or her family traditions. Ask about a specific practice and/or the celebration of a major holiday. Contrast these traditions with those of your family.

3.    A great deal of social life in postindustrial societies occurs in secondary groups. Indicator: primary versus secondary groups. List five groups in which you recently interacted. Which are primary and which are secondary groups? Can you have primary relationships in secondary groups? Vice versa?

4.    The postindustrial economy is heavily concentrated in the service sector. Indicator: the division of labor. Look at the Sunday classified ads in a major metropolitan newspaper. Count the total number of jobs on a page and figure out what percentage are service jobs. Then figure out the percentage that require a high school degree, a college degree, and additional training.

# CHAPTER 5

# Socialization

## Reviewing the Concepts

### LEARNING GOALS

*After studying this chapter, you should be able to:*

1. Discuss socialization and the three elements that comprise individual personality.

2. Present the views of Pavlov and Watson concerning the relative importance of genetic traits and socialization in determining human behavior.

3. Describe the ways in which biological predispositions and social influence are intertwined.

4. Summarize the evidence relating to the effects of childhood isolation on healthy socialization.

5. Discuss the concept of "self" and how it develops.

6. Describe Cooley's three-part theory of the looking-glass self.

7. Describe Mead's theory of the formation of the self through symbolic interaction, role-taking, and the generalized and particular other.

8. List the basic cognitive capacities that are associated with each of Piaget's stages of development.

9. Outline the process of human emotional development and the cultural factors that influence it.

10. Identify the key agents of socialization and the point in the life course at which they are most important.

11. Discuss the concept of a life course and why it is culturally relative.

12. Explain the connection between industrialization and the social inventions of childhood and adolescence.

13. Apply the idea of developmental socialization to mature adulthood and old age.

14. Describe how death is handled in a modern industrialized society and how our responses to death are learned and patterned by society.

15. Summarize the controversy surrounding the oversocialized view of man.

## IDENTIFYING KEY QUESTIONS AND THEMES

The human infant depends on other people for survival. *Socialization* is the process of social interaction through which human beings acquire personality and learn their society's way of life. As such, it is the essential link between the individual and society. Each individual operates, in part, on the basis of *personality,* or the fairly stable patterns of thought, feeling, and action that are specific to that person. Thus, personality includes three main elements: the cognitive component, the emotional component, and the behavioral component. At the same time, the individual is a member of a society, and as such shares common understandings about the basic rules of social life specific to that culture. The socialization process continues throughout the *life course*—the biological and social sequence of birth, childhood, maturity, old age, and death—as the individual adapts to changing conditions. However, the most important socialization occurs during the early years, when basic personality takes form.

### "Nature" and "Nurture"

*What part do instincts and genetic differences play in our behavior?*

The "nature versus nurture" debate originally was an attempt to establish human behavior as either primarily inherited (nature) or learned (nurture). Although the work of Pavlov and Watson, which supported the nurture viewpoint, held sway for the better part of this century, today most social scientists believe that we are the product not of either heredity or learning but rather of a complex interaction between the two. Biology imposes certain limits on human behavior and sets up basic potentials for each person, while socialization teaches us how to act on these limitations and potentials in culturally approved ways.

## Effects of Childhood Isolation

*What are the consequences of little or no human contact on human development? What is the quality of the evidence on which these conclusions are based?*

The effects of isolation on human development are devastating. Studies have proved beyond doubt that a child who lacks close bonds with at least one other person will not develop normally. Several sets of data support the importance of human nurturance to child development. Cases involving "feral" children, children allegedly raised by animals, show they possessed few human characteristics. Children deliberately raised in isolation were socially undeveloped and only limited improvements in socialization could be made once they were discovered. Studies of institutionalized children, such as those raised in orphanages, indicate they compared poorly in physical, cognitive, emotional, and social development with children raised in family settings. Finally, Harlow's experiments with monkeys reared in isolation show that without nurturance, even monkeys cannot develop normal social, sexual, or emotional behavior. Because isolation studies pose ethical dilemmas and cannot deliberately be conducted, results from existing cases must be interpreted cautiously.

## The Emergence of the Self

*What do sociologists mean by the concept of "self"? How does the self develop?*

Sociologists define the *self* as the individual's conscious experience of a distinct, personal identity that is separate from all other people and things. It is formed through interaction with other people. Charles Horton Cooley explained personality and its development in terms of the *looking-glass self*—a self-concept derived from a social "mirror" in which we can observe how others react to us. The responses of other people to our appearance, behavior, etc., give us information about our personal qualities. According to Cooley's three-step process, we imagine our own appearance, we interpret others' reactions to us—especially those of "significant others"—and we incorporate both views in our developing self-concept. Elaborating on Cooley's ideas, George Herbert Mead introduced the concept of *symbolic interaction,* the interaction between people that takes place through symbols, especially language. He pointed out that as a result of socialization, we can anticipate what other people expect of us and modify our behavior accordingly. *Role-taking* is the process of pretending to take, or actually taking, the roles of others in order to see one's self and the world from their viewpoints. As young children, we internalize the expectations only of the *particular other*—specific other people such as parents. Later in life, we internalize the attitudes and values of society as a whole—the *generalized other.* Through three stages of increasingly sophisticated role-playing (imitation, play, and games), children come to understand themselves and social life. Mead looked at socialization as an ongoing process, since the "I" (the unsocialized self) is never completely under the control of the "me" (the socialized self). The theories of both Cooley and Mead stress the link between the emergence of the self and social interaction.

## Learning to Think

*How does the mind develop? What are Piaget's stages of cognitive development?*

Jean Piaget studied cognitive development—the individual's mastery of intellectual capacities such as perceiving, remembering, and believing. According to Piaget, the human mind actively tries to make sense of the social world and matures through social interaction. His many experiments suggest cognitive development takes place through a sequence of stages—sensorimotor, preoperational, concrete operational, formal operational—moving from simple to more complex mental processes. If an individual is not involved in meaningful social interaction, that individual may remain fixed at a lower stage. Evidence suggests that the developmental *process* of cognitive socialization is universal, but that the *content* of what is learned is culturally variable. In a postindustrial society, computers are likely to play an increasingly important part in the education of young people. Sociologists are studying their possible impact on social relationships.

## Learning to Feel

*How are emotions socially created and controlled?*

Like cognitive abilities, humans learn emotions through a developmental process. Studies by Jerome Kagan and others indicate that children progress from reflexive reactions to their environment to interpreting, expressing, and responding to emotions on the basis of the shared cultural meanings of their society. Norms, one form of social control, guide when, where, and how emotions are expressed.

## Agents of Socialization

*What are the chief sources of influence in the socialization process?*

The four major *agents of socialization*—significant individuals, groups, or institutions that provide structured situations in which socialization takes place—are the family, the school, the peer group, and the mass media. The family is the single most significant agent of socialization in all societies. It is particularly important during childhood when youngsters are establishing their first close emotional ties, learning language, and beginning to internalize cultural norms and values. The agent of socialization formally charged by society with the responsibility of socializing the young in particular skills and values is the school. It provides training in such cognitive skills as reading and mathematics, and knowledge about a variety of subjects. Beyond this, children learn many attitudes and behaviors, such as punctuality, respect for authority, and competitive strategy, which will prepare them for later roles in the work force and in society. As they grow older, young people spend more and more time with their *peers*—people of roughly equivalent age and other social characteristics. Peers often exert a great deal of influence on adolescents in particular. Unlike the family or the school, the peer group is entirely centered on its own concerns and interests. The *mass media*—newspapers, books, television, radio, magazines, movies, records, and videos—act as a general socializing agent. Television, in particular, influences our perceptions of news events, different lifestyles, and the "in" things to buy, to name just a few. Some research indicates that violence on television encourages violent behavior in children, a position that continues to be hotly debated. Other agents, such as religious groups, clubs, and work organizations may influence socialization as well. In extreme cases, the individual may go through a process known as *resocialization,* that is, learning characterized by a sharp break with past ideas and socialization into very different norms and values. Often such resocialization occurs within a *total institution*—a place of residence where inmates are confined for a set period of their lives, where they are cut off from the rest of society, and where they are under the almost absolute control of a hierarchy of officials.

## The Life Course

*What are the various stages of the life course? How do ideas about the life course vary among cultures?*

The human life course, the sequence from birth to death, is artificially divided up into different stages by different cultures, according to the importance they attach to various times in the life span. Advanced industrialized societies emphasize childhood and the newly defined stage of adolescence, in part to education people for work roles. In emerging postindustrial societies, an additional stage in the life course—"youth"—is being created for people between the ages of 18 and 30 who are still in school or not yet settled into an occupation. In mature adulthood, developmental socialization builds on earlier experience to prepare people for the new roles of marriage, parenting, career, and retirement.

However a society delineates the life course, it is important that individuals be able to take on the different roles associated with each new stage they enter. Unfortunately, American society does not adequately prepare individuals to face old age, although the situation has improved somewhat within the past decade. Socialization for death is almost nonexistent. The modern technology that has significantly extended *life expectancy*—the length of life the average newborn will enjoy — has had little effect on the *life span* — the maximum length of life possible in the species. Death, then, belies our claim to human mastery of the world; research suggests this may lead us to deny it and exclude it from our thoughts. Societies such as the United States eliminate death from everyday experience by moving it from the context of the family to the bureaucracies of the hospital and nursing home. Although it seems like the ultimate personal experience, death, too, is a social process guided by societal norms and values governing how we treat the dying, which funeral rites we observe, and so forth. Fortunately, recent sociological research into death and dying has led to efforts, often through school courses and seminars, to improve socialization for death.

## Socialization and Free Will

*Has the importance of socialization been overstated? Are individuals active or passive in response to the process of socialization?*

Socialization is crucial if an individual is to learn the ways of society and develop a sense of self. However, the individual is not an "oversocialized" robot. Rather, we are all active agents in the socialization process, interpreting and blending the socializing experiences to which we are exposed. Individuals do not always obey all rules of society, nor do they behave identically in the same situations. Socialization provides broad limits for behavior, but leaves individual personalities room for variation within those limits.

## DEFINING CORE CONCEPTS

*After studying the chapter, write a sociological definition in your own words for the following core concepts. Then give an example from your own experience to illustrate your definition. Refer to the chapter to check your work.*

| Core Concept | Sociological Definition | Personal Illustration |
|---|---|---|
| agents of socialization | | |
| generalized other | | |
| life course | | |
| looking-glass self | | |

| Core Concept | Sociological Definition | Personal Illustration |
| --- | --- | --- |
| particular other | | |
| personality | | |
| resocialization | | |
| role-taking | | |
| self | | |
| socialization | | |
| symbolic interaction | | |
| total institution | | |

## PUTTING IDEAS TOGETHER

Although the nature vs. nurture debate is really a nonissue, it is important to understand that each human being has distinctive traits and potentials, which are shaped through social interaction. Thus each person's development results from the complex interaction of heredity and environment, including learning.

### The Changing Social Self

"ME"
(socialized self)

"I"
(unsocialized self)

Foundation of personality and other inborn talents will be shaped and modified through social interaction by various agents of socialization as the individual passes through the life course.

Socialization is the process of learning the ways of society. We are socialized throughout our life course, with different agents of socialization exerting more influence at various times. The general pattern, for purposes of summary, looks like this:

## Socialization

| Agents of Socialization of Greatest Importance | Stage in the Life Course | Examples |
|---|---|---|
| *Family*<br>*Mass media*<br>*(especially television)*<br>*School* | *Childhood* | Lee learns table manners from parents, the "acceptability" of violence from television, and the need to follow rules from school. |
| *School*<br>*Peers*<br>*Mass media* | *Adolescence* | School experiences teach Lee the social consequences of succeeding or failing; peers show Lee what behaviors win friends; media images influence Lee's aspirations and sense of identity. |
| *Mass media*<br>*Other agents* | *Mature Adulthood* | Lee's views of American life are shaped by the media, particularly television; the norms Lee adheres to are temporarily altered when s/he joins a cult; Lee's value system changes again upon entering big business. |
| *Other agents*<br>*(senior citizens groups;*<br>*geriatric institutions)* | *Old Age*<br>*Death* | Lee derives some satisfaction in belonging to a senior citizens group newly sponsored by the community. Still, feelings of despair often creep in and Lee fears the day s/he will face death in a nursing home. |

# Testing the Concepts

## MULTIPLE-CHOICE QUESTIONS

*After studying the chapter, try to answer each of the twenty-five questions below. Mark the alternative you think is correct; then look at the correct answer and explanation provided at the bottom of the page. Try to state why the other alternatives are incorrect, and check your understanding of the correct answer.*

1.  Which pair of terms contains two concepts with essentially the same meaning?
    a. I, Me
    b. generalized other, society
    c. self, particular other
    d. looking-glass self, family
    e. socialization, personality

2.  The textbook argues that socialization in American society has had its greatest failure in equipping us for roles in
    a. childhood.
    b. adolescence.
    c. the military.
    d. marriage.
    e. old age and death.

3.  The roles associated with the stage of childhood in the life course differ from society to society. One important determinant is
    a. the society's degree of industrialization.
    b. the presence of mandatory schooling.
    c. a cultural preference for large families.
    d. differences in life span.
    e. the practice of infanticide.

4.  The peer group is a significant agent of socialization, in part because it
    a. has a definite plan to make the individual conform to social rules.
    b. reinforces the teachings of the family.
    c. provides a recreational outlet for children.
    d. is an ascribed relationship, giving every person a position in society.
    e. allows exploration of relationships and topics that may be taboo in the family and the school.

5.  Regarding socialization, the isolation studies of Anna and Isabelle, as well as those of Harlow involving monkeys, show that
    a. isolation can help develop a sense of self-reliance.
    b. damage to children or monkeys raised in isolation can be reversed quickly by resocializing them, with few long-term effects.
    c. monkey behavior is instinctual, and the Harlow experiments are not applicable to the human cases of isolation.
    d. both human beings and monkeys show signs of

---

1.  **b.** *In Mead's terms, the generalized other represents the attitudes and viewpoints of society as a whole about how to behave. We internalize these expectations, forming the basis for self-evaluation and hence for self-concept. See page 123.*

2.  **e.** *Increased life expectancy has added old age to the life course. Most Americans are not prepared for the role of old person, nor does our culture allow much understanding of death. This focus on youth and corresponding denial of death can cause a great deal of pain and confusion. See page 136.*

3.  **a.** *Industrialized societies have more compartmentalized stages in the life course. Thus childhood is seen as a time of play and adolescence as a*

*time of self-discovery and occupational preparation. See page 132.*

4.  **e.** *The peer group is a voluntary group of members with relatively equal status. The peer group, particularly important during the adolescent stage of the life course, allows the exploration of relationships and topics in a nondirected fashion. This contrasts significantly with the more structured socialization experience found in the family and in the school. See pages 129–130.*

5.  **d.** *Anna and Isabelle were socially retarded due to their isolation from human contact. Harlow found that monkeys reared in isolation behave in some ways like human psychotics. See pages 119–121.*

maladjustment when denied early social interaction.

e. monkeys in isolation still meet their basic needs for food and sex; once these instinctual needs are met, there is no other harm.

6. Unlike the agents of socialization of the family and the school, the peer group

a. trains people to behave in negative, socially disapproved ways.

b. shapes the "I" but not the "me."

c. is insignificant because so much has been learned prior to adolescence.

d. is less direct and deliberate in its design.

e. is relevant for the adolescent stage of the life course only.

7. One agent of socialization is particularly important, because participation in it gives children an ascribed status in society. This agent is

a. the mass media.

b. the family.

c. the peer group.

d. a voluntary organization.

e. the school.

8. The concept of "generalized other" refers to

a. the general impression that others have of the self.

b. individuals other than the self, such as parents and friends, who play a part in socialization.

c. the attitudes of the self toward others in general.

d. the same concepts as Freud's term "ego."

e. the self's sense of the attitudes of society as a whole.

9. How does the unique genetic makeup of each child influence that child's socialization?

a. Biological traits predetermine the outcome of socialization.

b. Hereditary factors set the basic potential for a child.

c. The crucial determinant of *behavior* lies in the child's genetic makeup.

d. Socialization results from instincts transmitted through the child's genetic makeup.

e. Genetics determine personality, and socialization influences values and beliefs.

10. Charles Horton Cooley's theory of the self is based on the concept of

a. the looking-glass self.

b. the "I" and the "me."

c. the generalized other.

d. reference groups.

e. personality.

---

6. **d.** *The peer group is significant from adolescence through old age. Unlike the family or school, this agent of socialization is less deliberate. While the family and the school explicitly teach the young person the knowledge and rules of society, peer groups are powerful, but more indirect in influencing tastes, preferences, and behavior, and in contributing to self-image and self-esteem. See page 130.*

7. **b.** *The family into which we are born gives us an ascribed status in the class system of society, which influences later social interaction and socialization. For example, studies show that families socialize children differently depending on their social class position; thus, the values and expectations that children born in different classes learn are likely to be quite different. See page 128.*

8. **e.** *The generalized other refers to the attitudes and viewpoints of society as a whole. All of us take into account our perception of the expectations of the generalized other, both in forming our sense of self and in acting out our social roles. See page 123.*

9. **b.** *Heredity provides a basic potential. For example, people respond differently to each child based on physical appearance, especially gender. The child, in turn, responds to these messages and incorporates them as part of the socialization of the self. See page 118.*

10. **a.** *Cooley argued that the self is a social product, formed from the reflections we get from others. The looking glass is society, which provides a mirror in which we can observe others responding to our behavior. See page 122.*

11.  According to sociologists, what function do emotions, or learned feelings, serve that is most important to society in general?
    a.  social control
    b.  personal expression
    c.  private, intimate communication between two people
    d.  commonality of feeling across all cultures
    e.  a means of breaking away from expected norms

12.  Sociologist Dennis Wrong coined the term "oversocialized conception" of man. He used the term to argue that
    a.  human beings can be brainwashed relatively easily, as religious cults demonstrate.
    b.  too much socialization can confuse the individual.
    c.  sociologists have overemphasized the importance of socialization and have neglected the role of free will.
    d.  all the different agents of socialization try to get 'he individual to think a certain way.
    e.  we push children into assuming adult roles too early in life, before they are ready to play them.

13.  George Herbert Mead's theory of the self emphasizes
    a.  _he importance of symbolic interaction.

    b.  the need to avoid role-taking in order to develop a genuine sense of self-identity.
    c.  the importance of rewards and punishments to make people behave as society wishes.
    d.  the importance of understanding our own unique personality.
    e.  the looking-glass self.

14.  For which pair of emotions would the development of the looking-glass self be a precondition?
    a.  anger, curiosity
    b.  fear, pleasure
    c.  joy, anger
    d.  sadness, surprise
    e.  jealousy, pride

15.  For sociologists, the most important outcome of early socialization is
    a.  preparation for development of a gender role identity later in adolescence.
    b.  teaching older people about recent cultural changes.
    c.  completion of the socialization process before entering school.
    d.  development of a social self.
    e.  freedom of expression.

---

11.  a.  *Emotions such as pride, shame, guilt, and embarrassment serve as a control on our behavior. These learned feelings are part of what makes social life predictable, ensuring that people generally behave in socially approved ways. See pages 127–128.*

12.  c.  *Dennis Wrong argues that socialization is never predictable for every person; we react differently to the various agents of socialization. As individual human beings, we sometimes violate the expectations placed on us, exercising free will instead. Wrong criticizes social scientists, particularly behaviorists, who feel that people can be reinforced to do just about anything. See page 137.*

13.  a.  *Mead introduced the idea of symbolic interaction. He felt humans have the special ability to interpret the actions, language, and meanings of others through symbols and that we evaluate our "self" in terms of the*

*expectations we see presented by particular others and society as a whole. See page 123.*

14.  e.  *Children and adolescents must have a clear sense of self before they can understand the emotions of others. The "looking glass" provides a new social awareness that enables children to consider the judgments of others. See page 126.*

15.  d.  *Early socialization occurs in the first years of life and teaches us about the ways and expectations of society and how we, in particular, are to behave. We develop a social self in order to participate in society. See pages 115, 128.*

16. The *process* of cognitive and emotional socialization is
   a. universal in all societies.
   b. different for men and women.
   c. harmed by the use of impersonal computers.
   d. unleashed when a child is about three years old.
   e. not observable using current social science methods.

17. Socialization refers to
   a. the fact that human beings are basically social animals.
   b. the process by which people acquire personality and learn the way of life of their society.
   c. the tendency for people to interact with others in social situations.
   d. the process by which strangers become socially familiar with one another and form friendships.
   e. the training given a child by the family so that the child will know how to behave when starting school.

18. The ease with which we interact with others is most likely to be enhanced by
   a. role-taking.
   b. participation in a counterculture.

   c. isolation, so that one's unique qualities are not lost.
   d. the amount of exogamy in the family tree.
   e. the avoidance of deviant behavior.

19. Compared to other societies, advanced industrialized societies see childhood as
   a. a time to train for future work roles.
   b. a distinctive, child-centered time in the life course.
   c. a period when peer socialization is most significant.
   d. a scaled-down version of adult life.
   e. a time when socialization prepares a person for life's responsibilities.

20. Sociologists have documented differences in the child-rearing practices of working-class and middle-class parents. These differences are influential in producing
   a. the perpetuation of the class system.
   b. more heterogeneity in terms of how people choose to raise children.
   c. middle-class children who are better prepared for work than working-class children.
   d. working-class children who are more poorly disciplined than middle-class children.
   e. friction between the classes.

---

16. **a.** *The process of learning to think and to feel begins at birth. This process is universal, although the content of what is learned varies with the society. Primarily through laboratory methods, social scientists have been able to study infants and chart their development. See pages 125, 127.*

17. **b.** *Lacking instincts, human beings must learn about their society and how to survive with other human beings. Socialization is the process by which people acquire personality and learn the ways of their society. See page 115.*

18. **a.** *Role-taking provides us with a better understanding of ourselves and the social world. By pretending to take or actually taking the roles of others, we come to understand their viewpoints and to anticipate their responses. In this way, we learn more about*

*ourselves as well as how to successfully interact with others. See page 123.*

19. **b.** *Modern, industrialized societies see childhood as a distinctive phase in the life course, with few responsibilities and no economic obligations. These societies are child-centered, providing special activities and toys for children. The idea of childhood is a relatively recent one in human history. See page 132.*

20. **a.** *The style of parenting reflects the occupational experiences of the parents. Middle-class parents emphasize self-control and initiative, while working-class parents use physical discipline to reinforce the importance of obeying rules. Partly because of such influences, the social class of the family is an excellent predictor of the social class of the child. See page 128.*

21. The inadequate preparation for death in American society is a consequence of
    a. diverse religious convictions among the population.
    b. overconfidence in technology's power to extend the life span.
    c. the separation of the dying from the family into bureaucratic institutions.
    d. the society's general disregard of everything concerning the aged.
    e. the cultural emphasis on youth, which makes people unable to face the idea of their own death.

22. Social experiments on the effects of isolating infants and very young children are virtually impossible today, because
    a. research ethics rule out such experiments.
    b. they would be rejected as unscientific.
    c. there are no children available for such experiments.
    d. there are too many variables involved.
    e. before they could be carried out, children would already have learned too much.

23. If a sociologist argued that the development of the self depends on the human ability to take the roles of other people, the sociologist would be using
    a. a behaviorist approach.
    b. a psychoanalytic approach.
    c. a life course approach.
    d. a symbolic interactionist approach.
    e. a developmental approach.

24. As they play a card game, young Jack deals himself twice as many cards as he gives his Aunt Jane. When Jane asks if this is fair, Jack replies, "They're my cards!" According to cognitive theory, Jack is in which of the following stages?
    a. sensorimotor
    b. preoperational
    c. concrete operational
    d. formal operational
    e. role-playing

25. Much of the current knowledge of the development of cognitive abilities—reasoning, remembering, believing, etc.—is based on the work of
    a. John Watson.
    b. Jean Piaget.
    c. George Herbert Mead.
    d. Charles Horton Cooley.
    e. Ivan Pavlov.

---

21. **c.** *In preindustrial societies most people die in the family home. In modern industrialized societies, the dying are placed in hospitals and nursing homes, away from the ongoing life of the family and the community, making death a mysterious, often frightening experience. See pages 136–137.*

22. **a.** *The cases of Anna and Isabella occurred as the result of mistreatment by their parents. No researcher would deliberately deprive a child of necessary nurturance. See pages 118, 119–120.*

23. **d.** *Symbolic interactionists, particularly Mead, felt that taking the role of others is an important part of* human social development. This social process of role-taking is made possible by the shared meanings people develop through symbolic interaction. See pages 122–123.

24. **b.** *During the preoperational stage, children are highly egocentric: they see the world entirely from their own perspective. They are incapable of taking another person's perspective. See pages 124–125.*

25. **b.** *Piaget emphasized the internal processes of the mind as it matures through interaction with the social environment. His experiments showed that human beings gradually pass through four basic stages of cognitive development. See page 124.*

NAME

COURSE/SECTION NUMBER

# A CASE STUDY

Morgan's grandfather grew up during the 1930s, the time of the Great Depression. He doesn't speak too much about it, but occasionally when Morgan asks for money or gets an expensive gift, Grandpa has "that look" on his face. He seems to be repressing a story that would begin, "Now when I was a boy . . . " Morgan's father was in his late adolescence when the civil rights movement began and was in college as the protests against the war in Vietnam flared up. He was active in all these protests, burned his draft card, got arrested in a sit-in, and still gives his Joan Baez and Bob Dylan albums an occasional spin. Now Morgan is in his early 20s and is finishing college. He plans to go on to get his Master's Degree in Business Administration. He gets teased sometimes about being a "yuppie." He prefers to think of himself as ambitious and successful. Morgan has visited several advertising firms and knows the kind of work they do, the salaries and benefits, and even the proper clothing for a young account executive.

1.   Each generation in Morgan's family has been profoundly affected by the experience of coming of age during a particular historical period. Why do you think that adolescents and young adults are particularly affected by the events that occur during this part of their life course?

2.    Give a (hypothetical) example of how agents of socialization shaped the experience of each of the three generations of Morgans.

3.    How do the historic events in a person's life course become part of his or her "self"?

# Applying the Concepts

NAME

_____

COURSE/SECTION NUMBER

## APPLICATION EXERCISE ONE

Sociologists have noted that emotions are learned as part of socialization.

1.   Watch television and observe three situations in shows or commercials in which particular emotions were expressed. Describe each in detail. Next, indicate how a slight change in the script might make each an example of "improper" emotional behavior. For example, a man reprimanded by his boss bursts into tears rather than looking shame-faced, or a mother watching her toddler trip and fall laughs derisively rather than smiling sympathetically.

2.   Think of an occasion when you have "held your emotions in." Describe the situation, indicating why you felt it was necessary to be less expressive than you felt. In what ways were your emotions socially controlled?

3.   In part, growing up and passing through the life course results in increasing emotional maturity. Choose an example from your adolescence that shows emotional immaturity, then indicate how you have learned, through socialization and experience, to act differently in similar circumstances.

## APPLICATION EXERCISE TWO

NAME

COURSE/SECTION NUMBER

All of us are socialized throughout our lives. The messages we get vary according to the stage of the life course we are in. We can see this contrast in looking at socialization for college roles and socialization for old-age roles.

1.   Somehow, some way, you made the decision to come to college. Describe that decision, using terms such as "reinforcement," "socialization," "role-taking," "self," "particular other," and "looking-glass self."

2.   Many years of our lives will be spent at the old-age stage of the life course. Yet, as the textbook indicates, there is little socialization for old-age roles.

   a. What type of socialization are you or your parents experiencing in preparation for old age?

   b. Who are some of the models you will use in preparing for your old-age roles?

   c. The phrase "act your age" when used toward older people implies they are not acting in accordance with their roles. What behaviors are frowned on in old people? Try to identify five behaviors, unrelated to physical limitations of age, that are not acceptable old-age roles.

## APPLICATION EXERCISE THREE

NAME

COURSE/SECTION NUMBER

Consider the following passage from William Shakespeare's AS YOU LIKE IT.

> All the world's a stage,
> And all the men and women merely players;
> They have their exits and their entrances,
> And one man in his time plays many parts,
> His acts being seven ages. . . . At first the infant,
> Mewling and puking in the nurse's arms:
> Then the whining school-boy, with his satchel
> And shining morning face, creeping like snail
> Unwillingly to school: and then the lover,
> Sighing like furnace, with a woeful ballad
> Made to his mistress' eyebrow: then a soldier
> Full of strange oaths and bearded like the pard,
> Jealous in honour, sudden and quick in quarrel,
> Seeking the bubble reputation
> Even in the cannon's mouth: and then the justice,
> In fair round belly with good capon line,
> With eyes severe and beard of formal cut,
> Full of wise saws and modern instances,
> And so he plays his part. . . . The sixth age shifts
> Into the lean and slippered pantaloon,
> With spectacles on nose and pouch on side,
> His youthful hose, well saved, a world too wide
> For his shrunk shank, and his big manly voice,
> Tuning again toward childish treble, pipes,
> And whistles in his sound. . . . Last scene of all,
> That ends this strange eventful history,
> Is second childishness, and mere oblivion,
> Sans teeth, sans eyes, sans taste, sans everything.

Compare this passage with the discussion of the life course in the text, answering the following questions.

1.   Are the stages the same today as in Shakespeare's time, or different?

2.    Identify the principal agents of socialization for each stage in the passage. How do these compare with those listed in the text?

3.    What does Shakespeare have to say about socialization for death? Compare this with the kind of socialization you are likely to receive.

4.    Can you account for the differences between the passage and the text in sociological terms?

# CHAPTER 6

# Social Interaction in Everyday Life

## Reviewing the Concepts

### LEARNING GOALS

*After studying this chapter, you should be able to:*

1. Discuss symbolic interaction as an important part of social interaction.

2. Define and explain the importance of symbols.

3. Give examples of the variety of ways symbols are used in human interaction.

4. Contrast the focus of symbolic interactionists with that of functionalist and conflict theorists. Give three examples of topics an interactionist would be more likely to study.

5. Explain how role performances vary and why.

6. Summarize Goffman's dramaturgical approach to social interactions.

7. Discuss the concept of "impression management"; list mechanisms that are used to "keep face" during social interactions.

8. Define the focus of ethnomethodologists by indicating the type of social behavior they study and how they study it.

9. Note the importance of social psychology to sociology and the symbolic interactionist approach.

10. Explain the phenomenon of bystander apathy.

11. Describe body language and personal space in terms of nonverbal communication.

12. Discuss the idea of the social construction of reality and the process by which people act on their perceptions.

13. Review the examples in the text and find instances to illustrate the following concepts:

impression management                    dramaturgy

civil inattention                        front stage and back stage behavior

social construction of reality           nonverbal communication

symbol

## IDENTIFYING KEY QUESTIONS AND THEMES

*Social interaction* is the process by which people act toward or respond to other people. Unlike the rigidly instinctual behavior of animals, human interaction depends on the ability to reflect on and interpret the world. Due to the emphasis on the "micro," or small-scale, processes and structures of society, most studies of social interaction rely on the interactionist perspective.

### Symbolic Interaction

*Why are symbols important? What role do symbols play in human interaction?*

The many objects in our social world are important to us due to their symbolic meaning. Anything—a word, a gesture, or a tool—can be a *symbol.* According to the *symbolic interactionist approach,* humans give meaning to symbols, share these meanings with one another, and interact on the basis of the shared meanings. It is our concept of self, of an "inner person" that we think about as if it were an object outside ourselves, that makes it possible

to mentally take on the roles of others and interpret their behavior.

People use symbols to establish identities and convey certain meanings. For example, punks and nurses, though very different in many respects, both manipulate the symbols of dress and behavior: punks violate the social expectations of "straight" society by symbolically polluting themselves, while nurses symbolically rid themselves of pollution by conveying clean, competent professionalism. Likewise, apparently trivial social rituals, such as the door ceremony, are significant because they have deeper symbolic meaning: in this case, the dependent-female–independent-male relationship is reflected and reinforced. The fact that this ritual has become problematic suggests the ambiguity of symbolic meanings in times of cultural change.

### Dramaturgy

*How do we present our "self" in different situations? What does the dramaturgical approach say about our presentation of self? How do we facilitate symbolic interaction?*

Humans play many different roles and present a variety of

selves in everyday life, depending on the social situation and the audience. ***Dramaturgy*** is the approach to understanding social interaction that focuses on the participants as actors on a stage. Using this metaphor, we play out various parts and scenes according to the script where possible, and improvise when the script is ambiguous. Erving Goffman, the founder of the dramaturgical approach, developed a number of concepts to describe many subtle rules and rituals of social interaction. "Civil inattention," for example, is the unspoken rule of ignoring strangers in public even when we are aware of their presence.

Because we are deeply concerned with what others think of us, we present aspects of our selves that we believe will create a favorable impression on others, using the props and scenery of daily life. This is called "impression management." Often we have both a "back stage" and a "front stage" behavior for different audiences in a single situation, and we may work with other social actors ("teamwork") to create a successful scene. Participants in a social encounter may not always accept the impression we are trying to create, but they usually help us "keep face" by following along.

Much of what we consider to be polite or appropriate behavior consists of our mutual concern with impression management. A pelvic examination, especially if it is performed by a male physician, is an example of a very delicate social encounter. Doctor and patient participate in an elaborate ritual in order to ensure professional interaction and minimize embarrassment.

## Ethnomethodology

*How do sociologists study the rules of everyday life?*

In our day-to-day negotiations with each other we make many mutual assumptions that govern interaction. These shared understandings are important because they underlie so much of our social behavior. Yet, because we are almost unaware of these commonplace rules, it is hard for us to isolate and identify them for social researchers. Indeed, sociologists themselves have long overlooked the importance of these rules. ***Ethnomethodology*** is the study of how people construct and share their definitions of reality in their everyday interactions. This is accomplished by breaking the rules that conceal them. The

founder of this approach, Harold Garfinkel, set up experiments to violate rules of daily life by, for example, misusing commonplace phrases and noting the reaction. Ethnomethodologists focus special attention on language and the hidden meanings of words.

## Social Psychology

*What do social psychologists study? What are some key concepts and findings from their research?*

***Social psychology*** is the study of the influence of the social context on personality and behavior. For example, many researchers have studied the phenomenon of ***bystander apathy,*** that is, the unwillingness to help strangers in public emergency situations. Observation of many such cases suggests that the ambiguity of a situation and a lack of cues from others may immobilize even the most compassionate individuals. Likewise, bystanders may ignore property theft or damage for fear of overreacting and creating a wrong impression by intervening.

Stanely Milgram conducted a series of laboratory experiments in which subjects were asked to administer electric shocks to another person on the orders of an experimenter. People perceived the experimenter to be a legitimate authority and were willing to follow his orders even when they believed the victim was severely harmed as a result. Their behavior, like that of apathetic bystanders, was explained, not in terms of the personality characteristics of the individuals, but rather in terms of the situation as interpreted by the individual (and others).

## Nonverbal Communication

*What types of nonverbal communication are used in social interaction? What is the significance of nonverbal communication?*

A great deal of human interaction occurs not only through language but through ***nonverbal communication.*** Two important forms of nonverbal communication are "body language," such as gestures and facial expressions, and the manipulation of the physical space between people.

Facial expressions and hand gestures are the two most obvious forms of body language. However, many other, less readily noticeable kinds of body language, such as posture, positioning of legs, or inclination of the body, convey powerful messages. Because nonverbal communication is symbolic, much of it is culturally relative. With the exception of those facial expressions that convey such basic emotions as anger or amusement, for instance, gestures can be understood only by people of similar cultural background who attribute the same symbolic meaning to them.

People also communicate with one another by managing the space between them. Edward Hall studied attitudes toward personal space across several cultures and found variations in the amount and meaning of the space kept between strangers and acquaintances, with Americans requiring the most personal space. He identified four distinct zones of private space: intimate distance, personal distance, social distance, and public distance. Other studies have shown that people sit in different positions relative to one another depending on their level of intimacy.

## The Social Construction of Reality

*How do sociologists define reality? What is the implication of the possibility that different people operate from different definitions of reality?*

Sociologists define reality as the interpretations and meaning we give to what is around us. All knowledge and belief is created, linked to the particular social context and historical period in which it is produced. The American sociologist W.I. Thomas made an observation about reality that is known as the *Thomas theorem:* "If people define situations as real, they are real in their consequences." We act on the world as we see it, our interpretations having been shaped by social interaction with others. This *social construction of reality*—the process by which people create their understanding of the nature of their environment—involves three processes: (1) people create material and nonmaterial reality, called culture; (2) cultural creations become part of overall reality and are taken for granted; and (3) people learn about and accept their culture's reality through socialization.

The process becomes clearer when we consider the fact that we have had very different understandings of space and time, two of the most basic aspects of reality. Drawing on mathematical calculations, theological teachings, and various other explanations, and influenced by technological advances, cultural values, and diffusion of ideas, each society constructs its own reality. The important implication for sociologists is that different constructions of reality result in different actions.

## DEFINING CORE CONCEPTS

*After studying the chapter, write a sociological definition in your own words for the following core concepts. Then give an example from your own experience to illustrate your definition. Refer to the chapter to check your work.*

| *Core Concept* | *Sociological Definition* | *Personal Illustration* |
| --- | --- | --- |
| dramaturgy | | |

| *Core Concept* | *Sociological Definition* | *Personal Illustration* |
| --- | --- | --- |
| ethnomethodology | | |
| impression management | | |
| nonverbal communication | | |
| social construction of reality | | |
| symbolic interaction | | |

## PUTTING IDEAS TOGETHER

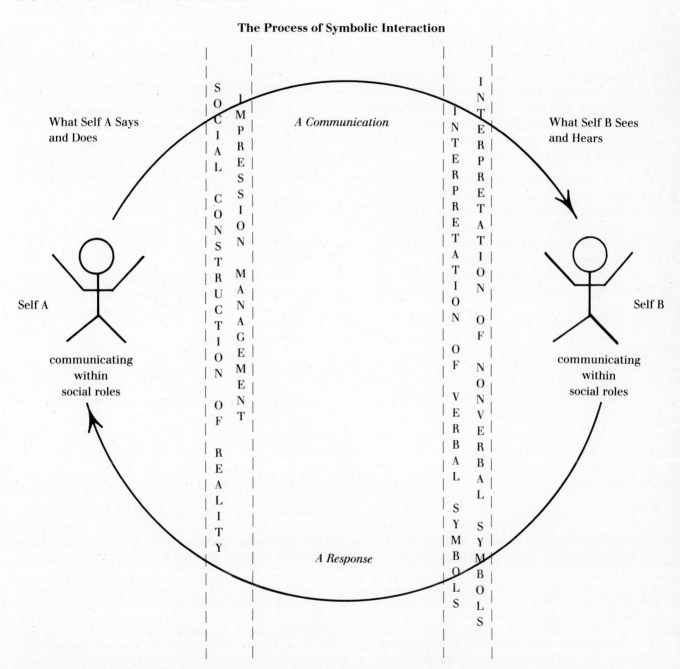

**The Process of Symbolic Interaction**

This cycle of symbolic interaction occurs within a common culture of shared symbolic meanings.

# Testing the Concepts

## MULTIPLE-CHOICE QUESTIONS

*After studying the chapter, try to answer each of the twenty-five questions below. Mark the alternative you think is correct; then look at the correct answer and the explanation provided at the bottom of the page. Try to state why the other alternatives are incorrect, and check your understanding of the correct answer.*

1.  Which of the following statements is *not* part of Goffman's dramaturgical approach to social interaction?
    a.  People construct props and scenery to give a certain impression about themselves.
    b.  Orderly social life is made possible by the unspoken rules of social interaction.
    c.  Impression management is an attempt to deceive people into thinking you are someone you are not.
    d.  Much of impression management involves teamwork.
    e.  When role expectations are unclear, people improvise.

2.  An ethnomethodologist would be most likely to study which of the following topics?

    a.  the mating practices of several primitive societies
    b.  the amount of racial prejudice in the United States
    c.  the unspoken rules of people who attend singles' bars
    d.  how honest people are in responding to questionnaires
    e.  the official hierarchy of a bureaucracy

3.  Ten-year-old Janet drinks milk directly from the carton, as she always does, but her parents have guests who might observe this behavior. Her father quickly pulls her aside and says, "Not in front of company." Goffman would describe this incident as an example of
    a.  ethnomethodology.
    b.  a poor self-concept.
    c.  civil inattention.
    d.  front stage and back stage behavior.
    e.  a negative sanction.

4.  At the family Thanksgiving gathering, Uncle Bill tells a joke he told everyone last year, but the group laughs and compliments him as if it is new. This is an example of
    a.  bystander apathy.
    b.  spoiled identity.
    c.  role-playing.
    d.  studied nonobservance.
    e.  impression management.

---

1.  **c.** *Goffman looked at the micro aspects of social life and how they resemble aspects of the stage. Impression management does not mean actors are attempting to deceive or be something they are not. Goffman says we all manage our impressions to present the best image in any situation. See page 149.*

2.  **c.** *Ethnomethodology is the study of the unspoken assumptions on which people act. Ethnomethodologists observe what people do and infer the rules underlying those actions. See page 151.*

3.  **d.** *People behave differently in public situations than they do privately. Goffman calls this difference front stage and back stage behavior. A family may cooperate to hide certain private, or back stage, habits from a more general audience. See page 149.*

4.  **d.** *In some cases, people who know one another will collectively overlook certain social mistakes to save the actor embarrassment. It is an implicit bargain to ignore an awkward situation. See page 150.*

5.  Ryan and Ethan, college buddies, went to a deli to have supper. The waitress, also a college student, was very friendly, and joked and talked with them during the course of the evening. Ryan thought she was looking for a "pick-up" and considered her behavior flirtatious, while Ethan passed it off as "nice" and her way of approaching all the customers. How would a sociologist best explain the difference in Ryan's and Ethan's views?
  a.  One is more sexist than the other.
  b.  They have different social constructions of reality.
  c.  They have different zones of personal space.
  d.  Their family backgrounds differ; one is conservative and the other more liberal.
  e.  One understands symbolic communication better than the other.

6.  What conclusion can be drawn from a comparison of body language and physical proximity patterns across several cultures?
  a.  Some gestures are universal.
  b.  Human instincts determine proximity.
  c.  Proximity is the same in most modern societies.
  d.  Body language and proximity patterns are basically culture bound.
  e.  Body language is hard to interpret even within a culture.

7.  What concept explains why a female patient can expose her body to a male doctor without embarrassment for either party?
  a.  ethnomethodology
  b.  role performance
  c.  maturity
  d.  back stage behavior
  e.  bystander apathy

8.  W.I. Thomas's phrase "If people define situations as real, they are real in their consequences" is most consistent with which concept listed below?
  a.  manifest function
  b.  social organization
  c.  social construction of reality
  d.  role playing
  e.  reinforcement

9.  A stranger approaches you in an airport. You avert your eyes and walk past him. Which of the following terms would best describe the mechanism you are using?
  a.  personal space
  b.  impression management
  c.  self-concept
  d.  civil inattention
  e.  labeling a deviant

---

5.  **b.** *Like the woman, each man has a social construction of the reality of the situation and is acting according to that understanding. Neither interpretation is right or wrong; each has a valid perception of what the woman's actions may mean. As a result, each responds differently, based on that definition of reality. See page 160.*

6.  **d.** *Body language and physical proximity patterns are symbolic behavior. Each communicates a message that can be understood by other actors. The meanings are defined by a particular culture; the same gestures may mean something quite different in another culture. See pages 157–158.*

7.  **b.** *When a male doctor and a female patient act within their specific roles, they minimize worry about a misinterpretation of his handling her body. The nurse and the "staging" of the examination help the doctor and patient maintain their role performance. See page 150.*

8.  **c.** *W.I. Thomas noted that people act on situations as they perceive them, regardless of what might have been intended or what might be seen as "real" by someone else. We all socially construct reality and act on that construction. See page 160.*

9.  **d.** *Although we are aware of the presence of strangers in public, we avoid eye contact with them at close quarters. "Civil inattention" is Erving Goffman's term for this unspoken rule. See page 148.*

10. The discussion of punk rockers' appearance and demeanor suggests that their outrageous behavior is a deliberate attempt to symbolically pollute themselves. What did the sociologist studying them conclude is their motive?

    a. finding diversions from their boring jobs

    b. gaining power over conventional society

    c. having fun

    d. taking advantage of their affluent position in society

    e. avoiding being mistaken for hippies

11. What is the significance of the door ceremony described in the text?

    a. It shows how trivial people can be.

    b. It reaffirms the battle of the sexes.

    c. It proves that people believe the ritual should be abolished.

    d. It makes fun of old-fashioned manners.

    e. It demonstrates the way in which small rituals reaffirm the social order.

12. Stanley Milgram's experiments on willingness to obey orders showed that people will harm others when

    a. they are misled about the harm they are actually doing to others.

    b. the authority giving the orders to inflict harm is seen as legitimate.

    c. they are mentally ill.

    d. they are under extreme stress and fearful.

    e. they have a grudge against the victim.

13. In the participant-observation study of nurses, the researcher noted how carefully they managed symbols of dress and manner. This is necessary

    a. to create a positive social identity.

    b. to be hygienic.

    c. to avoid being mistaken as doctors.

    d. to improve their back stage behavior.

    e. to follow hospital rules to the letter.

14. Ethnomethodologists often study the social world by

    a. breaking social rules to expose shared understandings.

    b. conducting surveys with very large samples.

    c. observing the types of symbols people use to communicate their ethnicity.

    d. taking careful notes of life in other cultures.

    e. asking people their assumptions about social interaction.

---

10. **b.** *Punk rockers are generally lower-class, unemployed or underemployed youth. Their deliberate attempt to dress and act outrageously gives them power in society. They relish their "spoiled identity" and the discomfort it causes conventional society. See page 146.*

11. **e.** *The fact that women expect men to open doors, and that men share this expectation, reinforces the existing social order in which men are regarded as more powerful, and women as more dependent. Confusion about traditional sex roles is evident in the hesitation both men and women feel as to whether to perpetuate this ceremony. Clearly, small acts of courtesy and habit support larger social patterns. See page 146.*

12. **b.** *Milgram ordered subjects to administer high-voltage shocks to actors playing the role of helpless victim. These orders were obeyed, largely due to the subjects' perception of Milgram as a legitimate authority who must have known what he was doing. See pages 155–156.*

13. **a.** *Nurses perform important, though often distasteful, duties in a hospital setting. They are poorly paid and do not enjoy the same prestige doctors do. To create and enhance their social identity, they carefully maintain a professional appearance and demeanor. See page 146.*

14. **a.** *By breaking social rules, ethnomethodologists discover the underlying assumptions on which people base their behavior. These assumptions are often taken for granted and cannot always be recognized by the individuals in their roles. See page 151.*

15. Which of the following research methods is most commonly used in symbolic interactionist research?
   a. existing records
   b. questionnaires
   c. face-to-face interviews
   d. experiments
   e. field observation

16. How do symbolic interactionists view the *macro* world and larger social institutions?
   a. There is little connection between the micro and macro world.
   b. The macro world is the framework that produces the rules for everyday life.
   c. Symbolic interaction occurs in the family, but not in other institutions.
   d. Social institutions are products of social interaction.
   e. There is little order in the daily activities of life we take for granted.

17. Social psychologists studied the responses of passersby who witnessed a person lying in the street or a person breaking into a car and taking objects from the car. They concluded that
   a. people intervened to give help, but not to stop a crime.
   b. people offered aid to an ill person if a number of other people were around.
   c. about half of the population could be expected to intervene in either situation.
   d. when no one else was around, people were afraid to act alone in either situation.
   e. bystander intervention was very low in both situations.

18. Salespersons often try to create a rapport with potential purchasers by acting as though they are personal friends. One way to do this would be to
   a. stand in the personal rather than the social zone.
   b. comment on other customers' spoiled identities.
   c. show the customer some front stage behavior.
   d. bring up some fancy technical language that the customer will not understand.
   e. use studied nonobservance to size up a customer before he or she comes up to ask for help.

19. How do sociologists explain instances of bystander apathy?
   a. Some individuals just don't want to get involved.
   b. There is too much litigation in our society; people are afraid to intervene.
   c. Many emergencies are ambiguous; people look for cues from one another for a definition of the situation and how to react.
   d. It is a phenomenon of big cities but not of small towns.
   e. People value their privacy.

---

15.  **e.** *The studies of punks and nurses and doctor-patient relationships were observational case studies. Sometimes the researcher is involved as a participant, while in other studies a detached role is preferable. Most people are not aware of, or will not acknowledge, the small rituals of everyday life. To uncover these rituals and discern social patterns, sociologists find observation to be an effective technique. See pages 145, 150.*

16.  **d.** *The small interactions of daily life set patterns of meaningful social interaction. These patterns are the basis for social institutions. See page 144.*

17.  **e.** *In both studies, people did not get involved. The* situations were ambiguous and passersby did not seem to know how to act. They may have taken no action because they felt awkward. See pages 153–154.*

18.  **a.** *By standing in the personal zone, a salesperson can imply a closer, more friendly relationship with a customer. Normally the zone of space in this relationship would be the social zone. See page 159.*

19.  **c.** *Bystander apathy is a group phenomenon. Individuals who are helpful or caring may not take action in a group situation. They wait to see how others define the situation and what others are doing. See page 153.*

20. The dramaturgical approach, founded by Erving Goffman, holds that social life is
    a. instinctive for human beings.
    b. determined by evolution.
    c. made possible by the tacit rules of social interaction.
    d. interesting because of its unpredictability.
    e. closely allied with behavior of other species in the animal kingdom.

21. Effective symbolic interaction depends on
    a. cooperation and friendly feelings between the parties.
    b. knowing the correct social role.
    c. formal education, at least to the point of literacy.
    d. language.
    e. shared meanings assigned to the symbols.

22. Erving Goffman calls our efforts to make ourselves appear favorable to others
    a. social lying.
    b. impression management.
    c. misdirection.
    d. a public relations default.
    e. putting on an act.

23. The railroad brought about a radical change in society's notion of time. What conclusion can be drawn from this fact?
    a. Science has replaced religion as the major belief system.
    b. Ideas of time are socially created and culture bound.
    c. The railroad is the social construction of a new reality.
    d. People resist change in the face of new inventions.
    e. Better transportation gets people together quickly.

24. Two people sit down for a competitive or formal occasion. They are likely to sit
    a. opposite one another.
    b. adjacent to one another.
    c. in a zone of public distance from one another.
    d. at right angles to one another.
    e. randomly.

25. Our ability to interpret the actions of others depends on the
    a. development of a concept of self.
    b. absence of intervening variables.
    c. degree to which our senses are tuned.
    d. total number of experiences we have assimilated.
    e. friendliness of our personality.

---

20. **c.** *Goffman's focus is on the small acts of everyday life. He makes an analogy between social life and the theater. Each of us is an actor playing a role. Many of our behaviors revolve around the unspoken cues we get from others. See page 148.*

21. **e.** *Meanings are assigned to symbols. Symbolic communication is effective to the extent that the meaning of these symbols is shared and understood by all. It can be discordant as well as pleasant, verbal or nonverbal. See page 144.*

22. **b.** *Goffman suggests that we all present an image we believe will create a favorable impression. Our efforts may not always be successful, but in any case, we are consciously advancing a certain side of ourselves over other aspects. See page 149.*

23. **b.** *Time is a social creation, and the ways in which it is measured, though shaped by technology, reflect a society's ideas about its importance. The United States and the Soviet Union, for example, handle time zones quite differently within their own countries, based on different cultural beliefs and political processes. See page 164.*

24. **a.** *Sitting opposite one another is the format chosen by people who are in formal or competitive situations. The manipulation of physical space communicates the relationship between the actors. See pages 159–160.*

25. **a.** *Because we have developed a social self through interaction with others, we can mentally put ourselves in the position of another person. This allows us to interpret their behavior with some accuracy and make social interaction meaningful. See page 145.*

## A CASE STUDY

NAME

COURSE/SECTION NUMBER

Frank and Rudy are two police officers in Troubled City. They have been partners on the regular squad car beat for eleven years. After all that time and the dangers they have faced together, they are good friends. In between radio calls, they cruise their beat and "shoot the breeze," telling jokes about the crazy characters they have seen over the years and the humorous situations they have had to untangle: a wino with his tongue stuck in a bottle; a cat caught in a tree during an electrical storm; chronic calls from a man who hears voices in his empty apartment; giving the mayor's car a ticket when it was parked in front of a risqué nightclub. Police work is not what is shown on television.

An outsider who observed Frank and Rudy during the course of a workday, would immediately note their politeness. Once they step out of the car, they put on their hats and their best behavior. They take most complaints seriously and remain as calm as possible with difficult and upset people. But they do not follow every rule in the book. For example, in the summertime they turn the other way when they see kids open up fire hydrants to cool off or spot illegally parked cars at the beach. They have their favorite neighborhoods and those they dislike patrolling because of the trouble they usually find. The Zonker neighborhood is known as the worst in the city among police officers, and Frank and Rudy avoid cruising through there except when called by headquarters to investigate a reported crime.

Some of their work has been very dangerous, of course. They have developed cues to detect which situations might be threatening. They are suspicious of the Zonker residents, of domestic violence calls, and of late-night calls for help from unidentified persons. In such circumstances one of them draws his gun and guards the other. They sense one another's movements and anticipate what the other will do next. So far, they have protected each other from harm.

1.   Reinforce your understanding of Goffman's terminology and the dramaturgical approach by citing examples of Frank and Rudy's impression management, front stage and back stage behavior, and civil inattention.

2.    Suppose Frank and Rudy were called to the Zonker neighborhood for a domestic violence call. How might they construct a reality for their behavior in this situation that would be different from a call for help from another neighborhood? What kind of nonverbal cues might they look for in one another's behavior?

3.    From what you know of police work, briefly outline a social psychological study that a sociologist might want to undertake. Consider an aspect of police work that would lend itself better to a symbolic interactionist approach than to a functionalist or a conflict approach.

# Applying the Concepts

NAME

COURSE/SECTION NUMBER

## APPLICATION EXERCISE ONE

Civil inattention refers to the act of overlooking people or events out of a sense of politeness. There are cases, however, where civil inattention is used to let people know their place. For example, a harried parent in a grocery store may appear to ignore a child's cries for treats as a way of telling the child to be quiet. Studied nonobservance is a similar social practice. We deliberately ignore someone if they belch out loud or slip getting off the bus, for example, to avoid adding to their embarrassment. Observe social life around you this week and see if you can identify an example of:

1. civil inattention as social control.

2. studied nonobservance as face-saving behavior for another actor or yourself.

3. civil inattention as a way to maintain social distance between people.

## APPLICATION EXERCISE TWO

Harold Garfinkel and other ethnomethodologists study the ordinary world as detached observers to uncover the commonplace rules of interaction. Select one of the situations below and play it out as long as you can. Record the reactions you receive, how you feel, and what rules of social life you are able to identify that might previously have been taken for granted.

1.    Begin a conversation about a family matter, a personal problem, or a fictitious illness you have with a stranger you meet on the bus or during a long elevator ride.

2.    Comment for five minutes on the physical appearance of a bank teller or store clerk (whom you do not know) in a complimentary fashion, going into some detail about aspects of their dress or looks. If possible, turn to another customer and ask them to verify your impressions. "Don't you agree that he (or she) has particularly lovely eyes?"

3.    Act in a formal way toward someone who is a close friend or date, addressing them as Mr. or Ms., for example.

4.    Be extremely courteous in a public place by opening doors for all passersby, greeting people with "Hello" or "Good Morning," looking at people directly, and giving them your biggest smile as they walk by.

Reactions:

## APPLICATION EXERCISE THREE

NAME
_____

COURSE/SECTION  NUMBER

Visit a dance club, singles' bar, or fancy restaurant. Observe nonverbal, symbolic communication, such as facial gestures, personal space, and body language. (Do not eavesdrop!) Complete the chart below with examples of the behavior you see. Remember that after a sociologist has carefully gathered data, he or she interprets it. Offer your explanations for the *patterned* social interaction you observe over the course of an hour.

*Describe five examples of nonverbal symbolic communication*

*Analyze the meaning of the symbols*

1.

2.

3.

4.

5.

Choose three "couples" and study the amount of personal space between them.
Describe the space and hypothesize about the intimacy of their relationship on
this basis.

*Describe the personal space*                              *Analyze the type of relationship you think they have*

Couple one

Couple two

Couple three

# CHAPTER 7

# Social Groups

## Reviewing the Concepts

### LEARNING GOALS

*After studying this chapter, you should be able to:*

1. List the characteristics of a group that distinguish it from an aggregate or category.

2. Contrast the features of primary and secondary groups.

3. Explain the importance of size to group interaction.

4. Give an example of each of the two leadership types and describe three leadership styles.

5. Identify ways in which individuals conform to groups.

6. List the functions of ingroups and outgroups.

7. Explain the importance of social networks.

8. Explain the importance of reference groups.

9. Characterize formal organizations.

10. Specify the features of an ideal-type bureaucracy according to Max Weber.

11. Identify the functions of the informal structure in a bureaucracy.

12. Contrast the importance of the bureaucratic form for modern society with its dysfunctions.

13. Explain Michels's "iron law of oligarchy" and give an example of a modern bureaucracy that supports the law and one that does not.

14. Discuss alternative forms of organization.

## IDENTIFYING KEY QUESTIONS AND THEMES

Human society is characterized by social interaction, frequently in the context of a *group,* a collection of people interacting together in an orderly way on the basis of shared expectations. Unlike *aggregates* (collections of people who happen to be in the same place at the same time) or *categories* (numbers of people who have never met but who share certain characteristics), groups shape both the personality and the behavior of the individual members. Every group has its own internal structure, boundaries, norms, values, statuses, and roles. Members interact for some purpose, whether it is to conduct business, have a good time, champion a political cause, or share affection. Sociologists have studied groups of all sizes and types because of the importance of group life to the well-being of the individual and the stability of the society.

### Primary and Secondary Groups

*In what ways do groups differ and how can they be classified?*

Sociologists distinguish between two types of groups. A *primary group* consists of a small number of people who interact over a relatively long period on a direct, intimate basis; each member often plays many roles. A *secondary group* consists of a number of people who interact on a relatively temporary, anonymous, and impersonal basis in terms of specific roles. Secondary groups can be either small or large and are organized to achieve certain goals.

The growth of secondary groups is a key feature of modern society.

### Small Groups

*What are the significant features of small groups? What processes are at work in group decision making? What types and styles of leadership occur in groups?*

A *small group* is one that contains few enough members for the participants to relate as individuals. It can be as small as a *dyad,* a group of two. Unlike all other groups, the members of a dyad must take account of each other. The addition of another member, forming a *triad,* significantly alters group interaction. As groups get larger than ten people, they need to develop more formal means of communication. One element that is always present in groups is leadership. A *leader* is someone who can consistently influence the behavior of others. Group leadership may be oriented toward the goals of the group or toward the quality of the interaction in the group. These types of leadership are called *instrumental leadership* and *expressive leadership,* respectively. Three common leadership styles are authoritarian, democratic, and laissez-faire. No single style is most effective for all situations. Preferences for one leadership style are culture bound; Americans find the democratic style of leadership most effective.

Groups are more effective in making decisions about "determinate tasks"—problems with a single solution—than they are about "indeterminate tasks"—problems that have no necessarily correct solution. Decisions are usually reached by consensus, with discussion bringing about greater agreement. In small groups, decision making follows a sequence of stages that includes gathering information, evaluating the information, and reaching a specific conclusion, as well as smoothing over differences to ensure continued group harmony. Small groups, in particular, seem to intensify the pressure to conform, and individuals may amend their opinions to stay in line with the views of others. The pressure toward group conformity may even lead an individual to give a response that he or she believes to be incorrect.

## Ingroups and Outgroups

*Why do groups have boundaries and how are they maintained?*

If a group is to survive, it must encourage a feeling of solidarity among its members and maintain a boundary separating them from nonmembers. All groups develop characteristics that distinguish "us" from "them." Thus members see themselves as an *ingroup* and other groups as *outgroups.* Banding together against the outgroup reinforces ingroup cohesion.

## Networks

*What are social networks? How are they used to link individuals and groups to one another?*

*Social networks* are the webs of relationships that link the individual directly to other people, and through these others, indirectly to a vast number of other people. Networks form a vital part of social life, contributing to a sense of "community," and helping to secure advice, job leads, and other tangible help. In fact, a well-developed network is crucial to many occupations that depend on "contacts."

## Reference Groups

*How do people use groups to guide and evaluate their own behavior?*

People compare their behavior, ideas, dress, manners, preferences, speech, and countless other lifestyle elements to the standards of certain groups. These *reference groups* may be ones to which the individual belongs or ones to which he or she mentally refers for norms.

## Formal Organizations

*What happens when a group becomes a formal organization? How did Max Weber study and characterize bureaucracies? Why do bureaucracies differ from one another and from the ideal-type characteristics Weber identified? What are some of the dysfunctions of bureaucracies?*

As our society has become larger and more complex, more of our relationships occur in large secondary groups, many of which are *formal organizations,* large secondary groups that are deliberately and rationally designed to achieve specific objectives. Sociologists categorize these organizations according to their purpose—voluntary, coercive, or utilitarian. To help meet their objectives, all formal organizations have a carefully designed structure that assigns specific positions, rights, and responsibilities to their members. The larger and more complex a formal organization becomes, the greater the need for a chain of command to coordinate the activities of its members. In a *bureaucracy,* activities are organized in a hierarchical way, with explicit rules and procedures for each status. The bureaucracy is the key to understanding the operation of formal organizations.

Max Weber studied bureaucracies and noted the trend toward logical, calculated procedures to efficiently meet organizational goals, a process he called *rationalization.* Weber analyzed the workings of bureaucracies by constructing an *ideal type,* an abstract description based on the characteristics held in common by real cases. In this way, Weber was able to describe the essential features of a bureaucracy, although not all bureaucracies would conform to the description in all ways. These features include (1) division of labor; (2) hierarchy; (3) rules and regulations; (4) impersonality; (5) written record-keeping; (6) administrative staff; and (7) career structure. The identification of these characteristics provided a benchmark against which real cases could be compared. Ideal-type analysis has been used to identify the features of many other types of social groups.

Modern researchers have altered Weber's ideas to account for the informal, primary relationships that exist in bureaucracies. People who work within bureaucracies modify procedures and rules. They form primary-group associations, collectively interpret their role expectations, and establish their own norms. This has led some sociologists to describe bureaucracies in terms of a **negotiated reality**—an organization that derives its existence and character from the social interaction through which the members continuously create and re-create it.

Even with the modifications brought about by the existence of informal networks, a number of dysfunctions are built into the bureaucratic structure. These include: (1) inefficiency in unusual cases—not all situations can be anticipated and not all solutions are covered by formal rules; (2) "trained incapacity" of bureaucrats, who may be unable to respond in new, imaginative ways due to previous bureaucratic training; (3) goal displacement, which occurs when the organization's original goals become secondary to the administration of the organization itself, or when the original goals are achieved and bureaucrats do not seek new objectives; (4) bureaucratic enlargement—the tendency of bureaucracies to grow and, over time, to expand in size and complexity beyond what is necessary; (5) authoritarian structure, which itself generates communication problems and internal friction related to various privileges; and, perhaps most serious, (6) bureaucratic personality, which develops when the rigidity and conformity associated with the bureaucratic structure leads to an insidious and alienating loss of personal freedom.

## The Problems of Oligarchy

*What is oligarchy? Why is it a problem associated with modern societies?*

According to the theorist Robert Michels, social, political, and economic power inevitably become concentrated in the hands of a few highly placed individuals. This concentration of power, called *oligarchy,* is present even in organizations built on socialist or democratic ideals. As Michels pointed out, most large organizations make use of the bureaucratic form to run efficiently. The hierarchy of decision making implicit in this structure tends to result in an unequal distribution of power at the top. The dilemma facing modern society is learning to benefit from the efficiency of modern bureaucracies without sacrificing individual freedoms.

## Other Forms of Organization

*What changes can be predicted for formal organizations of the future? What are the characteristics of the Japanese management style and collective decision making?*

The Japanese corporation, the collective, and various types of reformed organizations provide us with alternatives to bureaucratic-type organizations. In the future, job rotation, periodic sabbaticals, etc., may be instituted to help make the work environment more satisfying. Organizations will rely increasingly on the advice of highly trained professionals who do not fit easily into the hierarchy and are not easily replaced. This may lead to changes in traditional hierarchical relationships. Bureaucratic authority may be decentralized into smaller, more flexible units. Most important, the efficiency of bureaucratic procedures will have to be more effectively balanced against the pressing need for greater social control over bureaucracy itself.

## DEFINING CORE CONCEPTS

*After studying the chapter, write a sociological definition in your own words for the following core concepts. Then give an example from your own experience to illustrate your definition. Refer to the chapter to check your work.*

| Core Concept | Sociological Definition | Personal Illustration |
| --- | --- | --- |
| aggregate | | |

| Core Concept | Sociological Definition | Personal Illustration |
|---|---|---|
| bureaucracy | | |
| category | | |
| expressive leadership | | |
| formal organization | | |
| group | | |
| ideal type | | |
| ingroup | | |
| instrumental leadership | | |

| Core Concept | Sociological Definition | Personal Illustration |
|---|---|---|
| negotiated reality | | |
| oligarchy | | |
| outgroup | | |
| primary group | | |
| rationalization | | |
| reference group | | |
| secondary group | | |
| social network | | |

## PUTTING IDEAS TOGETHER

This chapter presents an array of different types of groups. Picture a continuum of groups ranging from the informal to the formal. Informal groups *tend* to have qualities that differ from formal groups. In general, informal groups are more likely to be small in size, exhibit intimate relationships, and prefer expressive leadership styles. As groups become more formal, they are likely to be larger, based on role relationships, and governed by instrumental leaders.

## Characteristics of Groups

| *Informal Groups Tend to Be* | *Formal Groups Tend to Be* |
| --- | --- |
| Primary | Secondary |
| Small | Large |
| Based on intimate relationships | Based on role relationships |
| Expressive in leadership | Instrumental in leadership |

Think about the following groups: your family, your fellow workers at your most recent job, your sociology class, and a club to which you belong. Do they lean more toward informal groups or formal groups?

Chapter 1 emphasized the basic insight of sociology: "Human behavior is largely shaped by the groups to which people belong and by the social interaction that takes place within these groups." Rather than being pawns to group life, we create it and contribute to it. This chapter explores some of the dynamics that characterize different types of formal organizations.

### Organizations: Their Structure and Decision-Making Patterns

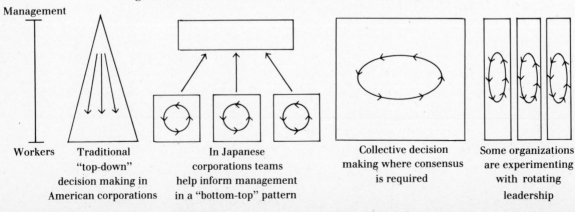

Management

Workers

Traditional "top-down" decision making in American corporations

In Japanese corporations teams help inform management in a "bottom-top" pattern

Collective decision making where consensus is required

Some organizations are experimenting with rotating leadership

# Testing the Concepts

## MULTIPLE-CHOICE QUESTIONS

*After studying the chapter, try to answer each of the twenty-five questions below. Mark the alternative you think is correct; then look at the correct answer and explanation provided at the bottom of the page. Try to state why the other alternatives are incorrect, and check your understanding of the correct answer.*

1.  People who identify and interact with each other in a structured way, based on shared values and goals, constitute
    a. a class.
    b. a group.
    c. an aggregate.
    d. an organization.
    e. a category.

2.  Which of the following would be an aggregate rather than a group or category?
    a. Citizen Band radio operators in the United States
    b. the American Association of Poodle Breeders
    c. fans attending a Bruce Springsteen concert
    d. the Chicago Bears football team
    e. all blond, blue-eyed women in Minneapolis, Minnesota

3.  United States citizens must submit tax forms by April 15. Some people will be audited by the Internal Revenue Service. Those who are audited constitute
    a. a category.
    b. a group.
    c. a criminal, secondary group.
    d. an aggregate.
    e. a class.

4.  The key components of a primary group that distinguish it from a secondary group are
    a. small size, instrumental tasks.
    b. a division of labor, interrelated statuses.
    c. face-to-face contact, small size.
    d. authoritarian leadership, informal structure.
    e. expressive leadership, determinate tasks.

5.  Which of the following groups would be *best* classified as a task-oriented voluntary organization on a college campus?
    a. the Young Republicans club
    b. the employees of the cafeteria
    c. the volunteers who gave blood at the Red Cross Drive held on campus
    d. Lynn, Mary, Joanne, and Dawnetta, four friends who have lunch every Friday
    e. the campus police

6.  Bureaucratic structure is beneficial in that it
    a. tends to be flexible and encourages innovation.
    b. tends to foster the feeling that employees are valuable to the work of the organization.
    c. is a structure ready and able to deal with any kind of situation and respond quickly to it.
    d. is designed to judge performance on the basis of seniority and merit, not favoritism.
    e. breaks down the divisions between different social classes.

---

1. **b.** *Groups are formed to meet instrumental and/or expressive needs its members have in common. The group's goals, internal structure, and role relationships bind the group together. See page 167.*

2. **c.** *Aggregates are groups of people assembled at a common place and time who do not function as a group. See page 167.*

3. **a.** *Members of a category share common characteristics, but they may not know one another or function as a group. See page 167.*

4. **c.** *Primary groups are characterized by a great deal of contact among the members. See page 168.*

5. **a.** *Membership in this club is voluntary. People join to help the group meet its goal of getting candidates elected, changing public opinion, and registering more Republican voters. See page 175.*

6. **d.** *Roles are assigned on the basis of seniority or merit, so presumably any given position is occupied by the person most qualified for it. See page 179.*

7. Let us assume that a good discussion leader for introductory sociology is one who tells students what to do and yet supports them as they try to learn the material. This leadership style would be best described as
    a. democratic and instrumental.
    b. authoritarian and instrumental.
    c. democratic and expressive.
    d. laissez-faire and instrumental.
    e. authoritarian and expressive.

8. Social scientists believe leadership in small groups is
    a. an inborn quality that some people possess and others do not.
    b. most effective in problem solving if it takes a laissez-faire form.
    c. culturally relative; some leadership styles work better in some cultures.
    d. not needed because the group is small and makes decisions by consensus.
    e. replaced by group pressure to conform.

9. One of the important functions ingroups serve is to
    a. promote conflict within other groups.
    b. raise the standards of membership in the group.
    c. encourage more leadership skills in members.
    d. enhance a feeling of "we-ness" and group solidarity.
    e. increase the publicity about the group and its goals.

10. A particularly fussy librarian who manages the University library system institutes new rules limiting which books can be checked out and shortening the time they are gone. This might be an example of which dysfunction of bureaucracy?
    a. authoritarian personality
    b. ideal type
    c. rationalization
    d. Parkinson's law
    e. goal displacement

11. A teenage girl who looks to fashion magazines for guidance on her appearance is being socialized by which type of group?
    a. a reference group
    b. a secondary group
    c. a peer group
    d. a media group
    e. an ingroup

12. A professor asks class members to grade one another as a group. Based on her knowledge of Asch's experiment with students' judgments of the length of lines, what will she guard against in this grading approach?
    a. the formation of ingroups and outgroups
    b. the emergence of the authoritarian leadership style
    c. the use of honor students as a reference group

---

7. **e.** *Directing group behavior toward the goal of learning course material is a sign of authoritarian leadership. The support given to students shows expressive leadership. See page 170.*

8. **c.** *All groups have leadership. The type of leadership chosen depends on what we have been socialized to see as most effective. See page 171.*

9. **d.** *Members of an ingroup identify with other members and see themselves as special. Pride in their membership strengthens the solidarity of this group as distinct from other groups. See page 173.*

10. **e.** *The librarian has lost sight of the library's main*

*purpose — to make books available to faculty and students for their needs. Instead, he is focusing on keeping order and control over the books, a displacement of the library's primary goal. See page 181.*

11. **a.** *Whether we are members or not, a reference group gives us guidelines about our behavior, looks, attitudes, and many other aspects of the lifestyle we choose. It is the basis for comparison between what we are and what we want to be. See page 175.*

12. **d.** *Asch found that subjects would give an incorrect answer in order to conform to the group decision, a clear indication of the power of peer pressure, particularly in small groups. See pages 172–173.*

d. the pressure on some students to conform to the group position

e. the speed with which large groups can reach a decision

13. Max Weber used the term "rationalization" to refer to

a. the tendency of small groups to become more rational in their decisions over time.

b. the skill of an effective expressive leader in a small group.

c. the replacement of traditional methods of social organization with rules and regulations.

d. the tendency of people to invent excuses for their behavior.

e. the growing shortage of resources from increased industrialization.

14. The best example of a formal organization is

a. three boys who form a club in their tree house.

b. the National Organization for Women.

c. your sociology class.

d. all voters for Ronald Reagan.

e. your high school class's tenth year reunion party.

15. A determinate task is handled most effectively in

a. a secondary group with a democratic leader.

b. a primary group with several leaders.

c. a small group with a laissez-faire leader.

d. a committee where everyone has an equal say in the decision.

e. a secondary group with an authoritarian leader.

16. When Ronald left his job as manager of the McDonald's franchise on Main Street, Linda took over. Customers are unaware of the change. What principle of formal organization does this illustrate?

a. the Peter Principle

b. the inflexibility of the bureaucracy

c. the "iron law of oligarchy"

d. the division of labor

e. the importance of roles with defined duties not based on personalities

17. The ideal-type analysis used by Max Weber involves

a. identifying and describing the common features of a social structure, although each case may differ in some respects.

b. arguing which changes are necessary in society to make life more ideal.

c. looking at different ways cultures handle problems and determining the superior method.

d. comparing real culture against ideal culture to discover the differences.

e. doing a survey to find out what the average person thinks about an issue.

---

13.  c. *According to Weber, one of the characteristics of an ideal-type bureaucracy is the use of standardized rules and procedures. He called this development rationalization, because it depended on rational thought about the most efficient way to do things. See page 177.*

14.  b. *A formal organization is a group that exists for a specific purpose and usually has rules, dues, officers, and procedures to meet its goals. See page 175.*

15.  e. *A determinate task (one with a single solution) will benefit by group effort—many individuals are more likely to come up with the correct solution than a given individual. However, once the solution has been found, a determinate task requires a single decision and someone*

*authorized to make that decision. Group decision making would not be as effective. See pages 170–171.*

16.  e. *The former manager could be replaced with someone who had the skills required to do the job, as laid out in the job description. While Ronald may have had some admirable personal qualities, it was his ability to do a standard job that mattered. See pages 178–179.*

17.  a. *By examining several examples of a social structure and identifying the features they share in common, the sociologist can construct an abstract description of the structure that reveals its essential characteristics and applies to most cases. See page 178.*

18. The informal structure in a bureaucracy is useful in that it serves to
    a. preserve the official channels of communication.
    b. help individuals interpret rules and bring them in line with what can reasonably be accomplished.
    c. allow workers to accept the inevitable red tape that will affect them.
    d. provide a chance for workers to release their hostile feelings and even subvert the work of superiors.
    e. reinforce the Peter Principle.

19. The corporation takes different forms in the United States and in Japan. In comparing the two countries, the corporation in Japan
    a. rewards the individual.
    b. is more bureaucratic in its decision making.
    c. offers greater job security and worker welfare.
    d. has a few executives who make all the decisions.
    e. looks for employees outside the corporation to promote to management positions.

20. A leader who does very little to direct or organize a group is using what sort of leadership style?
    a. democratic
    b. laissez-faire
    c. authoritarian
    d. consensual
    e. instrumental

21. If you wanted to build a social network, for the reasons described in the text, you would be wise to join
    a. a utilitarian organization.
    b. a coercive organization.
    c. an aggregate.
    d. a secondary group.
    e. a voluntary organization.

22. One of the most dramatic changes taking place in formal organizations today is
    a. the decline of the importance of reference groups.
    b. a more coercive management style.
    c. the rise of a special class of decision makers who have technological expertise.
    d. an emphasis on collective decision making and policies to foster self-fulfillment.
    e. a shift involving numbers of ingroups and outgroups.

23. Bill has joined the computer sales staff at IBM, which for him is
    a. a voluntary organization.
    b. a coercive organization.
    c. a utilitarian organization.
    d. a primary organization.
    e. an informal organization.

---

18. **b.** *The official policies of the bureaucracy are interpreted and sometimes bent to bring them in line with reality. The informal structure provides some degree of flexibility. See page 179.*

19. **c.** *The Japanese corporation has a teamwork philosophy, a "from the bottom up" decision-making process, lifetime job security, worker welfare programs, and a commitment to promote from within the company. See page 186.*

20. **b.** *A laissez-faire leader is easygoing and makes little effort to direct or organize the group. In the United States, laissez-faire leaders tend to be ineffectual because the group lacks directives and tackles problems in a haphazard manner. See pages 170–171.*

21. **e.** *Voluntary organizations, such as clubs, encourage people with similar interests to join together for education, study, recreation, and conversation. The informal contacts developed through networking can be useful to someone who is looking for a job, for example. See page 174.*

22. **d.** *American corporations are looking at new management styles that encourage employee participation in decision making, rotation of tasks, job-related education, periodic sabbaticals, and other policies that foster self-fulfillment. See page 187.*

23. **c.** *Bill's employment at IBM means he is working on assigned duties in exchange for his salary. Presumably the company has goals that will be met, in part, by his job performance. See page 175.*

24.  A student who wants to take an unusual combination of courses is likely to encounter a good deal of form-filling and other "red tape," because the rules of bureaucracies are designed for the typical case, not the unusual one. This problem is an example of

    a.  a dysfunction.

    b.  instrumental leadership.

    c.  bureaucratic personality.

    d.  ingroups and outgroups.

    e.  the Peter Principle.

25.  A sociologist argues that bureaucracies respond to certain needs in formal organizations and that bureaucratic structure promotes the efficiency and survival of such organizations. This sociologist is taking

    a.  a symbolic interactionist approach.

    b.  a functionalist approach.

    c.  a hierarchical approach.

    d.  a conflict approach.

    e.  an ideal-type approach.

---

24.  **a.** *A dysfunction is a negative consequence, although in this case probably an unanticipated one. The efficiency of the bureaucracy is realized when no exceptions are made to the rules. When a special case comes along, the standard rules do not apply, and they become dysfunctional to efficiency. See page 181.*

25.  **b.** *A functionalist would point to the various elements of bureaucratic structure and show how they promote the survival, efficiency, and goals of a formal organization. See page 181.*

## A CASE STUDY

Judy, Lori, Sarah, and Gerry all work for the Rin Tin Tin Can Company. Each one of them has worked at the company for over ten years. They see each other outside work, including participating in the company's bowling team: Rin Tin Tin Pins. Last month, Gerry received a temporary promotion to line supervisor. She became directly responsible to management for the quality of work turned in by Judy, Sarah, and the other line workers. Gerry tightened up on coffee breaks, "shushed" them when they talked while working, and kept a close eye on the time cards. She wanted to make this promotion permanent! After several weeks, Gerry noticed that she wasn't being invited for "after-work beers" with the others, and at bowling she was not included in the fun. She felt shunned and hurt by this behavior and thought, "Fine friends they turned out to be." Gerry did well in management's eyes, however, and was promoted to a permanent position at another station in the factory, away from her friends. She did not like the working conditions but felt she should keep this new job; after all, it was a promotion. At first she missed her days back on the line. But after a year in her new job, she was critical of the irresponsible attitudes of her former friends and the way they tried to get out of doing work whenever possible. Their interest in bowling seemed frivolous compared to her interest in Big Sisters of America, which she attended regularly with two other managers from the company.

1.   Identify a primary group in this example and explain how it functions.

2.   How do primary relationships develop from secondary groups, as evidenced in this study?

3.    What were Gerry's reference groups and how did they change over time?
How do reference groups operate in Gerry's life now?

4.    How do you explain the way Gerry's friends reacted to her promotion?

5.    What features of an ideal-type bureaucracy are apparent in this example?

# Applying the Concepts

NAME

COURSE/SECTION NUMBER

## APPLICATION EXERCISE ONE

In January 1986, stunned Americans watched as the space shuttle Challenger exploded, killing all seven astronauts aboard. In the wake of the tragedy, the Rogers Commission studied the causes of the accident and made recommendations for future space shuttle flights. In addition to small technical difficulties, the commission laid the blame on poor communication among NASA officials, disregard for the advice of the manufacturer of the O-rings, and a weak chain of command.

Almost any accident that appears to have a medical, technical, or scientific cause involves a problem with human decision-making abilities as well. Use the case of the shuttle accident, or a similar case from a recent news report, to answer the following questions.

1.   Looking at NASA (or another organization) as a small group, can you find any examples of peer pressure or "groupthink" that could have contributed to the accident in question?

2.   Looking at NASA (or another organization) as a bureaucracy, in what ways would you say the bureaucratic structure itself set up the conditions for possible miscommunication? What dysfunctions of bureaucracy are in evidence?

3.   What kind of leadership style do you think is most appropriate for a space shuttle mission or other highly technical and dangerous scientific venture? Should decision making be handled by a single individual? Or are most of the issues "indeterminate tasks" that are better solved by a group?

## APPLICATION EXERCISE TWO

NAME

COURSE/SECTION NUMBER

Think back to your high school days. Better yet, if it's available, take a quick look at your class annual. Recall the cliques that formed around athletics, school clubs, academic achievement, and social events.

1.   Give at least one example of an ingroup and an outgroup relationship.

2.   Characterize your social network. How has it changed since high school?

3.   Give an example of at least one personal reference group of which you were a member. What behaviors did you exhibit in line with this group?

4.   Give an example of at least one personal reference group of which you were not a member. What purpose did this reference group serve?

5.   You have probably changed considerably since you were in high school. What part did a shift in reference group(s) play in that change?

NAME

COURSE/SECTION NUMBER

# APPLICATION EXERCISE THREE

Ascension Morales is an El Salvadorian refugee who recently arrived in the United States with her five children. She needs to apply for temporary welfare benefits. Ms. Morales gets to the welfare office at her appointed time and waits for six hours before she is seen by her caseworker, Ms. Jackson. Through a translator, she assures Ms. Jackson that she has come to the United States with no more than a single box of possessions, yet the caseworker goes through the standard form, asking if she "owns a snowmobile," "has savings certificates," "owns any income property," and how she manages to live on so little. After six weeks Ms. Morales receives her benefits. She is notified by a form letter that her caseworker is now Mr. Fratney, but no change in her benefits results. When she returns to have her case updated, her file is lost and she must reapply, again completing the long entrance form. Ms. Morales experiences additional confusion because she has no Social Security card; given her alien status, Mr. Fratney threatens to withhold future checks unless she gets a card immediately. The seriousness of her special situation is explained to him. He softens, confers with his coworker, Ms. Hansen, and they agree to let it slip through; she can bring them her Social Security card when she gets it, and they will backdate its receipt. That way Ms. Morales will continue to get the assistance she needs.

1.    What elements of the formal bureaucratic structure identified by Weber are evident in Ms. Morales's experience?

2.    What evidence in this case can you find of the informal structure of a bureaucracy?

3.  How much social control is apparent in a bureaucracy of this type?

4.  Can you identify some of the dysfunctions of a bureaucracy evidenced in this case? Be sure to mention authoritarian structure and goal displacement.

5.  Relate an encounter you have had with a bureaucratic organization in which you experienced difficulties similar to those of Ms. Morales.

# CHAPTER 8

# Deviance

## Reviewing the Concepts

### LEARNING GOALS

*After studying this chapter, you should be able to:*

1. Define deviance as a sociological concept.

2. Discuss the concept of stigma according to Erving Goffman.

3. Identify means of social control and how they work.

4. Summarize Durkheim's argument about the functional aspect of deviance.

5. Explain the cultural-transmission theory of deviance.

6. Define the concept of anomie and explain how it relates to the structural-strain theory of deviant behavior.

7. Characterize Merton's five-part typology of deviance.

8. Link control theory to Durkheim's view of social solidarity.

9. State the labeling theorists' position on deviant behavior; define the concepts of primary and secondary deviance.

10. Explain how social power affects the definition of deviance and the consequences of the deviant label.

11. Compare the strengths and weaknesses of the four theories of deviant behavior.

12. Present information about the four types of crime and their rates of occurrence.

13. Describe the process of selecting the criminal.

14. Explain the various purposes of corrections; evaluate the goals of imprisonment in terms of implementation and results.

15. Explain how the features of a total institution bear upon rehabilitation.

16. Present a conflict theory analysis of class privileges and deviance.

17. Explain why mental disorder is classified as a form of deviance.

18. Give examples of the medicalization of deviance.

18. List four functions of deviance.

20. List four dysfunctions of deviance and their effects on society.

## IDENTIFYING KEY QUESTIONS AND THEMES

The fact that most people conform to most norms most of the time makes orderly social life possible. Yet social norms are often violated as well as adhered to. In fact, most of us are deviant from time to time, whether intentionally or not. Minor acts of deviance, such as expressions of personal idiosyncrasies, are usually tolerated. However, it is expected that the most important norms will be obeyed. Violation of such norms may result in stigmatization—a *stigma* is a mark of social disgrace that sets a deviant person apart from others who behave "normally." In sociological terms, then, *deviance* is behavior that violates significant social norms and is disapproved of by large numbers of people as a result. It is important to remember that deviance is relative. No act is inherently deviant; it becomes deviant only when it is socially defined as such. Therefore, it is possible for definitions of deviance to differ among cultures and to change over time. Sociologists are interested in how definitions of deviance develop and change, why people conform or deviate, and how society controls deviance.

### Deviance and Social Control

*Why doesn't more deviant behavior occur? What is social control and how does it work in our lives?*

People generally fulfill their roles in accordance with social norms. One reason for this conformity is an effective system of *social control,* the means to ensure that people generally behave in expected and approved ways. The most powerful form of social control is the basic socialization process by which new members of society learn its rules and the importance of following them. Through socialization, humans internalize the society's values and norms and keep themselves "in line" with social rules. However, the socialization process does not guarantee conformity in all instances. Society further enforces its norms through *sanctions,* both positive (rewards) and negative (punishments), using formal means, such as the police, or informal means, such as feedback from other people. The use of negative sanctions indicates a failure of social control.

Emile Durkheim pointed out that the presence of some deviance actually contributes to the effectiveness of social control. When deviants are identified and punished, social norms are reaffirmed for the rest of society. In applying sanctions and stigmatizing deviants, other people are made conscious of their own conformity, thereby strengthening their sense of solidarity.

### Explaining Deviance

*How can deviant behavior be explained? To what extent is deviance the fault of the individual or the society? Why does the amount of deviance vary so much among societies?*

Four basic sociological theories have been advanced to explain the presence of deviance, especially crime, in society: cultural-transmission theory, structural-strain theory, control theory, and labeling theory. No one theory provides a complete explanation, although each helps us better understand various forms of deviance.

According to *cultural-transmission theory,* deviance, like conformity, is behavior that is learned through interaction with other people. More specifically, deviant behavior is learned through *differential association,* or social relationships oriented toward particular types of people, such as criminals, who encourage a contempt for prevailing norms. Intensity of such contacts, age at which the contacts take place, and the ratio of contacts with deviants to contacts with conformists determine the likelihood of deviance. Cultural-transmission theory is especially useful when applied to gang behavior and recidivism. It is less useful in explaining how defiance arises in a culture or why it is defined as deviance in the first place.

*Structural-strain theory* looks at social strains that put pressure on some people to deviate. A key concept, which derives from Durkheim's work, is *anomie*—a condition of confusion that exists in both individual and society when social norms are weak, absent, or conflicting. Durkheim warned that modern societies are prone to anomie because their cultural diversity and rapid social change leave people confused about what constitutes acceptable behavior.

Robert Merton applied the concept of anomie to deviance, noting the discrepancies between socially approved goals and the availability of socially approved means of achieving them. People may respond in one of

CHAPTER 8   Deviance      161

five ways: (1) conformity, which occurs when both the goals and means of achieving them are accepted; (2) innovation, which occurs when the goals are accepted but socially disapproved means are used; (3) ritualism, which occurs when means are followed compulsively without regard to the goals; (4) retreatism, which occurs when both the goals and the means approved by society are abandoned; or (5) rebellion, which occurs when socially disapproved goals and means are substituted for approved ones. Structural-strain theory helps explain why people commit certain deviant acts, particularly crimes against property. It is not as helpful in terms of other forms of deviance, such as mental disorder or exhibitionism.

Durkheim also influenced *control theory,* which explains deviance as the outcome of a failure of social control. Unlike other theories, which focus on why people deviate, control theory focuses on why people conform, suggesting that people conform only because society is able to control their behavior. Hirschi outlines the four elements of a strong bond to society: attachment to specific other people; commitment to their stake in society; involvement in nondeviant activities; and belief in the value system of the society. The stronger the mutual ties of group members, the greater the social control for "normal" behavior. When social solidarity is high, people are less likely to deviate, conversely, when social bonds are weak, people are more likely to deviate. Control theory offers a plausible explanation for why some kinds of deviance are more likely to be present among certain types of people who lack close social bonds (it seems particularly applicable to juvenile delinquency). However, it is less useful in understanding deviance among high-status people, why deviance takes the forms that it does, or the possibility that some people have weak bonds with society because of their deviance, and not the other way around.

*Labeling theory* emphasizes the relativity of deviance and looks at the process by which some people are successfully labeled as deviant by other people. Because it focuses on the way in which people are perceived as deviant, and not on their acts, labeling theory follows in the interactionist tradition. More recently it has also incorporated aspects of the conflict approach to explain why some behaviors and people, and not others, are labeled deviant.

Early labeling theorists point out that most people behave in a deviant manner at one time or another. Most of this behavior can be called *primary deviance*—nonconformity that is temporary, exploratory, trivial, or easily concealed. The deviant act may pass unnoticed, and the individuals concerned do not regard themselves as deviant nor are they regarded as such by others. However, if the deviance is noticed and made public by significant others, the offender may be the object of a "degradation ceremony" in which he or she is accused of the deviant act, perhaps punished, and labeled a deviant. If the person consciously or unconsciously accepts the deviant label, develops a new self-concept, and behaves accordingly, the behavior becomes *secondary deviance.* Especially if forced into the company of other deviants, such individuals may enter into a "deviant career," whereby deviance becomes their master status. Borrowing from conflict theory, labeling theorists argue that the socially powerful members of society determine which acts and people are deviant and make those labels stick. Labeling theory helps us understand why certain people and acts—and not others—are considered deviant. Objections to labeling theory include the findings that, in many cases, labeling is not the most important influence on deviant behavior, that the labeling process may actually jolt the offender out of deviance, and that labeling theory encourages an indiscriminate sympathy for the underdog.

## Crime

*What is the relationship between crime and deviance? Who are the criminals in our society? Why are some criminals treated differently from others? How does the corrections system handle criminals? How can deterrence be enhanced?*

A *crime* is an act that has been formally prohibited by law, usually because it is too socially disruptive to be permitted and because it is difficult to control through informal sanctions alone. Like deviance, crime is defined within a culture at a given time, so its definition is subject to change. What may be regarded by one society as murder punishable by death may be regarded by another society as justifiable or even honorable.

In the United States, crime can be classified into four

general categories: (1) crimes of violence, (2) crimes against property, (3) crimes without victims, and (4) white-collar and corporate crime. The first two types of crime are regarded as most serious. The rate of violent crime in the United States has leveled off. Although Americans fear being attacked by a complete stranger, many violent crimes—particularly murder—occur between acquaintances or relatives and are intraracial. Black men run a disproportionately high risk of being murdered. The wide availability of guns here may be one explanation for the high rate of murder in the United States compared to other Western societies. Crimes against property (e.g., vandalism, arson, theft) have reached epidemic proportions in the United States. In recent years, the property-crime rate, like the violent-crime rate, has leveled off, reflecting a change in the average age of the population. As the proportion of young people between age 16 and 25 declines, so too does the crime rate. The third type of crime, victimless crime (e.g., drug use, gambling, prostitution), is very difficult to control both because it involves consent among the parties participating in the crime, who often feel no guilt at committing the offense, and because it is heavily infiltrated by organized crime. While white-collar and corporate crime is very costly in terms of its economic impact on society, it is generally regarded with more tolerance than other types of crime because the criminals are high-status people. To some extent, the public has come to expect tax evasion, computer fraud, etc., as a part of business life.

Statistics show that half of all those arrested for crime are young, male, urban residents, and that blacks are overrepresented. Yet surveys of the general population indicate that crime is spread through all social classes and that incidents of white-collar crime in particular are underrepresented in arrest statistics. In reality, it is difficult to characterize a typical criminal for several reasons: a great deal of crime is not reported, crime data generally reflect enforcement officials' emphasis on a limited number of "crime index" offenses, and, most significant, the majority of criminals escape detection.

When sociologists speak of "selecting criminals," they are acknowledging that the likelihood of a crime's being detected and reported and of a suspected offender's being arrested, prosecuted, convicted, and imprisoned depends largely on the seriousness of the crime and the social status of the offender.

Evidence shows that at each stage of the criminal justice process, decisions are affected by factors of age, race, gender, and, especially, class. If police and judicial officials expect persons of lower social status to commit more crimes and to be more dangerous, these expectations lead to selective perception of the criminals they encounter and a greater likelihood that lower-status criminals will be treated more severely.

*Corrections* are the sanctions and other measures that society applies to convicted criminals, including imprisonment, probation, and parole. Corrections are designed to: (1) punish the offender for the crime; (2) deter the offender and others from committing crimes; (3) remove the offender from society; and (4) rehabilitate the offender for possible reentry into society. For adults convicted of serious crimes, imprisonment is likely to be part of the corrections process. The high rate of *recidivism*—repeated crime by those who have been convicted before—suggests that certainly imprisonment alone does not result in successful long-term reform of criminals. As noted in Chapter 5, a prison is an example of a *total institution,* where all aspects of the residents' lives are controlled by custodial officials. Some sociologists argue that the very nature of a total institution limits the possibility of any rehabilitation, because it may lead to the inmate's becoming incapable of assuming normal social responsibilities. In the case of prison, it also ensures that criminals associate only with other criminals, which may predispose them to further crime. Imprisonment, then, is used as a last resort to protect society from dangerous and persistent criminals. However, the vast majority of convicted offenders undergoing corrections in the United States are put on probation or parole. Though many criminals repeat their offenses, their fate at the hands of the legal system may deter others from committing crimes. Studies show that deterrence is most effective when punishment is swift and certain.

Conflict theorists link class privilege to criminal deviance. According to this perspective, groups with power protect their interests by influencing what behavior is considered deviant, who is punished, and which type of punishment is set up to handle each offense. Conflict theory is also helpful in explaining how and why norms change. "Principled deviance"—socially disapproved acts committed out of moral conviction—may stimulate change in the status quo.

## Mental Disorder

*How is mental disorder a form of deviance? What is the medical response to such behavior? How do social factors shape the problems and its treatment?*

***Mental disorder,*** the psychological inability to cope realistically and effectively in daily life, is another important form of deviance. The confused, depressed, or difficult behavior typical of mentally disordered people violates social norms and thereby attracts the stigma of deviance. Mental disorder is widespread in the United States.

A medical model has been applied to mental disorder since the eighteenth century; late in the nineteenth century, psychiatry emerged as a specialized branch of medicine to treat mental disorder. Even with the many advances in medical science since then, the causes of mental disorder remain difficult to pinpoint and treatment has met with limited success. Psychiatrists generally rely on insight and subjective judgments as much as on medical skill in helping their patients. The most serious kind of mental disorder that does not result from physical damage to the brain is classified as ***psychosis,*** a profound mental disturbance involving such a severe break with reality that the affected person cannot function in society. The primary causes of mental disorder are thought to be earlier social and psychological experiences, coupled with certain biological factors that may increase a person's susceptibility. Social factors influence diagnosis of mental disorder, as is demonstrated by the high rate of disagreement among psychiatrists as to whether or not someone is psychotic and, if so, from which particular psychosis that person is suffering.

The ambiguity of the medical model has led some critics to charge that "mental illness" is not an "illness" at all, but a learned (albeit defective) means of dealing with the world. The application of labeling theory to mental disorder helps explain how some people are socialized into confusion, find a temporary escape from their role obligations by violating certain norms of reality, and once labeled as "mentally ill," never manage to shed the label or the deviant behaviors. Rates of mental illness, like the treatment received, vary by social class. Lower classes have a higher incidence of mental disorder than do upper classes, perhaps because their members experience greater stress, or perhaps they are more likely to be labeled as mentally disordered. The recent trend toward deinstitutionalization is resulting in an increase in the number of people suffering from a mental disorder who are out in society, rather than receiving professional care.

## The Medicalization of Deviance

*What is meant by the medicalization of deviance? What are the consequences of this phenomenon for society?*

***Medicalization*** is the process by which the influence of medicine is extended to areas of life that were previously considered nonmedical. In modern society, medicine is a major social institution whose doctors are regarded as powerful, prestigious professionals. The concept of "disease" is now applied to such deviant behavior as hyperactivity, obesity, and compulsive stealing: "offenders" are treated as "sick" people who need a cure, not punishment, to return to normal behavior. This shift, which greatly expanded the medical profession's area of influence, makes medicine an important agent of social control.

## The Social Implications of Deviance

*What have Durkheim and other sociologists identified as functional aspects of deviance? What are the dysfunctions of deviance for society?*

As Durkheim argued, some controllable level of deviance may actually be functional for society. (1) Deviance clarifies norms and defines the limits of social tolerance. (2) By collectively punishing deviance, conforming members of society reaffirm their shared norms and values and enhance their group solidarity. (3) Some acts of deviance are tolerated in that they serve as a safety valve for social discontent, allowing people to let off steam by violating the rules, yet preventing more serious attacks on the social order. (4) Deviant behavior may also be a useful sign of social change, indicating a shift in prevailing norms.

The dysfunctions of deviance are several and interrelated. (1) Since deviance violates social norms, its main dysfunction is disruption of the social order—social life is no longer orderly and predictable and common values are no longer reinforced. (2) As a result, people become confused about which norms and values should guide their behavior. (3) In an effort to reduce widespread deviant behavior, resources may be focused on social control rather than on other social needs, such as health care or education. (4) Lastly, deviance violates trust: we count on one another to behave according to accepted patterns of conduct; if such norms are broken, our mutual trust is undermined and the system of social control breaks down.

Whatever the consequences, deviance is an integral part of social life. Each theory of deviance suggests that modern societies—with larger populations, diverse subcultures, varied and possibly conflicting norms, inequali-ties among groups, and rapid social change—have more deviance than others. Not surprisingly, societies that em-phasize personal freedom and encourage people to test those freedoms, show a higher incidence of deviance as well. In this sense, deviance may be thought of as part of the price a free society pays for the liberty its members enjoy.

## DEFINING CORE CONCEPTS

*After studying the chapter, write a sociological definition in your own words for the following core concepts. Then give an example from your own experience to illus-trate your definition. Refer to the chapter to check your work.*

| *Core Concept* | *Sociological Definition* | *Personal Illustration* |
| --- | --- | --- |
| anomie | | |
| control theory | | |
| cultural-transmission theory | | |
| crime | | |
| deviance | | |
| differential association | | |

| *Core Concept* | *Sociological Definition* | *Personal Illustration* |
| --- | --- | --- |
| labeling theory | | |
| medicalization | | |
| primary deviance/secondary deviance | | |
| sanctions | | |
| social control | | |
| stigma | | |
| structural-strain theory | | |
| total institution | | |

## PUTTING IDEAS TOGETHER

Although most people conform to most social norms most of the time, deviance is an inevitable part of social living. Indeed, the great majority of us commit some deviant act(s) during the course of our lives. Yet, we all are part of a system of social control designed to keep behavior in line with important social rules. This system of social control enforces norms through subtle and informal means as well as through formal agents, such as police. The connection between social norms and social control is shown in the table below.

### Norms and Social Control

| Type of Norm | Form of Social Control to Ensure Conformity | Type of Sanctions Likely to Be Imposed | Type of Stigmatized Deviant |
|---|---|---|---|
| Folkways | Internalization of norms as part of socialization | Informal sanctions; social disapproval | The eccentric |
| (in between) | Threat of force | Serious social disapproval; fines | The petty criminal |
| Mores | Use of force | Serious social disapproval; possible arrest and imprisonment | The public menace |

Sociologists have developed four main theories of social deviance. Most of these theories indicate that deviance results from a unique interplay of individual and societal characteristics. Each theory comes out of a major theoretical perspective, studied in Chapter 1.

### Theories of Deviance and Theoretical Perspectives

| Theory of deviance | Cultural transmission | Structural strain | Control | Labeling |
|---|---|---|---|---|
| Theoretical Perspective of Primary Influence | Interactionist | Functionalist | Functionalist | Interactionist; Conflict |

# Testing the Concepts

## MULTIPLE-CHOICE QUESTIONS

*After studying the chapter, try to answer each of the twenty-five questions below. Mark the alternative you think is correct; then look at the correct answer and explanation provided at the bottom of the page. Try to state why the other alternatives are incorrect, and check your understanding of the correct answer.*

1. Which of the following statements about deviance is true?
   a. Deviance is statistically rare.
   b. Only a few people commit most of the deviant acts in a given society.
   c. Certain acts are always considered deviant in all societies.
   d. Deviance is a violation of significant social norms.
   e. Deviance means law breaking.

2. Which of the following general statements about mental disorder is supported by the text?
   a. Mental disorder is a form of illness, not of deviance.
   b. Mental disorder is rare and inconsequential in the United States.
   c. The causes of mental disorder are known even though the cures are not.

   d. Symptoms of mental disorder are culturally universal.
   e. Most mental disorder is learned and labeled in ways similar to other forms of deviance.

3. Some newspapers publish the names of prostitutes and their customers after they have been apprehended. According to Durkheim, what would be the value of this practice?
   a. It increases public interest in the news.
   b. Both parties are identified as law breakers; proper behavior for men and women is reinforced.
   c. It makes sex roles more equal.
   d. It embarrasses the families of the people involved.
   e. It validates the theory of deviant body types.

4. City residents and police in Jacksontown speak of the Linden area as "a bad neighborhood." Although different groups have lived in the Linden area over the years, the high incidence of deviance remains constant. Which of the following might best explain the deviance in Linden?
   a. cultural-transmission theory
   b. labeling theory
   c. prejudiced view of police
   d. genetic transmission of deviance
   e. structural-strain theory

---

1. **d.** *The definition of what is normal and what is deviant varies from culture to culture and from one point in history to another. Deviance refers to behavior that violates significant norms and is therefore disapproved by large numbers of people. See pages 191–192.*

2. **e.** *Mental disorder is socially defined deviance, as people choose unacceptable ways to cope with or drop out of reality. Far from an abrupt decision on the part of the individual, mental disorder stems from the subtle socialization process that occurs throughout the life course. It is estimated that one out of five U.S. adults suffer from mental problems. See pages 211, 213.*

3. **b.** *Durkheim felt that identification of deviant behavior provides a contrast to normal, desired behavior. Our society considers prostitution a violation of norms about sexuality. In these news accounts, both parties are held up to public scrutiny as law breakers, and normal behavior is reinforced in the process. See pages 193–194.*

4. **a.** *The cultural-transmission theory of deviance suggests that deviant norms are passed on from one cultural group to another in a particular area. When new cultural groups arrive, they are socialized to the deviant culture they encounter in that area. See page 194.*

5. Which of the following statements about the death penalty is supported by social science evidence?
   a. The death penalty is an effective deterrent to murder.
   b. The death penalty is used as a punishment primarily in the Western states.
   c. The death penalty is an effective form of retribution.
   d. The majority of Americans do not favor the death penalty.
   e. States that have the death penalty apply the sentence without regard to race.

6. Which of the following is a precondition for the medicalization of deviance.
   a. Medicine must be a major social institution; physicians must have high prestige.
   b. More cures must be found for catastrophic illnesses.
   c. Employers must offer health care as a part of their benefits package.
   d. Prisoners must receive the same quality of medical care as anyone else.
   e. Physicians must participate in continuing education programs so that they understand "deviant" diseases, such as alcoholism.

7. A sociological explanation for the lack of attention paid to white-collar crime would be that it
   a. does not involve much loss of money.
   b. is a victimless crime.
   c. is a new phenomenon.
   d. is committed by high-status members of society.
   e. is handled internally and does not require police or legal intervention.

8. Which theory of deviance has been most strongly influenced by the conflict perspective?
   a. labeling theory
   b. cultural-transmission theory
   c. structural-strain theory
   d. deviation theory
   e. alienation theory

9. A disproportionate number of apprehended criminals are likely to be
   a. under twenty-one.
   b. female.
   c. middle class.
   d. white.
   e. from rural areas.

---

5. **c.** *The death penalty is used primarily in Southern states for a small percentage of convicted murderers. Blacks convicted of killing white victims are disproportionately likely to be executed. There is little evidence that the death penalty deters murderers, but it is effective retribution and over 75 percent of all Americans support this form of punishment. See page 209.*

6. **a.** *Medicalization of deviance means that a wider range of disorders are defined as illness, and their treatment comes under the control of physicians. In premodern societies, the medical institution was peripheral to society and medical personnel were held in low esteem. Scientific advances moved medicine into a central position in modern society. See page 214.*

7. **d.** *White-collar crime is extremely costly in terms of the dollar amount of this illegal activity to society. It has been overlooked, however, because of the high status of many white-collar criminals. Society chooses instead to focus on criminals with less power. See pages 203–204.*

8. **a.** *The conflict perspective emphasizes the power of certain groups who are in a position to define what is deviant and what is normal. Both conflict theorists and labeling theorists are concerned with whose definitions of deviance prevail. See page 198.*

9. **a.** *Juveniles are arrested for more crimes than any other social group. See page 204.*

10.  In the movie "Nine to Five," three secretaries see no promotions or salary raises in their future. Their skills go unrecognized and their ambitions are blocked. They kidnap the boss and establish a variety of new, beneficial office procedures. What theory of deviance would a sociologist use to study these women?
     a. control theory
     b. feminist theory
     c. structural-strain theory
     d. "deviant career" theory
     e. labeling theory

11.  Which of the following statements best answers the question "Do prisons work?"
     a. Evidence indicates that prisons are the most economical means of carrying out the functions assigned to them.
     b. Prisons do punish criminals, even if they are not effective at rehabilitation.
     c. Prisons are effective in the protection of society, and in punishment and rehabilitation of criminals.
     d. The threat of prison has been shown to be a powerful deterrent to potential law breakers.
     e. Since most law breakers are caught and sentenced to prison, these institutions are effective protectors of the public's safety.

12.  According to control theory, what is the basis for "control" of deviance?

     a. the condition of anomie
     b. social solidarity
     c. the death penalty
     d. an individual's conscience and moral upbringing
     e. a restrictive society with clear-cut rules and penalties

13.  Which of the following sociological terms is most useful for understanding Erving Goffman's concept of "stigma"?
     a. looking-glass self
     b. *Gemeinschaft*
     c. endogamy
     d. rationalization
     e. civil inattention

14.  The significance of "secondary deviance" is that
     a. continued acts of deviance can be habit-forming.
     b. some deviant acts, if not most, are of minor importance.
     c. deviance is often a natural part of other major activities in life.
     d. young children who get involved in crime at an early age are likely to make it a life pattern if not stopped.
     e. once labeled deviant, a person may attempt to live up to that label.

---

10.  **c.** *The talents of these women are thwarted by social discrimination. Seeing no legitimate means for advancement, they seek to rise in their company through deviant acts. See page 195.*

11.  **b.** *Prisons are extremely costly to the taxpaying public, and despite goals for rehabilitation, seem to succeed only in isolating a select group of criminals from the public. See page 207.*

12.  **b.** *Durkheim argued that in a society with strong social solidarity, individuals would conform to shared norms and values and avoid deviant behavior. Their attachment to their society and its rules would serve as*

*an investment in, and a set of internal sanctions for, conforming behavior. See pages 196–197.*

13.  **a.** *Stigma is the mark of social disgrace that sets the deviant apart from those who consider themselves "normal." If the labeling process is effective, a person may come to accept this stigma as part of his or her self-image, the looking-glass self formed from the reactions of others. See page 191.*

14.  **e.** *The acceptance of a deviant label may predispose a person to behave according to deviant expectations. See page 198.*

15. The theory that both conforming and deviant behavior are learned as a result of the intensity of contact with significant groups that endorse conforming or deviant norms is
   a. structural-strain theory.
   b. symbolic interaction theory.
   c. labeling theory.
   d. conflict theory.
   e. cultural-transmission theory.

16. The article "The Saints and the Roughnecks" illustrates which point about deviance in society?
   a. Some people are deviant and others never are.
   b. Deviance is useful to the society.
   c. Eventually, most deviants are caught and punished.
   d. Definitions of deviance are selectively applied.
   e. The more religious a person is, the less likely it is that he or she will be deviant.

17. An example of a total institution would be
   a. the family.
   b. a public university.
   c. the mass media.
   d. a mental hospital.
   e. a church.

18. Which of the following kinds of society is most likely to produce deviance?
   a. a remote tribal group
   b. a modern pluralistic society like the United States
   c. a rural community
   d. a modern homogeneous society like Japan
   e. a newly reorganized society like Iran

19. Which of the following is a dysfunction of deviance?
   a. Others are motivated to conform.
   b. Social norms are clarified.
   c. Group solidarity is promoted.
   d. People become confused about what is right and wrong.
   e. Sanctioning those who break norms has a deterrent effect.

20. A college administrative official becomes obsessed with campus rules and regulations, losing sight of the objectives these rules were intended to achieve. In Merton's terms, this is an example of which response to a discrepancy between approved goals and means?
   a. primary deviance
   b. institutionalized evasion of norms
   c. ritualism
   d. retreatism
   e. authoritarian personality

---

15. **e.** *The groups with whom one associates provide norms for behavior. Some of these norms may be deviant in comparison to the dominant culture, while others may be conforming. See page 194.*

16. **d.** *These two groups of boys committed the same types of acts, but because of selective perception and labeling, they were treated in a different manner. See pages 219–221.*

17. **d.** *Inhabitants of a total institution submit to the almost absolute control of a hierarchy of officials; a mental hospital has rules and procedures that govern most if not all aspects of the patient's life. See page 207.*

18. **b.** *A large heterogeneous society may contain a variety of subcultures and competing norms. Rapid social change associated with such societies may lead to a gap between real culture and ideal culture. This lack of uniformity of belief in norms and appropriate behavior produces deviance. See page 216.*

19. **d.** *Deviance, particularly deviance that goes uncontrolled, leads to confusion over norms and values, which may result in social tension and low cultural integration. See page 215.*

20. **c.** *A person who becomes obsessed with means and loses sight of goals is called a ritualist. He or she favors the ritual of adhering to rules, even rules that have lost their purpose. See page 196.*

21. Crimes without victims differ from violent crimes (those with victims) in that they
    a. occur less frequently.
    b. are not pursued by formal law enforcement.
    c. involve a very small proportion of the population.
    d. include involvement by mostly lower-class criminals with previous records.
    e. are difficult to control; the established methods of social control do not work effectively.

22. A sociologist argues that lower-class youths join delinquent gangs because they are denied status in respectable society but can achieve it in the gang environment. Which theory of deviance is the sociologist using?
    a. labeling theory
    b. association theory
    c. cultural-transmission theory
    d. structural-strain theory
    e. retreatist theory

23. The public has reacted more vigorously and more negatively to drug abuse than to alcohol abuse because

    a. drugs are more dangerous.
    b. drug use is more widespread.
    c. less desirable types of people are associated with drug use.
    d. alcohol abuse affects only individuals, not everyone.
    e. drugs are used by minors and alcohol by adults.

24. Most murders and assaults in the United States are committed
    a. by relatives or acquaintances of the victims.
    b. by members of one racial group upon another.
    c. by people previously unknown to the victims.
    d. in the course of burglaries and robberies.
    e. by persons suffering from a mental illness.

25. The selection of criminals seems to be heavily influenced by
    a. the effectiveness of a community's police force.
    b. the willingness of citizens to report crimes.
    c. the social status of the criminal.
    d. the rate of recidivism.
    e. the record of previous offenses of criminals.

---

21. **e.** *Victimless crime is notoriously difficult to control, partly because there is no victim to press charges or testify, and also because offenders often regard the laws, not themselves, as immoral. See page 203.*

22. **d.** *Structural-strain theory explains why people commit deviant acts when they endorse either the goals or the means valued by society, but cannot reach those goals through socially approved means. In this case, lower-class boys cannot achieve a "respectable" status by legitimate means so they use deviant means to gain what status they can from fellow gang members. See pages 195–196.*

23. **c.** *Alcohol abuse is tolerated because it is used by people at all levels of society. Drug abuse has generally been associated with people who rebel against society. See page 199.*

24. **a.** *The largest proportion of murders and assaults are commited by persons known to one another. See page 200.*

25. **c.** *The social status of a criminal affects the perceptions of law enforcement and judicial officials. Lower-status criminals are more likely to be apprehended and are given stiffer penalties for their crimes. See page 206.*

# A CASE STUDY

NAME

COURSE/SECTION NUMBER

In nineteenth-century London, people with mental and physical handicaps were scorned, even feared, and certainly denied a decent quality of life. Many of the physically deformed were exploited as "freaks" in shows and carnivals. The "Elephant Man," so named for his severe bodily deformities, was one such individual. He was kept, in near bondage, in the carnival by a man who provided for his basic needs and pocketed the profits generated by the Elephant Man's appearances. Knowing he could not make it on his own in the "normal" world, the Elephant Man continued to live in the carnival with his exploitive master. Eventually, he was identified by a prominent doctor in London, who took an interest in his physical symptoms and hospitalized him for years of observation and medical testing. As their relationship progressed, the doctor sought to humanize the Elephant Man by bringing him into contact with his friends, members of London society's upper crust. Yet, the doctor was very much in control of the Elephant Man's life, telling him exactly how to behave, teaching him specific things, such as manners and elementary school lessons, but keeping him ignorant of other matters, such as sexuality. After a time, the Elephant Man became a "status symbol," someone to know, and the elite competed at lavishing attention on him and giving him expensive gifts. The Elephant Man's "normal" life within the confines of the hospital became infinitely more comfortable than it would have been had he remained in the carnival.

1.   Illustrate Goffman's concept of stigma. Was the Elephant Man deviant? Why or why not?

2.    What characteristics of a total institution are evident in the hospital and the carnival?

3.    How would you explain the change in society's view of the Elephant Man, from a freak to someone everyone wanted to know?

# Applying the Concepts

NAME

_____

COURSE/SECTION NUMBER

## APPLICATION EXERCISE ONE

Most of us have some physical trait or behavior that has elicited a negative reaction from others. In this exercise, think about a personal characteristic that other people have stigmatized.

1. What was the stigma and how do you know that it was a stigma?

2. To use Goffman's term, how did you "manage" this stigma? Did you change your behavior or feelings about yourself in some way?

3. Explain the relevance of labeling theory to your understanding and management of this stigma, or some other minor deviant behavior.

## APPLICATION EXERCISE TWO

Deviance may be readily observable on any school campus. Based on Merton's theory of deviance, construct a chart showing the five ways individuals may react to a discrepancy between approved goals and legitimate means for reaching them. Then, using the college scene as your guide, provide an example of each of the five types of reactions. You might consider such behaviors as cheating, plagiarizing, coming to class only when attendance is taken, and playing up to the instructor.

NAME

COURSE/SECTION NUMBER

## APPLICATION EXERCISE THREE

Look over today's newspaper for three examples of criminal behavior. One example should involve white-collar crime in either a business or a government setting. Attach these articles and use them as the basis for answering the following questions.

1.    Using the theories of deviance outlined in the text, offer an explanation as to why these particular people engaged in criminal activity. Which theory (theories) seems (seem) most useful in explaining why people *commit* crimes?

2.    Which theory is most useful in explaining society's *reaction* to the perpetrators' criminal acts? What formal and informal elements of social control are present in your examples?

3.   Pick one of your examples and use it to illustrate the steps involved in the labeling process.

4.   Provide a functionalist interpretation of crime. Then take a conflict theorist's point of view and show how definitions of crime, and the punishments that result, depend on the power structure of a society.

# CHAPTER 9

# Sexuality and Society

## Reviewing the Concepts

### LEARNING GOALS

*After studying this chapter, you should be able to:*

1. Indicate why human sexuality is a sociological issue.

2. Discuss the nature of the human sex drive.

3. Identify the three cultural universals found in every society.

4. Give examples of the culturally relative nature of conceptions of beauty, restrictiveness or permissiveness, and sexual conduct.

5.  Evaluate the degree of cultural variation in human relationships.

6.  Identify the traditional or historical bases for current sexual values in the United States.

7.  Critique the research that has been done on sexual behavior in America.

8.  List some of the recent changes, including dysfunctional changes, in sexual attitudes and behavior in the United States.

9.  Review the sociological evidence for the incest taboo.

10. Summarize the aspects of "normal" sexuality that encourage a high rate of rape in American culture.

11. Present a sociological view of the crime of rape.

12. Discuss the various types of male and female homosexuality, providing cross-cultural information when possible.

13. Describe the gay and lesbian community and explain how it differs from myths.

14. Contrast the four theories explaining the development of a homosexual orientation.

15. Discuss prostitution as an occupation.

16. Analyze prostitution from the functionalist, conflict, and interactionist perspectives.

## IDENTIFYING KEY QUESTIONS AND THEMES

Sexuality is important both to the individual and to society. Our interpersonal relationships often involve subtle and direct forms of sexual expression. On a larger scale, the sexual bond between husband and wife is the basis of marriage and family, the building block of society. Contrary to the view that sexuality is purely biological in nature, sociologists argue that human sexual behavior and feelings are learned primarily through socialization and thus conform to the prevailing norms of the society concerned. As such, sexuality is a sociological issue.

## The Nature of Human Sexuality

*What are the implications of a socially influenced sex drive?*

Research has shown that human sexual behavior is very flexible; we learn to attach a quality of eroticism to certain people, objects, acts, etc., depending on the particular socialization process we experience. The fact that the human sex drive is so flexible explains the powerful norms and taboos that exist to regulate it.

## Sexual Behavior in Other Cultures

*Are there any cultural universals? How do conceptions of beauty vary from society to society? What factors contrib-*

ute to restrictive or permissive sexual norms? How do attitudes about sexual conduct vary cross-culturally?

There are three *cultural universals*—practices that are found in every society: (1) the *incest taboo,* which regulates sexual contact among certain categories of relatives; (2) *marriage,* the socially approved mating arrangement between two or more people (*adultery,* sexual relations in which one or more of the partners is married to someone else, is forbidden in two-thirds of the societies studied); and (3) *heterosexuality,* or sexual orientation toward the opposite sex (although every society insists on some conformity to the norm of heterosexuality, *homosexuality,* or sexual orientation toward the same sex, and *bisexuality,* or sexual orientation toward both sexes, are accepted much more readily in some societies than in others). These cultural universals stabilize relationships within the family and ensure the survival of the society. Beyond these universals, however, substantial cross-cultural variations exist as far as sexual preferences and practices.

Societies vary a great deal in their conceptions of beauty, for example, with more specificity given to standards for female attractiveness than for male attractiveness. There are few, if any, universal standards of female beauty.

The degree of sexual *restrictiveness,* or insistence on adherence to narrowly defined sexual norms, and of sexual *permissiveness,* or acceptance of some nonconformity to sexual norms, also varies a great deal from one society to another. Cultural comparisons show North American societies to be more restrictive in terms of sexual practices. Most other cultures allow or encourage premarital sexual contact, and a significant number allow some form of adultery.

There is also wide cross-cultural variation in the norms governing sexual conduct, in terms of preferences for particular positions, times, places, partners, and erotic stimuli. However, cross-cultural evidence must be interpreted carefully because much of it deals only with the sexual practices of small preindustrial societies. While comparable studies have not been made of modern industrial societies, existing evidence suggests that sexual behavior in these societies is less variable. As more and more societies become industrialized, sexual practices are likely to differ much less radically from those of Western nations. Nevertheless, evidence from preindustrial societies, both past and present, is important in that it highlights the interplay between biological potentials and cultural norms.

## Sexual Behavior in America

*What are the bases for the sexual norms in the United States? How have they changed and what predictions can be made about the future?*

The most striking feature of sexuality in America is the tension between, on the one hand, a tradition of highly restrictive standards promoted by the *ideal culture* and, on the other, the permissive practices reflected in the *real culture.* Thus the sexuality we actually express differs from that based on traditional moral values founded in Judeo-Christian teachings. Beginning with the Old Testament, Western culture strongly emphasized the procreative purpose of sex and generally disapproved of sex for pleasure. The New Testament cast an even more negative light on sexuality and strictly prohibited sex outside marriage. By the Middle Ages, sex was strongly equated with sin and further restricted. Subsequent centuries were marked by alternating periods of restrictiveness (particularly among the early Puritans and nineteenth-century Victorians), and relative permissiveness. The *double standard,* an unspoken code of conduct for men and women that emphasized the importance of purity and chastity for women but tolerated greater sexual freedom for men, compounded the general embarrassment and guilt that came to be associated with sexuality. Traditional values persist in America today as can be seen in current laws regulating private sexual behavior and in institutions such as education and the media.

Social scientists have only recently begun to study American sexuality. This research is often limited and unreliable owing to the difficulty of surveying a representative, random sample of the population. Studies done by Alfred Kinsey in the 1940s and 1950s are useful for the mass of data they provide. Not only do these studies describe the sexual practices of more than 18,000 American males and females; they show the gap between the values of ideal culture and the ways Americans actually behave. In fact, a sexual revolution had taken place in the experimental years of the "roaring twenties" that was primarily the result of sexual attitudes catching up with social behavior. Due to the restrictive atmosphere, the full extent of the changes went largely unrecognized until the Kinsey reports, after which the atmosphere in America became a good deal more permissive. With the introduction of the birth-control pill, permitting a separation of sex for reproduction and sex for pleasure, a second revolution, from the mid-1960s to the mid-1970s, took place, bringing sweeping changes to many areas of sexual and social life. These changes include: more permissive attitudes about sex; an increase in the number of people who engage in premarital sex; a gradual erosion of the double standard; a high rate of teenage pregnancy and illegitimacy; greater popularity and availability of **pornography**—pictorial and written material intended to arouse sexual excitement—certain kinds of which have been shown to correlate with sexually violent attitudes; and an explosion in the incidence of sexually transmitted diseases, the most ominous of which is AIDS. Thus far, the 1980s have been a period of relative stability; in fact, researchers generally agree the sexual revolution is over. Perhaps the most important outcome of the tumultuous 1960s and 1970s is the widespread acceptance of newer concepts of sexual morality. Particularly significant is the redefinition of sexual morality in terms of mutual consent rather than absolute rules of right and wrong.

## The Incest Taboo

*What are the social functions of an incest taboo? What is the sociological view of this cultural universal?*

Every known society has a taboo prohibiting sexual relations between specific categories of relatives, almost always between parent and child and brother and sister. Common-sense thinking may suggest that the taboo is instinctive or that it exists to prevent the physical and mental degeneration that may result from inbreeding. However, both these positions are refuted by scientific explanations showing that the incest taboo is learned for social, not biological, reasons. First, the incest taboo encourages marriage outside one's own group and thus the formation of bonds with others, linking families and helping to ensure the survival of society. Second, within a given family, the incest taboo clearly delineates various statuses, thereby eliminating a great deal of potential confusion. Third, the incest taboo reduces sexual rivalry and jealousy among relatives; the family institution is more stable as a result.

## Rape

*What is known about the crime of rape? What connections exist between acceptable social relations between the sexes and criminal acts such as rape?*

**Rape** is a crime of violence in which the domination of one person and the humiliation of another takes a sexual form. About 87,000 rapes are reported in the United States each year, but these cases probably represent only one-tenth the number of incidents that actually occur. One reason rape is so underreported is that victims feel unable to undergo further traumatization by submitting to police interrogation, medical examination, and often hostile court proceedings. Another reason is that most rapes are committed by an acquaintance of the victim, and many victims fear that they themselves will be blamed—particularly in the case of "date rape." This fear on the part of the victim reveals social confusion about the crime of rape and the nature of normal sexual relations in general. It is important to note that rape is virtually unknown in some societies. In fact, the incidence of rape appears to depend on cultural factors. Rape-prone societies often have male gods, accord women low status, and encourage male aggression. In the United States, the social relations of the sexes are characterized by two cultural features relevant to rape: inequality between men and women and a tendency for men to view women as sex objects. Incidents of sexual harassment in the workplace and in other social situations evince the general male belief that any and all sexual attention is flattering to women, or at least will be tolerated by them. Not surprisingly, women report very negative feelings about unwanted sexual advances.

The crime of rape is an extreme manifestation of culturally approved activities in which men dominate women. In most cases, it is not an act of sudden impulse carried out by a "sick" individual lacking other sexual outlets. On the contrary, the majority of rapes are planned in advance and seem to have little to do with lust. Rapes are intended to bolster the aggressor's feelings of power, superiority, and masculinity by humiliating and degrading the woman. As far as the victim is concerned, the effects of rape are devastating, involving physical and emotional damage and the disruption of personal, social, familial, and sexual life.

## Homosexuality

*What is the incidence of homosexuality in the United States? What are the characteristics of the gay and lesbian community? How do we learn our sexual orientation?*

Homosexuality occurs worldwide and throughout history. While there is a good deal of evidence about male homosexuality, much less information is available about female homosexuality, or lesbianism. In any given society where male homosexuality is accepted, it takes one of three forms: pederasty, involving a relationship between a man and a boy; transvestism, in which certain men assume the social and sexual role of women; or homophilia, in which both partners are adult men who play otherwise conventional male roles. Although homophilia is common in the United States, pederasty is, cross-culturally, the most widespread form of socially accepted homosexual behavior. The cross-cultural evidence on lesbianism is fragmentary, but the behavior seems to be generally less common than male homosexuality and appears most often to take the homophilic form. At various periods in history, homosexuality has been accepted, rejected, tolerated, and condemned. In general, Western attitudes have been negative because Western moral tradition tolerates sexual acts only within marriage, for reproductive purposes.

Most individuals are not exclusively heterosexual or homosexual but have a preference for one type of relationship over the other. Kinsey assessed homosexuality on the basis of a 7-point scale, ranging from exclusively heterosexual to exclusively homosexual orientations. Most Americans stand somewhere along the continuum rather than at either end. Subsequent studies indicate that approximately 10 percent of the population can be considered exclusively or predominantly homosexual.

Although gay men and lesbians constitute a major subgroup of the U.S. population, their sexual preference is not readily known to others and myths about homosexuality persist. Many homosexuals "pass" as heterosexuals, while others seek companionship and a more accepting environment in the gay and lesbian communities found in most major urban areas of the United States. Such communities offer homosexuals the opportunity to meet, shop, dine, and enjoy leisure activities without the stigma experienced in "straight" society. The great majority of homosexuals form long-lasting, affectionate relationships; in fact, lesbian relationships appear to be even more enduring than heterosexual relationships. Nevertheless, it is true that gay men are more promiscuous as a group than heterosexuals, although the recent AIDS epidemic has produced a trend toward more traditional practices of dating and settling down with a single partner.

Attempts to identify biological factors that may predispose individuals to homosexuality have been unsuccessful, as the incidence of homosexuality has varied greatly from one historical time and place to another. Homosexuality, like other sexual behavior, is learned. Four theories have been offered to explain how people learn their eventual sexual orientation and, in particular, why some become homosexual. (1) A common popular view is that homosexuality is caused by early childhood experiences, but no discernible pattern has been found. (2) Another hypothesis concerns the effects of the family environment on homosexuality. Again, no factors could be identified to predict homosexuality or heterosexuality for certain family types. (3) The social-learning view argues that if homosexual behavior is reinforced, the individual will tend to repeat the experience, and a homosexual identity may result. However, the strength of the social stigma against homosexuality makes it unlikely that a theory of rewards and punishments alone can explain individuals' sexual preferences. (4) The self-labeling approach suggests that both heterosexual and homosexual behaviors are learned through a similar process involving self-definition, usually occurring in late childhood or adolescence. After experiencing a mild sexual attraction for another male, for example, a boy might label himself, or be labeled by others, as a homosexual. In time, the person may become trapped within that lable, eventually defining himself exclusively in those terms. Cultural beliefs strongly influence the self-definition that the individual ultimately makes.

## Prostitution

*What are the types of prostitution in the United States? Why do some people choose prostitution as an occupation? Why does prostitution exist within a society? Can prostitution be eliminated? What do functionalist, conflict, and interactionist theories say about prostitution?*

**Prostitution** is the relatively indiscriminate exchange of sexual favors for economic gain. Prostitution violates social norms governing appropriate sexual relations, and is against the law in the United States and in many other countries. Although other forms of prostitution exist, notably men-for-men prostitution in large cities, by far the greatest number of prostitutes are women offering their services to men. Ranked from low to high status and income, female prostitution takes the following forms: streetwalker; housegirl; and call girl. Male prostitutes catering to men solicit in gay bars, on certain streets, or through "escort agencies," while those catering to women often work through private introductions.

Most prostitutes drift into the role, perhaps by accepting a casual sexual offer or by coming in contact with a prostitute or a pimp, and serve a period of apprenticeship before considering it their occupation.

Despite social stigma, prostitution continues to be a well-established social institution. Functionalists argue that from the prostitute's point of view, the occupation can offer higher earnings than a "straight" job, less tedium, and a greater possibility of forming relationships with higher-status individuals. From the customer's point of view, prostitution offers convenient sex without obligations or emotional entanglements that might undermine the family system in the way more affectionate extramar-

ital affairs sometimes do. Conflict theorists are critical of this approach, arguing that prostitution, like any other institution, reflects the power relationships in the society. As conflict theorists point out, prostitutes are generally young, have little education, come from lower-class backgrounds, and are alienated from their families. They enter prostitution because their only economic resource is their sexual availability, then become trapped in a dangerous, exploitive situation that is far more beneficial for the pimps and the clients than it is for them. Interactionist researchers have tended to concentrate on the dynamics of the human relationships involved in prostitution. One focus, for example, is on the process whereby the new prostitute is resocialized by the pimp and other prostitutes — learning how to solicit, how to recognize undercover cops, etc. — and acquires a new set of values that help to maintain a relatively stable self-concept. Taken together, all three theories contribute to a more comprehensive understanding of prostitution.

In spite of efforts to eradicate it, prostitution has survived for centuries. Because it is a victimless crime and laws against prostitution are difficult to enforce, some countries have legalized prostitution in order to control it. The suggestion that prostitution be legalized in the United States has met with resistance, however, because people fear a decline of public morality. Either way, prostitution cannot be completely eliminated in a sexually restrictive culture, for it arises in response to those very restrictions.

## DEFINING CORE CONCEPTS

*After studying the chapter, write a sociological definition in your own words for the following core concepts. Then give an example from your own experience to illustrate your definition. Refer to the chapter to check your work.*

| *Core Concept* | *Sociological Definition* | *Personal Illustration* |
| --- | --- | --- |
| cultural universals | | |

| *Core Concept* | *Sociological Definition* | *Personal Illustration* |
| --- | --- | --- |
| double standard | | |
| ideal culture/real culture | | |
| incest taboo | | |
| restrictiveness/permissiveness | | |

## PUTTING IDEAS TOGETHER

Human sexual behavior and feelings are learned primarily through the socialization process and generally conform to the prevailing norms of the society concerned. The enormous amount of variation in sexual practices can be explained by cultural differences. We could classify societies in terms of:

### Degree of Permissiveness and Restrictiveness

*sexually permissive*                                                    *sexually restrictive*

### Discrepancy Between Real and Ideal Culture

*overlap of real and ideal culture*              *a gap between real and ideal culture*

### Attitude Toward Homosexuality

*tolerant of homosexuality*                                      *hostile toward homosexuality*

The United States would be placed on the right-hand side of each of these continua. Remember that all societies have some form of incest taboo and encourage (among other sexual options) heterosexual, genital intercourse.

Sociologists have studied the connection between approved sexual behavior and deviant sexual acts. In some cases, deviance occurs when normal sexual acts take place with improper partners, as in the case of incest. In other cases, sexual acts are considered deviant even with a culturally acceptable partner: laws in some states forbid certain sexual acts even between consenting adults within the context of marriage. Rape and prostitution are examples of deviance stemming from attitudes about normal sexuality. The table below summarizes some sample connections between cultural norms and deviant sexual acts.

| *Cultural Norms in the U.S. for Sexuality* | *As They Show Up in the Deviant Acts of* | |
| --- | --- | --- |
| | *Rape* | *Prostitution* |
| Male dominance. | Rape is almost entirely a crime in which men take control of women against their will. | Men frequent male or female prostitutes at will, to meet their own needs. |
| Males have intense sexual needs that must be satisfied. | Men are presumed to be out of control because they are tantalized by women. | Mates may not be able to provide all the sex a man needs, so he seeks it elsewhere. |
| Women are seen as sexually passive objects. | Women need to be pushed into sexual acts, and although they protest, they actually "like it." | An economic transaction is permissible; no feelings are involved. |
| Double standard. | Women are blamed for their victimization, for not guarding their sexual access and for being "promiscuous." | Fallen women, or prostitutes, are good only for the sexual services they provide; they are stigmatized and arrested, while customers are not. |

# Testing the Concepts

## MULTIPLE-CHOICE QUESTIONS

*After studying the chapter, try to answer each of the twenty-five questions below. Mark the alternative you think is correct; then look at the correct answer and explanation provided at the bottom of the page. Try to state why the other alternatives are incorrect, and check your understanding of the correct answer.*

1. According to the self-labeling theory of homosexuality,
   a. people with homosexual tendencies are more likely to become bisexual if their society offers bisexuality as an option.
   b. both homosexual and heterosexual behavior are learned through a similar process.
   c. once a person has engaged in a homosexual act, he or she becomes homosexual.
   d. society has nothing to do with homosexuality; the individual chooses that definition of self in spite of the pressure to be heterosexual.
   e. homosexuals have lower self-esteem than do heterosexuals.

2. Which of the following statements implies a functionalist analysis of prostitution?

   a. Prostitution is socially useful; for example, it permits men to have nonemotional sexual experiences outside the context of marriage that may be less dangerous to the family system than extramarital affairs.
   b. Prostitutes are generally from lower-class backgrounds and tend to have a history of promiscuity and alienation from their families.
   c. Prostitution is fundamentally immoral and ought to be controlled by every possible legal means.
   d. Prostitution is yet another example of the exploitation of women by men; women are seen only as sex objects.
   e. The increase in venereal disease and illegitimate births among prostitutes is a function of prostitution.

3. In Western societies, homosexuality has generally been regarded negatively; sociological analysis suggests the reason for this is that
   a. homosexuality is unnatural.
   b. homosexual acts are nonreproductive and thus do not contribute to the survival of society.
   c. kings, emperors, and others in positions of power were heterosexual.
   d. homosexuality is practiced by less than 2 percent of the U.S. population, a clear minority.
   e. homosexuality is esthetically offensive.

---

1. **b.** *Self-labeling theory recognizes the flexibility of the human sex drive and sees sexual orientation—be it homosexual or heterosexual—as the result of a process of self-definition, whereby people label their sexuality and then operate within that definition. Thus, people may have homosexual contacts and still think of themselves as heterosexuals. Cultural beliefs strongly influence the self-labeling process. See page 244.*

2. **a.** *Functionalist theory looks at the consequences of prostitution for society, without endorsing it or* criticizing it. One function prostitution serves is the provision of sexual variety in a society with strong norms for monogamy. See page 246.*

3. **b.** *Human sexuality in Western societies is associated with reproduction rather than with recreation and enjoyment. According to this traditional orientation, sexual activity without the possibility of procreation is unjustifiable; consequently, homosexuality is regarded negatively. See page 242.*

4. Surveys of American sexual practices reveal that
   a. adultery is a rare practice for both males and females (Kinsey).
   b. use of prostitutes, at least once, as a sexual outlet, is confined to a minority of men (Kinsey).
   c. there has been little or no change in the "double standard."
   d. there is a remarkably high degree of conformity to traditional sexually restrictive values.
   e. there is a wide discrepancy between traditional sexual norms and sexual behavior.

5. American laws that attempt to regulate the private sexual behavior of consenting adults
   a. are similar to the laws found in most advanced industrial countries.
   b. have few parallels in other advanced industrial societies, except for the Soviet bloc.
   c. have been ruled unconstitutional by the Supreme Court.
   d. are remarkably permissive compared to most other industrial societies.
   e. include high penalties for offenders.

6. Kinsey provided a wealth of statistical data in a volume called *Sexual Behavior in the Human Male.* Even though it is one of the best studies ever done, his research is flawed by a problem common to sex surveys. The problem is that
   a. the questions asked are too intimate.
   b. respondents exaggerate their sexual conquests.
   c. the answers are shocking to the researchers, leading them to censor their reports.
   d. it is difficult to get a representative, random sample of the population; answers therefore cannot be generalized.
   e. no one reads these reports because they are quickly out of date.

7. The "double standard" refers to the Western notion that
   a. sexual behavior should be regulated by government laws and religious teachings, which sometimes do not coincide.
   b. Christians should have a higher moral standard about their sexual behavior than other people.
   c. people brag about having more sexual experience than they really do.
   d. heterosexuality is normal, whereas homosexuality is abnormal.
   e. men ought to be allowed more sexual freedom than women.

---

4. **e.** *A wide gap still exists between sexual norms about how Americans ought to behave and how they actually do behave. Additionally, Americans are much more cautious about sexual practices others engage in than they are about their own behavior. See page 232.*

5. **b.** *American laws, reflecting restrictive attitudes about sexual behavior, limit the sexual practices of consenting adults for the preservation of the morals of society. These laws are often not enforced, because they are difficult to control. Most other Western societies are considerably more liberal about consensual sex. See page 231.*

6. **d.** *The refusal rate on sex surveys is higher than for surveys on other topics. Refusals are not random; people in certain social classes, reflecting particular sexual attitudes and practices, are more likely to refuse. Thus, the generalizability of the results is questionable. Like Kinsey's research, most sex surveys are based on volunteer respondents; those who volunteer to talk about sexual topics are members of a special group. See page 232.*

7. **e.** *Sexual norms differ for men and women. In Western societies, men are presumed to have greater sexual needs and are freer to take advantage of various sexual outlets. Women are expected to be passive and to keep their sexual feelings under control. Until recently, fidelity and virginity were considered crucial for women, but not for men. This dual set of norms is called the double standard. See page 230.*

8. Sociology approaches the human sex drive by
   a. treating it as a biological drive for reproduction.
   b. recognizing it as so flexible that societal norms are necessary for stability.
   c. regarding human sexual behavior as rigid and predictable.
   d. seeing the flexibility of the sex drive as requiring equally flexible norms for sexual behavior.
   e. trying to point out to people that restricting sexual behavior and pornography is a losing battle.

9. Recent studies of sexual behavior in the United States show that
   a. sexual behavior is more restrictive than the norms would suggest.
   b. norms and values are catching up with actual behavior.
   c. there is an increase in the double standard.
   d. sexual practices are changing but attitudes are not.
   e. pornography is directly linked to sex crimes.

10. On the basis of the 1986 Attorney-General's Commission on Pornography and other earlier studies of pornography, which of the following statements is supported by available evidence?

   a. Exposure to pornography has a detrimental effect on young people's sexual preferences.
   b. Pornography should be banned altogether because it causes sexual misconduct.
   c. Less pornography is available in the United States today than at any other time since the 1920s.
   d. Pornography does affect *attitudes,* if not behaviors, of readers/viewers.
   e. As many women as men read and see pornography.

11. Which of the following conclusions accurately describes prostitution as an occupation?
   a. Prostitutes tend to drift into the occupation.
   b. Male prostitutes are homosexuals themselves, just like their clients.
   c. Prostitutes generally regret their choice of occupation.
   d. Conflict theory argues that prostitution contributes to the maintenance of the family system.
   e. Female prostitutes typically have a strong father attachment and transfer this relationship to their clients.

---

8. **b.** *The immense variety of human sexual expression is evidence for the importance of societal norms in guiding sexual behavior. Human sexual behavior and feelings are learned through socialization and generally conform to prevailing norms of the society concerned. See page 224.*

9. **b.** *By their own admission, people in the United States have long been engaging in more sexual behavior than they approve of for themselves or for others. However, the gap between real and ideal culture is closing. Greater acceptance of sexual permissiveness and sex for nonreproductive purposes has resulted in more consistency between moral beliefs and the sexual practices that have been occurring for some time. See page 232.*

10. **d.** *Although the link between pornography and behavior is undetermined, there is a link between pornography and attitudes. Pornography orients the reader/viewer to attitudes that degrade women and condone violence as part of sexual pleasure. The increased availability of "kiddie porn" and hard-core porn make this link an especially sobering one. See pages 234–235.*

11. **a.** *Recruitment into prostitution is rarely an abrupt decision. On the contrary, most people drift into prostitution—perhaps by accepting a casual offer from a potential client or by meeting another prostitute or a pimp—and serve a period of apprenticeship before finally defining themselves as prostitutes and relying on the occupation as a major or sole source of income. See page 246.*

12.  Which approach to the learning of homosexuality or heterosexuality is consistent with the theoretical perspective of symbolic interaction?
    a.  social learning
    b.  family environment
    c.  biological factors
    d.  cultural norms
    e.  self-labeling

13.  Prostitution has been called the world's oldest profession. The text argues that prostitution cannot be eliminated
    a.  in a sexually restrictive society.
    b.  unless it is legalized.
    c.  until churches change their teachings.
    d.  without a change in the family system.
    e.  until adultery becomes a more common and accepted practice.

14.  From cross-cultural data concerning beauty, which of the following generalizations can be made?
    a.  There is a strong cross-cultural tendency for women to prefer tall muscular men.
    b.  Breasts are universally considered a sexual stimulus.
    c.  More is known about female than male beauty

because of the universal importance placed on physical appearance for females.
    d.  Within a culture, ideas of beauty remain fairly stable over time.
    e.  Cultures universally prefer muscular men as the standard for male attractiveness.

15.  Which of the following statements about rape, according to your text, is *not* a myth?
    a.  Rape is an act of sudden impulse.
    b.  Rapists rarely have alternative sexual outlets.
    c.  Rapists seek sexual satisfaction from their crime.
    d.  The dynamics present in sexual harassment exist to a more extreme degree in rape.
    e.  Women who have had a great amount of sexual contact are less affected by the crime of rape than sexually inexperienced women.

16.  Cross-cultural evidence shows that almost every society
    a.  prohibits premarital sexual activity.
    b.  has norms promoting genital, heterosexual intercourse within marriage.
    c.  values similar facial features in defining beauty.
    d.  considers prostitution illegal.
    e.  prefers virginity at time of marriage.

12.  **e.** *The self-labeling theory argues that people develop a homosexual or heterosexual self-image based on the signals they receive from others. Eventually they take one sexual definition as their social construction of reality and act in accordance with this definition. Thus any person, regardless of background and independent of biology, develops a sexual sense of self. See page 244.*

13.  **a.** *In a sexually restrictive society, such as the United States, monogamy is a strong cultural value. Prostitution is a response to these restrictions. See page 247.*

14.  **c.** *There are no universal standards for beauty, though some patterns of preference exist. Even ideas about which physical characteristics are sexually arousing are socially defined within a culture. In all cultures, however, female beauty is defined more precisely than male attractiveness, because of the*

*importance that has been placed on physical appearance in determining women's social value. See pages 225–226.*

15.  **d.** *The basic objective of rape is domination and control: the satisfaction for the attacker is not primarily sexual but is based on power over, and humiliation of, the victim. To a lesser degree, sexual harassment involves the same dynamics in that the harasser's advances are unsolicited and unwanted. See pages 238–239.*

16.  **b.** *Societal norms promote heterosexual, genital intercourse within the context of some stable, socially-approved arrangement between two or more people to ensure reproduction and survival of the society. Norms may encourage a variety of other sexual practices as well, but the biology of reproduction dictates the importance of genital intercourse. See page 225.*

17. One generalization that can be made about homosexuals is that they are
    a. discriminated against in all societies.
    b. identifiable by their appearance.
    c. unable to maintain a single sex-role identity.
    d. represented in about 2 percent of the United States population.
    e. usually in stable, long-lasting relationships.

18. Which of the following statements is true about teenage pregnancy in the United States relative to teenage pregnancy in other culturally similar countries?
    a. U.S. welfare benefits are more generous, encouraging teenage pregnancy.
    b. The United States has the lowest rate of teenage pregnancy in the Western world.
    c. The U.S. rate of teenage pregnancy was high in previous decades, but is dropping.
    d. Teenagers in the United States have less sexual freedom and are less sexually active.
    e. U.S. teenagers are less likely to use contraception than their peers in other countries.

19. Cross-cultural studies of sexuality indicate that compared to other cultures, the United States
    a. has more restrictive attitudes toward sexual behavior.
    b. is one of the few cultures where adultery is not punishable by death.

    c. has parents playing a larger role in sex education.
    d. has an earlier average age of intercourse for boys and girls.
    e. is more accepting of homosexual behavior than other cultures.

20. The textbook argues that rape is a crime of violence with origins in *approved* patterns of interaction between the sexes, such as
    a. the positive feelings men inspire in women when making sexual advances toward them.
    b. the commitment implied by sexual contact.
    c. the inability of men to control their sexual desires.
    d. the central importance of sexuality in the lives of men and women.
    e. inequality between the sexes and the tendency for men to view women as sexual property.

21. We still do not understand many aspects of human sexuality, in part, because
    a. of social inhibitions on sex research.
    b. too many studies have been done on sex, resulting in widespread confusion.
    c. female sexuality has been overemphasized.
    d. sex is an emotional subject that does not lend itself to rational consideration.
    e. sex is an individual matter and few generalizations are possible.

---

17. **e.** *The great majority of homosexuals form stable, long lasting relationships. This is especially true among lesbians. The AIDS scare has heightened the desirability of monogamous relationships. See page 243.*

18. **e.** *There is a gap between the sexual freedom that many American teenagers enjoy, and the sparse information and limited access they have to contraception. This age group is sexually active and vulnerable to unplanned pregnancies. The rate of births to unmarried teenagers is growing. See pages 233–234.*

19. **a.** *U.S. legal and normative codes concerning sex are more restrictive than those of many other societies because of the religious base of many of our sexual values. Many "primitive" cultures in the Ford and Beach*

*study allowed a greater range of sexual behavior. See pages 227, 229, 231.*

20. **e.** *The cultural norms that promote male domination of women, as well as the view of women as sex objects, encourage the attitude used to justify many forms of sexual exploitation: men are allowed to use women for their own purposes. Rape is the extreme, brutal form such notions can take. See pages 239–240.*

21. **a.** *Research on sex is difficult to conduct. The subset of people willing to discuss such topics produces a response bias. Additionally, respondents may not report their attitudes or behavior completely or accurately out of a desire to give socially acceptable answers. See page 232.*

22. Cross-cultural evidence on human sexual behavior shows
    a. the interplay between biological potentials and cultural norms learned through socialization.
    b. the influence of many inborn sexual preferences.
    c. that sexual perversion is the dominant norm in some societies.
    d. that primitive peoples have little sense of sexual morality.
    e. the overall sexual satisfaction of heterosexual couples in particular.

23. One reason for the existence of a universal incest taboo is that
    a. it is instinctive.
    b. our ancestors realized that inbreeding causes degeneration and created the taboo to prevent it.
    c. the family might otherwise disintegrate under the strain of jealousy and role confusion.
    d. people have a natural revulsion against sexual intercourse with close relatives.
    e. it brings new genetic material into the population.

24. Social and biological scientists generally agree that
    a. human sexual behavior is fairly uniform.
    b. human sexual behavior is instinctive.
    c. human sexual behavior is entirely different from that of higher primates.
    d. the human sex drive is so flexible that it is not difficult to imagine all human beings engaging in all types of sexual behavior.
    e. homosexuality is the result of chromosomal defects.

25. Compared to homosexual men, lesbians cross-culturally
    a. have higher social approval, as evidenced in sociological studies.
    b. are more often the subjects of social science research.
    c. tend to have more sexual partners.
    d. more often relate adult woman to adult woman (homophilia).
    e. are aware of their homosexuality earlier in life.

---

22. **a.** *Humans have certain inborn needs for sexual activity, and genital, heterosexual intercourse is necessary for the survival of the species. But past these few biological necessities, the immense variation in human sexual expression can only be explained by the variety of cultural norms governing sexual practices. See pages 224, 228.*

23. **c.** *The intimacy of the family requires specific norms regulating sexual contact between the members to prevent random pairings and the feelings of jealousy and confusion that would inevitably result. See page 237.*

24. **d.** *There is no biological reason why individuals cannot engage in every type of sexual expression. The fact that they don't, and that different groups show different sexual preferences, is the result of socialization. See page 224.*

25. **d.** *Cross-cultural evidence on lesbianism is fragmentary. Existing studies show few cultures that specifically approve of lesbianism; most appear to tolerate or not notice it. Lesbianism generally takes the homophilic form; relations involving pederasty or transvestism are quite rare. See page 241.*

# A CASE STUDY

NAME

COURSE/SECTION NUMBER

*Cosmopolitan* magazine is known for its provocative material and sexually suggestive magazine covers. Recently the magazine conducted a survey of its readers' sexual practices. Readers were asked to fill out a questionnaire inside the magazine and send it in—and thousands of readers responded. Helen Gurley Brown, the magazine's editor, appeared on many talk shows describing the "astounding" revolution in sexual practices evidenced in the survey results: for example, at least a third of the women had had sexual intercourse over their lunch hours; many women reported multiple sexual encounters, sometimes with twenty or more different partners within a month; readers also indicated experience with a wide variety of sexual acts.

1.   What methodological concerns would you raise in assessing the merit of this study?

2.   Do these results indicate changing sexual behavior, or could you offer alternative explanations?

3.    On the basis of these survey results, how well can we differentiate between sexual attitudes and behavior? How might you design a study to do this?

# Applying the Concepts

NAME
_____

COURSE/SECTION NUMBER

## APPLICATION EXERCISE ONE

In this exercise, you will conduct a content analysis of television commercials. There has been a great deal of controversy recently about the use of explicit sexual messages to sell products. You will look at the symbolic messages contained in these commercials and construct an argument about the meaning and significance of these messages.

1.   Select five television commercials that involve actors/actresses selling a product, at least in part, through sexual innuendo and complete the chart below. Describe each commercial and what product is being sold. Indicate whether the commercial shows a man, a woman, or a couple. Identify some of the characteristics of the actors/actresses that provide evidence for our culture's definition of beauty (for example, many commercials feature actresses with long hair, styled in a way that would be very impractical for the average American woman). Finally, comment on the sexual implications that can be inferred from the commercial.

| *Commercial* | *M/F/Couple* | *Idea of Beauty* | *Sexual Message* |
|---|---|---|---|
| *(1)* | | | |
| *(2)* | | | |
| *(3)* | | | |
| *(4)* | | | |
| *(5)* | | | |

2.    After examining your five cases, comment on any trends you see as far as the use of sex in advertising. Since most of us do not actually resemble the actors/actresses in the commercials, what messages are we likely to receive? What about people who are older, of another race, homosexual, or physically handicapped? How do commercials address these and other groups?

## APPLICATION EXERCISE TWO

NAME
_____

COURSE/SECTION NUMBER

There is a great deal of cross-cultural variation in sexual behaviors and attitudes. There are many variations within a culture as well.

1.   Select three subcultures in which you feel comfortable either as a participant or an observer. Examples might include a homosexual or heterosexual subculture, racial, ethnic, or religious groups, small-town or large-city subcultures, as well as age subcultures. Your task is to obtain information about these subcultures in an ethical way. You might interview members of the subcultures and ask about such things as sexual rules or norms and the relative importance of sexual activity in everyday life. You might also note key words (argot) each subculture uses to discuss sexual matters. Decide what characteristics you will compare, and gather whatever evidence you can.

Subculture 1

   Distinctive Features:

Subculture 2

   Distinctive Features:

Subculture 3

Distinctive Features:

2.    Describe the similarities and differences among the subcultures and try to account for these differences in sociological terms.

## APPLICATION EXERCISE THREE

Changes in sexual attitudes and behaviors in the United States are evidenced in the marriage manuals of different time periods. Go to the library and select three manuals that were written at least five years apart, or compare modern manuals that have a religious orientation to ones that do not. Or, look at the books on teenage sexuality or sex education curricula. What social changes can you document using these sources?

NAME

COURSE/SECTION  NUMBER

# UNIT 3

# Social Inequality

# CHAPTER 10

# Social Stratification

## Reviewing the Concepts

### LEARNING GOALS

*After studying this chapter, you should be able to:*

1. Define social stratification.

2. Discuss the social implications of inequality based on position within a stratum.

3. Contrast the features of a caste system and a class system.

4. Evaluate the extent to which the Soviet Union is a classless society.

5. Explain the concept of social mobility and distinguish between the two different kinds of social mobility.

6. Summarize Marx's analysis of social class.

7. Summarize Weber's analysis of social class.

8. Describe how sociologists use socioeconomic status (SES) as a measurement of social position.

9. Explain how stratification systems are maintained.

10. Discuss ideology, false consciousness, and class consciousness as they relate to Marx's view of stratification.

11. Summarize the functionalist perspective on stratification, indicating the strengths and limitations of its analysis.

12. Summarize the conflict perspective on stratification, indicating the strengths and limitations of its analysis.

13. Present Lenski's theory of the sociocultural evolution of stratification, indicating the way in which the theory combines aspects of both the conflict and functionalist perspectives.

14. Discuss social stratification in the United States; describe the gap between the value of equality and the unequal distribution of wealth.

15. Contrast C. Wright Mills's views on the concentration of power in the United States with those of David Riesman.

16. Describe the ways in which prestige is distributed in the United States.

17. Explain the three methods sociologists use to analyze the American class system.

18. Identify the social classes in the United States and the features of each.

19. Specify some of the factors that are correlated with social-class membership.

20. Explain the typical patterns of social mobility in the United States.

21. Compare the intergenerational mobility of the United States with that of other industrialized countries.

22. Explain the two ways poverty is defined and indicate which groups in the United States are most likely to experience poverty.

23. Explain why American public opinion does not support more social policies to aid the poor.

## IDENTIFYING KEY QUESTIONS AND THEMES

All societies differentiate among their members, giving certain groups of people greater access to social rewards such as wealth, prestige, and power. *Social inequality* is the term used to describe this unequal distribution of social rewards. As societies have become more and more complex, inequality among whole categories of people (as opposed to particular individuals) has appeared. Like layers of rock, the members of such societies are grouped into "strata" with others in a similar social position. This kind of inequality is actually built into the social structure and passed down from generation to generation, primar-

ily through the family. *Social stratification,* then, is the structured inequality of entire categories of people, who have different access to social rewards as a result of their status in a social hierarchy. Almost all people now live in stratified societies, although different social characteristics determine the formation of strata and the amount of movement between strata. Sociologists are interested in the features of social stratification because people's location in the social hierarchy is linked to almost every other aspect of their social lives. That is, persons within a stratum share the same *life chances,* or probabilities of benefiting or suffering from the opportunities or disadvantages their society offers.

## Stratification Systems

*How do social stratification systems differ? What are the characteristics of a caste system and a class system?*

One way to categorize the various social stratification systems is to look at the boundaries between classes. In a closed, or "caste," system, the boundaries between strata are very clearly drawn, and there is no way for people to change the status given them at birth. In an open, or "class," system, on the other hand, the boundaries between strata are more flexible, and changes in position can occur. Some societies, such as the Soviet Union, claim to be "classless."

A *caste* system is a closed system based on *ascribed statuses.* A common feature of caste societies is the fact that they insist on *endogamy,* or marriage within the same social category. Additionally, caste societies recognize *ritual pollution,* types of contact or proximity between members of different castes that "contaminate" the superior class. Today, only two rigid caste systems exist—in South Africa and in India.

An open system based primarily on economic statuses is called a *class* system. Boundaries between the classes are more blurred than those in a caste system. An individuals' status is usually based on the economic position of the family breadwinner. People may rise above, or fall below, the class of their parents; and/or they may marry someone of another class. Class membership, then, is an *achieved status,* for it depends to some extent on talents and efforts over which the individual has some control. Almost all societies now have class systems. Generally, agricultural societies have two classes: a small class of wealthy landowners and a large class of poor peasants. In industrial societies, there are usually three main classes: a small and wealthy upper class, a fairly large middle class, and a large working class. Great Britain is one example of a modern society with distinct class lines.

A *classless society* is one with no economically based strata. No modern industrial society is classless. The Soviet Union and other communist-ruled countries for which classlessness is a central goal operate at an intermediate stage of socialism: classes have been formally abolished but a small group of individuals, usually leaders of the communist party, receive more privileges than other citizens.

## Social Mobility

*How do people move from one social status to another? What are the forms of social mobility in modern societies?*

Sociologists look at stratification systems and the chances they offer people for *social mobility,* or movement from one social status to another. Such movement can be upward or downward. Sociologists are especially interested in *intergenerational mobility,* or movement up or down the social hierarchy by family members from one generation to the next.

Social mobility takes two different forms, each with its own source. *Exchange mobility* involves changes in people's social statuses as they exchange places with one another at different levels of the hierarchy. The more open the society, the greater the exchange mobility. However, this form of mobility accounts for only a small percentage of social movement in modern societies. *Structural mobility* involves changes in people's social statuses as a result of changes in the structure of the economy. Ongoing mechanization and automation continue to pull many people from low-status jobs into higher-status service-sector positions based on economic factors that may have little to do with their individual efforts and talents. In all stratified societies, even open ones, social mobility is limited. Most people remain within the social class of their parents.

## Analysis of Class

*What did Marx and Weber say about the criteria for class membership?*

It is often difficult to determine a person's status in a class society when the boundaries between strata are blurred. Two early sociologists, Karl Marx and Max Weber, advanced important theories about class membership. Marx defined a class as all those people who share a common relationship to the means of economic production. In his view there are two classes, the dominant class made up of those who own the means of production, and the subordinate class made up of those who work for them. In such a society, the relationship between the classes is one not only of inequality but also of exploitation. The dominant class seizes the profit, or *surplus wealth,* produced by the subordinate class and uses it themselves. This exploitation is the main source of class conflict.

Of course, Marx's view of class was shaped by the times in which he lived. Ongoing industrialization has meant a rapid expansion of the middle class, many of whom work for their fellow citizens rather than for capitalists. Most industry is now run by large corporations and managed by nonowners. Thus the ownership and control of the means of production are separate. Indeed, a "new class" of well-educated experts may be emerging.

Weber built on Marx's view by offering a multidimensional approach to class analysis. He broke the single concept of class into three distinct but related elements: wealth, or economic status; prestige, or social status; and power, or political status. Thus he allowed for the possibility that an individual may rank highly on one dimension of class membership, and lower on the other two. In practice, however, these three dimensions are usually closely associated because one of them can often be "converted" into either of the others. Based on Weber's work, sociologists studying class membership now use the concept *socioeconomic status (SES)*, which takes into account a complex of factors, such as years of education, income, type of occupation, and residence, to assess people's social positions.

## Maintaining Stratification

*How do stratification systems survive? What did Marx say about the control of resources and the role of ideology?*

In order for a stratification system to survive, two factors seem to be important: the ruling class must control the resources necessary to preserve the status quo, and the general society must believe that the prevailing inequality is "natural" or "right."

Marx emphasized the influence of the economic base of society over all other aspects of culture and social structure. In his view, other social institutions, such as education, religion, and government, tend to reflect the interests of those who control the economy rather than those who do not. Members of the ruling class act in their common interest to maintain their advantage. Based on greater resources of wealth, power, and prestige, their *social networks*—webs of relationships that link the individual directly to other people, and through these others, indirectly to even more people—tend to be stronger than those of other strata, allowing them far more "leverage" in society. Therefore, a stratification system survives for as long as the resources of the beneficiaries outweigh those of the disadvantaged groups. Change may come about if the lower stratum mobilizes its collective resources—usually through a social movement or, in extreme cases, through revolution. Violent class conflict is unusual, however, because the existing social inequality has become a tradition. That is, stratification systems gain *legitimacy,* the generally held belief that a given political system is valid and justified.

An *ideology* is a set of beliefs that explains and justifies an actual or potential social arrangement. Marx noted that the dominant ideology in any society is always the ideology of the ruling class, which supports its privileged position. The members of subordinate groups fail to realize the source of their oppression and attribute their position to bad luck or fate, a subjective understanding Marx called *false consciousness,* for it did not coincide with the objective facts of exploitation. Only if members of the lower stratum gain a *class consciousness,* or an objective awareness of their common plight and interests as an oppressed group, will they begin to question the legitimacy of the stratification system. According to Marx, class conflict is the inevitable outcome.

An ideology is a complex belief system, often comprising religious, political, economic, and other ideas. In modern capitalist societies, such as the United States, inequality is justified as a way of providing incentives and rewarding achievement. However, most Americans work very hard but experience very little social mobility. Individuals tend to blame their lack of mobility on their own failings rather than on a stratification system that depends on a large lower stratum that has to be filled by somebody.

## Stratification: A Functionalist View

*How do functionalists explain stratification? What are the strengths and weaknesses of this theory?*

Functionalists argue that stratification is universal and contributes to the stability and survival of society. Without justifying inequality, functionalists explain that the unequal distribution of social rewards occurs because roles demanding scarce talents or prolonged training are filled by the ablest individuals, who are then rewarded for their skills. This analysis was once popular with American sociologists, because it fit the American value of individual achievement. However, it has come to be criticized for overlooking the fact that some roles of relatively low social value receive high rewards and that, in some cases, social status is ascribed or inherited instead of being achieved in proportion to talent and effort. Actually, the functionalist view shows how inequality among individuals might be functional to matching skilled people with demanding roles, but it cannot show that stratification among categories of people helps society work more effectively. In fact, stratification may have dysfunctions, or negative social effects. Because people in lower strata are denied access to social roles, society does not benefit from their talents, and social relations are strained or disrupted.

## Stratification: A Conflict View

*How do conflict theorists explain stratification? What insights did Marx provide and which of his predictions failed to materialize?*

The conflict perspective, which derives from the ideas of Marx, argues that tension and competition are powerful factors in shaping culture and social structure. Stratification exists because the rich and powerful members of society are determined to maintain their advantage. The key to changing the balance of power is class conflict whereby the subordinate class eventually overthrows the ruling class, and thus becomes the new ruling class. Some of Marx's predictions about a capitalist industrialized economy were inaccurate. He did not anticipate the replacement of individual capitalists by corporations, the emergence of a large middle class, or the conditions under which revolutions would occur. However, he did sensitize modern theorists to the importance of conflict over scarce resources (and competition among groups for control) as well as to the role of ideology in supporting the interests of the dominant class. In so doing, Marx made a powerful case against stratification as a functional necessity, providing ample evidence that stratification is, in fact, the outcome of structured inequality and the ideology that perpetuates it.

## A Synthesis?

*How does Lenski's theory of sociocultural evolution synthesize the functionalist and conflict perspectives?*

A synthesis of the two perspectives is found in the influential theory of Gerhard Lenski, which explains why some types of societies are more stratified than others. Essentially Lenski argues that the basic resources a society needs in order to survive are allocated in the way the functionalists claim, but that surplus resources are distributed unequally, through conflict between competing groups. Inequality may sometimes be functional, but most societies become much more stratified than they need to be. Using the idea of *sociocultural evolution,* Lenski traced patterns of stratification from hunting and gathering societies to industrial societies, noting that the economic mode of industrialism at first results in a wide gap between the rich and the poor, but that it eventually brings relatively more equal distribution of wealth, power, and prestige due to its reliance on a skilled, educated, and mobile labor force.

## Social Stratification in the United States

*How are wealth, power, and prestige distributed through the class system in the United States?*

Although equality is a core value in American culture, the United States is a very unequal society. There are striking differences among social classes in terms of wealth, power, and prestige. Conflicting values, such as those emphasizing white supremacy, male superiority, and economic competition have mitigated against the value of human equality.

Wealth, the most obvious sign of stratification in the United States, contains two components—assets (property such as real estate and stock) and income (earnings such as salaries and wages). Contrary to the trend in most industrialized countries, in the United States, wealth of either kind has not become more equally distributed: the bulk of the nation's wealth is owned by a small minority of the population, primarily people with earnings from capital investments and/or positions in large corporations. The rising standard of living for all Americans since World War II has obscured the wide gap between rich and poor. Under current government policies, there will be greater income inequality in the immediate future. Despite these disparities in assets and income, however, overall living standards have been improving, as reflected in a real median income that has more than doubled and a decline in the proportion of the population living in poverty.

Power, like wealth, is distributed unequally. The progress made by voting-rights acts has been offset by the concentration of power at the upper levels of government and the corporate economy. Two basic views address the unequal distribution of power. C. Wright Mills argues that the American society is dominated by a "power elite" consisting of high officials in government and corporations (elite model). David Riesman claims that a variety of powerful interest groups struggle for advantage, and tend to counterbalance one another in the long run (pluralistic model). In either view, the ordinary voter has little or no political influence, and the United States is, in effect, run by a "governing class" of power holders who are likely to be male, white, middle-aged, Protestant, and wealthy. Tax loopholes favoring the rich have served as a striking example of the powerful serving their own interests.

Differences in prestige seem less significant in the United States than gaps in wealth and power. Although some people have a great deal of prestige and others are social outcasts, most Americans treat one another relatively equally. Compared to other societies, there are few outward signs, in the form of clothing or manners, for example, showing superiority or inferiority. The symbols of prestige that do exist have become available to an increasing number of Americans as a result of the expansion of white-collar jobs. The earnings associated with most jobs result in a comparable material lifestyle, which fosters the belief that everyone is equal.

## The American Class System

*How have sociologists studied the class system in the United States? On what basis is America divided into classes? What are some of the correlates of class membership? How much social mobility is there between classes? What factors relate to mobility?*

Sociologists use three basic methods to analyze the American class system. The first is the "reputational" method, in which the researcher asks people to describe stratifica-tion as they see it in their own community. The second is the "subjective" method, in which the researcher asks people what class they think they belong to. The third approach is the "objective" method, in which the researcher ranks people into classes based on such measures of socioeconomic status as income and occupation. Although each approach has advantages and disadvantages, all methods have given a generally similar view of the American class system. Most sociologists accept the division of the United States population into the following social classes: upper class (1 to 3 percent); upper-middle class (10 to 15 percent); lower-middle class (30 to 35 percent); working class (40 to 45 percent); and lower class (20 to 25 percent).

Although the upper class is very small, its members own more than three-quarters of the nation's wealth and are the most powerful people in the country. The upper class consists of people who have inherited wealth, and those who have recently become wealthy. Together, the upper- and lower-middle class lead the distinctive lifestyle that dominates American advertising, politics, and education. The upper-middle class consists of high-income business and professional people who are concerned with career advancement and have high aspirations for their children; the lower-middle class consists of average-income people, such as small-business operators, teachers, nurses, sales representatives, and middle-management personnel who share most of the values of the upper-middle class, but lack the educational or economic advantages that would permit them to enjoy the same lifestyle. Blue-collar workers, whose jobs typically involve manual labor, compose the upper-lower, or working, class. A higher proportion of nonwhites and less-educated people are represented in the working class. Members take great pride in being "respectable" and putting in a hard day's work. The lower class consists of the "disreputable poor." This class includes the chronically unemployed, the unskilled, the homeless, the illiterate, welfare dependents, and other impoverished people often thought to be worthless by the general society. The American class system tends to reproduce itself from generation to generation.

One of the reasons social class is so important is that it correlates closely with many other social characteristics, including political behavior, marital stability, religious affiliation, educational achievement, health, values and attitudes, child-rearing practices, and criminal behavior. This correlation suggests the enormous impact of social class on life chances.

Social mobility, or movement from one social status to another, does not occur as extensively as Americans might believe. Although most Americans enjoy higher statuses than their parents did (measured as intergenerational mobility), often the gain is small and takes place within a social class, as opposed to between social classes. Mobility to high statuses is limited by too many people seeking too few statuses. On the other hand, short-distance mobility has been enhanced by the increased demand for white-collar workers in a technical and service economy. Thus the United States appears to have relatively little exchange mobility, and a great deal of upward structural mobility. Two factors are strongly associated with upward mobility: the higher an individual's social-class background and education, the better that individual's prospects for upward mobility.

Intergenerational mobility in the United States is similar to that of other industrial societies, except that a much higher proportion of people with working-class backgrounds graduate from high school and reach professional status. Of course, not all intergenerational mobility is upward. About a quarter of American men are downwardly mobile relative to their fathers. Economic fluctuations can trigger downward mobility. For example, many workers who are laid off from their jobs either cannot find employment again or must accept lower-paying jobs.

## Poverty

*How is poverty defined? Who are the poor? What are some of the causes of poverty? What are Americans' attitudes about the poor?*

There are two ways to define poverty. *Relative deprivation* describes a situation in which people are unable to maintain the living standards considered normal in their society. *Absolute deprivation* refers to a situation in which people cannot afford minimal standards of food, clothing, shelter, and health care. The latter definition is often used by the U.S. government to establish an annual income designated the "poverty line"; people having less than this amount are considered poor.

Poverty is particularly prevalent among female-headed households, children, and minority groups. The poor are a highly diverse group including people working full-time for low wages, the recent poor, people who are poor for a short time, and an underclass comprised of the chronically poor. The problem of the homeless is one tragic indication of poverty in America.

The United States could eliminate absolute poverty through the use of subsidies; however, this approach runs up against Americans' myths about the poor. Many people still hold the belief that the poor are unwilling to work and prefer to live off others. Public assistance is kept to a minimum in order to provide incentives to work. However, only 5 percent of the poor are able-bodied men; the vast majority of the poor are children, aged people, disabled persons, or mothers of young children. Because Americans endorse the value that success is a matter of individual initiative and that people are rewarded accordingly, they tend to "blame the victim," to focus on the faults of the poor rather than on the social forces that create poverty. Ironically, Americans do not object to financial assistance to the nonpoor in the form of tax breaks, for example.

Poverty, like wealth, is a social characteristic, resulting from a complex interaction of the individual and the social environment. In a class system, based on an unequal society, there are bound to be those who are more and less fortunate. However, it is important to remember that social stratification is socially constructed, and therefore, socially modifiable.

## DEFINING CORE CONCEPTS

*After studying the chapter, write a sociological definition in your own words for the following core concepts. Then give an example from your own experience to illustrate your definition. Refer to the chapter to check your work.*

| *Core Concept* | *Sociological Definition* | *Personal Illustration* |
| --- | --- | --- |
| absolute deprivation | | |
| achieved status | | |
| ascribed status | | |
| caste | | |
| class | | |
| class consciousness | | |
| classless society | | |
| endogamy | | |

| Core Concept | Sociological Definition | Personal Illustration |
|---|---|---|
| exchange mobility | | |
| false consciousness | | |
| ideology | | |
| intergenerational mobility | | |
| life chances | | |
| relative deprivation | | |
| ritual pollution | | |
| social mobility | | |

| *Core Concept* | *Sociological Definition* | *Personal Illustration* |
|---|---|---|
| social network | | |
| social stratification | | |
| socioeconomic status (SES) | | |
| sociocultural evolution | | |
| structural mobility | | |
| surplus wealth | | |

## PUTTING IDEAS TOGETHER

Social stratification means social inequality. Stratification systems vary widely from one society to another according to how open or closed they are. Open systems of social mobility are based primarily on class distinctions, while closed systems are based on caste distinctions. In all cases, ideology legitimates the wealth, power, and prestige of the ruling class and justifies the inequality present in the society. We can classify societies' stratification systems as follows:

Type of Status of Primary Importance

| ascribed | | achieved |
| :--- | :--- | ---: |

Type of Stratification System

| caste | | class |
| :--- | :--- | ---: |

Type of Mobility System

| closed | | open |
| :--- | :--- | ---: |

Example:                       Example: none;
India                             not possible
                                   by definition

Amount of Mobility Likely for the Individual

| nonexistent or low mobility | | some mobility |
| :--- | :--- | ---: |

Example:          Example:          Example:
USSR              Great Britain     USA

The class system in the United States reflects inequalities in wealth, power, and prestige. Sociologists who have studied the American class system conclude that these three elements are somewhat separate, as Weber suggested. Wealth, or economic status, as determined by the family breadwinner's occupation is the predominant basis for assignment of social class. Power, or political status, is closely associated with wealth; wealth can be converted into power. The symbols of prestige, or social status, are somewhat more available to more Americans. A composite of these three measures of social class might look like this:

**The Bases for Social Class**

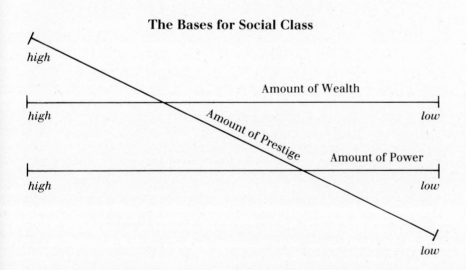

The upper class would be in the upper left-hand section of this diagram, and the poor in the lower right-hand section.

The chapter describes the three major approaches sociologists use to determine social class and the two ways in which poverty can be defined.

| *Method for Determining Class Membership* | *The Basis or Standard for the Definition* |
| --- | --- |
| *reputational method* | respondents describe stratification as they see it in their own community |
| *subjective method* | respondents place themselves in categories according to the class they think they belong to |
| *objective method* | researcher uses an index of socioeconomic status and ranks respondents accordingly |

| *Method for Determining Poverty* | *The Basis or Standard for the Definition* |
| --- | --- |
| *absolute deprivation* | minimal standards of food, clothing, shelter, and health care |
| *relative deprivation* | living standards customary in the society |

# Testing the Concepts

## MULTIPLE-CHOICE QUESTIONS

*After studying the chapter, try to answer each of the twenty-five questions below. Mark the alternative you think is correct; then look at the correct answer and the explanation provided at the bottom of the page. Try to state why the other alternatives are incorrect, and check your understanding of the correct answer.*

1. Social stratification will continue to exist in the United States as long as
   a. the ascribed position we get from our family remains important to life chances.
   b. the prejudiced attitudes of the average person change so slowly.
   c. there are inherent differences in the capabilities of the two genders.
   d. a sizable portion of our population does not take advantage of opportunities for upward mobility.
   e. the proportion of blue-collar jobs to white-collar jobs decreases.

2. A stratification system survives primarily because
   a. the system's very existence proves its worth in a given culture.
   b. it is enforced by laws backed up by the military and the police.
   c. such systems represent a natural order.
   d. there is no way to make life chances more equal than they already are.
   e. all classes or castes accept its legitimacy.

3. Which of the following social classes would you expect to have the highest incidence of most diseases?
   a. the upper class
   b. the upper-middle class
   c. the lower-middle class
   d. the working class
   e. the lower class

4. Which *pair* of features is essential to the maintenance of a caste system of social stratification?
   a. an agricultural economy; racial differences
   b. class consciousness; income differences
   c. ascribed statuses; endogamy
   d. exogamy; extended families
   e. power elite; status inconsistency

---

1. **a.** *Our initial position, or status, in society depends on the family into which we are born. We are assigned a racial status, and we work from our family's social class background. Some mobility can occur through individual efforts, but our starting points are unequal. See pages 253–254.*

2. **e.** *People at all strata must believe in the legitimacy of a stratification system if it is to survive. Those in the lower strata accept their subordinate positions as valid and justified. See pages 261–262.*

3. **e.** *The rates of most diseases are highest for the lowest social classes. Reasons include safer working conditions and better standards of nutrition in the higher classes. In addition, the higher classes can afford a better quantity and quality of health care. See page 273.*

4. **c.** *A caste system must have clearly defined boundaries separating social strata. Membership is an ascribed status designed to maintain the purity of the castes. Endogamy further assures that caste boundaries do not become blurred. No vertical mobility is possible in such a system. People must grow up, marry, have children, and die within their caste. See page 254.*

5. Which of the following statements supports a conflict perspective of social stratification?
  a. Physicians are scarce because it is in the medical profession's interests to ensure that they are.
  b. Physicians are scarce because few people will sacrifice their social life for the sake of rigorous medical training.
  c. Lawyers receive high salaries because they do the work others do not have the patience or skill to perform.
  d. Lawyers receive high salaries because they struggle through years of schooling that others do not consider worth the effort.
  e. Doctors and lawyers deserve respect and high incomes.

6. Laura, mother of two, is a single parent who lives in a middle-class neighborhood and works as a real estate agent, making $20,000 a year. Her former husband, Frank, lives in a lower-middle-class section of town and makes $20,000 a year as an assembly-line worker at Ace Motors. According to Weber, Frank and Laura have the same
  a. economic status, or wealth.
  b. family.
  c. political status, or power.
  d. community.
  e. social status, or prestige.

7. Attitude surveys on poverty in the United States show a general belief that
  a. the poor have brought on their own misery through lack of work.
  b. welfare assistance is inadequate to support life above the poverty level.
  c. unemployment is at the root of the poverty problem.
  d. a minimum family income should be provided for all United States citizens.
  e. the educational and employment opportunities of the poor are severely restricted.

8. The range of incomes among the members of the Shorewood Country Club is great, but all manage to pay their dues and maintain a similar lifestyle. On which of the dimensions of stratification identified by Weber do these members have a common position?
  a. wealth
  b. prestige
  c. power
  d. honor
  e. none—they are not equally ranked

---

5. **a.** *Conflict theorists argue that those in positions of power and privilege use various resources, such as educational credentials, to protect their position. For example, medical schools deliberately restrict the number of students they accept, turning away many qualified applicants. The resulting scarcity of physicians keeps salaries and the demand for services high and enhances the prestige of doctors as well. See pages 265–266.*

6. **a.** *Weber argues that there are three dimensions of class: wealth, power, and prestige. While Frank and Laura would have different rankings on prestige and power, they do have similar incomes, giving them a similar ranking on economic status. See page 260.*

7. **a.** *One of the major cultural values in the United States is the belief in hard work for advancement. Many people regard poverty as a sign of a person's lack of initiative and unwillingness to work. Despite evidence pointing to structural causes, Americans tend to blame the victims for their impoverished conditions. See page 278.*

8. **b.** *The members of this country club enjoy similar prestige. In the United States, the symbols of prestige are less unequally distributed than are wealth and power, chiefly because the nation has become predominantly middle class. See page 270.*

9. A middle class as we know it in the United States
   a. would be unthinkable outside an industrial society.
   b. is a necessary component of every society that hopes to survive.
   c. emerged among human societies with the accumulation of wealth and a food surplus.
   d. limits the state's power and responsibilities.
   e. shows that the gap between the very rich and the very poor has been reduced.

10. Which of the following statements is basic to Lenski's theory of stratification?
   a. The stratification system of the United States is not questioned by subordinate groups.
   b. Most societies are not as stratified as they need to be.
   c. Stratification systems offer different life chances because of the circumstances of birth and therefore do not make use of individual talent.
   d. A society's surplus resources are distributed through conflict among competing groups
   e. Societies will evolve to a classless state.

11. Feminists have been working to improve the position of women in today's society; others, such as Phyllis Schlafly, suggest that women "have it good."

How would Marx describe the collective thinking of the latter group?
   a. relative deprivation
   b. false consciousness
   c. oppression of lower classes
   d. provocation conflict
   e. dominant ideology

12. The text presented several ways in which social class can be measured. Which sociological tool for studying social-class structure is likely to be more useful in small communities?
   a. the reputational method
   b. the objective method
   c. the selective method
   d. the subjective method
   e. the experimental method

13. The Soviet stratification system is distinctly different from that of the United States in that there is
   a. a lack of economic differences among the citizenry.
   b. no "leisure class" supported by accumulated wealth.
   c. no allotment of special privileges for government officials.
   d. more wealth accumulated by inheritance than by capital investment.
   e. more exchange mobility.

---

9. **a.** *With industrialization, a greater variety of occupations becomes possible and the amount of wealth is more evenly distributed. The basic division between land owners and laborers is broken down. A middle class of artisans, busiensspersons, and other nonlanded workers emerges and expands with continued industrialization. See page 266.*

10. **d.** *Lenski's theory combines elements of functionalist and conflict theory. He believes that the basic resources a society needs for survival are allocated the way the functionalists claim, but that surplus resources are distributed the way the conflict theorists claim—through struggle among different groups. See page 266.*

11. **b.** *Marx used the term "false consciousness" to describe a subjective understanding that does not*

*correspond to the objective facts. Thus, members of an oppressed group are not aware of their oppression or attribute it to factors beyond their control. See pages 262–263.*

12. **a.** *The reputational method asks people to describe stratification as they see it in their own community. Such a method presumes some knowledge of others in the community, and therefore its use is best suited to a small town or neighborhood. See page 271.*

13. **b.** *Soviet law does not allow the accumulation of wealth or the presence of a leisure class or aristocracy. Strict inheritance laws restrict the wealth passed on to succeeding generations. Citizens are required to work and contribute to the society, rather than live off the wealth of their ancestors. See page 257.*

14. Which of the following is a *disadvantage* of the objective method of analyzing a class system?
    a. It ignores people's beliefs about their status and relies on the judgment of the researcher.
    b. It can produce distorted results, because people may have a mistaken idea about their own status.
    c. It asks only about income as a measure of social class.
    d. It is only useful in small communities where people know one another.
    e. The results are more likely to be influenced by the wording of the questions.

15. Which of the examples below would be better explained and classified by Weber's categories of social stratification than by Marx's categories?
    a. Two friends go through school together and now work in breweries, but at competing firms.
    b. An Asian refugee comes to the United States with hopes of a better life and cannot find work.
    c. Migrant workers pick lettuce at subsistence wages while the farm owners increase their profits.
    d. The son of a bank president completes his higher education and goes to work for the bank management.

    e. *Time* magazine carries a story of a janitor who writes country music hits on the side and continues to do janitorial work.

16. If a society were described as having low intergenerational mobility, we would guess that the society also
    a. values ascribed status more than achieved status.
    b. is highly industrialized.
    c. has a rapidly expanding economy.
    d. has a great deal of downward mobility.
    e. has a large number of available roles.

17. If a presidential order gave all U.S. citizens at least a standard middle-class income and severely taxed those whose salaries were above this amount, functionalist theorists argue that this policy would be dysfunctional for society, because
    a. there would be no social classes.
    b. ascribed statuses are not taken into account.
    c. vertical mobility is harmful to society.
    d. there would be no monetary motivation to take on different roles.
    e. class conflict would result.

18. The term "life chances" refers to
    a. life expectancy.
    b. social respectability.

---

14. **a.** *A researcher using the objective method establishes class criteria; people are ranked into classes according to such measures of socioeconomic status as occupation and income. The translation of the respondent's score into a class grouping is, therefore, a matter of the judgment of the researcher. See page 271.*

15. **e.** *Marx defined class in terms of economics. Weber acknowledged the importance of economics, but added the dimensions of power and prestige as bases for social rankings. In this case, a person of low power and prestige has a high income, a situation Marxian analysis did not explain. See page 260.*

16. **a.** *When no persons experience upward or downward mobility, it is likely that there are structural obstacles to mobility. Such societies usually have ascribed statuses based on a closed, or caste, system of stratification. See pages 254, 257.*

17. **d.** *If incomes were equalized, the monetary incentive to undergo extensive training and to commit oneself to high-powered, stressful, dangerous, unpleasant, or extremely important jobs would be reduced. Functionalists argue that a stratification system that offers higher rewards for such pursuits is functional for society as a whole because the ablest individuals are motivated to take on the most demanding roles. See page 264.*

18. **e.** *In a stratified society that has an unequal distribution of social rewards, an individual's likelihood of benefiting or suffering from the opportunities or disadvantages of that society differs by social class. The life chances of the wealthy are better than those of the poor. See pages 254, 273.*

c. the infant mortality rates for different racial and ethnic groups.

d. traffic accident rates in different areas of the country.

e. the probability of having access to the benefits society offers.

19. Ronald Reagan's first appointments to his cabinet were, with one exception, white, upper-class, middle-aged men. Seven of the cabinet members were highly educated. Most had business backgrounds rather than government experience. This cabinet was evidence for

    a. a pluralistic theory of government.

    b. the mobility that is possible through education.

    c. sex differences in administrative talent.

    d. the power of the presidency.

    e. an elite theory of government.

20. Weber's three criteria of class membership have been translated into a measure of social position sociologists call

    a. surplus wealth.

    b. occupational prestige rankings.

    c. socioeconomic status.

    d. control of the means of production.

    e. the Protestant ethic.

21. After receiving her high school diploma twenty years ago, Janice went to work at a toy factory where she's been employed ever since. When the factory began laying off workers, Janice's daughter, Pam, knew she would have to look for work different from her mother's. After Pam graduated from high school, she took a position as a word processor in a law firm. This example involves _____ mobility.

    a. selective

    b. exchange

    c. familial

    d. matrilocal

    e. structural

22. Structural mobility is likely to be greatest in

    a. agricultural societies.

    b. preindustrial societies.

    c. modern industrial societies.

    d. feudal societies.

    e. hunting and gathering societies.

23. The son of a peanut farmer becoming president of the United States would be an example of

    a. economic mobility.

    b. intergenerational mobility.

    c. structural mobility.

    d. horizontal mobility.

    e. class mobility.

---

19. **e.** *C. Wright Mills argued that American society is dominated by a power elite consisting of people with overlapping bases of power in government, the corporate world, the military, and the upper social classes. The cabinet appointees are not a random group, but one composed of individuals with the kind of power described in Mills's elite model. See page 269.*

20. **c.** *Socioeconomic status, or SES, is a measure used by social scientists based on Weber's dimensions of wealth, power, and prestige—factors that are highly correlated with one another. See page 261.*

21. **e.** *The change in the structure of the economy (increased automation, growth of service industries) translates as social mobility for Janice. She is employed in a higher-status, white-collar job, although her education and career aspirations are the same as her mother's. See page 258.*

22. **c.** *Structural mobility is produced through changes in the structure of a society's economy. In the past 100 years or so, the mechanization of agriculture and the automation of industry have eliminated many low-status blue-collar jobs; at the same time, service industries and government and corporate bureaucracies have grown, creating many new, higher-status white-collar jobs that must be filled. Under such structural conditions, social mobility is guaranteed for a large part of the population. See page 258.*

23. **b.** *Social mobility that occurs across a generation, from parent to child, is called intergenerational mobility. It can be upward or downward. See page 257.*

24. If a sociologist defined poverty in terms of an inability to maintain the living standards customary in the society, he or she would be using the concept of
    a. cultural deprivation.
    b. absolute deprivation.
    c. life chances.
    d. relative deprivation.
    e. an "under class."

25. The social networks of the upper classes differ from those of the lower classes in that the upper classes use them as a means to
    a. socialize with friends.
    b. meet new people.
    c. give service to their community.
    d. build "cultural" capital.
    e. secure employment.

---

24. **d.** *Relative deprivation is a situation in which people may be able to afford basic necessities but are unable to maintain the standard of living considered normal in their society. Relative to other people, they are poor and disadvantaged. See page 276.*

25. **d.** *Because the social networks of high-status individuals link them to others with similar resources of power, wealth, and prestige, they have far more "leverage" in society. In effect, they build "cultural" capital — access to the best education, highest-paying jobs, etc. — thereby reinforcing their privileged position. See page 261.*

## A CASE STUDY

NAME

COURSE/SECTION NUMBER

In 1980, the Anaconda Copper Mine in Anaconda, Montana was closed. Corporate officials justified this action saying that the cost to comply with pollution standards was prohibitively high, leaving them with no choice but to close the mine. As its name implies, Anaconda is a company town, with 70 percent or more of the town formerly directly or indirectly employed in the mine. The pit workers and smelters tried to get help from management and union officials, but many of these people were stockholders in the corporation or served on the board of directors that made the decision to close. Even the congressman's brother was an official with the mine, and refused to use his influence to keep the mine open. While the company writes off the mine closing as a tax loss, the workers, having no other employment opportunities in the area, line up for unemployment and welfare benefits. In all likelihood, most of the town will be out of work for some time. Housing prices dropped with the announcement of the mine's closing. Thus many of the residents cannot afford to move to other locations where jobs might be available.

1.   What kind of mobility are the mine workers experiencing?

2.   Assuming they have some unemployment benefits and savings, would they be considered poor? Try to determine the social class of the average miner before and after the mine's closing.

3.   If you were a sociologist projecting the future "health" of this community, what kinds of problems would you expect area residents to have as a result of their new social standing?

4.   How is power distributed in this community? Would Mills's model or Riesman's be the more applicable here?

5.   Pick either a functionalist or a conflict perspective and analyze this situation accordingly.

# Applying the Concepts

NAME

_____

COURSE/SECTION  NUMBER

## APPLICATION EXERCISE ONE

One of the basic arguments of conflict theorists is that the ideology, or the way of thinking of the dominant class, justifies its own superior position. If all the members of society, rich and poor, believe that the characteristics that are most valued and preferred are the ones the rich possess, then this system of stratification gains legitimacy.

1.  Some of the key values in American culture are presented in Chapter 3 of the textbook. These values, based on the work of sociologist Robin Williams, are listed in the chart below. Following the examples used with the first two values, identify the norms that are based on the remaining values and indicate how the class system of the United States is supported and maintained by these norms and values.

| A Basic American Value | A Norm Based on This Value | An Illustration of How These Norms and Values Benefit the Dominant Class |
| --- | --- | --- |
| Achievement and success | Competition for wealth, power, and prestige | Creation of capital; the rich get richer. |
| Work ethic | Hard work | Work by the lower classes creates profits for the upper classes. |
| Fulfillment of the individual | | |
| Efficiency and practicality | | |
| Progress | | |
| Material comfort | | |

| A Basic American Value | A Norm Based on This Value | An Illustration of How These Norms and Values Benefit the Dominant Class |
|---|---|---|
| Equality for all | | |
| Freedom for all | | |
| Democracy | | |
| Science and rationality | | |
| Nationalism-patriotism | | |

2.   How would conflict theorists explain the endorsement of these values and norms by people in the lower classes who may be hurt by this ideology?

## APPLICATION EXERCISE TWO

Social class has been studied by functionalist and conflict theorists since sociology began. Social class can also be studied from a symbolic interactionist perspective. In this exercise, you will examine the social classes in your community.

1. In the next day or so, observe your surroundings with an eye trained on social-class differences. Then give an example of a behavior or lifestyle preference for each of the categories below as they differ from social class to social class.

NAME
_____

COURSE/SECTION NUMBER

| Preferences in: | Upper Class | Middle Class | Lower Class |
|---|---|---|---|
| Sports activities | | | |
| Table manners or manners in public places | | | |
| Cultural activities | | | |
| Choice of cars | | | |
| Family size | | | |
| Choice of pets | | | |

2.    Try to think of an activity in which you have been involved or in which you could take part in the near future where most of the people are of a social class different from your own. For example, a working-class person might venture into an exclusive clothing store. A middle-class person might visit the welfare office on the first day of the month. Or you might consult the list of activities in the preceding section and enter into a situation different from those in which you usually interact. Do you feel uncomfortable when mingling with people of different social classes? What problems in symbolic interaction occur?

3.    Think of a movie, old or new, that you have seen in which social class is an important part of the plot. For example, there are many old movies about forbidden love between a person from the upper class and one from a lower social class. Briefly summarize the social-class differences shown in the film and comment on the role that popular culture, for example, film, plays in maintaining class divisions.

## APPLICATION EXERCISE THREE

NAME
_____

COURSE/SECTION NUMBER

1.   How should poverty be defined, in relative or absolute terms? Why?

2.   Many social policies have been proposed to deal with poverty. Based on your reading of this chapter, evaluate each of these in terms of their likelihood of success.

   a. A guaranteed annual income for every family that would keep all citizens at least at the poverty line.

   b. More federal jobs to reduce unemployment.

c. Elimination of welfare and reliance on the free-market economy; jobs would have to come from the private sector.

d. An extremely progressive income tax; each household would be taxed on its total income with no deductions.

e. A flat 10 percent tax on all income for all groups, no deductions.

f. Other proposals you have heard on the subject.

# CHAPTER 11

# Inequalities of Race and Ethnicity

## Reviewing the Concepts

### LEARNING GOALS

*After studying this chapter, you should be able to:*

1. Give a social definition of race, ethnicity, and ethnic group.

2. List the important features of a minority group.

3. Explain assimilation and pluralism as two patterns of race and ethnic relations.

4. Give examples of the following patterns of race and ethnic relations: legal protection of minorities, population transfer, continued subjugation, and extermination.

5. Explain why there is no well-developed functionalist theory of race and ethnic relations and why functionalists focus on the dysfunctions of racial and ethnic inequalities.

6. State the conditions necessary for the development of racial and ethnic inequalities according to conflict theorists.

7. Explain why racism persists (use the concepts "ideology," "colonialism," "self-fulfilling prophecy," and "false consciousness").

8. Distinguish between prejudice and discrimination, using examples based on Merton's typology.

9. Summarize social-science research on stereotypes, authoritarian personality, irrationality, scapegoating, and social environment as sources of prejudice.

10. Contrast legal and institutionalized discrimination; review the ways each form of discrimination might be eliminated.

11. Trace the social position of black Americans from slavery to the present.

12. Indicate the variations among Hispanic-American groups and their social positions in the United States today.

13. Outline the social position of the American Indians in the United States from the arrival of white immigrants to the present.

14. Describe the immigration experience of Asian groups to the United States and their current social position.

15. Discuss the importance of white ethnic heritage and the part it plays in American society today.

16. Assess affirmative action as a means to redress patterns of racial and ethnic discrimination.

17. Characterize U.S. immigration policy and its consequences for the American population.

18. Identify possible future patterns of race and ethnic relations in America.

## IDENTIFYING KEY QUESTIONS AND THEMES

All societies differentiate among their members. Often distinctions are made with regard to people who share similar physical characteristics, socially defined as a "race," and those who share similar cultural traits, socially defined as an "ethnic group." The extraordinary physical and cultural diversity of our species has been a source of conflict and inequality throughout history.

### Race and Ethnicity as Social Facts

*What do sociologists mean by race and ethnicity? What is the social significance of race and ethnic groupings?*

As a result of adaptations to various environmental conditions, the human species shows a remarkable degree of racial diversity. As far as we know, these evolutionary differences affect only physical characteristics (and not psychological characteristics such as intelligence or artistic ability).

For years, anthropologists used three major categories—Caucasoids, Mongoloids, and Negroids—in an effort to divide the human species into races on the basis of physical features. Most social scientists today acknowledge the futility of such attempts at classification (for one thing, different populations have been interbreeding for thousands of years), and consider the term "race" to have no scientific meaning at all.

The sociological interest in race derives from its significance as a social fact—people attach meanings to physical differences, real or imagined, between human groups. Thus individuals are grouped with others sharing certain physical characteristics, receive different treatment because of these characteristics, and come to regard themselves as "different." From a sociological viewpoint, then, *race* is a category of people who are regarded as socially distinct because they share genetically transmitted physical characteristics. Application of the ***Thomas theorem***—"If people define situations as real, they are real in their consequences"—to race relations teaches us that it matters little whether social beliefs about race have any biological basis; if people believe in racial differences, it is their beliefs, not the objective facts, that will influence race relations.

Whereas race refers to physical features, ethnicity describes cultural features that may be handed down from generation to generation. These features include language, religion, national origin, rituals, habits, or any other distinctive cultural trait. An ***ethnic group***, then, is a category of people who, as a result of their shared cultural heritage, come to be seen as socially distinct. Sociologists recognize that ethnic differences are learned rather than inherited.

### Minority Groups

*What are the characteristics of minority groups?*

Migration, missionary work, colonization, and other processes associated with industrialization have made modern societies large and heterogeneous. Today most societies contain ***minority groups***—peoples whose physical appearance or cultural practices are unlike those of the dominant group, making them susceptible to different and unequal treatment. A minority group has many distinguishing features. (1) The members of a minority group suffer various disadvantages at the hands of another group. (2) A minority group is identifiable by visible social characteristics. (3) The members of a minority group have a strong sense of "oneness," "a consciousness of kind" with others in their group. (4) Membership in a minority group is not voluntarily; it is an ascribed status. (5) By choice or necessity, members of a minority group generally marry within the group. Although it is the exception rather than the rule, a "minority" can be a numerical majority (in South Africa, the white population dominates the much larger black population). Thus, the term "minority group" refers to a social relationship, rather than to a numerical relationship, with the dominant group.

### Patterns of Race and Ethnic Relations

*What are the possible patterns of interaction between minority groups and dominant groups?*

The inequality between dominant groups and minority groups within a society may appear in one of six basic patterns of interaction. (1) In some cases, minority-majority differences are eliminated because minorities are assimilated, or absorbed, into the dominant culture, taking on new cultural and/or physical traits over time. (2) Some societies show a pattern of pluralism in which minorities maintain their distinctive cultural and physical traits and coexist with the dominant group. (3) Minorities are protected by law in some societies. (4) In situations of intense hostility between groups, population transfers remove the minority groups to other locations on a forced or voluntary basis. (5) In some cases, the dominant group fully intends to maintain its advantage, and openly exercises its privileged position at the expense of the minority groups. Historically, continued subjugation is a common policy. (6) The most extreme form majority-minority relations may take is *genocide*—the extermination of entire populations.

All six patterns of race and ethnic relations have been in evidence at different points in the history of North America.

## Intergroup Relations: A Functionalist View

*How do functionalists approach racial and ethnic inequalities? What are the dysfunctions of racial and ethnic inequalities for society?*

While functional theorists generally explain persistent social features in terms of their positive effects on society, in the case of racial and ethnic inequalities, they have concentrated on the dysfunctions that such antagonisms have on society. Merton points out that a social feature can be functional for one group but dysfunctional for others. However, as the example of slavery in the United States reveals, in the long run, racial and ethnic inequality is harmful to all of society. Functionalists also point out that some measure of *ethnocentrism,* and the feelings of group solidarity it engenders, are almost unavoidable and can be functional for the group's survival. But in the extreme, these same attitudes lay the groundwork for the exploitation and oppression of other groups.

## Intergroup Relations: A Conflict View

*How do conflict theorists explain racial and ethnic inequalities? How and why do these inequalities develop?*

The conflict viewpoint is helpful in identifying why racial and ethnic inequalities develop. According to conflict theorists, the following three conditions must be met: (1)

there must be two or more identifiable racial or ethnic groups; (2) there must be competition between the groups for valued resources; and (3) the groups must be unequal in power, enabling one of them to secure scarce resources at the expense of the other(s). The more the groups compete, the more negatively they view one another.

The dominant group develops a set of beliefs about the supposed inferiority of the minority group(s) and, thereby, justifies its own supremacy. Thus conflict theorists emphasize competition for valuable resources, not the racial and ethnic differences themselves, as the basis for racial and ethnic stratification. Only when minority groups gain greater equality with the dominant group is the conflict among groups reduced. Evidence shows that racial intolerance is most acute among lower-status members of the dominant group who want to preserve their relative advantage over the minorities.

## Racism

*What is racism? What is the significance of an ideology of racism? What are the causes of racism?*

A dominant group always tries to legitimate its interests by means of an *ideology,* a set of beliefs that explains and justifies some actual or potential social arrangement. One such ideology is *racism,* the belief that one racial or ethnic group is inferior to another and that unequal treatment is therefore justified. Many racist ideologies center on making economic inequalities seem "right" or "natural." *Colonialism* is the formal political and economic domination of one nation by a more powerful one. European colonialism, which lasted from the fifteenth century to the mid-twentieth century, is a prime example of the exploitation of raw materials and indigenous labor, seizure of land, and imposition of a system of rigid stratification used to secure economic interests. This era of colonial expansion was marked by an intense racism among European peoples, for they needed a way to justify their subjugation of others. Although open and systematic racism of the kind that led to the wholesale enslavement of blacks, or the extermination of Jews in Nazi Germany, is rare today, racism in other forms is commonplace.

The ideology of racism justifies existing inequalities, and reinforces them through the *self-fulfilling prophecy*—a prediction that leads to behavior that makes the prediction come true. For example, the dominant group denies the minority group opportunities to achieve high-status positions because of its alleged inferiority, and thereby forces the minority group into taking low-status positions. It then points to the minority group's lack of achievement as proof of inferiority. Minorities often accept the ideology that justifies their oppression, a state that Marx called *false consciousness.* When this occurs, minorities' subjective understanding of their situation derives from the dominant group's ideology rather than from the objective facts of their oppression. Once the members of a subordinate group develop an objective awareness of their common plight as an oppressed group, they begin to challenge the legitimacy of the system and social conflict is the inevitable outcome.

## Prejudice and Discrimination

*What are prejudice and discrimination? What are the sources of prejudice? What forms can discrimination take?*

Prejudice and discrimination, found in any situation of inequality between racial and ethnic groups, refer to two related, though different, phenomena. *Prejudice* is an irrational, inflexible attitude, usually negative, toward an entire category of people. It is always rooted in generalizations and thus ignores differences among individuals. *Discrimination* is unequal treatment of people, usually negative, on the basis of their group membership. La-Piere's study with a Chinese couple illustrated the practical difference between the two concepts. As Merton indicates, there are actually four possible combinations that people can approximate: unprejudiced nondiscriminators; unprejudiced discriminators; prejudiced nondiscriminators; and prejudiced discriminators. Merton's typology is useful in explaining discrepancies between people's beliefs and their actions.

Prejudiced thought always involves the use of a *stereotype*—a rigid mental image that summarizes whatever is believed to be typical about a group. These stereotypes result in a view of the world that is not checked against reality. In most cases, a prejudiced person fits his or her observations of a particular group's behavior into the stereotype, thus reaffirming the original stereotype. Although some measure of stereotyped thinking is almost unavoidable, certain persons are more likely to exhibit prejudice and rely on stereotypes than others. Adorno found that some people have a distinctive set of traits that together form an *authoritarian personality.* Those exhibiting this psychological makeup tend to be intolerant, insecure, highly conformist, submissive to superiors, and domineering to inferiors. Another consistent feature of prejudiced thought is irrationality. Adorno found that prejudiced people often believe mutually contradictory statements about groups they dislike. Other studies show that prejudiced people may be hostile toward groups of which they have no knowledge—even toward purely fictitious groups. *Scapegoating*—placing the blame for one's problems on a relatively powerless individual or group—is another factor that can contribute to prejudice. Scapegoating typically occurs when members of one group feel threatened but cannot attack the real source of the threat; instead, they vent their frustrations on some weak and despised group, thereby enhancing their sense of superiority over another. Prejudice is not only a matter of individual personality traits. Certain social environments may tend to foster or discourage prejudice. In general, if groups interact regularly in an equalitarian and cooperative manner, there is likely to be little prejudice among their members. Conversely, under conditions of inequality, competition, and minimal contact between groups, prejudice can flourish.

Discrimination occurs when the dominant group feels that it is entitled to social advantages and uses its power to get them at the expense of minority groups. Discrimination takes two basic forms. Unequal treatment, on the grounds of group membership, that is upheld by law is called *legal discrimination.* The second form of discrimination is *institutionalized discrimination*—unequal treatment, on the grounds of group membership, that is entrenched in social customs. Because institutionalized discrimination is more indirect and subtle, it is very difficult to change. Even when laws are amended and discrimination is outlawed, social customs based on unequal treatment persist, resulting in such patterns as segregated housing and the concentration of minority groups in low-status jobs.

## Race and Ethnic Relations in the United States

*What minority groups are present in the United States? What have been the patterns of majority-minority relations for each group?*

An important value in American society is equal opportunity for all citizens, yet there are many social inequalities in our society based on racial and ethnic differences. Although the United States prides itself on being a "melting pot" for the diverse peoples that have made their homes here, inequalities of power, wealth, and prestige tend to follow racial and ethnic lines. The first settlers were white Anglo-Saxon Protestants; to a considerable extent, their descendants have maintained political and economic control of the American society, setting the standards for the entire nation. The degree to which other groups have successfully incorporated themselves here depends on two factors. The first is their similarity to the dominant "WASP" group: the greater the racial and ethnic dissimilarities to the dominant group, the greater the social inequalities that persist. The second factor shaping the destinies of the various minorities is the unique historical circumstances surrounding each group's arrival in the United States and its entry into particular labor markets. The influence of both sets of factors can be traced by looking at the experiences of the main minority groups in America.

Black Americans are the largest minority within this country and represent almost 13 percent of the population. The history of black slavery shapes black-white relations to this day. Even after the emancipation of slaves in 1863, white dominance was assured by depriving blacks of the vote, the use of terror tactics such as lynchings, and segregation. Legal reforms (such as the landmark decision in 1954 banning school segregation) and social change brought about by the emergence of a powerful civil rights movement finally resulted in some improvement in status for black Americans. The racial turmoil of the 1960s led to an important change in black goals and black self-image. The emphasis was no longer on assimilation, but on "black power" in a plural society that recognized the validity of black culture. Important gains since the changes of the 1960s include a rapid narrowing of the gap between blacks' and whites' average years of school-

ing, an increase in the number of blacks holding elective office, and a greater concentration of blacks in middle-class jobs. However, in many other respects, blacks have made little or no progress. Institutionalized discrimination still persists throughout the United States. Blacks remain underrepresented at the higher levels of the political system. The economic position of blacks has actually worsened relative to that of whites. One-third of all black Americans live below the poverty line. Social problems such as illegitimate births, teenage pregnancies, single-parent households, welfare dependency, drug abuse, unemployment, and crime are disproportionately acute for the black population. Despite the success of many blacks, the great majority remain trapped in an "underclass" at the bottom of the stratification system. In trying to understand why this might be so, some social scientists look to historical factors that have resulted in the intertwining of race and class in the United States. As Thomas Sowell points out, the tradition of slavery, and then marginal farm employment, did not prepare blacks for entry into an industrial labor market. Moreover, unlike other immigrants to industrialized areas, blacks arrived at a time when the manufacturing base of cities was disappearing. Informal barriers such as racial prejudice and lack of skills kept most of the new arrivals mired in the ghettos. W. J. Wilson argues that the black underclass is now a subculture with a life all its own that tends to reproduce itself in subsequent generations. How to penetrate this underclass and create real opportunities, especially for unskilled workers, is an unresolved problem.

The Hispanic population of the United States, composed of several different groups, numbers around 15 million persons and may soon surpass the black population as the largest minority. Chicanos or Mexican-Americans, Puerto Ricans, and Cubans, the three largest groups, along with those from Central and South America, share a common language (Spanish), religion (Catholicism), and a tradition of relative economic deprivation. Yet there is considerable diversity among the groups as well. The Chicano population is heavily concentrated in the southwestern United States and includes increasing numbers of migrant workers and illegal aliens who are among the poorest minorities in this country. Although Chicanos have traditionally worked as farm laborers, mechanization of agriculture has pushed many into the cities in search of other employment, where some 80 percent live in ghettos, or barrios. Chicanos have resisted attempts to "anglicize" their children, insisting on bilingual education. Unlike other minorities, Chicanos are able to maintain close ties with their country of origin and keep their ethnic identity and language intact. The Puerto Ricans are a people of mixed Spanish, African, and Indian descent, many of whom now live in New York City, primarily in ghetto areas. They are one of the most impoverished groups in the nation, which may explain the fact that, unlike any other minority group, more return home each year than come to the United States. The Cuban population is concentrated in Miami and consists of many middle-class, well-educated people who fled the Castro regime. Cubans have been considerably more successful economically than other Hispanic groups. However, a second wave of Cuban immigration in 1980 has posed a significant problem for the United States since most of the immigrants were unskilled, and several thousand were criminal or mentally disordered.

Few groups in the United States have suffered crueler treatment than the original inhabitants of the country, the American Indians. Their fate at the hands of the white man included population transfers to reservations and outright genocide. The 1.4 million Indians in the United States today respresent 500 highly diverse tribal groups. Conditions of unemployment, poverty, and alcoholism characterize life in the depressed urban areas, where a third reside, and on the reservations, where the remainder live. Indians have mobilized forces in recent years and are demanding the return of illegally seized lands as well as respect for their culture, including the right to self-determination on their reservations.

With notable exceptions, Asian-Americans are the only minority group that has approached any real degree of equality with whites. They represent some 2 percent of the population, the largest groups being the Chinese, Filipinos, and Japanese. While the Chinese remain relatively isolated from the American mainstream, retaining their language and other cultural traditions, the Japanese are relatively well assimilated into American society and have attained high educational and economic standards. There are now about 1 million Filipino-Americans, soon to be the largest Asian ethnic group. Recent immigrants from Indo-china still have relatively low social and economic status. In general, however, Asian-Americans have been highly successful, much more so than other minorities, largely because of their educational achievements. The tight-knit Asian family fosters the high value placed on education.

The various groups of "white ethnics," among them the Irish, the French, the Italians, and the Poles, encountered considerable discrimination upon immigrating to the United States and made great efforts to adopt the values and customs of the dominant WASP society. Many white ethnics have been absorbed into the middle and upper classes of American society. Working-class ethnics tend to remain close to traditional ways and to identify their cultural heritage as a point of strength and pride. In recent years, white ethnics of all classes have demonstrated a renewed interest in their unique backgrounds, which has contributed to the growing pattern of pluralism in the United States.

## Affirmative Action

*What is affirmative action? How successful are affirmative-action programs?*

In an attempt to eradicate patterns of discrimination that have become structured into social and economic life, federal and local governments have turned, in part, to affirmative-action programs designed to ensure that racial minorities (and women) are not discriminated against in terms of access to higher education, employment, or promotion. The programs set goals and timetables for the hiring of minorities in government agencies and other large organizations that receive government contracts or funds. While very few of these goals are completely attained, affirmative-action programs have been very successful at expanding minority-group opportunities. Not surprisingly, they often come under fire: what is "affirmative action" to one group is "reverse discrimination" to another.

## The New Immigration

*What are the consequences of immigration policies for racial and ethnic relations? Who are the current immigrants to the United States?*

The pattern of immigration to the United States and the

laws regulating such entry have changed markedly over the past hundred years, with important consequences for racial and ethnic relations. Immigration into this country was largely unregulated until the exclusion of the Chinese in 1882. After a period that saw restrictions in the form of a quota system, which gave preference to Europeans, immigration laws were changed to admit those who have close relatives who are U.S. citizens, those with exceptional skills, and those who are political refugees. About 400,000 legal immigrants arrive in the United States each year, accounting for about two-thirds of all immigration in the world. An additional 3.5 to 6 million people are illegal immigrants to the United States. Asians and Hispanics now account for more than 80 percent of all immigration to this country. Both groups are growing in size and power, with some backlash from American-born citizens, whose ancestors probably were immigrants themselves.

## The Future

*How are American intergroup relations changing? Will inequalities based on race and ethnicity increase or decline?*

In general, American intergroup relations are improving, but we are far from the cultural ideal of equality. Three main options appear possible for the future pattern of race and ethnic relations: (1) Anglo-conformity, whereby minorities are expected to conform to the dominant white culture; (2) melting pot, involving a new blend of all racial and ethnic groups; and (3) cultural pluralism, whereby coexisting groups preserve their own traditions and culture, at the same time exhibiting loyalty to broader national unity. At this point, cultural pluralism seems to be the most likely future for American race and ethnic relations.

## DEFINING CORE CONCEPTS

*After studying the chapter, write a sociological definition in your own words for the following core concepts. Then give an example from your own experience to illustrate your definition. Refer to the chapter to check your work.*

| *Core Concept* | *Sociological Definition* | *Personal Illustration* |
|---|---|---|
| authoritarian personality | | |
| colonialism | | |
| discrimination | | |

| *Core Concept* | *Sociological Definition* | *Personal Illustration* |
| --- | --- | --- |
| ethnic group | | |
| ethnocentrism | | |
| false consciousness | | |
| genocide | | |
| ideology | | |
| institutionalized discrimination | | |
| legal discrimination | | |
| minority group | | |

| Core Concept | Sociological Definition | Personal Illustration |
|---|---|---|
| prejudice | | |
| race | | |
| racism | | |
| scapegoating | | |
| self-fulfilling prophecy | | |
| stereotype | | |
| Thomas theorem | | |

## PUTTING IDEAS TOGETHER

Even in a country such as the United States, formally committed to equality, there are striking inequalities based on race and ethnicity. The chapter distinguishes between prejudice and discrimination. Prejudice refers to irrational, inflexible attitudes toward a category of individuals, whereas discrimination refers to unequal treatment of people on the grounds of their group membership. Consider these differences between prejudice and discrimination and what can be done to reduce their incidence.

| Response to Minority Group | By Whom? | Example | Necessary for Change |
|---|---|---|---|
| PREJUDICE, or attitudes about minorities (*authoritarian personality*) | Individual | Person thinks all members of group X are lazy | Sufficient evidence contradictory to that person's stereotypes to result in attitude change. |
| DISCRIMINATION, or unequal treatment of minorities | Individual | Person refuses to rent an apartment to minority | Penalties for the behavior, by formal or informal sanctions |
| *Legal* discrimination | Society | Minority group not allowed to vote | Changes in law or enforcement to give voting rights. |
| *Institutionalized* discrimination | Society | Minority group members systematically overlooked for job and other opportunities | Policies such as affirmative action and busing to change patterns of majority-minority relations. |

The various minority groups in the United States have received different treatment at the hands of the dominant white majority. The text outlines six patterns of race and ethnic relations.

## Patterns of Race and Ethnic Relations

| | *Primary Patterns Associated with U.S. Minority Groups* | Blacks | Hispanic-Americans | American Indians | Asian-Americans | White Ethnics |
|---|---|---|---|---|---|---|
| *least severe* | Assimilation | | | | X | X |
| | Pluralism | X | X | X | X | X |
| | Legal Protection | X | | X | | |
| | Population Transfer | | X | X | | |
| | Continued Subjugation | X | X | X | | |
| *most severe* | Extermination | | | X | | |

# Testing the Concepts

## MULTIPLE-CHOICE QUESTIONS

*After studying the chapter, try to answer each of the twenty-five questions below. Mark the alternative you think is correct; then look at the correct answer and the explanation provided at the bottom of the page. Try to state why the other alternatives are incorrect, and check your understanding of the correct answer.*

1. With regard to the sociology of race and ethnicity, the concept of pluralism refers to
   a. a situation in which several racial groups are present.
   b. a situation in which different racial and ethnic groups maintain their identities and traditions.
   c. constitutional provisions for preventing a majority from obtaining a plurality of votes in elections.
   d. the assimilation of minority groups by the majority group.
   e. the reduction of social distance between minority groups, which increases the contact they have with one another.

2. Which of the following statements about race and ethnicity in the United States is true?
   a. American Indians have high educational achievement but low employment.
   b. The gap between the median income for blacks and whites has narrowed steadily since 1970.
   c. Most Chicanos are migrant workers and live in rural areas.
   d. One early policy toward American Indians was genocide.
   e. Asian-Americans are rapidly catching up to blacks in educational and occupational achievements.

3. The sociological study in which LaPiere and a Chinese couple visited some 250 hotels and restaurants in the United States demonstrated that
   a. minority groups specialize in certain types of work.
   b. the Chinese have the highest mobility of any racial minority in the United States.
   c. there is a difference between the concepts of prejudice and discrimination.
   d. certain minority groups are more outgoing than others in dealing with the WASP majority.
   e. people do not discriminate publicly in restaurants to the degree they might privately.

---

1. **b.** *Pluralism is a state of society in which several different groups coexist, maintaining their respective culture and traditions, perhaps as a number of subcultures within the dominant culture. See page 288.*

2. **d.** *Native Americans were massacred so that their land could be taken and settled by whites. Bounty was often paid for the scalps of Indians. Genocide is the most* extreme pattern of majority-minority relations. See page 304.

3. **c.** *LaPiere's study illustrated the practical difference between prejudice and discrimination. For example, a person can be prejudiced without discriminating, as this study indicated. See page 293.*

4. Regarding the black experience in the United States, after the racial upheavals of the 1950s and 1960s, the pattern of the 1970s and 1980s seems to be
   a. pluralism, with greater self-confidence among blacks and a greater sense of community.
   b. increasing antagonism, with a real potential for disastrous conflict.
   c. integration, with both blacks and whites working toward the full acceptance of blacks into white society.
   d. continued black subservience with only superficial token concessions by whites.
   e. almost complete assimilation of blacks into the white culture.

5. Concerning racial and ethnic relations in the United States, which of the following statements is true?
   a. America is a "melting pot."
   b. the dominance of white, Anglo-Saxon, Protestant Americans has largely disappeared over the years due to assimilation.
   c. Southern European whites have been assimilated rather easily into American society.
   d. The best prediction for future racial and ethnic relations is one of pluralism with some conflict.
   e. Black Americans will continue to be the largest minority group in the United States through the 1990s.

6. On St. Patrick's Day, there are large parades and other festivities in major cities in the United States. What would be the best *sociological* explanation for the continuation of these celebrations in this country year after year?
   a. White ethnic groups are trying to assimilate into the mainstream culture.
   b. White ethnic groups have never fully assimilated into WASP culture; this is a way to celebrate and share their unique cultural heritage.
   c. These events show non-Irish people the amount of intergenerational mobility the Irish have achieved.
   d. The Irish, as a minority group, have suffered low self-esteem and these events seek to correct that condition.
   e. It is a good excuse to celebrate.

7. An American Indian applies for a job and is turned down because the white employer says "all Indians are drunks." The applicant is upset by this rejection and goes to a bar to socialize with his buddies. In terms of the ideology of racism, the Indian's behavior is an example of
   a. continued subjugation.
   b. assimilation.
   c. prejudiced nondiscrimination.
   d. self-fulfilling prophecy.
   e. the authoritarian personality.

---

4. **a.** *The black-pride movement instilled a sense of self-confidence in the black community and a desire to retain the features of black culture rather than assimilate into white culture. Civil rights advances have broken down some of the barriers separating blacks and whites; a pattern of pluralism is emerging. See pages 299–300.*

5. **d.** *Although the pattern of race relations is difficult to predict because there is no national consensus on goals, pluralism, in which each group retains its own racial and ethnic features, is likely in the future. See page 309.*

6. **b.** *White ethnics often retain distinctive cultural*

*rather than racial features that distinguish them from the dominant culture. Ethnic festivals such as St. Patrick's Day emphasize the contributions of these groups to the United States and implicitly demonstrate that they are not fully assimilated. See page 307.*

7. **d.** *The ideology of racism justifies existing inequalities and reinforces them through the self-fulfilling prophecy. The job applicant is confronted with the stereotype associating alcohol use and American Indians. He may believe the accusation has some truth in it and even applies to him. His own behavior fulfills the stereotype; and his self-image as an American Indian with a drinking problem is reinforced. See page 292.*

8.  Under which circumstances is assimilation likely to occur most readily?
   a.  when the minority group is large
   b.  when the level of education, income, or prestige of the minority group is low and they are not threatening to those in power
   c.  when the minority group is similar to the dominant groups in both cultural and biological traits
   d.  when the minority group is close to its homeland
   e.  when the minority group does not have a strong religious affiliation as part of its heritage

9.  Which of the following is a means of undoing institutionalized discrimination?
   a.  educating people not to be prejudiced
   b.  enacting laws to punish people who are prejudiced
   c.  busing children to achieve racial balance in the schools
   d.  eliminating information on race from job applications
   e.  having consciousness-raising sessions so people can determine whether they are racist

10.  A rigid mental image of a person that is based on whatever is believed to be typical about other members of that group is called
   a.  false consciousness.
   b.  an authoritarian personality.
   c.  scapegoating.
   d.  a minority group.
   e.  a stereotype.

11.  Which racial minority in the United States has come closest to achieving equality with the whites?
   a.  blacks
   b.  Chicanos
   c.  American Indians
   d.  Puerto Ricans
   e.  Asian-Americans

12.  Sociologists define a minority group as one that
   a.  is a numerical minority in a society.
   b.  tries to gain additional members by recruitment.
   c.  is in a disadvantageous position because of the power exercised by the dominant group.
   d.  is racially distinct from the dominant group in a society.
   e.  makes fewer contributions to the society and thus deserves to receive fewer rewards.

---

8.  **c.** *Assimilation is the blending of cultures so that previous differences are diminished. This blending is more likely when the original differences are minimal. Groups with similar ethnic heritages, such as European immigrants to the United States, can be assimilated more easily than groups with very different cultures. See page 297.*

9.  **c.** *Institutionalized discrimination is based in social customs that are longstanding and therefore difficult to eliminate. While changing individual attitudes is important, the overriding patterns of society are the problem to be addressed. Busing breaks the pattern of residential segregation and thus also breaks the pattern of school segregation. See page 296.*

10.  **e.** *A stereotype is used to categorize people based on physical and/or cultural characteristics that are assumed to be typical of all people in a similar category. See page 294.*

11.  **e.** *Asian-Americans have been the most readily assimilated minority group in the United States. The high value placed on education and industriousness blend well with American values. Japanese have assimilated more readily than Chinese; Filipinos will soon be the largest ethnic group in the Asian population. See pages 305–306*

12.  **c.** *A minority group suffers unequal treatment at the hands of the dominant group because of a socially visible characteristic, usually an ascribed status, that distinguishes its members from the dominant culture. See pages 286–287.*

13.  A sociologist gave a tour of Big City, indicating the patterns of racial and ethnic relations there. In one neighborhood, he illustrated the pattern of *assimilation* by pointing out that
   a. blacks now dominate this once Italian neighborhood.
   b. Asian refugees coexist with white ethnic groups, each with their own customs.
   c. bitter racial strife developed with the increase in Cubans settling there permanently.
   d. the various white ethnic groups were indistinguishable from one another in terms of current cultural practices.
   e. there are five Polish delis within 3 blocks of each other.

14.  Compared to other minority groups, American Indians have experienced to a greater degree which *pair* of patterns of majority-minority relations?
   a. population transfer; extermination
   b. assimilation; genocide
   c. pluralism; legal discrimination
   d. continued subjugation; pluralism
   e. legal protection of minorities; assimilation

15.  Which *pair* of concepts explains why racist ideology can continue?
   a. self-fulfilling prophecy; false consciousness
   b. ethnocentrism; biological inequalities
   c. assimilation; class consciousness
   d. legal discrimination; melting pot
   e. prejudice; affirmative action

16.  With which of the following statements would a functionalist be likely to agree?
   a. Racism is the natural outcome of conflict between two groups.
   b. Racism is an outcome of extreme ethnocentrism.
   c. People who take pride in their own customs will become victims of racism.
   d. Racism disappears when the conditions that gave rise to it disappear.
   e. Racism is an attitude that is functional to the ideals of American culture.

17.  Which of the following conditions is *not* seen by conflict theorists as a necessary condition for the development of racial or ethnic inequalities?
   a. socially visible group characteristics
   b. competition for valued resources
   c. power inequalities between groups
   d. laws favoring the dominant group
   e. economic inequalities between groups

---

13.  **d.** *Various groups of white ethnics may have settled a neighborhood, but after a time they dropped the more distinctive features of their original culture and adopted those of the dominant American culture. The basic similarities between white ethnic groups make assimilation more likely. See page 288.*

14.  **a.** *The experience of the American Indian at the hands of whites has been one of extermination and population transfer to reservations. See page 304.*

15.  **a.** *Racism is an ideology or belief system about the inferiority of a racial or ethnic group. In order to continue, all ideologies must be seen as legitimate by most of the people affected by them. Racism is perpetuated by the self-fulfilling prophecy; minorities are treated in such a way that they appear to live up to the stereotypes about them. False consciousness refers to the inability of the oppressed groups to recognize their oppression. See pages 291–292.*

16.  **b.** *A certain amount of ethnocentrism is inevitable and even functional to group solidarity. However, ethnocentric attitudes in an extreme or aggressive form lead to racism and the oppression of a minority group. See page 290.*

17.  **d.** *The dominant group directs many outward and subtle acts of oppression against a minority group. No law is needed to enforce this domination. In fact, racism, for example, often occurs when laws exist to prevent it. See page 291.*

18.  Which of the following groups would sociologists consider a minority group?
    a.  brain surgeons
    b.  poodle owners
    c.  ex-convicts
    d.  Cuban refugees
    e.  Japanese industrialists

19.  Which of the following characteristics of the Hispanic population in the United States helps explain its low power base and inability to promote its own interests?
    a.  The population is geographically concentrated in just a few states.
    b.  The Spanish language is a common characteristic.
    c.  It is too small.
    d.  Many Hispanics are native-born Americans.
    e.  There is considerable diversity among the various Hispanic groups.

20.  The racial turmoil of the 1960s produced which of the following outcomes for black Americans?
    a.  significant economic gains as black incomes move closer to white incomes each year
    b.  increased educational gains, moving closer to white high school and college enrollment figures
    c.  a preference on the part of blacks for greater assimilation with whites

    d.  a perception, shared with whites, that significant strides were made in eliminating discrimination
    e.  all of these have occurred

21.  The racial differences we see today among humans
    a.  represent the division of the human family into different species.
    b.  are of comparatively recent evolutionary origin—10,000 years at the most.
    c.  evolved as human populations adapted to their differing environments.
    d.  are accompanied by different inherited psychological characteristics.
    e.  are the same as those that were present 50,000 years ago.

22.  In his work on the "authoritarian personality," Adorno found that
    a.  there is a correlation between fascist, ethnocentric, and anti-Semitic attitudes.
    b.  the concept of the authoritarian personality was a myth.
    c.  authoritarianism is as common among radicals as among conservatives.
    d.  the experience of prejudice and discrimination tends to make members of oppressed groups authoritarian.
    e.  people in positions of authority are likely to be less racist than the general public.

---

18.  **d.** *A minority group must have socially identifiable characteristics and little power over or access to valued resources. See page 287.*

19.  **e.** *Hispanics include many diverse ethnic groups, such as Chicanos, Puerto Ricans, Cubans, and groups from South and Central American countries. The shared language belies the many differences between the groups. See page 301.*

20.  **b.** *The gap between blacks' and whites' average years of schooling has narrowed rapidly. Economic gains, when compared to whites, have not improved as quickly in recent years. See page 300.*

21.  **c.** *The adaptations humans have made to their environments have produced the racial differences seen today. These racial differences have continued to evolve over the last 50,000 years. See page 284.*

22.  **a.** *The authoritarian personality is one characterized by intolerance, dislike for ambiguity, aggressive behavior toward "inferiors," and submissiveness to "superiors." Adorno found that people who display the authoritarian personality are prejudiced toward many groups. See page 294.*

23. Slaves often seemed to accept their masters' view that they were inferior. Although this attitude was sometimes a deliberate pretense, it seems that many slaves unquestioningly accepted their inferior status. This is an example of what Marx called

    a. continued subjugation.
    b. class consciousness.
    c. false consciousness.
    d. institutionalized inferiority.
    e. ideological victimization.

24. A northern doctor moves to Mississippi. Although she personally disapproves, she maintains the separate waiting rooms for blacks and whites established by her predecessor, since this is expected by her more affluent white patients. According to Merton's typology, the doctor is

    a. an unprejudiced nondiscriminator.
    b. an unprejudiced discriminator.
    c. a prejudiced nondiscriminator.
    d. a prejudiced discriminator.
    e. an authoritarian personality.

25. Schools in the United States used to be segregated by law, but are now largely segregated as a result of segregated residential patterns. This change marks a shift from

    a. institutionalized discrimination to legal discrimination.
    b. assimilation to legal discrimination.
    c. legal discrimination to institutionalized discrimination.
    d. prejudice to pluralism.
    e. prejudice to deinstitutionalized discrimination.

---

23.  **c.** *False consciousness is the term used by Marx to describe the failure to realize one's own oppression and to identify with others in a similar situation. Lacking an understanding of the objective facts of their exploitation, many slaves accepted their masters' ideology that defined them as inferior, rather than looking on that viewpoint as the whites' way to justify black enslavement. See page 292.*

24.  **b.** *Merton separated the concepts of prejudice (attitude) and discrimination (behavior), noting that an individual can be prejudiced without discriminating and* vice versa. *In this case, the doctor is not prejudiced herself, but discriminates against blacks to appease her white patients. See page 293.*

25.  **c.** *Even though laws that segregated schools have been removed, institutionalized discrimination, informal discrimination entrenched in social customs, continues. In the United States, most people live in neighborhoods with others of the same race. This situation has produced residential segregation, which, in turn, contributes to institutionalized discrimination. See page 296.*

# A CASE STUDY

It has been predicted that the 1990 U.S. census will show Hispanic-Americans to be the largest minority in this country. The United States has dealt with race relations in terms of black-white relations for so many years that the predominance of Spanish-speaking peoples will result in many changes. The area of East Los Angeles, California, has one of the largest Hispanic populations in the United States. Many of the residents are lifelong American citizens; others are recent immigrants; and some are illegal aliens. The high unemployment rate in the city of Los Angeles has exacerbated racial tensions. Some members of the black community allege that illegal aliens and other immigrants (Asian refugees and Cuban refugees) are taking the jobs that used to be held by blacks. The power structure of Los Angeles does not reflect the presence of a large Hispanic population: Hispanics enjoy little or no representation on the city council, the school board, or other government bodies such as the police and fire departments. Government-funded welfare programs have been placed primarily in black neighborhoods. While East Los Angeles is relatively healthy in terms of its own organizations, it has received little help from the outside. As a community, it seems to be shunted off from the rest of the city.

1.    What if an argument were made that Hispanics should be elected to the city council and the school board, and that a certain percentage of Hispanics should be represented in the police department, fire department, and schools? Is this a legitimate commitment or racism in the name of quotas?

2.    From time to time, Hispanics have been nominated for a few minor city offices. Some of the qualified candidates have met with resistance from the East Los Angeles community; even though they are ethnically Hispanic, they allegedly do not represent the views or experiences of the community. How would you explain a situation like this?

3.    Review Merton's four-part model of prejudice and discrimination. Then imagine that you are a mayoral candidate making a campaign speech to a group of white businesspeople. From the point of view of each of the four types of persons Merton described, write a sentence explaining your position on some issue concerning majority-minority relations in East Los Angeles.

4.    With the Hispanic population so heavily concentrated in East Los Angeles, how would you characterize the pattern of majority-minority relations in the city of Los Angeles? In your view, what are the consequences of such a pattern?

5.    How might the idea of the self-fulfilling prophecy explain why some of the East Los Angeles residents live up to stereotypes about their community, as far as purported gang activity, heroin use, and low-rider cars?

# Applying the Concepts

NAME

_____

COURSE/SECTION  NUMBER

## APPLICATION EXERCISE ONE

1.   Look at television commercials or advertisements in popular magazines. Describe which racial stereotypes are in evidence (or are being broken). For example, for many years the Frito-Lay company used the Frito Bandito as its mascot, portraying Mexicans as robbers and untrustworthy characters. Public pressure forced this commercial off the air. How important is popular culture in supporting or changing racial stereotypes?

2.   How are stereotypes culturally transmitted through humor, e.g., ethnic jokes, popular television shows, etc.?

## APPLICATION EXERCISE TWO

NAME

COURSE/SECTION NUMBER

1.   Some racial and ethnic minorities have adopted the ways of WASP culture, becoming fairly well assimilated into the American mainstream. Still, there are many traits we associate with one racial or ethnic group or the other. For example, the use of hand gestures while speaking is associated with Italians. Hip, colorful clothing is associated with black males. A looser concept of time and punctuality is associated with American Indians and Hispanic groups. How can these differences be maintained within ethnic subcultures while common norms and values prevail for the United States as a whole?

2.   What are some of the intended outcomes of bilingual or multilingual education? What is your view of the results of these efforts?

3.   What is your opinion of affirmative-action programs as a means to eliminate patterns of racial and ethnic discrimination?

4.   Give an example from your own experience, or one from a recent newspaper or television report, that shows the patterns of:

    a. pluralism

    b. assimilation

# APPLICATION EXERCISE THREE

NAME

COURSE/SECTION NUMBER

Select one of the minority groups presented in the text and describe its relationship to the dominant culture in the United States.

1.    What are the historical circumstances surrounding this group's arrival in the United States? Which pattern(s) of treatment did it receive from the majority group? To what extent has the group been assimilated? On what evidence are you basing your judgment?

2.    What evidence of discrimination against this group can you present? Why did discrimination take these forms rather than others?

3.    Obtain a copy of a magazine that is written for this minority group.
Examples include: *Ebony, Jet, Mujeres, Red Power.* How do these publications
differ from the mainstream magazines in the United States?

4.    What aspects of this group's culture have become part of the dominant
culture? Consider words, foods, traditions, dances, music, and other lifestyle
aspects.

# CHAPTER 12

# Inequalities of Gender and Age

## Reviewing the Concepts

### LEARNING GOALS

*After studying this chapter, you should be able to:*

1. Distinguish between sex and gender and explain the concept of gender roles.

2. Cite biological evidence in discussing differences between the sexes.

3. Cite psychological evidence in discussing differences between the sexes.

4. Cite cross-cultural evidence in discussing differences between the sexes.

5. Evaluate the functionalist view of gender inequality in traditional and modern societies.

6. State the conflict view of gender inequalities.

7. Explain the ideology of sexism and the role religion has played in maintaining gender inequality.

8. Discuss the implications of America's transformation from an agricultural to an industrial economy for gender roles.

9. Present an ideal-type analysis of American gender roles and indicate the effects of traditional roles on male-female interaction.

10. Describe the three main elements of the psychological process by which children learn gender roles, beginning in the family.

11. Indicate the ways in which the school and the media reinforce traditional gender roles.

12. Explain the wage gap between male and female workers and note policies that may help to close the gap.

13. Compare gender roles today with those likely to exist in the future.

14. Explain the concept of a life course consisting of basic stages marked by rites of passage.

15. Contrast the position of the elderly in preindustrial and industrialized societies and account for the differences.

16. Summarize the "disengagement" view of aging, explaining why it is consistent with the functionalist perspective in general.

17. Summarize the conflict view of age inequality; describe the power base of the aged.

18. Discuss ageism in American society, citing evidence from the text and from personal experience.

19. Describe the field of social gerontology.

20. Indicate the significance of a cohort and of age structure in understanding the experience and meaning of aging in a society.

21. Assess the situation of the aged in America today; list three major problems the elderly face.

22. Assess the well-being of America's children.

23. Explain the idea of the graying of America and predict the social consequences of this trend.

## IDENTIFYING KEY QUESTIONS AND THEMES

Sex and age are ascribed statuses. All societies use these two characteristics to differentiate among their members. In terms of sex, there is a general cross-cultural pattern of male domination. Age, too, has been (and continues to be) strongly associated with social inequality. In traditional societies, the old often have the greatest access to wealth, power, and prestige; however, in modern societies, these resources go to the middle-aged, while the elderly may take on the characteristics of a minority group.

## Gender and Society

*What is the connection between sex and gender and what significance does each have for society?*

Human beings can be divided into two categories based on *sex*—the biological distinction between males and females. The significance of sex is that all societies elaborate this biological fact into social ideas about "masculinity" and "femininity," which refer to *gender*—the culturally learned differences between men and women, such as differences in clothing styles or occupational patterns. Thus men and women are taught to be socially different on the basis of their biological characteristics. Because a person occupies the status position of male or female, he or she is expected to play certain roles associated with that status. *Gender roles* are the behavior patterns, obligations, and privileges that are considered appropriate for each sex. Because the social statuses of the sexes are generally unequal, these gender roles tend to reflect and reinforce sexual stratification. In the past twenty-five years, people in Western society have challenged the traditional relationship of the sexes, opening up many new possibilities.

## How Different Are the Sexes?

*What does evidence from biological, psychological, and cross-cultural research tell us about differences between men and women? How do sociologists interpret this evidence and explain sex differences?*

In terms of biological evidence, men and women differ from one another genetically, hormonally, and anatomically. The differences in their genes, which provide the inherited blueprint for their physical development, are revealed in chromosomal composition, hereditary disorders, life expectancy, resistance to disease, and tolerance for pain and malnutrition. Differences in hormones, chemical substances that are secreted by the body's various glands, may affect aggressiveness and sex drive, although individual differences in age and temperament seem to be equally important in explaining behavior. Additionally, the sexes differ in terms of anatomy, or physical structure and appearance, including their reproductive system, height, weight, body fat, body hair, and musculature. The fact that male anatomy gives men the potential to dominate women by force is a socially important distinction.

It is difficult to draw conclusions from the many studies of psychological differences between men and women because the effects of biological and social influences are intertwined. As a result, most psychological research has focused on infants who have undergone little socialization. Studies show some evidence of sex-linked personality differences in newborn infants. Yet, from birth, parents treat babies in subtly different ways on the basis of sex, so the case is not proved. Some of the most important literature on sex-linked behavior concerns children who

have been raised as a member of the opposite sex. Such studies indicate that an infant can easily be raised as a member of the opposite sex, but that after the age of three or four, it is difficult to resocialize that child to the original gender role. The present consensus among researchers is that there are probably some predispositions toward minor variations in the behavior of the sexes at birth, but that these are not clear-cut differences and can be overridden by cultural learning.

Cross-cultural research documents a wide range of gender-role patterns. Anthropologist Margaret Mead studied preindustrial societies and found male and female roles quite different from our own. The overall cross-cultural tendency points to a strong pattern of male dominance both in preindustrial and industrialized societies. The pattern is particularly evident in terms of political power—there is no record of any society in which women were/are the politically dominant sex. Another cross-cultural feature, the *division of labor* between men and women, helps explain why. Around the world, women are socialized for child-rearing and home maintenance tasks, while men are responsible for tasks outside the home and those involving heavy physical activity, like hunting or fighting. The overall conclusion from cross-cultural evidence is that there is a strong general pattern in dominance, personality, and work, but that this pattern is not inevitable, as shown by the many cultural variations in gender-role behavior. Sociologists who focus on the striking gender inequality that does characterize most societies explain its sources and persistence in terms of the functionalist and conflict views, among others.

## Gender Inequality: A Functionalist View

*How does the functionalist perspective account for gender-role differences? How are these differences functional or dysfunctional?*

Functionalist theorists assume that if all societies encourage gender differences, they must serve some positive purpose for society. The division of labor by sex seems to be a highly functional pattern in traditional, preindustrial societies. Duties are allocated to particular people who are socialized to play the roles involved. The requirements of childbearing and child-rearing are assigned to women, while men take on the responsibilities of hunting, and defending the family. However, under such a system, the female inevitably becomes dependent on the male for food and protection. Male dominance assures that men's activities and personality traits will be more highly regarded and rewarded in society. Over time, these patterns become structured and passed down from generation to generation as "natural" and "right."

Two functionalist theorists, Parsons and Bales, argued that traditional gender roles are still functional in a modern society. Men play the "instrumental" role, focusing on relationships between the family and the outside world. The "expressive" role is played by the female, who is responsible for the nurturant relationships within the family. Each role contributes to a smoothly functioning whole. Functionalist theory explains how traditional gender roles and sexual inequalities arise. However, it is criticized for promoting the status quo and being out of touch with men and women in modern, industrialized societies. Longer female life expectancy and the fact that most jobs require little physical labor have blurred the distinction between men's and women's worlds. Furthermore, the theory overlooks the dysfunctions to society of denying half the population the opportunity to play the roles linked to the other sex.

## Gender Inequality: A Conflict View

*What does a conflict perspective contribute to an analysis of gender-role differences? How are gender-role inequalities maintained and reinforced?*

A conflict analysis may offer a better explanation of why sexual inequalities persist in a modern, industrial society. Although women are found at all levels of the social-class hierarchy, at any given position they generally have inferior status to men at the same position. Conflict theorists argue that sexual inequality, like any other structured social inequality, is based on a conflict of interest between the dominant and subordinate group. By maintaining sexual inequalities, society prevents women from making the best use of their talents, thus protecting the opportunities of the higher-status male group. Since the existing arrangements of society perpetuate male dominance, men have little motivation to change them. The underlying source of sexual inequality, in the view of conflict theorists, is the economic inequality between men and women. Analyses of horticultural, pastoral, agricultural, and early industrial societies show that men make greater economic contributions and have correspondingly more power, prestige, and wealth than do women. In advanced industrial societies, and particularly in emerging postindustrial societies, the economic contributions of women increase relative to men, and inequalities between the sexes begin to diminish. As the percentage of employed women in the United States continues to climb, changes in gender roles are the likely result.

## Sexism

*What is the ideology of sexism? How does this ideology create a false consciousness?*

**Sexism** is an **ideology,** or set of beliefs, that legitimates unequal social arrangements on the basis of sex and makes them seem "right." To varying degrees, both men and women accept the sexist ideology that gender characteristics and sexual inequalities are rooted in the natural order. Like most ideologies that justify some form of social inequality, sexism is endorsed by major world religions and by prominent denominations in the United States. The sexist belief in the superiority of men has wide-ranging implications. For example, women are commonly viewed as the sexual property of men and are expected to be submissive to them. One sign of women's acquiescence to this notion is the great lengths to which they have historically gone to make themselves attractive to men. Indeed, women have generally accepted views of their "natural" inferiority, a condition Marx called *false consciousness* — a subjective understanding of one's situation that does not accord with the objective facts. Only when the subordinate group loses this false consciousness and becomes aware of the situation of oppression will it challenge the social order and demand that changes be made. The women's movement has worked at consciousness-raising to help make women and men aware that inequality is socially created and can be changed.

## Gender Roles in America

*How have changes in the economy affected gender roles? What personality traits are considered appropriate for men and women? How does routine social interaction reveal and reinforce the inequality between the sexes?*

With the transformation of America from an agricultural to an industrial society, traditional gender roles shifted. Men left the home to work in the factory, leaving women isolated from the economy. Women's lack of economic clout carried other restrictions—women were not allowed to vote, make contracts, or own property. At the turn of the century, early feminists lobbied for changes, and in 1920, succeeded in securing women's right to vote. Traditional gender roles shifted again in the 1940s when women were temporarily employed in the industrial jobs vacated by men serving in World War II. Although women proved themselves capable of filling these jobs and doing heavy work, social norms were slow to change and most returned to the housewife role in the postwar years. In the 1960s, a new women's movement emerged and lobbied for social changes in an effort to give women equal status with men. Not surprisingly, these efforts met at first with resistance from men and women as well. Although legislation in 1963 guaranteed equal pay for men and women, the Equal Rights Amendment to the Constitution was never ratified. American gender roles are now far more flexible than those in most other societies. However, traditional norms still exist and guide behavior. People are negatively sanctioned for behavior that deviates too far from what is expected. The persistence of clearly defined gender roles is reflected in the personalities, interpersonal relations, and workplace experiences of men and women.

Even in a diverse society such as the United States, there is some consensus as to the personality traits that are most desirable for each of the sexes. The American woman is generally expected to be conformist, passive, caring, affectionate, sensitive, and dependent. In relationships, she does not take the initiative, and often places more emphasis on romantic involvement than on sexual gratification. Her self-image is linked to her attractiveness to men, her success at romantic involvements, and her fulfillment of nurturant roles for husband and children. The American man is expected to be self-reliant, competent, independent, and competitive. He is expected to take the initiative in sexual relationships and to care more about sexual gratification than romantic involvement. He has power and authority in both the work world and the family. Since his self-image derives mainly from his achievements outside the home, his work is a major

focus of his life. These gender-linked personality traits may have advantages and disadvantages for each sex. For example, women have a longer life expectancy, but their dependent role is not socially valued; men have greater access to wealth, power, and prestige, but suffer from stress-related problems brought on by these responsibilities. Currently, American gender roles are in a state of flux; however, certain ethnic groups and lower socioeconomic classes tend to adhere to traditional patterns.

Many routine interactions between men and women reflect and reinforce traditional role relationships. Research on these subtle interactions reveals the importance of differences in such things as the titles and names we use, our manipulation of physical space, as well as the way we direct a conversation. Men still dominate in these realms, reinforcing the inequality of the sexes.

The basic gender characteristics expected of the sexes are learned in the course of socialization, first in the context of the family very early in life and later in peer groups, schools, and the mass media, where they are reinforced. From the time they are born, boys and girls are socialized differently by their families. Each is taught to follow the expectations for one gender and to avoid the behavior or interests of the other gender. As a result of this training, gender roles are learned quickly and effectively. The psychological process by which children learn these roles consists of *conditioning* through reward and punishment, *imitation* of older children and adults who serve as role models, and *self-definition*, during which children learn to identify themselves with the appropriate gender. Schools reinforce traditional gender roles in many ways. Analyses of textbooks reveal an overwhelming proportion of males in the more prestigious and desirable roles. Additionally, many curricular and extracurricular activities segregate boys and girls. Teachers and counselors may channel boys into vocational activities and training for high-prestige occupations, discouraging them from pursuing interests traditionally considered "feminine," while girls often gain little prestige from being bright and may not be encouraged to continue with their schooling. The mass media perpetuate gender-role stereotypes, particularly by portraying women as sex objects or as domesticated housewives. Market research has shown these advertising approaches to be effective, which is evidence that at least certain gender stereotypes have been internalized by most men and women. Goffman's research reveals the subtlety of many advertisements that reinforce sexual stereotypes by showing men in command, conveying authority, as women adorn the scene or bicker over which detergent to use.

## Men, Women, and Jobs

*How do the occupational patterns of men and women differ? What factors explain the wage gap? What factors contribute to occupational segregation and limited occupational mobility for women?*

The inequality of men and women is reflected in their unequal earnings. The wage gap significantly affects people's sense of self-worth, their economic independence, and their social prestige and power. Although large numbers of women have entered the work force, their incomes are only about 60 percent that of their male counterparts. This gap will probably persist as long as women, on average, have less education and job experience than men, family responsibilities take women in and out of the labor force, and employers continue to discriminate against women in terms of salaries, promotions, and job titles. As a result, women workers are overrepresented in certain occupations, known as "pink collar" jobs, that have lower pay and prestige.

For many women in female-dominated jobs, then, the concept of "equal pay for equal work" has little meaning. Some people insist that social policies must provide "equal pay for comparable work" if the pay gap is to be corrected. However, such efforts at "comparable worth" have met with resistance by government and employers who fear additional costs. A minority of women have entered traditionally male occupations, but an even smaller number rise to the top positions in these fields. The old-boy network and institutional discrimination, as well as the prejudices of individual men, have limited women's job mobility. Furthermore, women's socialization does not adequately prepare them for the management style that is valued in the male-dominated professions.

## Gender Roles Today

*What are the implications of changing gender roles? What will the future hold for men and women?*

Changes in gender roles have important implications for the workplace, the family, and the relationships of the sexes. Although a great deal has changed, working women still do the majority of housework, for example. Many women enjoy the benefits of employment outside the home, yet they struggle to reconcile the conflicts of work, children, and relationships. One of the most dramatic changes in the family is that most American children are now in day care. Additionally, women's economic independence means they can leave unhappy marriages or raise children on their own. The divorce rate has increased as has the number of women heading households. Unfortunately, women's lower incomes have collided with these changes resulting in a condition called the "feminization of poverty," in which 57 percent of the poor are female. For their part, many men have generally reacted positively to more flexible gender-role expectations, which, of course, affect their own possibilities as well. In the future, the most probable pattern is one in which many alternative lifestyles and roles will be acceptable for men and women. American culture emphasizes personal development and is very open to experimentation and change. Biological sex will decline as a determinant of choices, as individual human qualities come to serve as the primary measure of worth and achievement.

## Age and Society

*What is the significance for the aged of the transition from preindustrial to industrialized societies? How is the life course socially created? What are rites of passage?*

The human life course is both a social and a biological process. Each society imposes its own culturally defined "stages" on the continuous process of human aging. Traditional societies recognize the stages of childhood, maturity, and old age, while modern societies recognize six stages—infancy, childhood, adolescence, young adulthood, middle age, and old age. Each stage may include *rites of passage,* formal ceremonies that mark an individual's transition from one age status to another. All societies distribute different rights and responsibilities to individuals on the basis of their ascribed status as members of a particular age category. As with gender roles, age roles result in social inequalities. As a general rule, preindustrial societies grant the greatest power and prestige to the old; industrialized societies, on the other hand, accord rewards to the middle-aged and devalue old age. This pattern can be explained in terms of the relative economic and social usefulness of the aged in each type of society. In most preindustrial societies, the aged are respected for their knowledge, wisdom, and experience. The typical family is a large *extended family* that consists of many relatives living in close proximity; authority rests with the oldest male. In industrialized societies, on the other hand, the status of the aged is different. The knowledge explosion and the need for technical expertise means that formal education, and not the experience accumulated over a lifetime, is the key to wisdom and socially valued experience. The economic status of the aged also changes markedly as the ownership of land becomes a less significant source of wealth. In an industrialized society, new sources of wealth are created, and the main beneficiaries are middle-aged executives and other professionals. The role of old people in the family changes as well: they no longer head the family unit, since in industrialized societies the extended family gives way to the *nuclear family* in which married couples and their dependent children live apart from other relatives. As the elderly are deprived of meaningful roles in society, their political, economic, and social power declines, resulting in low status.

## Age Inequality: A Functionalist View

*How do functionalist theorists explain the status of the elderly in industrialized societies? How does the process of disengagement ensure transition of roles between the age strata?*

Industrialization has changed the rights and responsibilities of the aged. But the unequal status of the elderly is not inevitable. Functionalist theorists have tried to explain the situation of the elderly in an industrialized society in terms of "disengagement." Proponents of this view argue that the status of the elderly is the result of a mutual process of disengagement, in which society gradually withdraws from the elderly, while they surrender their roles to younger members of society. This slow process of disengagement provides an orderly transfer of roles from older to younger persons, and ensures the survival of the society. Functionalists explain changes in the status of the young, too, in terms of the importance of social stability,

arguing that compulsory education prepares young adults for work roles and keeps them out of the work force until they are ready to take on those roles.

## Age Inequality: A Conflict View

*How do conflict theorists explain the status of the elderly in industrialized societies? Why are the elderly at a disadvantage?*

According to the conflict perspective, various age categories are really social strata. They are ranked in a hierarchy of power, prestige, and wealth, and are in competition for scarce resources. Thus the interests and gains of one stratum may be at another's expense. Conflict theorists assert that in preindustrial societies all workers, young and old, were needed to ensure the society's survival. In industrial societies, on the other hand, there is a surplus of labor, so the young are kept out of the work force by lengthy, compulsory schooling, while the elderly are forced to retire, giving up their work roles to the middle-aged. In the conflict view, the most powerful age stratum in any society is able to secure a larger share of the society's resources for itself. The declining status of the aged in industrialized societies results from the loss of power, wealth, and prestige to the middle-aged. Any improvement in the status of the elderly, therefore, would have to come about through a change in the power relationships among the age strata.

## Ageism

*What evidence is there for an ideology of ageism? What are the consequences of such an ideology?*

The dominant stratum in an unequal society usually uses an ideology to justify its position. *Ageism* refers to the belief that one age category is in some respects inferior to other age categories and that unequal treatment is therefore justified. Like racism and sexism, ageism takes no account of individual differences in ability, talents, or experience. Rather, the negative stereotypes of lower or nonexistent economic contributions, infirmity, senility, dependence, crankiness, forgetfulness, sexlessness, and rigidity are attributed to the elderly as a category. No matter how unfair or inaccurate these stereotypes are, they are used to exclude the aged from equal participation in society. Ageism against the elderly is often subtle, but pervasive. For example, television commercials feature young, attractive people and rarely present older characters, in keeping with a market that promotes products designed to perpetuate a youthful appearance. People's attitudes toward their age reveal ageist bias as well. Middle-aged people and women, in particular, are socialized to value youthfulness and often understate their age.

## Social Gerontology

*How does social gerontology explain the process of aging? What problems do the elderly face? Why is America's real poor its children?*

In America, the aged are considered to be those sixty-five years or older. *Social gerontology* is the study of the social aspects of aging. Sociologists in this subdiscipline examine the influence of social forces on the aged and the aging process, and the impact of the aged and their needs on society. Aging involves three related processes: (1) physical aging—maturation of the body; (2) psychological aging—changes in the personality; and (3) social aging—the transitions from one social status to another over the life course. All three processes occur at different and uneven rates for any given individual. The experience and meaning of aging also change from one social and historical context to another. Sociologists use the concept of a *cohort,* a category of people born during the same time period, to analyze these factors. Another influence on the meaning of aging is a society's *age structure,* the relative proportion of different age categories in the population. If a particular age stratum, such as old people, is in a majority, it may place demands on a society for special social programs, or it may command more political power.

Social gerontologists have documented the wide variety of lifestyles of the aged. Many draw great satisfaction from the final stage of the life course. American society is now treating its older members much better than before, as evidenced by the declining poverty rate of the aged. However, the elderly still have some distinctive problems, especially poor health. More than 75 percent of those over sixty-five suffer from some chronic ailment, brought on by biological aging, that can usually be treated but not cured. Senility is perhaps the most notorious disability of the aged, yet it is rare in people under seventy-five. The high incidence of poor health among the elderly is compounded by higher medical expenses and lower incomes. Medicaid and Medicare cover only part of the bill. Another problem the aged face is the loss of a work role and the sense of identity it provides. Despite laws against age discrimination, many people in late middle age face layoffs, or pressure to retire early. Retirement is a relatively new phenomenon that only became possible with the advent of Social Security. Mandatory retirement has been abolished for all but a few jobs because it discriminates against the aged, many of whom are capable of working well past the retirement age. Isolation is also a serious problem for the elderly. Their social networks dwindle with the disability and death of friends and spouses. Many older people fear the loss of their independence as a result of illness or financial difficulties. In American society, we place a high value on independence, making it difficult for formerly self-sufficient adults to turn to their children or the government for help. Yet, with advanced age, most people have to rely on some outside help. Although only a small percentage of the elderly are in a nursing or old-age home at any given time, the great majority die in such a setting.

Many of America's aged live on frugal incomes, supplemented by Social Security, very close to the poverty line. However, America's real poor are its children. About 22 percent of Americans under the age of eighteen live in poverty, with even higher rates for black children. This trend is linked to the poor economic condition of many mothers. The high rate of divorce and single-female–headed households sets up a group of people highly vulnerable to financial distress. Unfortunately, many poor children will perpetuate the cycle of poverty by having children at a young age, completing little schooling, and working at marginal jobs. Unlike the aged, children are not a powerful voting block and their plight has received little attention. Americans tend to think that poverty is the fault of its victims, and to be unwilling to help the poor through government relief or other programs. While more than 30 percent of the total federal budget is spent on older Americans, only 3 percent goes to children.

## The Graying of America

*What is the significance of an aging population structure in the United States?*

Due to an increase in life expectancy and a decline in the birth rate, the American population structure is changing and growing older. This "graying of America" will bring about a variety of social changes, some of which are already in evidence. Government and social services will have to prepare for middle-aged and older persons. Changes will be made in marketing and advertising in an attempt to attract this group of consumers. The commer-

cial world, such as nursing homes, funeral homes, the health professions, continuing education programs, and other services linked to middle and older ages, will grow. The elderly are already an effective political group, and their power is likely to be enhanced. In short, the age category of individuals over sixty-five will increase in size and social influence in the coming years.

## DEFINING CORE CONCEPTS

*After studying the chapter, write a sociological definition in your own words for the following core concepts. Then give an example from your own experience to illustrate your definition. Refer to the chapter to check your work.*

| *Core Concept* | *Sociological Definition* | *Personal Illustration* |
| --- | --- | --- |
| ageism | | |
| age structure | | |
| cohort | | |
| gender roles | | |
| division of labor | | |

| *Core Concept* | *Sociological Definition* | *Personal Illustration* |
|---|---|---|
| extended family | | |
| false consciousness | | |
| ideology | | |
| nuclear family | | |
| rites of passage | | |
| sexism | | |
| sex | | |
| social gerontology | | |

## PUTTING IDEAS TOGETHER

All societies have criteria to differentiate among their members. Two ascribed statuses, sex and age, have been used to assign social roles and social rewards. The process of differentiating people by sex and age usually results in social inequalities. The particular culture within which this process occurs sets the stage for the form the inequalities will take, how serious they are, how likely they are to change, and the specific privileges accorded one group over another.

### Visible Biological Differences

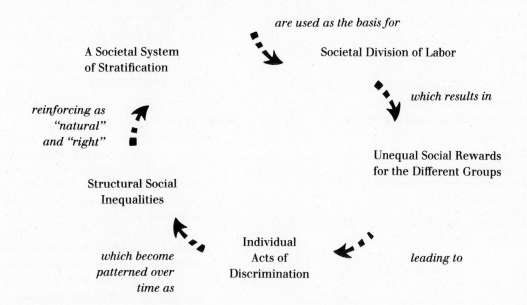

A Societal System of Stratification

*are used as the basis for*

Societal Division of Labor

*which results in*

*reinforcing as "natural" and "right"*

Unequal Social Rewards for the Different Groups

Structural Social Inequalities

*which become patterned over time as*

Individual Acts of Discrimination

*leading to*

Functionalist and conflict perspectives offer explanations for differentiation of gender and age roles as well as how the division of labor changes with industrialization. These explanations are shown below.

|  | *Functionalist Perspective* | *Conflict Perspective* |
|---|---|---|
| *Why Gender and Age Roles Exist and Are Maintained* | These distinctions form a reasonable division of labor and contribute to a smoothly functioning society. | The dominant group's ideology protects their privilege; oppressed groups have a false consciousness and do not question existing arrangements. |
| *Why Gender and Age Roles Will Change* | Societal needs will shift, and all parts of society will adapt to this change; ascribed statuses are not functional in an industrial society. | The power base of society will shift as women and the elderly gain an awareness of their oppression and demand changes. |

# Testing the Concepts

## MULTIPLE-CHOICE QUESTIONS

*After studying the chapter, try to answer each of the twenty-five questions below. Mark the alternative you think is correct; then look at the correct answer and the explanation provided at the bottom of the page. Try to state why the other alternatives are incorrect, and check your understanding of the correct answer.*

1. Regarding gender roles, both the functionalist and conflict views agree that
   a. existing gender-role patterns are primarily social in origin.
   b. women are to be regarded as a minority group.
   c. a modern family needs two adults who will divide the household, childcare, and income-earning responsibilities.
   d. the traditional relationship between the sexes must be radically changed.
   e. gender roles are not important in modern, industrialized societies.

2. Jean, biologically a boy, is raised by his parents as a girl. It may be expected that he will
   a. have great difficulty in making any adjustments to his biological sex identity after the age of three or four.
   b. resist this imposed gender role vigorously, and probably with success.
   c. throw off this training as soon as he gains a degree of independence, although this might not be until mid-adolescence.
   d. begin to resist his "female" role and strongly assert his masculine role at about age four.
   e. become celibate due to confusion about his own sexual identity.

3. Compared to the category of people over sixty-five, American children
   a. have a higher standard of living.
   b. have more social services directed to them.
   c. if once poor, will remain poor, unlike the elderly.
   d. have more public sympathy and more political power.
   e. receive one-tenth of the amount the government spends on the elderly.

4. Which of the following examples best illustrates the idea of gender differentiation?
   a. Jack has a beard; Mary cannot grow one.
   b. Janet wants to get married and raise a family when she grows up; Larry wants to be a fireman.
   c. Alice and Nancy argue that the Equal Rights Amendment will protect the rights of both men and women.
   d. In a celebrity sports contest, the female athletes are given a handicap to make up for their lesser physical strength compared to the male athletes.
   e. After their baby was born, Ted felt jealous of the relationship his wife had with their child.

---

1. **a.** *Gender-role behavior is learned through socialization and varies considerably by culture. Functionalists feel the division of labor between men and women promotes social stability, while conflict theorists see the relationship as unequal and exploitive. Both groups support the idea that gender-role behavior is not biologically based. See pages 318–319.*

2. **a.** *Gender-role socialization is so pervasive and subtle, and important to the self-concept and the division of labor in society, that by the time a child has reached the age of three or four, a strong sense of maleness or femaleness has developed. This image is difficult to change. See page 316.*

3. **e.** *American children have the highest poverty rate of any age group. Yet government subsidies favor other groups, including the elderly. Children receive one-tenth the amount of government funding given to the elderly. See page 339.*

4. **b.** *Gender differentiation refers to characteristics based not on biological sex but on social definitions of gender. See page 314.*

5.  Which of the following viewpoints implies a functionalist approach to gender roles?
   a.  The family works more efficiently if the husband and wife play different roles.
   b.  Traditional gender roles are preserved because the dominant group, the men, benefits from them.
   c.  Men enjoy superior status because social norms ensure that women are relegated to inferior status.
   d.  Young children are aware of the existence of two sexes, and define themselves as members of one or the other.
   e.  One of the functions of the battle of the sexes is to keep each sex from understanding the other.

6.  Women's roles have changed a great deal in the past twenty-five years; for example, more than half of all American women now work outside the home. Which of the following accurately reflects one of many impacts this has had?
   a.  Many female-headed households are caught in a syndrome known as the "feminization of poverty."
   b.  Women earn comparable salaries/wages for comparable work thanks to equal-pay legislation.
   c.  Men do approximately half of the housework when their wives are employed.
   d.  Women's decision to work outside the home is a major cause of divorce.
   e.  Once women work their way into male dominated jobs, they have the same opportunity to rise to the top.

7.  Aging is accompanied by certain health problems. Which of the following statements about the health of the elderly is accurate?
   a.  A large proportion of people under seventy-five are senile.
   b.  Most ailments suffered by the elderly can be cured with adequate medical care.
   c.  More than three-quarters of the elderly suffer from chronic ailments, and as a group the elderly are disproportionately represented among hospital populations.
   d.  Medicaid and Medicare pay the bulk of elderly people's medical bills.
   e.  Most of the elderly people are quite ill and require hospitalization.

8.  Ideologies like sexism and ageism depend on
   a.  a biologically ascribed status for categorizing people.
   b.  laws to enforce them.
   c.  evidence from social science research on which stereotypes are based.
   d.  a cultural value of social equality.
   e.  individuals who defy the stereotypes generally associated with their category.

9.  The graying of America will result in
   a.  a higher birth rate.
   b.  endorsement of mandatory retirement.
   c.  new marketing strategies aimed at older people.
   d.  higher incomes for the postretirement elderly.
   e.  greater stigma on the old.

---

5.  a.  *According to functionalists, the division of labor within a family is most efficiently defined on the basis of sex. All duties can be completed in a smooth and coordinated fashion because each sex has specific roles to play. See pages 318–319.*

6.  a.  *The large number of female-headed households has resulted in a "feminization of poverty." Women's depressed wages and insufficient support from children's fathers have contributed to the serious conditions of poverty plaguing so many women and children. See page 330.*

7.  c.  *Most of the elderly suffer from chronic diseases that can be treated but not cured. Although the aged*

*represent only 12 percent of the total population, they use a third of all hospital beds each year. See page 337.*

8.  a.  *Sexism and ageism, like racism, distinguish among people on the basis of a single biological characteristic. Such ideologies ignore individual differences and fail to recognize that many differences among the strata they create are caused by social factors. See pages 320, 334.*

9.  c.  *The American population is getting older as the birth rate drops and life expectancy increases. As a result, a greater proportion of the population will be in the upper age brackets and thus the target of marketing efforts to gain their business. See page 341.*

10.  The disengagement view of aging is consistent with a functionalist theory because
   a.  it assumes a smooth, natural withdrawal of the old person from society.
   b.  most elderly people do not look forward to retirement.
   c.  it encourages the elderly to develop new activities, roles, and relationships.
   d.  interaction between the aging person and society increases.
   e.  society does not have to be concerned about the welfare of the elderly.

11.  Conflict theorists would be most interested in which of the following social trends of aging?
   a.  the wealth that the elderly have accumulated over the years
   b.  the high incidence of illness among the elderly
   c.  increased life expectancy due to medical technology
   d.  mandatory Social Security for all employees
   e.  the growing politicization of the elderly

12.  A group of friends, all born in 1950, meet again at their college reunion. They reminisce about their college experiences, rock music, protests over the war in Vietnam, and "the good old days." Which term would be helpful in understanding their experience as young adults during this turbulent time?
   a.  life course
   b.  cohort
   c.  age structure
   d.  stratification
   e.  age inequality

13.  Many elementary schools have tried to hire male teachers in the early grades, arguing that role models must be available to young boys if they are to consider such careers in the future. This argument is consistent with which psychological process by which children learn gender roles?
   a.  conditioning
   b.  self-definition
   c.  schooling
   d.  imitation
   e.  role-playing

---

10.  **a.** *The disengagement view of aging holds that old people withdraw from society and that society relieves them of their major family and work roles. This allows younger people to take on work roles and older people to gradually separate themselves from society until the time of their death. Because this slow transition is not disruptive to the stability of society, it is consistent with the functionalist view of social structure and social change. See page 333.*

11.  **e.** *The elderly are growing in number and power. As an age group they recognize society's ageist ideology. The elderly will demand a greater slice of the social benefits and will compete with other groups for the scarce resources of society. See page 334.*

12.  **b.** *A cohort is a category of people born during the same time period who thus experience history in a similar manner as they pass through the life course. The concept is important because it links individuals at a given life-course stage to a common history; the events that correspond to a particular cohort's life-course stage significantly shape the socialization experiences of that cohort. See page 336.*

13.  **d.** *Young children tend to imitate older children and adults of the same sex. Such persons serve as role models for positions the children may eventually assume. Lacking male teachers, young boys may not identify with the possible career choice of elementary-school teacher. See page 327.*

14.  Which of the following statements accurately
describes women's participation in the labor force?
   a.  The average woman spends about one-quarter
      of her working life bearing and raising children.
   b.  Women's participation in the labor force adds to
      the unemployment rate of men.
   c.  The median income of women is comparable to
      men's when qualifications are held constant.
   d.  Institutionalized sexism reduces women's
      training and motivation for prestigious jobs.
   e.  Jobs traditionally held by men are the only
      places for women to achieve.

15.  Conflict theorists could use cross-cultural evidence
to support their argument that equality between the
sexes depends on
   a.  increases in the economic contribution of
      women relative to men.
   b.  more social support for mother and wife roles.
   c.  attitude changes on the part of men in terms of
      recognizing women's contributions.
   d.  women and men having interchangeable tasks.
   e.  men experiencing some of women's roles.

16.  If we knew that a society values the aged, we would
guess that the society also
   a.  emphasizes religious values.
   b.  has a nuclear family form.
   c.  is preindustrial.
   d.  has diversified occupational opportunities.
   e.  has a longer life expectancy.

17.  Many members of the Supreme Court and the
Congress are over sixty-five. How would we explain the
important jobs they hold at this age?
   a.  Their high-status occupations and individual
      qualities exempt them from stereotypes about
      their age category.
   b.  Men are affected by age status as much as women.
   c.  These individuals are exceptional for their age in
      terms of both mental and physical health.
   d.  Age is related to economic power but not to
      political power.
   e.  These individuals entered their careers at an
      older age than do most people.

18.  Which of the following agents of socialization has
been among the most resistant to changing gender-role
stereotypes?
   a.  school sports
   b.  media advertising
   c.  school curricula
   d.  individual parents
   e.  employers

---

14.  **d.** *The employment patterns of our society have channeled women into particular occupations that are lower in status and salary than male-dominated jobs. Stereotypes about the kinds of jobs women should hold and the kinds of skills they are predisposed to possess have limited women's opportunities and motivation for higher education and job advancement. See page 328–329.*

15.  **a.** *As economic power is gained, social status rises. The general trend toward income equity between men and women in industrialized countries has brought with it a reduction of sexism. In general, women who work outside the home and earn an income have more power both in and beyond the home. See pages 319–320.*

16.  **c.** *In preindustrial societies, the aged are respected for their wisdom. As important sources of information,* they are socially useful. The extended family form, as well as the ownership and control of property by the older members of society, reinforces this powerful and honored position. See pages 332–333.*

17.  **a.** *These individuals have achieved personal power through their prestigious positions. The magnitude of this power overrides the ageism they might encounter based on their biological age. Positions such as these are not as closely linked to mandatory retirement or other age restrictions as other occupations. See pages 335–336.*

18.  **b.** *Mass media advertising has continued to portray women as sex objects or as witless housewives dedicated to trivial tasks. Even so-called liberated images of women usually involve only small variations on these basic themes. See pages 327–328.*

19. Many social scientists, like Margaret Mead, have conducted cross-cultural research on gender roles. Which of the following generalizations is *most often* supported by cross-cultural evidence?
    a. There is a general pattern of male dominance.
    b. Women are discouraged or prohibited from doing heavy work.
    c. Women are thought to have low or passive sexual appetites.
    d. As women take on men's jobs, their status rises.
    e. Gender roles are more equal in primitive and developing societies than is the case in industrialized societies.

20. Which of the following trends is *not* likely to contribute to more egalitarian gender roles in the future?
    a. a more diversified economy
    b. women adopting the characteristics and roles of males
    c. increasing sexual permissiveness
    d. greater educational achievement for women
    e. consciousness-raising efforts on the part of women and men

21. A significant change in the population structure of the United States is that
    a. we, as a people, are growing older.
    b. because of the birth rate, the nation is actually getting younger.
    c. the median age of the population has remained about the same for the last 100 years or so.
    d. the median age of the population has been going down for the last 100 years or so.
    e. more female babies are born than are male babies.

22. The main reason for the discrepancy between the quantity and quality of female and male employment is
    a. overt discrimination on the part of individual employers.
    b. the large portion of a woman's life devoted to pregnancy and childcare.
    c. the inability of women to make the hard decisions and take the tough action required at the upper levels of management.
    d. occupational segregation.
    e. the differences in men's and women's inborn abilities.

23. Which of the following would be an example of "false consciousness"?
    a. A man campaigns for women's liberation.
    b. A woman regards traditional gender roles as "natural" and does not question them.
    c. A woman claims that traditional gender roles have given women a false sense of inferiority.
    d. A group of women start a consciousness-raising group.
    e. A man thinks the government report on women's earnings is untrue.

---

19. **a.** *There is a general pattern of male dominance in societies, according to cross-cultural research. As a group, men are politically dominant in all societies. These unequal social arrangements are learned and vary from one society to another. See page 316.*

20. **b.** *To achieve sexual equality, both men's and women's personality characteristics and roles will have to change. Men and women will want to explore a wide variety of lifestyle options. Individual preferences and skills will take precedence over the ascribed characteristic of sex in allocating social roles. See page 331.*

21. **a.** *In the United States, increased life expectancy and a lower birth rate have resulted in an older population. The median age of the American population is increasing. See page 340.*

22. **d.** *Men and women are channeled into different jobs. This occupational segregation has limited women's participation in the labor force and kept their salaries significantly below those of men doing similar work. See pages 327, 329.*

23. **b.** *Karl Marx coined the term "false consciousness" to refer to the discrepancy between objective and subjective consciousness. Women who think they are in a position of equal or higher social value than men have not seen, in Marx's view, their own exploitation. See page 321.*

24. Which of the following statements implies an interactionist perspective on gender roles?
    a. A sex-based division of labor is useful for society because it allows individuals to specialize and thus perform their roles more efficiently.
    b. Traditional roles are damaging the economy, because they prevent half the population from making full use of its talents.
    c. By challenging traditional gender roles, the women's movement can bring about social change in this area.
    d. When conversing with women, men talk more and interrupt more, reinforcing their position of power.
    e. The gap between the earnings of men and women reveals discrimination on the part of men.

25. According to Parsons and Bales, the mother takes which role in the family?
    a. the instrumental role
    b. the maternal role
    c. the expressive role
    d. the matriarchal role
    e. the passive role

---

24. **d.** *Interactionist theorists look at the micro, or small, interactions between people. Our gender roles are learned through socialization, and we are often not aware of the powerful conditioning that leads us to play our roles differently as males and females. See page 326.*

25. **c.** *These two functionalist theorists see men in the instrumental role and women in the expressive role as far as the division of labor in the family. Men enact their role as breadwinners, while women support their husbands and children emotionally. See page 318.*

## A CASE STUDY

A recent letter to an advice-to-the-lovelorn columnist read like this:

Dear Blabby:

I am a fifty-eight-year-old widow and pretty well put together, if I do say so myself. After waiting around eighteen months for some eligible man to appear, I finally hooked Bill. We've been dating for about a year. Now Bill wants to take a winter cruise. He says he will foot the bill if we stay in one stateroom. The shipping line does not have rooms for singles, and there is a discount for couples as an incentive to go.

I say let's get married first and then cruise on our honeymoon. He says why should we get married at our age, especially since I'd lose my late husband's Social Security. He says it pays for us to stay single. But I worry about what my children and grandchildren will think if I go off on a cruise with a man. Are you going to tell me to "wake up and smell the coffee"? I've had enough years without a man and enough coffee klatches and bridge games with the girls to make me do anything to hold onto this guy!

1.   What elements of sexist ideology are present or might be inferred from what this woman has written?

2.   What are the role expectations for widows? For widowers? If the woman had been widowed at age thirty, would her story be different? Why?

3.  What does the grandparent role involve? Is it gender related or is it more neutral?

4.  If you were to rewrite this letter and the man's and woman's roles were reversed, or the couple were thirty years younger, what changes would you have to make in the story to make it believable?

5.  How are interpersonal relations affected by societal expectations? Why isn't this issue limited to the two people involved? In what ways are they running up against institutional sexism and ageism?

# Applying the Concepts

NAME

_____

COURSE/SECTION NUMBER

## APPLICATION EXERCISE ONE

Select three cartoons from the magazines you currently read, and attach them to your paper.

1.   Indicate the source of the cartoons and the kind of audience to which the magazines are directed.

2.   Identify the gender-role behavior shown in these cartoons. Choose one cartoon showing traditional male behavior, one showing female behavior, and one showing heterosexual couples. Try to indicate why the cartoons are funny in terms of the gender roles they portray.

3.   How important is popular culture, like cartoons, in supporting or changing gender-role expectations?

## APPLICATION EXERCISE TWO

NAME

COURSE/SECTION NUMBER

Think back to your own childhood and adolescence and the major influences in terms of your gender-role socialization. While socialization is a continuing process, we can often identify critical events that had an important impact on our learning. For example, a young man whose mother returns to work or leaves the family through divorce may take on roles traditionally associated with women, such as cooking and household management. For each of the major agents of socialization listed below, see if you can identify some of those critical events for you. If any of these were marked by rites of passage, note that as well.

family

school

peers

the media

## APPLICATION EXERCISE THREE

NAME

COURSE/SECTION NUMBER

The United States is said to have a "youth culture" that values young people and their roles and disregards the elderly. In this exercise you will be asked to think about an old-age culture.

1.  How are people socialized for old age? What reference groups and role models are available to us? Give some examples of how the media portray the elderly. What is the underlying message?

2.  Give at least one example from recent experience in which the age of an elderly person was seen as his or her master status. For example, an older person forgets to signal and other drivers yell out "You old codger, get off the road" or "Hey, lady, get back in your rocking chair." We can't imagine shouting the same insults to a young person, even though, statistically, young drivers are far more hazardous than elderly drivers.

3.    Many older people live in senior-citizen communities in Florida or the Sun Belt. Others have chosen to live in neighborhoods, condominiums, or apartments where most of the residents are the same age. In some cases, children are prohibited from such establishments. Assess the possible effects of this "age ghetto" form of living.

4.    The proportion of elderly persons (over sixty-five) in the total population will increase each year, as birth rates have declined and life expectancy has increased. The elderly constitute a powerful voting block and will lobby for issues that benefit them. What effect will this power base have on the youth culture?

# UNIT 4

# Social Institutions

# CHAPTER 13

# The Family

## Reviewing the Concepts

### LEARNING GOALS

*After studying this chapter, you should be able to:*

1. List the basic characteristics of the family.

2. Discuss the importance of marriage and kinship to the family.

3. Describe the functions the family performs for its members and for society.

4. Explain the conflict theorists' view of oppression within the family.

5. Present evidence of American family violence and the explanations for it.

6. Explain the universal presence of the incest taboo.

7. Describe some cross-cultural variations in families.

8. Using correct terminology, indicate the six dimensions sociologists use to analyze families.

9. Indicate the changes that have occurred in family patterns with increasing industrialization and urbanization.

10. Outline the functions and dysfunctions of the nuclear family form.

11. Characterize the typical American family and describe some of the variations in these patterns.

12. Discuss the importance of romantic love as a basis for marriage in Western culture.

13. Identify the factors involved in the homogamous mate-selection process observable in the United States.

14. Describe the difficulties family members may face in coping with divorce.

15. Specify four major factors related to marital breakdown.

16. Discuss the social problems faced by black families in the United States.

17. Summarize the controversy surrounding the abortion issue.

18. Evaluate the possible future of the family—including various marital forms, sexual patterns, and living arrangements—as revealed by the nine alternatives noted at the end of the chapter.

# IDENTIFYING KEY QUESTIONS AND THEMES

The family is the fundamental social unit in every society. While families take many different forms, sociologists have identified several common characteristics. A *family* is a relatively permanent group of people related by ancestry, marriage, or adoption, who live together, form an economic unit, and take care of their young. The family plays an integral part in linking individuals to society and ensuring continuation of the species through reproduction and socialization of children.

## Marriage and Kinship

*What are the basic responsibilities of family? Why is marriage important for society? What is the importance of kinship?*

Unlike other animals, human beings are not bound by a breeding season. The year-round sexual relations of human beings encourage mates to form stable, long-lasting bonds. The longer period of dependency of the human infant reinforces these bonds; for several years after birth, adult care-givers are essential to an infant's survival. Typically, women are assigned the child-rearing responsibilities while men are expected to take care of the family's economic activities. The result has been a universal pattern in which men and women establish permanent bonds maximizing the efficiency of their respective duties: hence, the family.

Most of us spend our lives in two families: the *family of orientation,* into which we are born, and the *family of procreation,* which we create ourselves. Families are formed through *marriage* — a socially approved mating arrangement between two or more people. Whatever form the marriage takes, it expresses the commitment of the marriage partners to one another and to society as a whole. Marriage also serves as the basis for a society's distinguishing *legitimate birth* from *illegitimate birth.* Children born to a mother and father who are not married are regarded as illegitimate and may receive different and unequal treatment from society.

The family is connected to other relatives, or kin. *Kinship* is a social network of people related by common ancestry, adoption, or marriage. Our kin connections are an important part of social organization. In traditional societies, contact with kin may be the basis for economic activities, a common household, and various kinds of help and emotional support. In modern societies, families may exist somewhat more separately from the kinship network, yet retain important emotional ties with some close relatives.

## The Family: A Functionalist View

*What are the basic functions of the family institution?*

Functionalist theorists are interested in the ways the family institution helps maintain the social order, as well as the survival of individuals. Research has identified several universal family functions, including (1) regulation of sexual behavior, (2) replacement of members, (3) socialization, (4) care and protection, (5) social placement, and (6) emotional support. While other social institutions can fulfill some of these functions, the family takes primary responsibility for them in every culture.

## The Family: A Conflict View

*Why are family relationships significant for other social relationships? What is the significance of gender-role inequalities within the family? How do conflict theorists explain violence among family members?*

Conflict theorists do not dispute the importance of the family's social functions; however, they do emphasize the fact that the family is the principal institution in which the dominance of men over women has been expressed. Marx's colleague, Engels, argued that the relationship between the spouses in marriage is the model on which other forms of oppresssion are based, particularly that between capitalist and worker. Indeed, analyses of wedding rituals and legal codes consistently reveal gender inequalities based on male privilege.

The extent of conflict in the family is evident in the astonishing amount of family violence that has been documented in the past two decades, particularly in American families. This violence may involve verbal and/or physical abuse, including murder, wife-beating, and child abuse. Sociologists suggest that the causes of this violence lie both within and outside the family. Because close relationships involve intense emotions, there are more occasions for tensions and conflict to arise. In addition, many people use the family as a place to vent frustrations: family members may carry problems from the outside back into the family, redirecting their aggression at those who will listen. Most significantly, violence is more likely to take place in an atmosphere that has traditionally emphasized male dominance and female subservience rather than equality. In view of the fact that one of its functions is the provision of care and protection for its members, the state of the modern family suggests it may be under more pressure than it can bear.

## Family Patterns

*What is the cross-cultural range of family variation? What is the significance of a universal incest taboo? How do sociologists classify family types?*

Cross-cultural research documents the wide range of marriage, family, and kinship patterns. Each culture endorses its patterns as the proper ones and may resist, or at least be concerned about, change. Yet the family, like any other social institution, must inevitably change over time.

Every society has an *incest taboo,* a powerful moral prohibition against sexual contact between certain categories of relatives. However, the taboo is applied to different relatives in different cultures. Cultural variations are also present in expectations about whom one will marry and why. In advanced industrial societies, it is generally assumed that marriage is founded on romantic love between the partners and that the choice of a mate should be left to the couple. In most traditional societies, however, marriage is regarded as a practical economic arrangement or a matter of family alliances. Norms dictate the choice of desirable mates and, in these societies, it is the parents who do the selecting. In addition, research reveals the existence of cultural differences on such matters as the role of the biological father in the family, acceptability of multiple spouses, premarital or extramarital sexual activity, children born outside the marital relationship, preferred age at marriage, and desirable level of involvement with kin.

The wide range of family patterns can be analyzed in terms of six basic dimensions.

(1) Depending on the number of partners, marriages may be either *monogamous,* involving one spouse of each sex, or *polygamous,* involving a spouse of one sex and two or more spouses of the opposite sex. In a polygamous union, if the husband has more than one wife, the marriage form is called *polygyny;* if the wife has more than one husband, it is called *polyandry.* Although most societies favor polygyny, the bulk of the world's population lives in societies that insist on monogamy.

(2) All societies set criteria for preferred marriage partners. Some social groups expect and require members to marry outside the group, a pattern called *exogamy.* Other groups prefer ingroup marriages, a pattern called *endogamy.* Endogamy is associated with minority groups, in part, as a means of maintaining their group solidarity.

(3) After marriage, couples in traditional societies often live either with or near the husband's relatives, a custom known as *patrilocal residence,* or with or near those of the wife, a custom known as *matrilocal residence.* In modern societies, they are likely to establish *neolocal residence,* a new residence apart from relatives.

(4) The patterns of authority between husband and wife may take the form of a *patriarchy,* favoring male authority, or a *matriarchy,* favoring female authority. Male dominance is the cross-cultural norm, although the newly emerging pattern is one of *egalitarian marriage,* in which husband and wife have more or less equal power in the family.

(5) Descent may be traced and property passed on in three basic ways. Under the *patrilineal system,* descent and inheritance pass through the male side of the family; under the *matrilineal system,* they pass through the female side. Under the *bilateral system,* which is more common in the United States, descent and inheritance are traced through both sides of the family.

(6) All family systems can be roughly categorized into one of two types. In the *extended family,* more than two generations of the same kinship line live together. The extended family is commonly found in traditional, preindustrial societies. The *nuclear family,* which

occurs in virtually all modern industrialized societies, consists only of the parents and any dependent children they may have.

## The Transformation of the Family

*What changes have occurred in family patterns with increasing industrialization?*

The larger social processes of industrialization have significantly changed family patterns. In general, people are focusing less on their family responsibilities and more on their desires for self-fulfillment as individuals. Current trends indicate a preference for the nuclear family, monogamy, neolocal residence, egalitarian authority, fewer kinship ties, and marriage based on the emotional commitment of two individuals.

There are several reasons why the nuclear family is better adapted to the conditions of the modern world: (1) life in an industrial society offers and requires geographic mobility; (2) a wide range of economic opportunities offers individuals the potential for greater social mobility; (3) formal organizations and institutions can assume many of the functions once performed by the extended family; (4) children become an economic liability rather than an asset, meaning that small families are advantageous; (5) the ascribed status derived from the family becomes less important than the achieved status of the individual members—individualism is an outstanding feature of industrial and postindustrial societies.

There are, however, a number of dysfunctions accompanying this preference for the nuclear family: marriage partners can turn only to one another for emotional and tangible support, so crises like prolonged illness or unemployment of a breadwinner are highly disruptive; expectations of romantic love may be unrealistic, leading to disenchantment and unhappiness; finally, there are no socially approved roles for elderly family members.

## Marriage and Family in America

*What is the American family pattern? How does romantic love influence American mate selection? What are the features of courtship in the United States? How do sociologists explain the relatively high rate of marital dissolution?*

The "typical" American family is monogamous, endogamous, neolocal, increasingly egalitarian, bilateral, and nuclear. Of course, there are many ethnic and social-class variations on this pattern.

The basis for marriage in American society and other industrialized nations is supposed to be romantic love. The importance of romantic love and, in fact, the ways one recognizes and experiences it are learned through socialization. Agents of socialization, particularly the mass media, emphasize the importance of romantic love as a basis for marriage.

The emphasis on romantic love is consistent with the preference for a nuclear family system. Romantic love helps young people (1) transfer loyalties from their families of orientation to one another and to the new family they will become. It also serves as (2) an incentive to marry in a society that does not require it. Additionally, romantic love provides the couple with (3) emotional support in overcoming the difficulties they will face in establishing a life of their own without significant kin assistance.

The courtship system in the United States uses the practice of dating for the selection of a mate. Although Americans have a great deal of personal freedom in choosing a marriage partner, probably more so than any other society, the process is not random. In general, the American mate-selection process produces *homogamy,* marriage between partners who share similar social characteristics. These characteristics include (1) age, (2) social class, (3) religion, (4) education, (5) racial and ethnic background, and (6) propinquity.

The divorce rate in the United States is believed to be the highest in the world. Divorce constitutes official recognition that a marriage has failed. Divorced individuals may face social stigma, economic difficulties, emotional problems, and intense concerns for the well-being of their offspring. Although children are present in over 70 percent of the families that break up through divorce, evidence suggests that the experience of divorce may be less traumatic for children than remaining in a conflict-ridden home. Unfortunately, economic difficulties for divorced women and children are increasing, since ex-wives often do not receive alimony at all and collect only a fraction of the necessary child support.

The social characteristics of divorce-prone couples are well-established. In general, divorces are more common among urban couples, those who marry very young, have short engagements, and whose friends and relatives disapprove of the marriage. Statistics also indicate that the greater a wife's ability to support herself, the more likely she is to leave an unhappy marriage; that partners who have been married before are more likely to become involved in subsequent divorce; and that most divorces take place early in the marriage—half within the first seven years—and the longer a marriage has lasted, the less likely it is to end in divorce.

Beyond these individual factors, certain social factors are related to marital breakdown. As noted, (1) the nuclear family is highly vulnerable to stress, both from without and within; (2) the emphasis on romantic love as the basis for marriage may lead to the conviction that fading romantic love is a sufficient basis for divorce; (3) the traditional division of labor between a male breadwinner and a female housekeeper and child-rearer is changing dramatically—womens' growing economic independence makes it easier for them to divorce their mates, and it challenges the relationship on which the nuclear family has been based; finally, (4) increasing sexual permissiveness in conjunction with the development and widespread availability of contraceptives facilitates the pursuit of relationships outside of marriage for recreational purposes, rather than simply for reproduction.

## Current Issues

*How has the black family fared in recent years? How do Americans feel about the abortion debate?*

Although a third of the black population has now entered the middle class, the plight of those who remain trapped in the ghetto has become more acute in the past two decades. Poor black families face a number of social problems, including a high rate of illegitimate births, an increasing number of single-parent households (usually female-headed), and living conditions below the poverty line. These families are isolated from middle-class families, black and white, and have little opportunity to break free of the self-perpetuating desolation of the ghetto. Coupled with high rates of unemployment and persistent racial discrimination, the problems repeat themselves in succeeding generations and have worsened in recent years. Many leaders now recognize that any solutions de-

pend on programs and changes based not only on government intervention but also on the involvement and commitment of the black community.

One in four pregnancies in America is terminated by abortion, and in some areas the rates are much higher. This volatile political issue brings together personal, moral, and religious values with ambiguous evidence about, and much controversy over, the human status of the fetus. Attitudes differ about the rights of the unborn versus the right of women to control their own bodies, as well as the rights and responsibilities of biological fathers. New medical technology, which makes it possible to keep fetuses alive earlier in the course of pregnancy but also makes it safer for women to wait longer to have an abortion, compounds the issue's complexities. Not surprisingly, opinion polls show public confusion over the question of abortion, with one survey indicating that 40 percent of Americans wonder whether their own position on abortion is right—regardless of whether they are "prolife" or "prochoice." In any case, the abortion rate and surrounding debate can be understood only in the context of the social changes affecting many aspects of American life.

## The Future of the Family

*What are the current trends in American family life? What are some of the emerging alternatives to the nuclear family?*

Demographics show that the traditional American family with male breadwinner, female housekeeper, and dependent children in the home is no longer the prevailing family pattern in the United States. In fact, it exists in fewer than one of every ten households in America. The sharp increase in the number of women in the work force is changing not only the American economy but the American family as well. By looking at current trends and emerging alternatives, we gain important insights into the future of the American family. The single-parent family is becoming the most common alternative to the nuclear unit, with most households headed by young, low-income, single mothers. The increased rate of divorce and growing number of people who marry more than once (serial monogamy) will result in a corresponding rise in reconstituted families comprised of children from spouses' previous marriages. Other changes in the established nuclear family pattern include cohabitation, or "living together" before or instead of marriage—a relatively common type of arrangement today, particularly among young people; communal living; childless couples; "open" marriage, which may involve sexual exchange of partners ("swinging"); gay couples and gay-parent families; and an increasing number of people who prefer to remain single. Because the United States is a pluralistic society with an emphasis on individual choice, it is likely that while Americans will explore a range of alternative lifestyles, they will continue to marry and endorse the nuclear family form.

## DEFINING CORE CONCEPTS

*After studying the chapter, write a sociological definition in your own words for the following core concepts. Then give an example from your own experience to illustrate your definition. Refer to the chapter to check your work.*

| *Core Concept* | *Sociological Definition* | *Personal Illustration* |
|---|---|---|
| bilateral system | | |
| egalitarian marriage | | |
| endogamy/exogamy | | |
| extended family/ nuclear family | | |
| family | | |

| Core Concept | Sociological Definition | Personal Illustration |
|---|---|---|
| family of orientation/<br>    family of procreation | | |
| homogamy | | |
| incest taboo | | |
| kinship | | |
| legitimate birth/<br>    illegitimate birth | | |
| marriage | | |
| matriarchy/patriarchy | | |

| *Core Concept* | *Sociological Definition* | *Personal Illustration* |
| --- | --- | --- |
| matrilineal system/<br>  patrilineal system | | |
| matrilocal residence/<br>  patrilocal residence | | |
| monogamy | | |
| neolocal residence | | |
| polyandry/polygamy | | |

## PUTTING IDEAS TOGETHER

Family relationships are important both to individuals and to the larger society. The process of industrialization is associated with a major, global change in family patterns. As in other industrialized societies, Americans have witnessed the emergence of a pluralistic pattern of family types in response to a rapidly changing economy.

## The Transformation of the Family

| Characteristics of the preindustrial family | Characteristics of the industrial family | Factors underlying the shift |
| --- | --- | --- |
| extended family | nuclear family | a fundamental shift in emphasis from kinship responsibilities to individual self-fulfillment; and the suitability of the nuclear family to rapidly changing modern society |
| kinship is the basis for social status | individual achievement is the basis for social status | ascribed characteristics of sex and family name are less important; achieved statuses are more important |
| low geographic mobility | high geographic mobility | jobs often require relocation |
| patrilocal residence* | neolocal residence | the couple forms a unit distinct from that of the parents |
| patriarchal authority* | egalitarian authority | gender roles are more egalitarian |
| patrilineal inheritance* | bilateral inheritance | children of both sexes are more equally valued |

*Male-dominated families are the norm in nearly all societies; in a few cases, female-dominated families reverse the above patterns.

A sociological study of the family must take into account a given society's patterns of courtship, marriage, and marital breakdown. Despite growing pressures both from without and within, the institution of the family remains the fundamental social unit in every society. However, the modern family is a different group, formed in a different way, on the basis of different assumptions than the traditional family.

## The Pattern of Family Formation

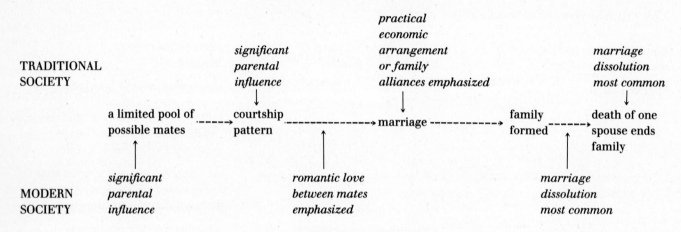

# Testing the Concepts

## MULTIPLE-CHOICE QUESTIONS

*After studying the chapter, try to answer each of the twenty-five questions below. Mark the alternative you think is correct; then look at the correct answer and the explanation provided at the bottom of the page. Try to state why the other alternatives are incorrect, and check your understanding of the correct answer.*

1. The family's regulation of sexual behavior is a function
   a. useful only in modern society.
   b. specifying who may mate with whom and under what circumstances.
   c. useful primarily in early societies lacking laws to protect the rights of women and children.
   d. made fundamentally obsolete by the sexual revolution.
   e. accomplished by the incest taboo in our society.

2. Which of the following is an example of exogamy?
   a. In Australia, in two neighboring tribes, a member of one tribe may only marry a member of another tribe.
   b. Two people get married, divorce, and marry each other again.
   c. An Asian society assumes that parents will choose their children's mates.

   d. American teenagers go out on dates and generally conduct their courtship away from home.
   e. At the turn of the century, Mormon men were allowed to have, and expected to have, several wives.

3. The text outlines changes in the family as a result of increasing industrialization. Provision of which of the following functions of the family has become more important for the *nuclear family* as a result of these changes?
   a. educating the young
   b. maintaining intergenerational family ties
   c. providing continuity and security
   d. caretaking of the elderly
   e. determining social-class standing

4. Among poor black families, half of all births are illegitimate; half of all families are headed by one parent; half of all births are to teen mothers; half of all children live in poverty. How do sociologists explain this perilous situation?
   a. lack of individual initiative
   b. heavy use of drugs and alcohol
   c. a self-perpetuating underclass of the educationally and economically disadvantaged
   d. an easier life on welfare
   e. discrimination that has kept all black families in the lower-class ghettos

---

1. **b.** *There is considerable cultural variation in sexual behavior. The formation of a family, according to societal rules, indicates special relationships between people related by blood or marriage. All cultures have norms about sexual activity within the family. Far from being a random occurrence, sexual behavior is regulated within the family unit to maintain social order. See page 349.*

2. **a.** *Exogamy means marrying outside one's group. These tribes have a norm for exogamy, perhaps as a means to build alliances by exchanging kin through marriage. See page 354.*

3. **c.** *The number of functions performed by the family has declined, but the family as a source of security and continuity has become critical in industrial societies. Some sociologists argue that the family is more important today, because it provides security in an increasingly complex world. See pages 350, 356.*

4. **c.** *While some black families have stable employment and middle- and upper-class incomes, many are trapped in a cycle of unemployment or underemployment and a lack of education that repeats itself with each generation. Sociologists look to larger societal forces rather than to the characteristics of individuals to explain why poor black families are in peril. See page 363.*

5. Below is a list of common assumptions about marriage in the United States. Which assumption is best supported by evidence from social science research?
    a. Marriages are not arranged by parents and thus people randomly pick their spouses in ways sociologists cannot accurately predict.
    b. Marriage is happiest when children are present.
    c. Marital infidelity (sex outside marriage) is a rare behavior because of our societal value on monogamy.
    d. Most men and women would like to marry sometime during their lives.
    e. The personal-choice method of mate selection allows people to pick someone they like and thus reduces the probability of divorce.

6. A family, as inclusively defined in your text, consists of all the following *except*
    a. adult members who assume responsibility for their offspring.
    b. a monogamous, endogamous, nuclear, neolocal, bilateral pattern.
    c. a group of people who are related to one another.
    d. a relatively permanent group of people who live together.
    e. members who form an economic unit for the consumption of goods and services.

7. A social network of people related by common ancestry, adoption, or marriage is called
    a. a family.
    b. a community.
    c. kinship.
    d. siblings.
    e. a family of orientation.

8. From a sociological viewpoint, romantic love as a part of mate selection might be considered
    a. old-fashioned in today's world because it emphasizes the needs of the individual over the couple.
    b. a cause of strain and disruption to an extended family system.
    c. the one factor of stability in the uncertain setting of the medieval peasant's family life.
    d. a way to ensure endogamy and a patrilocal pattern.
    e. particularly functional in a hunting and gathering society.

9. One likely explanation for the universal presence of the incest taboo is that it promotes some amount of
    a. exogamy.
    b. polygamy.
    c. egalitarianism.
    d. assimilation.
    e. monogamy.

10. Cross-cultural research on the family shows the universality of

---

5. **d.** *Americans are very committed to marriage. The proportion of Americans who marry sometime during their lifetime is one of the highest in the world. See page 369.*

6. **b.** *Although the family system in the United States is typically monogamous, endogamous, nuclear, neolocal, and bilateral, this pattern is not seen in most other cultures in the world. See pages 348, 358.*

7. **c.** *Kinship is the larger group of people to whom one is related and with whom one has reciprocal rights and responsibilities. See page 349.*

8. **b.** *When mate selection is based on romantic attraction, the influence of parents and other kin is* reduced. *Romantic love focuses on the partner one will marry, not on his or her family. See pages 357, 359.*

9. **a.** *Exogamy is marriage outside one's group. In general, immediate family members are discouraged or prohibited from marrying one another by the incest taboo, which protects against the jealous rivalries that might result. See pages 352, 354.*

10. **b.** *All societies have a marriage institution that binds individuals to the larger society. Marriage usually involves some culturally prescribed ritual, such as a wedding by a religious official, which marks social approval of the union of people to form a family unit. See page 349.*

a. a preference for mates of much the same age.

b. a socially approved mating arrangement between two or more people.

c. the expectation that biological fathers are responsible for the economic well-being of their children.

d. disapproval of extramarital sexual contacts.

e. a preference for monogamy.

11.  The text describes trends and alternatives for future family patterns. Which of the following lifestyles is most commonly practiced in the United States?

a. communal living

b. remaining single

c. open marriage

d. serial monogamy

e. remaining childless

12.  Which one of the following statements accurately describes the abortion dilemma in the United States?

a. The controversy temporarily subsided in 1973 with the Supreme Court's decision in favor of a woman's right to abortion.

b. New medical technology, making it possible to keep fetuses alive earlier in the course of pregnancy, has helped clarify the abortion issue.

c. Opinion polls show confusion on the part of the public over the abortion issue.

d. The decreased use of abortion as a means of

after-the-fact birth control is one hopeful sign amid all the controversy.

e. About one in eight pregnancies is now terminated through abortion.

13.  "Open" marriage and cohabitation, perhaps as a prelude to marriage,

a. permit greater personal freedom while retaining mutual commitment.

b. undermine marriage as a desirable lifestyle.

c. provide a greater opportunity for legal sexual relationships.

d. change patterns of mate selection and lower the divorce rate.

e. are consistent with traditional religious values.

14.  Mork and Mindy got married and, according to custom, moved in with her family. Soon after the marriage, Mork's dad died, leaving Mork all his estate and, according to custom, leaving nothing to Mork's sister, Pork. The couple was happily married and, according to custom, Mindy took another husband, Windy. This family can be described as

a. monogamous, patrilineal, patrilocal.

b. patrilocal, nuclear, polygamous.

c. extended, neolocal, matrilineal.

d. matrilocal, patrilineal, polyandrous.

e. crazy.

---

11.  **d.** *Even after divorce, people are eager to marry again. In fact, the marriage rate for divorced people is higher at all ages than the rate for single or widowed persons. Divorce is on the rise, so a pattern of serial monogamy is likely to be the norm. See page 367.*

12.  **c.** *Far from ending the controversy over abortion, the Supreme Court decision inflamed it. New medical technology has only complicated the picture. About one in every four pregnancies in America is now terminated by abortion, a grim reminder that abortion is being used as a means of after-the-fact birth control. At the root of the controversy is a basic value judgment about the human status of the fetus. Polls indicate that the American public wonders whether their own position on*

abortion is right—regardless of whether they are "prolife" or "prochoice."

13.  **a.** *Some aspects of monogamous marriage have not been satisfying to many Americans. Variations in living arrangements are aimed at retaining the security and commitment associated with monogamous relationships while, for example, making women's and men's roles more satisfying, clarifying marital obligations, and expanding sexual boundaries along mutually satisfactory lines. See pages 367–368.*

14.  **d.** *The couple's residence with the wife's family is matrilocal; inheritance through the male line is patrilineal; marriage involving one wife and more than one husband is polyandrous. See pages 354–355.*

15. The extended family system
    a. tends to be dysfunctional in traditional societies.
    b. excludes old people due to its reliance on a system of neolocal residence.
    c. encourages incest.
    d. can impede an individual's social mobility.
    e. is unstable in times of crisis.

16. Each of the following is a major cause of marital breakdown in the United States, *except*
    a. stress on the nuclear family
    b. couples' decisions to have smaller families
    c. the changing role of women
    d. sexual permissiveness
    e. the fading of romantic love

17. According to conflict theorists, the significance of the relationship between spouses is that it
    a. is the model on which other forms of oppression are based, such as the relationship between capitalist and worker.
    b. provides a refuge from the outside world.
    c. allows women a domain of their own and thus enhances their power.
    d. emphasizes the important values of love and commitment.
    e. provides for legitimate children.

18. Which of the following statements about courtship and marriage in the United States is best supported by research?
    a. Most Americans choose mates on the basis of certain personality characteristics.
    b. Parental involvement is considered appropriate at the pre-engagement stage.
    c. The courtship system leads to random pairing of men and women.
    d. The practice of dating has little relationship to the reality of marriage.
    e. The mate-selection process is homogamous.

19. The nuclear family form associated with industrialization is dysfunctional with regard to
    a. job demands in the modern workplace.
    b. modern society's emphasis on achieved statuses.
    c. a crisis such as a death in the family or chronic unemployment.
    d. intimacy within the nuclear family.
    e. keeping the family small.

20. According to the textbook, which of the following trends in the American family is *not* expected to increase significantly in the next decade?
    a. women entering the work force
    b. young people postponing marriage
    c. smaller family size
    d. the number of illegitimate births
    e. participation in a communal lifestyle

---

15. **d.** *The extended family provides an individual with an initial social-class position. In societies where the extended family system is strong, individuals tend to adhere to their original class position and to maintain kin obligations, which tie them to a particular geographic area as well as to particular occupations. Thus, an individual's potential mobility is constrained by the original kinship bond. See page 356.*

16. **b.** *Sociologists cite many causes for the collapse of modern American marriages. Because children have become an economic liability rather than an asset, couples' decisions to limit family size is not likely to be a major source of marital discord. See pages 357, 362–363.*

17. **a.** *Family relationships are the basis for other relationships of unequal power, according to Marx and Engels. They noted the unequal distribution of power in the family. See pages 350–351.*

18. **e.** *Americans tend to marry people like themselves who share major social characteristics such as religion, racial and ethnic background, social class, education, and age. See page 360.*

19. **c.** *Nuclear families are often isolated from kin and must weather crises without significant help. Jobs pull families apart geographically and may lead to a dissolution of the bonds of shared experience. The amount of assistance a family can expect in times of trouble may be limited. See page 357.*

20. **e.** *The proportion of Americans who are choosing a communal lifestyle is small. Communal living gained in popularity in the 1960s, but participation has since leveled off; nevertheless, communes certainly represent an alternative family system. See page 368.*

21. The fact that human sexual relations are not restricted to a brief breeding season
   a. encourages reproduction.
   b. offers an incentive for people to change relationships frequently.
   c. encourages the formation of stable, long-lasting bonds between mates.
   d. is biologically significant, but not sociologically relevant.
   e. encourages promiscuity and sexual variety.

22. The Toda of India practice female infanticide. It is not surprising, therefore, to learn that their society has the custom of
   a. polygamy.
   b. polyandry.
   c. exogamy.
   d. endogamy.
   e. homogamy.

23. In the United States, the fastest-growing alternative to the nuclear family unit is the single-parent family. What is one of the characteristics of this family form?
   a. Ex-spouses share custody of children in most cases.
   b. Men provide alimony to their former wives in most cases.
   c. Women remarry very quickly, more so than their ex-husbands.
   d. Most ex-spouses didn't want to get married in the first place, but did want to have children.

   e. Women and children experience economic hardship, while men's incomes rise after the divorce.

24. On the basis of what we know about divorce-prone partners, which of the following marriages would you consider most likely to end in divorce?
   a. Tommy and Julie, both college graduates from middle-class backgrounds, get married.
   b. Phil and Mary, a rural couple, marry after four years of courtship; he is a Methodist and she is an Episcopalian.
   c. David and Jenny, both teenagers, fall deeply in love and marry four months later.
   d. Bob and Linda, a middle-aged couple, are approaching their twenty-seventh year of marriage.
   e. Martha and Bruce, an orthodox Jewish couple, have been married one year.

25. Which of the following statements is accurate about the growing number of people who choose to remain single?
   a. Most single people are homosexual.
   b. Single people indicate they have not yet found the "right partner."
   c. About 10 percent of the population will choose a permanent single lifestyle.
   d. Most single people have been divorced and have a negative view of marriage.
   e. Single people who cohabit generally follow a promiscuous lifestyle.

---

21.  **c.** *The mating season of many animals occurs at a fixed time during the year. Males and females may pair for that time period only. Humans have the potential to mate year round. This fact, coupled with the long period of gestation and infant dependency, encourages more permanent relationships. See page 348.*

22.  **b.** *The shortage of females created by infanticide would make it impossible for every man to have one wife. Thus women have more than one husband, a practice called polyandry. See page 354.*

23.  **e.** *The incomes of divorced women with dependent children drop dramatically when they set up their own households. Alimony is rare and even court-ordered child support is not always paid. Women whose work*

*skills and experience have been limited to homemaking and child-rearing are often at a particular disadvantage in terms of earning enough money to support their families. Men's incomes rise as a result of divorce. See page 361.*

24.  **c.** *In U.S. culture, two of the best predictors of divorce are age at marriage and length of courtship. Couples who marry very young and whose courtship is brief are more likely to get divorced. See pages 361–362.*

25.  **c.** *There is likely to be an increase in the number of people who remain single throughout life, from about 5 percent now to about 10 percent or more by the end of the century. See page 369.*

# A CASE STUDY

NAME

COURSE/SECTION NUMBER

Jack and Liz are both college graduates with degrees in business. They met at State University and were married after graduation. Jack is an East Coast city boy, with a strong Catholic background. Liz comes from a small family living in a suburban area in the Midwest. Now their jobs have taken them to the West Coast. After two years of marriage, Jack and Liz are beginning to have frequent arguments and have resorted to physical as well as verbal attacks on one another in the heat of battle. Both are worried about the depth of their anger, and fear one may become violent enough to cause serious physical harm to the other. Jack and Liz find their present circumstances especially shocking, because during their six-month courtship, they never even fought, much less hit one another or threw objects as they do now. Finally, they seek the help of a counselor and tell her they no longer have feelings of love for one another and wish to get a divorce.

1.    What features of the nuclear family make situations like this most likely?

2.    What features of their mate-selection process may be influencing (but not necessarily causing) the troubles this couple is now experiencing?

3.    To what degree do Jack and Liz have the characteristics of divorce-prone people? What about violence-prone people?

4.    What functions could their families of orientation perform?

# Applying the Concepts

NAME
_____

COURSE/SECTION  NUMBER

## APPLICATION  EXERCISE  ONE

Starting with yourself, make a family tree going back to your great-grandparents. You may use real or fictitious names as you prefer. Under these names, write relatives' primary occupation during most of their lifetime, their religion, ethnicity/race, and the number of children they had. Comment on the amount of social mobility in your family and the evidence for endogamy or exogamy. (If you cannot construct a tree that includes great-grandparents, explain some of the social reasons for the omissions.)

## APPLICATION EXERCISE TWO

We know, statistically, that the so-called normal American family pattern is by no means predominant. That is, most families do not have both parents pesent, with children at home, a male breadwinner, and a female housekeeper not employed outside the home. Yet, to some degree, alternatives to the "normal" family are considered deviant. From among the people you know or can be introduced to, select *one* of the following alternative family forms:

a single person, committed to that lifestyle
a childless couple
a cohabiting couple
a single parent, male or female, with children at home
a divorced couple with joint custody of children
a couple in an open marriage with a nonmonogamous pattern of sexuality
a person who was divorced after many years of marriage
a couple in which the woman is at least ten years older than the man
a cohabiting homosexual couple
a person who has been married three or more times

Set up an interview. Ask those involved how they arrived at this lifestyle, how they feel about it, and what reactions they have received from others. Comment on whether they see themselves as deviant. Why or why not? Can you see yourself in this lifestyle?

## APPLICATION EXERCISE THREE

NAME

COURSE/SECTION NUMBER

Popular culture often reflects the attitudes of the "average" American about family life. Examine examples of this popular culture to determine their message.

1.   Listen to popular songs on the radio about romantic love, and find one with a message about how women should act when in love. Now find an example for men and one for heterosexual couples. What themes are present in these three songs? How does socialization occur through popular culture? How do the media contribute to socialization?

2.     Watch television and select programs that show different types of family life. You might want to try a "model" family, like the one depicted on "The Cosby Show" or "Family Ties," or a new family form (e.g., "One Day at a Time," "The Brady Bunch"). Or, look at reruns of traditional families such as those on "Father Knows Best," "Leave it to Beaver," and "The Donna Reed Show." Think, too, about the soap-opera families on "Dallas" and "Dynasty." Try to pick an example of what seems to be a "good" family and an example of an unhappy family or one that we should pity or reject. Describe the two families. Be as specific as possible about the roles shown for the family members.

3.     If possible, interview a parent or grandparent, asking about the popular culture during their courtship. Ask for examples of songs that showed romantic love and for radio or television programs that portrayed family life. Can you make any conclusions about the contrast between the era in which they grew up and were socialized and your own experience?

# CHAPTER 14

# Education

## Reviewing the Concepts

### LEARNING GOALS

*After studying this chapter, you should be able to:*

1. Describe how education has changed with the rise of industrialism in the United States.

2. Contrast the characteristics of American education with the educational systems in other industrialized nations; discuss the commitment to mass education in the United States, the utilitarian emphasis of education in the United States, and community control of schools in the United States.

3. Present the functionalist view of the purposes of education.

4. Indicate some of the latent functions of education.

5. Present a conflict view of education and the influence of schooling on social mobility.

6. Describe schools as formal, bureaucratic organizations.

7. Assess the functions and dysfunctions of competitiveness in schools.

8. Explain how the self-fulfilling prophecy operates in schools.

9. Summarize the connection between education and social inequality.

10. Discuss the relationship between class, race, and educational achievement; explain which factors affect students' chances of educational success.

11. Evaluate competing positions on the use of IQ tests to assess students from diverse racial, ethnic, and class backgrounds.

12. Assess the equality of educational opportunity in the United States on the basis of the degree of segregation of the schools.

13. Indicate the findings of the Coleman report.

14. Evaluate the effectiveness of busing as a means to correct racial imbalances within school systems.

15. Present Jencks's view of the effectiveness of education as a way to reduce social inequality.

16. Summarize the major criticism leveled against the American educational system and the basic strategies designed to remedy declining academic standards.

17. List the distinguishing features of a profession, and describe the effect of increasing professionalization on the educational system.

18. Present Randall Collins's argument regarding the United States as a "credential society" and the implications for education and society in general.

# IDENTIFYING KEY QUESTIONS AND THEMES

The educational institution today is substantially changed from that found in preindustrial societies. With the rise of industrialization, schooling has come to be viewed as a social necessity. Many of the new economic roles available today require specialized knowledge and skills. The general information explosion along with the expectation of an educated populace has resulted in the formalization of education as a central social institution in all industrialized societies. Sociologists define *education* as the systematic, formalized transmission of knowledge, skills, and values. Education figures prominently in American life and is the largest single industry in the United States.

## Characteristics of American Education

*What is the basis for America's commitment to mass education? What is the significance of the utilitarian emphasis in schools? How does the American system of community control differ from other societies' management of schools?*

American education has several characteristics that distinguish it from education in other societies. In the United States, it is taken for granted that everyone has a basic right to at least some kind of formal education and that this schooling should be free and compulsory. In other societies, education is a privilege available to a small segment of the population or, if state-supported, may be limited to the first few grades. The extension of educational opportunities within the United States has resulted in a lowering of academic standards, compared to those of other industrialized countries. In Britain, France, and Japan, for example, rigorous examinations separate students; educational privileges are granted only to those at the top. The American system entitling every child to twelve years of education is based on the belief that public education benefits the entire society.

Not only is education considered valuable in and of itself, but it is used as a means to address a variety of social goals. Since the nineteenth century, American schools have been oriented toward serving a wide range of utilitarian purposes. For example, schools have been asked to "Americanize" immigrants; provide compensatory help for the poor; and solve various social problems such as drug addiction, teenage pregnancy, and a high rate of car accidents among youth. There is little evidence that these programs have had much effect. Yet the American faith in education persists.

In most other countries, education is regulated by the national government. In the United States, however, the schools are regarded as the concern of the community they serve, and decisions about the schools are made by local school boards and residents. One consequence of local control is the remarkable diversity in what is taught; another result is differences in educational expenditures among communities, indicating unequal educational opportunities.

## Education: A Functionalist View

*What are the manifest and latent functions of education?*

The functionalist perspective explains the central importance of the schools by emphasizing the part they play in maintaining the social order as a whole. Several distinct functions of education can be identified.

(1) Schools assist with cultural transmission, providing students with the knowledge, skills, and values deemed important by their society.

(2) Education can further social integration, bringing young members of various subcultures into a common culture, contributing to a relatively homogeneous society with shared values.

(3) Schools assist students with their personal development and occupational choices. The higher an individual's level of education, the more likely he or she is to have a broad and tolerant world view.

(4) Education connects with the economic order by screening and selecting students for the range of available occupations. The training an individual receives in school provides the credentials needed to obtain employment, which is directly linked to future life chances.

(5) Educational institutions serve an innovative function, as they add to the cultural heritage by developing new knowledge and skills. At the college level, faculty engage in *basic research*—systematic inquiry that is concerned with establishing new knowledge. *Applied research*—systematic inquiry that tries to find practical uses for existing knowledge—is increasingly pursued outside the college context.

(6) In addition to these **manifest functions**— consequences that are recognized and intended, education also has **latent functions**—consequences that are generally unrecognized and unintended. For example, schools serve as "babysitting" agencies; promote the formation of youth cultures; act as a "marriage market" for college students looking for mates; and teach habits such as punctuality and obedience to authority that will be helpful as students take on work roles.

## Education: A Conflict View

*What is the relationship between education and social mobility?*

The conflict perspective focuses on the ways different social groups use education as a means of getting or keeping power, wealth, and prestige. Schooling is an important influence on **social mobility,** or movement from one status to another. Students (and their parents) compete for the best educational credentials that are crucial to getting the best jobs.

Conflict theorists emphasize that the schools do not so much create the existing class system as reproduce and legitimate it. In all societies, there is a direct correlation between the social class of the parents and the educational achievement of their children. Children of the upper and middle classes are far more likely to continue their education at the college and university level. Since students start school with different advantages and are tracked into different curricula and career paths that maintain those advantages, the educational system is not really fair at all.

## Inside the School

*In what ways are schools bureaucratic organizations? What are the consequences of competition within the school? How is the self-fulfilling prophecy part of schooling?*

Every school is a miniature social system with its own statuses and roles, subcultures and cliques, traditions and values. One of the most obvious features of the school is that it is a bureaucracy with rationalized procedures, a leadership hierarchy, and an emphasis on uniform procedures to attain efficiency. As a result of this bureaucrati-zation, schools are necessarily quite regimented, and individuals must adapt to administrative needs. Schools emphasize obedience, conformity, and regimentation, especially in the early grades, to keep things running smoothly. Like all formal organizations, the school contains many informal groups. Peer groups and cliques are especially important because they may emphasize norms and values consistent with, or in opposition to, the goals of the school. Usually these peer groups do not value academic goals.

The educational system emphasizes competition as appropriate preparation for economic roles in a capitalist society. Unlike students in other countries, American pupils compete with one another for better grades. Intense competition has been shown to be dysfunctional, as students concentrate on strategies to get good grades, rather than on acquiring knowledge.

The result of academic competition is that some students are identified as successful, and others as failures. These labels can have an important impact on their later academic careers. The labeling process may involve a **self-fulfilling prophecy**—a prediction that leads to behavior that makes the prediction come true. Students come to accept the expectations of their teachers or peers and behave accordingly. Rosenthal's classic experiment shows that teachers' expectations for a child, even when based on bogus information, result in different treatment and, as a result, different academic achievement. School policies regarding grading, tracking students according to their perceived ability levels, and counseling students toward certain vocational paths, all supplement the self-fulfilling prophecy and reinforce social-class distinctions.

## Social Inequality and the Schools

*How do schools perpetuate social-class differences and privileges? What is the controversy surrounding IQ scores?*

People do not have equal opportunity to achieve educational success. Their educational opportunities are strongly influenced by the social class of the family into which they were born. By reinforcing the advantages that some people already have over others because of an accident of birth, schools preserve social inequalities. Many sociologists have researched the connection between social class and educational achievement, finding striking differences in the educational achievement of pupils of the same intelligence level, depending on social class. These important class differences can be explained by several different factors: (1) the cost of education; (2) family expectations for students' achievement; (3) cultural background, which prepares students differently for school; (4) language problems; (5) teacher attitudes toward nonconforming students; (6) the labeling of a child as dull or bright, which may result in a self-fulfilling prophecy about how much education the child should seek; and (7) peer-group influence.

Educational achievement is highly correlated with intelligence as measured on IQ tests. However, IQ scores are stongly influenced by social-class background so that, once again, it is class (not measured intelligence) that is the critical factor. Lower-class whites and members of disadvantaged minority groups perform poorly on IQ tests compared to middle- and upper-class whites. The issue of race and intelligence became especially controversial when Jensen implied that the overall differences in blacks' and whites' IQs could be partially explained by hereditary factors—a view that has met with strong criticism on many fronts. Although the exact nature of "intelligence" is still not known, it is generally agreed that intelligence involves two factors: an innate, inherited element that sets a limit on a person's intellectual potential, and a learned, environmental element that determines how far that potential will be fulfilled. IQ tests measure knowledge in a limited range of fields; thus they are not so much a test of intelligence as a test of academic aptitude. Because IQ tests use language and assume some background knowledge on the part of the pupil, they are "culture-bound." Children raised in a culture or subculture other than that of white middle-class America are at a disadvantage in having had little exposure to the knowledge, skills, and experience demanded by these tests. In short, racial and social-class differences on IQ tests can be explained by cultural factors. Despite this fact, IQ tests are used as the basis for labeling and tracking students and, as such, perpetuate social inequalities.

In the hope that greater social equality will result, most modern societies have made attempts to equalize educational opportunity, largely by redrawing the lines of school districts and combining previously separate vocational and academic schools. In the United States, a major obstacle to achieving a relatively similar educational experience for all children was legal discrimination in the South, resulting in racially segregated schools, and institutionalized discrimination in the North, as evidenced by residential segregation. The Supreme Court struck a crucial blow to segregation in 1954, when it ruled that segregated schools were inherently unequal and ordered them to desegregate. However, progress was slow until the civil rights movement and racial disturbances of the 1960s galvanized government action.

At this time, James Coleman and a team of sociologists were asked to investigate racial inequalities in schools. Contrary to expectation, the researchers found similar school expenditures and other measures of educational quality between predominantly black schools and predominantly white schools. Coleman's crucial finding was that achievement in school was less related to school characteristics and more related to pupils' social-class background. This finding had a crucial impact on national educational policy. Some people argued that minority pupils suffer from "cultural deprivation," or deficiencies in their home background that poorly prepare them for competition in school and in the larger society. Thus, programs of "compensatory" education were designed to make up for these weaknesses. Such programs generally have not been successful in the long term. Busing was another social policy implemented to correct racial imbalances within school systems. However, it has often met with resistance from white and nonwhite parents who resent federal interference in local community control over education. Furthermore, school desegregation seems to have negligible benefits for the minority children it seeks to help. Coleman himself came to feel that busing is counterproductive in that it hastens "white flight" from the central cities to the suburbs, leaving city schools with high minority enrollments.

Christopher Jencks strongly questions the belief that social inequalities can be significantly reduced by equalizing educational opportunity in the schools. Jencks argues that the source of inequality lies outside the school and reflects discrepancies in the larger society. In his opinion, Americans should shift their focus from equality of opportunity to equality of social and economic results. This suggestion implies a redistribution of wealth that is unlikely to occur; yet the suggestion shows both the continuing faith Americans have in their schools and the magnitude of the problem of inequality.

## A Crisis of Quality?

*What criticisms are being leveled against the American educational system? What changes are being introduced to combat the problems underlying these criticisms?*

Recent reports on American education have criticized the schools for failing in their most basic teaching mission. Such warnings are not unusual. In previous decades, the curriculum was modified to emphasize math and science (to compete with the Soviets in the "space race") and then changed again to create an "open" classroom environment responsive to individual needs. In the 1980s, the call is for a "back to basics" approach in light of declining scores on SATs and similar tests and high rates of illiteracy. To some extent, the changing criticisms of the schools reflect broader social fashions. However, it appears that the schools are failing to educate students as well as in the past. Experts have pointed to several factors that may contribute to the decline of academic standards: (1) permissive child-rearing; (2) changing family patterns; (3) the impact of television; (4) an overburdened curriculum; (5) inferior teachers; (6) discipline problems; (7) education fads and frills; and (8) greater educational access, which has brought in students with a wider range of abilities. To combat these problems, educational policy-makers are emphasizing a traditional curriculum with more rigor and homework, as well as efforts to recruit and reward better teachers.

## The "Credential Society"

*What are the consequences of the emphasis on educational credentials? How are credentials used in the marketplace? Why do professions and consumers of education press for higher educational credentials?*

The increase in high grades, especially in light of declining test scores, is a result of "grade inflation" brought on by pressure from parents and pupils to improve student "achievement." The entire system has been distorted away from the search for knowledge and toward the acquisition of credentials. Randall Collins describes the United States as a "credential society" that places over-

whelming importance on various diplomas, degrees, etc. Educational qualifications have become crucial to securing a place in the job market. However, recent evidence reveals a disjuncture between the jobs in demand and the spiraling insistence on credentials. The level of skills required in most jobs has not increased, even though these jobs now demand more advanced degrees. Formal qualifications allow employers to screen and select applicants more easily and foster the belief that better-educated workers are more productive, despite studies indicating little or no correlation between educational achievement and job performance or productivity. Thus good grades are poor predictors of career success because most curricula provide students with a basic education and not job-related skills. In fact, many college graduates end up working in fields unrelated to their major subjects.

Educational credentials, however, do mean prestige and higher earnings due to the value the job market places on them. Blau and Duncan's landmark study of social mobility found that the amount of education attained was the single most important factor affecting whether a son achieved a higher status than his father. Because higher education is a scarce and valued resource, it is the key to social mobility. Conflict theorists argue that the expansion of the American educational system is directly attributable to pressure from the professions, which insist on high membership qualifications and from consumers of education (students and parents), who seek the prestige, power, and wealth associated with those credentials.

A *profession* is an occupation requiring extensive, systematic knowledge of, or training in, an art or science. Professions maintain boundaries between themselves and lay persons by demanding specific credentials, licensing, or training as part of entering the profession. These requirements increase the profession's prestige and the autonomy and income of those who practice it.

The consumers of education are equally aware of the direct relationship between educational credentials and social mobility. Students are shifting toward college majors that link them more directly to high-paying jobs. Fewer students choose the liberal arts as a course of study; more students elect coursework in business and the professions. This strategy of pursuing credentials, rather than the subjects one enjoys, may backfire. Sociologist

Randall Collins argues that even in a postindustrial society, many jobs do not require a college education, much less additional postcollege training. Insistence on needlessly high qualifications means that some people are denied jobs they could do, but for which they lack the specific credentials, while other poeple are wasting time and money on attaining educational credentials that will not be relevant to the work they actually do. A trend toward employer preference for the liberal arts graduate, who has broader training and can learn to work in many settings, is now beginning to take hold.

## DEFINING CORE CONCEPTS

*After studying the chapter, write a sociological definition in your own words for the following core concepts. Then give an example from your own experience to illustrate your definition. Refer to the chapter to check your work.*

| *Core Concept* | *Sociological Definition* | *Personal Illustration* |
| --- | --- | --- |
| applied research | | |
| basic research | | |
| education | | |
| latent function/manifest function | | |
| profession | | |

| *Core Concept* | *Sociological Definition* | *Personal Illustration* |
|---|---|---|
| self-fulfilling prophecy | | |
| social mobility | | |

## PUTTING IDEAS TOGETHER

Functionalist theorists have identified outcomes of the social institution of education that are important to any society. In the United States these functions are tempered by particular characteristics of American education: commitment to mass education, utilitarian emphasis, and community control.

## Basic Functions of Education in American Schools

| *Function of Education* | *American Example* |
|---|---|
| Cultural transmission | Community control ensures that the skills and values of a particular region are emphasized. |
| Social integration | Commitment to mass education brings all citizens into the educational institution and encourages the development of a relatively homogeneous society. |
| Personal development | Tracking is an attempt to provide education for children in line with their abilities. |
| Screening and selection | Competition is stressed to identify the most able students and to prepare them for future economic roles. |
| Innovation | Research has a utilitarian emphasis; we believe that scientific knowledge will solve many social problems. |

One of the persistent controversies in American schools surrounds the issue of equality of education. While most social scientists who have studied schools agree that the goal of equality has not been met, there is disagreement about the source of the inequality and the feasible solutions that should follow.

## Inequality Within Schools and Social Policies

| Problem Is With | Source of the Inequality | Resulting Social Policies and Programs |
| --- | --- | --- |
| student | biological differences (Jensen) | none—nothing can be done |
| school | unequal school facilities | busing or equalization of school funding |
| society | backgrounds of students (Coleman) | compensatory education |
| | reflection of social inequalities (Jencks) | redistribution of wealth on a societal level |

# Testing the Concepts

## MULTIPLE-CHOICE QUESTIONS

*After studying the chapter, try to answer each of the twenty-five questions below. Mark the alternative you think is correct; then look at the correct answer and the explanation provided at the bottom of the page. Try to state why the other alternatives are incorrect, and check your understanding of the correct answer.*

1. James Coleman studied equality of school opportunities and found
   a. no major gap between the achievements of black and white students.
   b. great differences between predominantly black and predominantly white schools.
   c. achievement in all schools is related to the social-class background of the pupils.
   d. achievement in all schools is related to the characteristics of the schools.
   e. Nonwhites had lower IQs than whites, and the source of the difference is genetic.

2. Rosenthal conducted an experiment, reported in your text, by causing teachers to believe that certain of their students would spurt ahead in learning during the school year. What did the results of this experiment teach us about education?
   a. Bright students achieve more when matched with bright teachers.
   b. Slow learners may be helped if they can be identified to the teacher as needing special help.
   c. Natural intelligence will shine through no matter what group a student is in.
   d. The self-fulfilling prophecy is one important factor explaining student academic performance.
   e. Teachers can judge the abilities of students with considerable accuracy.

3. In its broadest sense, "education" is almost synonymous with "socialization." The distinguishing feature of education in modern industrial societies is that it
   a. develops new knowledge.
   b. involves the transmission of culture.
   c. facilitates the learning of skills.
   d. has become an institutionalized, formal activity.
   e. involves social interaction.

4. Below is a list of skills Jack learned in school. Which one would you consider a latent function of schools?
   a. Jack can read at a tenth-grade level but is in the twelfth grade.
   b. Jack learned to type in his typing course and is qualified for a typing job.
   c. From his civics class, Jack learned about the U.S. government and how to vote.
   d. The discipline in school taught Jack to obey authority, which will help him in later job situations.
   e. Weekly physical education classes helped Jack to stay in good physical shape despite his addiction to Twinkies.

---

1. **c.** *Contrary to expectations, Coleman found that school facilities were roughly equivalent for black and white schools. The gap between the achievement of black and white students was explained on the basis of social-class differences. See page 387.*

2. **d.** *The expectations teachers held for the pupils identified as "spurters" were different than those for the other students, and the "spurters" performed accordingly. Even though the "spurters" had been chosen randomly, they fulfilled the expectations of the teachers and outperformed the "nonspurters" presumably*
because the teachers' attitudes toward them had a positive influence on their progress. See pages 383–384.

3. **d.** *Modern industrialized societies organize education into a formalized activity outside the home, handled by trained professionals. Education is the systematic, formalized transmission of knowledge, skills, and values. See pages 375–376.*

4. **d.** *Although American schools strive to produce "sound minds in strong bodies," they also have the latent function of teaching certain habits, such as punctuality and obedience to authority, that are later useful in the workplace. See page 380.*

5. One source of opposition to busing by both white and nonwhite parents is racist attitudes. Beyond these feelings, what characteristic of American education is inconsistent with a social policy like busing?
    a. a commitment to mass education
    b. faith in education to solve social problems
    c. a utilitarian emphasis
    d. attention to the personal development of the individual student
    e. community control of schools

6. The proportion of the population holding a college degree has increased rapidly in recent years because
    a. of increased minority enrollments in high schools.
    b. a college degree has become an essential credential in obtaining better-paying jobs.
    c. of the renewed interest in education for education's sake.
    d. of competition from two-year schools.
    e. the content of most jobs has changed, necessitating advanced knowledge and skills.

7. Education has both manifest and latent functions. Which of the functions below is a *manifest* function?
    a. serving as a "babysitting" agency
    b. transmitting culture
    c. functioning as a "marriage market"

    d. permitting the formation of distinctive youth cultures
    e. teaching habits of docility and obedience to authority

8. If a sociologist were studying the significance of peer groups in schools, which of the following research questions would most likely be posed?
    a. Which student activities are the most fun?
    b. What happens to a person who is left out of peer groups?
    c. How do peer groups generate school spirit?
    d. What makes one student more popular than another?
    e. How do peer groups encourage or discourage academic achievement?

9. A crucial insight of the conflict perspective on education is that
    a. in a mass society, education is more common and more competitive.
    b. people do not have equal opportunities to achieve success.
    c. education is not connected to life chances.
    d. people have unequal abilities.
    e. students will perform better when high standards are set for them.

---

5. **e.** *The American education system differs from that of the other industrialized countries in its commitment to local decision making. The concept of the neighborhood school is highly valued and is challenged by attempts to bus students from one district to another, whatever the reason. See page 378.*

6. **b.** *A higher number of high school graduates are continuing on to college because many jobs now require a college degree, where a high school diploma was previously considered sufficient. The United States has become a "credential" society in which overwhelming importance is attached to the educational qualifications that give people an edge in the competition for power, wealth, and prestige. See pages 391–393.*

7. **b.** *A manifest function is a deliberate consequence.*

*One of the goals of education is the transmission of culture, providing young people with the knowledge, skills, and values the society considers important. See pages 378, 380.*

8. **e.** *Peer groups have a significant influence on members' academic motivation and career plans. Social-class values held by students and their friends reinforce or discourage the goal of academic achievement, particularly with regard to the importance placed on college plans. See pages 382, 385.*

9. **b.** *Conflict theorists argue that the inequalities of the larger society are reinforced by the schools. When students begin school, they do not begin with equal opportunities; thus it is not surprising that their academic achievement reflects these inequalities. See pages 380–381.*

10. According to Jencks's research on schools,
    a. the schools alone cannot be used to change society.
    b. attempts to equalize educational opportunities will significantly reduce social inequality.
    c. economic inequality is caused by lack of educational achievement.
    d. attempts to equalize educational opportunities will greatly affect student academic performance.
    e. parental involvement in schools is the key to better quality education.

11. Sociologists argue that IQ tests measure
    a. culturally learned knowledge.
    b. native intelligence.
    c. learning potential.
    d. creativity.
    e. genetic differences by race.

12. Recent reports have raised questions about the quality of American education. Which pair of remedies seems to be supported?
    a. "back to basics" curriculum; hire better teachers
    b. more discipline in schools; more foreign-language classes
    c. culture-free IQ tests; more rigid tracking
    d. open admissions policies in colleges; exit exams to graduate
    e. voucher system for private schools; more busing to achieve integration

13. The finding that "cultural deprivation" was a cause of performance differences between black and white schoolchildren resulted in which educational policy?
    a. compensatory education programs
    b. teacher workshops
    c. greater parental involvement in schools
    d. attention to the problems of grade inflation and declining standards
    e. education against discriminatory racial attitudes

14. Competition for grades in school can be justified as
    a. a way to identify which students should go on to college.
    b. an essential part of the socialization necessary in a capitalist society.
    c. a way to motivate most students to learn.
    d. a culturally universal tendency that cannot be avoided.
    e. an essential part of developing self-discipline.

---

10. **a.** *Jencks argues that the social inequalities in society are so entrenched that schools cannot be expected to significantly reduce them. Even when schools provide equal opportunities, pupils are differently equipped to take advantage of them. See pages 388–389.*

11. **a.** *IQ tests have been shown to be biased toward white, middle-class students who have had more exposure to the topics, vocabulary, experiences, and concepts measured by the tests. IQ tests, then, assess this culturally learned knowledge more than they test native intelligence. See page 386.*

12. **a.** *The current trends in educational policymaking show a return to the basic subjects and a reduction of electives and special courses. In addition, incentives have been established to hire and reward better teachers. See page 391.*

13. **a.** *The Coleman report's findings led to the conclusion that cultural deprivation was often the cause of the differences in students' performance in school. One way to address these background deficiencies was to offer compensatory programs to help students make up for the knowledge and skills they might have missed at home. See page 387.*

14. **b.** *Schools prepare students for adult roles. Competition for grades can be seen as preparation for the intense competition for economic roles that characterizes the job market in a capitalist society such as the United States. See page 383.*

15.  Which of the following seems to contribute to declining academic standards in public schools?
  a.  grade inflation
  b.  high salaries, which attract poor teachers who are just out for the money
  c.  permissive child-rearing practices at home and inadequate discipline at school
  d.  lack of innovative teaching methods
  e.  a more difficult curriculum

16.  The fact that schools are bureaucratic organizations makes which of the following educational goals the most difficult to achieve?
  a.  efficient organization of students by age, subject, and ability
  b.  procedural uniformity
  c.  exposure to the informal structure of a peer group
  d.  development of individual creativity
  e.  reinforcement of important values such as obedience, conformity, and competition

17.  Which of the following hypothetical school courses would be most in line with the utilitarian emphasis in American education?
  a.  philosophy of the Western world
  b.  industrial arts
  c.  sex education
  d.  introduction to sociology
  e.  creative writing

18.  How do conflict theorists explain the expansion of American education in recent decades?
  a.  Professions insist on high qualifications to protect their own interests.
  b.  High qualifications are a response to job needs.
  c.  A college degree produces increased mobility for the individual.
  d.  The more professionalized an occupation, the better service it delivers.
  e.  Schools teach the specific job skills necessary for successful careers.

19.  The United States attaches an overwhelming importance to educational qualifications for various kinds of employment. Which of the following statements about the "credential society" is accurate?
  a.  Most jobs in the expanding economy require a college education.
  b.  Employers have found that higher education is a good predictor of worker productivity.
  c.  Most college graduates work in the field of their major subjects.
  d.  College grades are a good predictor of occupational performance.
  e.  Credentials are used by employers in screening job applicants.

---

15.  **c.**  *Standardized tests reveal a steady decline in academic standards. Among the factors that may be contributing to this decline are permissive child-rearing practices, which may deprive children of the self-discipline necessary for academic success, and lack of discipline in schools. See pages 390–391.*

16.  **d.**  *As a bureaucracy, a school must emphasize its goals and the standardized procedures of its operation. Because students must conform to the administrative needs of the bureaucracy, their individuality is diminished. See pages 381–382.*

17.  **c.**  *The American educational system reflects the strong conviction that the schools can be used to solve social problems. While sex-education courses aimed at reducing the rate of teenage pregnancy, or drug-*

*education programs, have not had the impact educators had hoped, faith in education as a cure-all persists.*

18.  **a.**  *A profession is a self-monitored occupation, controlled by its members. Fellow professionals set the standards for licensing, education, and entrance into the profession. In some cases, standards for membership are set very high, making access to the profession difficult. This creates a higher demand for the available services of that profession. See pages 392–393.*

19.  **e.**  *Although there is little evidence to support a connection between educational achievement and performance on the job, employers continue to value academic degrees in the belief that highly educated graduates will make more productive workers. See page 392.*

20. The American educational system's unique blend of features shows that
    a. social equality can be ensured by education.
    b. a college education is not critical for job advancement in an industrial society.
    c. mass education usually brings a lowering of academic standards.
    d. schools do not vary greatly from community to community.
    e. it is difficult to teach values within a standard curriculum.

21. Which factor has the most important influence on pupils' academic achievement?
    a. their social-class background
    b. the amount of money spent on the schools they attend
    c. the intelligence of the individual student
    d. the motivation and industriousness of the individual student
    e. the amount of parental encouragement

22. Peter Blau and Otis Duncan found that the most important factor affecting whether a son moved to a higher social status than his father's was
    a. the degree of ambition displayed by the son.
    b. the amount of education the son received.
    c. urban versus rural residence.
    d. personality.
    e. the quality of the son's early school experience.

23. In which respect is the American educational system different from that of other advanced industrial societies?
    a. The percentage of high school graduates who go on to college is significantly smaller.
    b. There is a far greater emphasis in the United States on community control of schools.
    c. Other countries have had a commitment to mass education far longer than the United States.
    d. A lower proportion of American youth graduate from high school.
    e. The U.S. standards for college entrance are higher.

---

20. **c.** *In the United States, all young people are expected to attend school. Education is offered free of charge as a basic right of citizenship. This mass effort means that there is a heterogeneous group of student abilities within the school system, and standards must be lowered to accommodate their diversity. See page 376.*

21. **a.** *The social-class background of students is associated with their preparation and motivation for school, and serves as an important predictor of their school achievement. See page 384.*

22. **b.** *Education is related to social mobility. A high level of education is a scarce and valued resource for which people compete. Those who gain an educational advantage usually attain an employment advantage as well. See page 392.*

23. **b.** *One of the key characteristics of American schools is the emphasis on community control. While other countries have a standardized, national curriculum, Americans prefer a diversity of educational options guided by the preferences of the local community. See page 378.*

24. The schools in the United States have always served a "melting pot" function, in that they help assimilate young members of ethnic, racial, religious, or other minorities into a common culture. This is an example of which function of education?
    a. innovation
    b. screening and selection
    c. social integration
    d. cultural deprivation
    e. personal development

25. An educational idea pioneered in the United States is that
    a. every child should attend school.
    b. education should be tailored to the economic needs of a society.
    c. religious education is superior to secular education.
    d. smaller classes are better.
    e. schools should weed out poor students so that only the best go to college.

---

24. **c.** *As immigrants enter American society, they are taught the ways of their new culture. This process of Americanization, usually accomplished in the schools, integrates the members of various subcultures, encouraging them to conform to basic societal norms. See page 379.*

25. **a.** *The idea of mandatory, free education for all citizens is a feature of American schooling, unequaled anywhere in the world, that is very much in line with a commitment to an educated voting public in a democratic government. See pages 376–377.*

## A CASE STUDY

NAME

COURSE/SECTION NUMBER

Secretary of Education, William Bennett, has proposed a voucher system for the nation's elementary and secondary schools. Each child would be given a voucher for a certain dollar amount of education; parents could then choose the school that best fit their children's needs, whether it be a public institution or a private one. Not only would this tax-funded voucher plan help support the private schools, Bennett argues, but it would increase competition among schools and result in better educational programs. Segregation in schools would be reduced, since the quality of a program would attract students of all races, without government interference or busing. Schools could specialize in the arts, science, foreign language, or other disciplines thereby improving the educational opportunities open to all students.

1.    In what ways do you think the voucher system would improve the quality of education for America's children?

2.    What, if any, pitfalls do you see in the plan? Which, if any, of Secretary Bennett's assumptions do you question?

3.    How might Coleman or Jencks respond to this idea? What would you guess their comments and criticisms might be?

4.    Which principles of American education might this plan violate? Which principles does it reinforce?

# Applying the Concepts

## APPLICATION EXERCISE ONE

You are aware that some educators, parents, and sociologists believe IQ tests are culturally biased to favor white, middle-class children. Design an IQ test of ten items (or more) that would be culturally biased to favor another racial or ethnic group, an age group, a gender group, or some other subculture. (Be sure to provide the right answers!) For example, a test on sports items might favor males, or a test on songs and political events during the Depression might favor older people or history buffs. How might your test be used to discriminate against some groups?

## APPLICATION EXERCISE TWO

Reflect on the community or communities in which you spent most of your youth. If you lived in a very rural area, think about the surrounding county.

1.   What was the social-class structure of the community?

2.   How did the various elementary schools and high schools differ in terms of what kinds of children went where? Which were "good" schools and why?

3.   Did your school use tracking or a similar device to separate students according to their perceived abilities? If so, how rigid were the boundaries between the tracks? Did tracking perpetuate the class structure?

4.   Give specific evidence from your school experience to support each of the functionalist theorists' arguments regarding the functions of education.

5.   Give specific examples of how your school experience taught you the American values of success, equality, competition, patriotism, and outward conformity.

6.   Using the college or university you are currently attending, explain, from a conflict theorist's viewpoint, how the school intentionally or unintentionally maintains social-class inequalities.

## APPLICATION EXERCISE THREE

The text states that Americans place so much faith in their public schools that there is a tendency to expect the schools alone to solve many social problems.

1.    Do schools primarily promote social change, or respond to it? What evidence supports your answer?

2.    Interview three nonrelatives in your community, asking them what they think the schools should be doing differently. Should schools emphasize education or training? How much social change do they expect from schools?

3.   Provide examples from your own experience of situations in which your school attempted to remedy social ills.

4.   Evaluate the text's contention that schools are expected to solve social problems but do not do a very good job of it.

5.   What evidence do you find in support of or in opposition to the text's suggestion that the American educational system reflects our credential-conscious society? Give an example of educational achievement as a credential in your life, or in the lives of the people you know.

# CHAPTER 15

# Religion

## Reviewing the Concepts

### LEARNING GOALS

*After studying this chapter, you should be able to:*

1. State the sociological definition of religion, based on the work of Durkheim.

2. Relate the process of socialization to the development of religious beliefs.

3. List topics of interest to a sociologist studying religion as social behavior.

4. Distinguish among the characteristics of four types of religions.

5. Define theodicy and its social functions.

6. Outline Durkheim's approach to the sociology of religion and his key findings.

7. Provide examples of four social functions of religion.

8. Compare and contrast the elements of religion with those of functionally equivalent belief systems.

9. Summarize Marx's view of religion in society.

10. Illustrate Marx's argument that religion legitimates the dominant class.

11. Contrast the views of Marx and Weber on the relationship between religion and social change.

12. Explain Weber's "Protestant ethic" thesis and the current evidence for it.

13. Use Islamic fundamentalism to discuss religion and social change.

14. Identify the features of the following religious organizations: an ecclesia, a denomination, a sect, and a cult, and give a current example of each.

15. Discuss the characteristics of religious life in America.

16. Compare the religiosity of the American people with that of other nations and discuss the social consequences of these differences.

17. Specify the correlation of Americans' political and social attitudes with their religious affiliation.

18. Explain the recent decline of traditional religions in the United States.

19. Identify the factors that have led to a fundamentalist revival in the United States.

20. Discuss the influence of religion on politics.

21. Characterize the religious sects and cults that have recently become popular in the United States.

22. Define the concept of secularization and explain how it is measured; describe the relationship between industrialization and secularization.

23. Discuss various predictions for religious life in the United States in future years.

## IDENTIFYING KEY QUESTIONS AND THEMES

Religion, like the family, is a universal social institution that takes a multitude of forms. The early sociologist Emile Durkheim studied many religions and noticed that they all possessed a single common feature: a sharp distinction between the *sacred*—anything that is regarded as part of the supernatural world and, as such, inspires awe, reverence, and deep respect—and the *profane*—anything that is regarded as part of the everyday world and, as such, may be considered familiar, mundane, even corrupting. The sacred is approached through a *ritual*—a formal, stylized procedure, such as prayer, incantation, or ceremonial cleansing, that recognizes the extraordinary, supernatural, and often dangerous qualities of the sacred world. In light of the great cross-cultural variety of religious practices, sociologists define *religion* as a system of communally held beliefs and rituals that are oriented toward some sacred, supernatural realm.

## The Sociological Approach to Religion

*How have sociologists approached the study of religion? How do sociologists deal with value judgments based on their own religious preferences?*

Sociologists argue that religious convictions of any type are learned through socialization, a process that begins with the initial religious training provided by the family. Therefore, a person's religious convictions are influenced by the historical times and social context in which that person happens to live. The fact that a religion is culturally learned does not bear on whether it is "true." Like other empirical sciences, sociology is not concerned with the validity of any religion, for it simply is not equipped to address such an issue. While individual sociologists may hold certain religious views, they study religious behavior objectively regardless of their own beliefs. Sociological research, then, is directed at the social rather than the theological aspects of religion and focuses on the mutual influence of religion and society.

## Types of Religion

*How do sociologists classify the wide range of world religions?*

The scientific method is useful to sociologists of religion in terms of bringing conceptual order to their field. Many sociologists classify religions according to their central belief, resulting in four main categories:

(1) *Simple supernaturalism* is a type of religion, common to preindustrial societies, in which believers assume that supernatural forces influence human events for better or worse.

(2) *Animism* is a type of religion that recognizes active, animate spirits operating in the world. These benevolent or evil spirits may be found both in humans and in the world of nature. People may try to influence them through the use of *magic,* or rituals intended to harness supernatural power for human ends.

(3) A type of religion that is based on a belief in god(s) is called *theism.* With the help of religious officials such as pastors, rabbis, and priests, humans engage in religious ceremonies to worship a god or gods. Some societies practice *polytheism,* a belief in a number of gods, usually ranked in a hierarchy of power and importance. *Monotheism* is a belief in a single supreme being: Judaism, Christianity, and Islam are the only monotheistic religions in the world, but they have the largest number of adherents.

(4) Some religions, such as Buddhism, are based on *transcendant idealism* and are less concerned with worship of a god than with sacred principles of thought and conduct aimed at the development of an individual's potential for religious consciousness. Religions of this type are characterized by reverence for life, truth, and tolerance of other beliefs.

Although most religions do not try to win converts, several of the major world religions have attempted to do so. A common feature of these religions is that they have a convincing *theodicy,* an emotionally satisfying explanation for the great problems of existence, such as the origins of life, human suffering, and death. A theodicy provides its believers with a world view, giving them an understanding of, or justification for, the presence of evil and misfortune in the world.

## Religion: A Functionalist View

*What were Durkheim's early contributions to the study of religion? What functions of religion have sociologists identified? What are examples of functional equivalents of religion?*

Durkheim was impressed by the fact that religion is universal in human society, and he wondered exactly what function it served; he concluded that religion plays a vital role in maintaining the social system as a whole. In his classic study, *The Elementary Forms of Religious Life,* published in 1912, Durkheim argued that every society needs a religion or some belief system and the rituals that go with it. Without a common religion, individuals in the society pursue their private interests, and social solidarity declines as a result.

Modern sociologists have expanded on Durkheim's investigation of religion and social cohesion, identifying four social functions of religion: (1) religion fosters social solidarity by uniting believers and bringing them together to enact various rituals based on shared values and beliefs; (2) religious teachings provide a theodicy that addresses ultimate questions about existence and explains human events that might otherwise seem beyond comprehension; (3) social control is promoted by adherence to religious teachings that reinforce the more important values and norms of a society; (4) religion provides individuals with psychological support in the uncertainty of the world.

As Durkheim emphasized, a society requires some shared set of beliefs to ensure its cohesion. Although religion may meet this need, other belief systems may serve as a *functional equivalent*— a social or cultural feature that has the same purpose. Examples of these functional equivalents include humanism, fascism, communism, and various self-help psychology movements. The essential difference between such belief systems and religion is that only the latter is directed toward the supernatural.

## Religion: A Conflict View

*How did Karl Marx view the place of religion in society? How are religious views related to social conflict?*

The conflict approach to religion is shaped by the views of Karl Marx, who referred to religion as the "opium of the people." He saw religion as a form of false consciousness and as a tool used by the dominant group to justify its privileges. Like Durkheim and others, Marx argued that religion is socially created. But, for Marx, belief in religion was a profound form of human *alienation,* the situation in which people lose their control over the social world they have created and find themselves "alien" in a hostile social environment. Thus, people create gods, religious rituals, and roles for religious officials and later lose awareness that they have done so; religion becomes something "natural" and "right," rather than something man-made.

Substantial historical evidence supports Marx's claim that the dominant religion in any society legitimates the interests of the ruling class; the Dutch Reform Church's support of apartheid in South Africa is but one example. So-called classless societies usually downplay or repress religion. Yet the role of religion in social conflict is not limited to the legitimation of the existing order. Religion is often present in conflicts between societies or between groups with different faiths within a society; frequently, however, religious differences are more an ideological justification of the conflict rather than its actual cause. Religion can also be used to challenge the existing order and to point out its divergence from religious principles, as in the liberation movement in Latin America.

## Religion and Social Change

*How did Max Weber explain the relationship between religion and social change? Why do fundamentalist movements develop?*

Contrary to Marx's view that religious ideas merely reflect material conditions, and thus that religious changes are simply a reflection of social changes, Max Weber held that under certain conditions religious ideas could *influence* social change. In his classic study of the *Protestant ethic*—a disciplined, moral commitment to regular, conscientious work and deferred gratification—Weber demonstrated that the behaviors necessary for capitalism to develop—hard work, frugal living, and reinvestment—were connected to the emergence of Protestant puritanism, especially Calvinism. Weber identified tenets of early Calvinism that promoted these behaviors and argued that

other religions did not provide the same incentives for the kind of social and economic change associated with the rise of capitalism. Although Weber's hypothesis concerning the connection between the Protestant ethic and capitalism is generally supported, there is some competing evidence. Both Weber and Marx made modern sociologists aware that the material and nonmaterial components of culture influence one another in different ways at different times.

Islam is a major world religion claiming the allegiance of a fifth of the entire human population. In recent years, religious fervor has erupted into violent political action, a development inspired by *fundamentalism*—a commitment to, and reliance on, the basics of religious doctrine. This return to traditional ideas, affecting all aspects of personal conduct and social life, comes at a time when rapid modernization has led to uncertainty, turmoil, and the erosion of familiar values. Muslim societies fear Westernization and the threat it poses to community solidarity. Identification of an alien enemy—such as labeling the United States the "Great Satan"—and reinforcement of traditional religious doctrines help to retard wrenching social change.

## Religious Organizations

*How have sociologists classified the variety of religious organizations? How does the organization of a religion affect the types of beliefs and practices a religion emphasizes?*

Religious organizations can be classified into one of four basic types. The *ecclesia* is a religious organization that claims the membership of everyone in a society or even in several societies. State churches are an example. Because of the all-encompassing nature of these organizations, they are powerful bureaucracies within the society and have bases of power that overlap those of state authorities. The *denomination* (or "church") is one of two or more religious organizations that claim the allegiance of a substantial part of the population. Denominations are well-established, relatively tolerant, bureaucratic organizations that operate within the mainstream of society. The *sect* is an exclusive, less formally organized religious body, usually one that has split off from a denomination. Its members are generally recruited through conversion and frequently are of lower socioeconomic status. The beliefs of sects tend to be dogmatic and fundamentalist and are often hostile to political authority. The *cult* is the most loosely organized and most temporary of the religious organizations. Its belief system is independent of religious tradition and has few coherent doctrines; membership is open to almost anyone who wants to join. The members of a cult usually have low commitment to the group and tend to drift in and out of it. Cults appeal to people who, disenchanted with traditional religion, are drawn to the personal experiences the cult offers. Because they are the most common, sociologists generally focus on denominations and sects. Sects are continually formed as groups break off from denominations in search of doctrinal purity. Although most new sects are short-lived, some survive and prosper, occasionally growing into denominations from which new sects break off; the Methodists are one such example.

## Religion in the United States

*How important is religion in American life? What are the consequences of religious pluralism? What trends are important in American religion?*

Religion plays an important role in American life and has several distinctive characteristics. (1) The United States has no official, established religion; indeed the Constitution specifically separates church and state. No religion can be declared illegal simply because of its beliefs and practices. Thus there is freedom of religion. (2) Yet, the overwhelming majority of Americans belong to a religious organization. In fact, the United States has one of the highest rates of church or synagogue attendance, testimony to the breadth of religious commitment. (3) This involvement fosters an implicit assumption that Americans should be religious, that religiosity is a value in itself. Often religious values are invoked in connection with patriotism and good citizenship. (4) There is a considerable degree of religious pluralism in the United States as evidenced by the many organizations representing a variety of religious views. (5) This pluralistic pattern reinforces Americans' general tolerance of religious diversity. (6) Religion is also a source of personal and group identity. Certain ethnic groups are associated with, and held together by, a common religion. (7) Sociologists have identi-

fied certain social characteristics that tend to correlate with participation in particular religious organizations. These include socioeconomic status, educational standards, political views, and attitudes toward social issues, such as sexual morality and abortion.

The institution of religion in America is changing. Established religions are on the decline. The Roman Catholic Church, the major Protestant denominations, and mainstream Judaism are all experiencing a decline in commitment as evidenced by dwindling membership and attendance, greater deviation from traditional religious doctrine, and the current trend toward interfaith marriages, which weaken solidarity and allegiance to a particular organization. At the same time, Protestant fundamentalism is growing, as the conservative wing of a larger Protestant movement—evangelism. The fundamentalists' domination of the "electronic church," combining preaching and fund-raising with television and radio programming, has greatly enhanced their strength. The revival of the fundamentalist message, based on a literal interpretation of the Bible, is, for the first time, being facilitated at least in part through political means.

Although the Constitution protects against the involvement of the state in religion, there is no law against religious participation in the affairs of the state. This trend toward political involvement of religious organizations, particularly with respect to fundamentalist movements, reflects the general American pattern of "civil religion," in which various sacred elements are used to sanctify and celebrate the American way of life. For example, the Pledge of Allegiance and prayers in the legislature draw on religious values, but are sufficiently broad to be acceptable to almost anyone. Other political issues, such as clergy recommendations about voting, or the desirability of school prayer, are much more controversial.

Many new sects and cults have appeared in the United States in the past two decades. Some of the more enduring ones include the Hare Krishna, the Unification Church, and Scientology. These groups tend to differ significantly from traditional American religious organizations and sometimes strain the American tolerance for diversity of religious beliefs. Charges of greed and hedonism have been leveled against the leaders of those new movements that seem fraudulent and exploitative. Extreme methods of indoctrination practiced by some groups cause concern on the part of parents and public officials who fear young people will be drawn into the movements and possibly even brainwashed. Because their rituals and beliefs seem unusual in light of traditional religious practices, new religions tend to generate suspicion and hostility; however, the intolerant reactions they sometimes provoke are inconsistent with the principles of religious freedom and civil liberties upon which the United States was founded. Of course, shifts in allegiance from established denominations to new religions is not a recent phenomenon—it has occurred at several points in U.S. history. What is new is the extent of religious pluralism. Many Americans use religion as a way of asserting and establishing their identities; the wide variety of religious outlets means Americans can choose the religious organizations that best suit their needs at a particular point in their lives. In particular, these new affiliations appeal to those who may be seeking the self-fulfillment and meaning they cannot find elsewhere.

## Secularization: Fact or Myth?

*What do sociologists mean by secularization? What is the evidence for secularization?*

As industrialization increases, societies tend to become more secular and more worldly in their institutions, values, and beliefs. *Secularization* is the process whereby religion loses its social influence. The most obvious outcome of secularization is the tendency of traditional religion to become a separate and distinct institution with only a limited role in society; questions of daily life are no longer organized around religious rituals. In these highly diversified, modern societies, religion's sphere of influence is circumscribed by other institutions such as science and education, and religious commitment, if it exists at all, tends to be a part-time rather than an all-encompassing orientation. Sociologists have noted a decline in membership and attendance figures for different religious organizations and an increase in the proportion of the population not formally involved in any religion. Other measures of secularization include financial contributions, the prestige of the clergy, the ratio of secular to religious marriages, and the number of religious publications. Although attitude polls show a general decline and sometimes collapse of religious commitment in the industrialized nations, most Americans continue to express a belief in God or a universal spirit and indicate they have a religious preference. Advanced industrialization usually erodes traditional religious institutions; however, sociologist Peter Berger suggests this has not been the case in the United States (and Canada) because the churches in North America have stayed closer to the center of society by becoming secularized themselves. Sociologists believe that the trend toward religious diversity will continue in the postindustrial future. Particularly during periods of rapid social change, people may look to religion for answers as they have done in the past. Traditional and new forms of religion will provide a diverse set of responses to the search for stability and meaning. Questions regarding the purpose of life and the nature of morality are unanswerable by science; thus some orientation to the sacred or supernatural will prevail to provide the sense of understanding and solidarity critical to the maintenance of society.

## DEFINING CORE CONCEPTS

*After studying the chapter, write a sociological definition in your own words for the following core concepts. Then give an example from your own experience to illustrate your definition. Refer to the chapter to check your work.*

| *Core Concept* | *Sociological Definition* | *Personal Illustration* |
| --- | --- | --- |
| alienation | | |

| *Core Concept* | *Sociological Definition* | *Personal Illustration* |
| --- | --- | --- |
| animism | | |
| cult | | |
| denomination | | |
| ecclesia | | |
| functional equivalent | | |
| fundamentalism | | |
| magic | | |
| monotheism/polytheism | | |

| Core Concept | Sociological Definition | Personal Illustration |
|---|---|---|
| profane | | |
| Protestant ethic | | |
| religion | | |
| ritual | | |
| sacred | | |
| sect | | |
| secularization | | |
| simple supernaturalism | | |

| *Core Concept* | *Sociological Definition* | *Personal Illustration* |
|---|---|---|
| theism | | |
| theodicy | | |
| transcendent idealism | | |

## PUTTING IDEAS TOGETHER

Sociologists of religion differ in the importance they ascribe to the interrelationships between religion and society.

### Social Significance of Religion

| | | |
|---|---|---|
| *Durkheim and other functionalists* | Maintenance of social solidarity | Example: Common beliefs and rituals bind people together. |
| *Marx and other conflict theorists* | Maintenance of social inequality | Example: The dominant groups in society use religion to justify their privileges. |
| *Max Weber* | A response to, and a source of, social change | Example: The Protestant ethic was conducive to the development of capitalism. |

There are four basic types of religious organizations. They differ in several ways.

## Types of Religious Organizations

| Ecclesia | Denomination | Sect | Cult |
|---|---|---|---|

### Number of Followers

| most | | | fewest |
|---|---|---|---|

### Zeal of Followers

| lowest | | | highest |
|---|---|---|---|

### Longevity

| long-standing | | | short-lived |
|---|---|---|---|

### Overlap with Political State

| high | | | low or hostile |
|---|---|---|---|

### Degree of Organization

| tight or bureaucratized | | | loose |
|---|---|---|---|

### Social Class Affiliation

| generally higher | | | generally lower |
|---|---|---|---|

# Testing the Concepts

## MULTIPLE-CHOICE QUESTIONS

*After studying the chapter, try to answer each of the twenty-five questions below. Mark the alternative you think is correct; then look at the correct answer and the explanation provided at the bottom of the page. Try to state why the other alternatives are incorrect, and check your understanding of the correct answer.*

1. Judaism, Christianity, and Islam are examples of which type of religion?
   a. transcendant idealism
   b. fundamentalism
   c. simple superstition
   d. monotheism
   e. animism

2. The end result of secularization is that
   a. people no longer interpret the world only through religion.
   b. the basic elements of religion change.
   c. religion performs more important functions for society.
   d. Marx's interpretation of the relationship between society and religion proves accurate.
   e. religious beliefs are more directly applied to the everyday aspects of life.

3. Judging from the polls and surveys on the subject of religion in the United States, Americans are
   a. a remarkably irreligious people.
   b. indicating a renewed faith in religiosity.
   c. more likely to belong to a religious organization and attend worship regularly than those in other advanced, industrialized societies.
   d. split about evenly between believers and atheists.
   e. members of secular religions more often than of traditional denominations.

4. Religious commandments such as "Thou shalt not kill" and "Thou shalt not commit adultery" can be described as serving which social function of religion?
   a. discouraging fundamentalism
   b. addressing eternal questions about existence
   c. providing social control
   d. relieving personal anxiety
   e. limiting personal freedom

5. In the United States, which of the following statements about the correlation between religion and social attitudes is accurate?
   a. Jews are generally the most liberal on social issues.
   b. The influence of religion is such that all believers are more concerned about social issues than are nonreligious people.
   c. Protestant denominations are associated with liberal political positions.
   d. Catholics are most conservative on issues of sexual morality, but not so on social issues.
   e. Catholics are likely to vote with the Republican party.

---

1. **d.** *Monotheism is the belief in a single supreme being. Although Judaism, Christianity, and Islam are the only three monotheistic religions in the world, they have the greatest number of adherents. See page 400.*

2. **a.** *Religion becomes a separate and distinct part of life. Religious beliefs do not dominate or orient the individual's thinking as they once did. See page 419.*

3. **c.** *Religious commitment in the United States is remarkably strong. Americans attend religious services at a rate higher than that of people in most industrialized societies. See pages 411, 419–420.*

4. **c.** *Modern sociologists have elaborated on Durkheim's ideas concerning the functions of religion. Commandments and other religious teachings provide guidance about appropriate behavior while reinforcing important values, thus enhancing social control. See pages 401–402.*

5. **a.** *Opinion polls indicate that Jews have the most liberal views about social issues. They are particularly supportive of civil liberties. See page 412.*

6. With which of the following statements about religion would both Marx and Durkheim agree?
   a. Religious rituals promote social cohesion and serve a useful social function.
   b. Religion is socially created.
   c. Religion leads to social change.
   d. Religion contributes to false consciousness.
   e. The Protestant ethic culminated in capitalism.

7. The Hare Krishna movement has successfully recruited new members for the sect. Which feature of this group's religious practices would be most in line with Durkheim's view of the functions of religion?
   a. soliciting money at airports rather than taking regular jobs
   b. performing a number of group rituals each day
   c. belief in one almighty god figure
   d. maintaining close ties with family members, whether Krishna or not
   e. maintaining the status quo of social relationships in the larger society

8. The fundamentalist movements in the United States and Iran are similar in many ways. Which of the following statements is true only for the United States?
   a. Political leaders endorse religious pluralism and separation of church and state.
   b. A sizable percentage of the population is self-identified as fundamentalist.
   c. Believers hold to literal interpretations of the scriptures.
   d. Religious life affects political life through lobbying and interest groups.
   e. Believers may reject evidence of evolution or other discoveries in favor of religious interpretations.

9. The Catholic church in the United States is an example of
   a. an ecclesia.
   b. a denomination.
   c. a sect.
   d. a cult.
   e. a theodicy.

10. Weber's view of religion differs from that of Marx on which of the following issues?
   a. the extent to which the supernatural is part of religious beliefs
   b. whether civil religion can withstand the development of capitalism

---

6. **b.** *Both theorists agree that humans create religion and its rituals. As sociologists, neither Marx nor Durkheim comment on the validity of one religion over another. Marx argued that after humans create religion, they lose sight of that fact, which leads to alienation. Durkheim emphasized the functional aspects of religion. See pages 401, 403.*

7. **b.** *A religious group enhances social cohesion through the rituals it performs, giving its members a "we" feeling, reaffirming common values, and emphasizing the group's relation to the sacred. See pages 401, 417.*

8. **a.** *The U.S. Constitution calls for the separation of church and state. Thus the state may not favor or penalize one religious belief relative to another. However, religious groups can affect political life and have become*

increasingly active in supporting particular candidates and pieces of legislation. In Iran, no such separation exists; religious leaders are also political leaders. See pages 407–408, 414–416.*

9. **b.** *A denomination is a religious organization whose membership includes a sizable proportion of the population. While in other countries, such as Spain, the Catholic church might be considered an ecclesia, or state church, in the United States, Catholics are one of several major religious groups or denominations. See page 409.*

10. **c.** *Marx felt that religion maintained the status quo and limited social change. He compared religion to an opiate that prevented people from making necessary changes. Weber, in studying the Protestant ethic and the rise of capitalism, felt that under certain circumstances religion contributed to social change. See page 406.*

c. whether religion promotes social change or inhibits it

d. whether rituals are a basic element of religion

e. whether or not religion is socially created

11. Emile Durkheim pointed out that one feature common to all religions is

a. belief in a supreme being or at least some godlike entity.

b. a relationship between earthly mortality and afterlife.

c. a distinction between the sacred and the profane.

d. the belief that God (or a god) created the universe.

e. a group of religious leaders set apart from the laity.

12. Emile Durkheim concluded that religion is universal to all human societies because

a. it is part of our primitive past.

b. every individual is superstitious.

c. religion explains ultimate realities.

d. it is vital in maintaining the social system as a whole.

e. every culture must have one god.

13. Religion is probably here to stay because

a. the material investment in church properties will ensure continuation.

b. there are gaps in our understanding of life's mysteries that science alone cannot answer.

c. a deeply embedded social habit is difficult to change.

d. it is a means of social control.

e. attendance falls off and rises again with a new generation.

14. Communism is a belief system but not a religion because it

a. claims to have access to ultimate truth.

b. has no orientation toward the supernatural.

c. regards all views other than communism as false.

d. claims to be able to explain human suffering.

e. is future-oriented and offers a vision of a better life.

15. Sociological data on religion in the United States support the hypothesis that

a. churchgoers are less prejudiced than other people.

b. Protestants have the most liberal views on social issues.

c. people in public office are not supposed to be religious.

d. religion is a politically controversial institution.

e. there is considerable religious pluralism.

---

11.  **c.** *Despite the differences in world religions, the distinction between the sacred or supernatural world and the profane or ordinary world is always present. See page 398.*

12.  **d.** *Durkheim was impressed by the universality of religion in human society. In 1912, he published his classic study of religion in which he concluded that the community solidarity and sense of shared beliefs inspired by religion gave it a vital function in maintaining the social system as a whole. See page 401.*

13.  **b.** *Many events in life have no scientific explanation;* *even in a highly technological society, religion will serve as a guide and a support for human behavior. See page 421.*

14.  **b.** *A functional equivalent of religion is a belief system that is compelling to adherents and directs behavior. Because it is not oriented toward the supernatural, communism may be considered a functional equivalent, not a religion. See page 402.*

15.  **e.** *Most societies have only a few religious organizations. In the United States many groups exist, representing a wide range of faiths. Religious pluralism is extensive in this country. See pages 412, 418.*

16. Karl Marx's view of religion was that
    a. it produces orderly social change.
    b. Christian beliefs are superior to other world religions.
    c. the dominant religion in any society legitimizes the interests of the ruling class.
    d. the Protestant ethic aided the development of capitalism.
    e. religious conflict is unlikely to occur when an ecclesia is present.

17. The spirit worship practiced by many American Indians is which type of religion?
    a. animism
    b. theism
    c. transcendant idealism
    d. theodicy
    e. simple superstition

18. Secularization is
    a. on the decline in the United States.
    b. easily measured by sociological research.
    c. accelerated by urbanization and modernization.
    d. the basis for voting patterns in the national elections.
    e. evidenced by the low level of church attendance in the United States.

19. In the United States, civic affairs and religion have been closely intertwined, leading some sociologists to speak of the society's "civil religion"—a vague nondenominational conviction that
    a. challenges the existing social structure and allocation of resources.
    b. provides a religious alternative for the young and socially disadvantaged who may not be part of a religious group.
    c. emphasizes religious differences among the dominant churches in American society.
    d. makes fun of people who are religious, because God's existence cannot be proved.
    e. unifies members of a religiously pluralistic society by giving them a sense that Americans are a godly people.

20. Which of the following statements accurately describes fundamentalism in the United States?
    a. Fundamentalists comprise a political force and communicate effectively via TV and radio.
    b. Fundamentalist religions are relatively small splinter groups.
    c. Fundamentalist religions are active in social justice campaigns, leading the fight for civil rights and the ERA.
    d. Fundamentalist religions attract a small minority of adherents who truly believe in the church's teachings.
    e. Fundamentalists favor greater emphasis on civil religion and secular humanism.

---

16.  c. *To Marx, religion was an ideology justifying the status quo and maintaining the privileged position of the dominant class. The appeal to sacred authority rationalizes unequal opportunities and life chances. Oppressed groups endorse the same ideology that keeps them oppressed. See page 403.*

17.  a. *Animism is the belief in active, animate spirits. Rain dances, for example, were appeals to spirits in nature to help humans. See pages 399–400.*

18.  c. *Urbanization and modernization are associated with secularization. In modern societies, new institutions erode the social influence of religion. Religion becomes a separate institution with a limited role. See page 419.*

19.  e. *Some sociologists argue that Americans share a worship of the American way of life and use various sacred elements to sanctify it. This "civil religion" may serve as a unifying force, particularly in a religiously pluralistic society such as the United States. See pages 414–415.*

20.  a. *Fundamentalist religions often use "electronic churches" to convey their message and to appeal for funds across the airwaves. Several fundamentalist church leaders have been politically active (one tele-evangelist, Pat Robertson, has even had presidential aspirations), strongly urging followers to vote in particular ways on controversial issues. See pages 413–415.*

21. Which of the following statements implies a functionalist perspective on religion?
    a. The persecution of cults is a tactic used by the ruling class to divert the attention of the underclass from economic and political injustice.
    b. Religion serves as a form of social cement, providing people with shared values and thus enhancing the solidarity of the society.
    c. Religious conflicts usually mask deeper economic conflicts.
    d. The interaction between preacher and congregation varies markedly among various types of religious organizations.
    e. Killing other people in the name of religion has a shock value that functions to disband violent groups.

22. In the Zoroastrian religion, the universe is seen as a battleground between evenly divided forces of good and evil. A victory for evil is caused by the failure of human beings to throw their weight on the side of good. This belief is an example of
    a. a functional equivalent of religion.
    b. secularization.
    c. theodicy.
    d. fundamentalism.
    e. magic.

23. In Marx's terms, which of the following would be an example of religious alienation?

    a. A person rejects the religious beliefs of the community and so feels "alien" within it.
    b. A conquered people are forced to give up their religion.
    c. People create a religion, lose sight of the fact that it is socially created, and allow the religion to order their lives.
    d. A person embraces communism.
    e. A person raised in a particular religion practices it only on holidays.

24. Max Weber attempted to explain the development of modern capitalism in terms of the "Protestant ethic," which is a belief in
    a. rewards in heaven, not on earth.
    b. mysterious "signs" of God's favor.
    c. a static social structure as integral to the natural order.
    d. thrift, hard work, and deferred gratification.
    e. a desire to live for today and enjoy the money you earn.

25. Sects may gain respectability over time, because
    a. their views become more fundamentalist.
    b. they become more interested in the sacred and thus don't "bother" anyone.
    c. their practices begin to approximate those of accepted denominations.
    d. they restrict membership to those who give continuing proof of their commitment.
    e. they shun worldly corruption.

---

21. **b.** *Functionalists look at the consequences of religion in terms of enhancing the stability of a society. The shared beliefs held by members of a religion form a common bond among them, stabilizing the society. See page 401.*

22. **c.** *A theodicy is an overarching explanation for the large problems of life. This view of the battleground explains all kinds of earthly events for believers in the Zoroastrian religion. See pages 400–401.*

23. **c.** *According to Marx, people lose sight of the fact that religion is socially created and take it for granted as "natural" or "right." This loss of control over the social*

*world produces a sense of alienation that prevents people from seeing the objective reality of this situation, much less changing it. See page 403.*

24. **d.** *The particular beliefs of Calvinists—thrift, hard work, and deferred gratification—were conducive to the development of capitalism, most particularly to the idea that money earned in excess of subsistence was to be reinvested as capital for future profits. See pages 405–406.*

25. **c.** *Most sects tend to be short-lived; however, some gradually become denominations. This shift always involves a gain in social respectability and a loss of fervor. See pages 409–410.*

NAME

COURSE/SECTION NUMBER

# A CASE STUDY

Thailand is an almost totally Buddhist country. Although it welcomed missionaries of all faiths for a number of years, the running joke among missionaries there is that gaining one convert makes for a "very good year." Members of the Thai government are Buddhist and ceremonies on state occasions include religious ritual. Almost all young Thai men serve for some time in a monastery as part of their voluntary religious training. Monks are so revered and cared for by the people that they need no other income to lead a secure life.

Buddhism focuses on the transcendence of life's trials. Practitioners try not to do evil or kill any living thing. The teachings of the Buddha instruct followers to pursue a middle path, neither denying oneself all worldly pleasures, nor becoming greedy about material gains. It is thought that the purity of following the middle path will release a person from the chain of earthly suffering and death.

The pervasive nature of Buddhism in Thai society led foreign governments to regard it as a key factor in the country's rather laissez-faire attitude toward modernization. The U.S. government attempted to channel foreign aid to Thailand using Buddhist monks as agricultural extension agents. The monks were supposed to teach crop production, better health, and support for the current government, which was sympathetic to the United States. As it turned out, the plan was very ineffective. The monks did not regularly carry through their assigned tasks nor did they show enthusiasm for them.

1.   What kind of religion is Buddhism (supernaturalism, animism, theism, or transcendent idealism)? Is Buddhism a(n) denomination, cult, sect, or ecclesia?

2.   In what ways is Buddhism a theodicy?

3.   How does Buddhism function within Thailand? What would Durkheim see as the functions of this religion?

4.   Why was using the highly respected monks for political purposes a failure?

5.   How does socialization to Buddhism affect the modernization and development of Thailand?

# Applying the Concepts

NAME

COURSE/SECTION NUMBER

## APPLICATION EXERCISE ONE

Select a religious group, not your own, that you wish to study. If possible, interview one or more practitioners of that faith and attend a religious service or meeting held by the group.

1.   How are the four functions of religion listed in the text evidenced in the practices of this group?

2.   Review Marx's theoretical approach to religion in which he argued that religion serves the dominant classes to legitimate the status quo. What specific ideas and practices of the group you are studying support this point of view? (Remember, this is not a criticism of anyone's religion.)

3.   Summarize in a paragraph or two the changes this religious group has experienced over time. Has it gone from a sect to a denomination? Is it a newly formed group? Has its membership increased or declined?

# APPLICATION EXERCISE TWO

_____

NAME

_____

COURSE/SECTION NUMBER

Look through the newspaper or news magazines for two examples of the connection between religion and social change. Choose an article on religion and politics as one of your examples.

1.  Use the functionalist perspective to demonstrate how religion retards social change.

2.  Use the conflict perspective to demonstrate how religion encourages social change.

## APPLICATION EXERCISE THREE

The text states that traditional denominations may be on the decline. There has been an increase in sect and cult membership as well as a continuing trend toward secularization.

1.   Some belief systems, such as transcendental meditation, est, psychotherapy, and pop psychology, seem to be "religions" for many people. Choose one of these belief systems and show how it fulfills the functions of religion. Is this belief system a functional equivalent of religion?

2.   Present a case study of secularization as you have observed it or read about it. (Think about what precipitated it, which institutions gained influence, which lost influence, etc.)

# CHAPTER 16

# Medicine

## Reviewing the Concepts

### LEARNING GOALS

*After studying this chapter, you should be able to:*

1. Contrast the institution of medicine in preindustrial and industrial societies.

2. Explain the social impact of endemic and epidemic disease.

3. Discuss social influences on disease.

4. Describe the field of epidemiology and how it contributes to understanding disease.

5.  List some of the social factors related to AIDS.

6.  Explain how the Hippocratic theory and the germ theory shaped the development of medicine and the role of doctors.

7.  Outline the professionalization of medicine and its consequences on doctors' prestige, autonomy, and income.

8.  Describe the socialization process for doctors and nurses.

9.  Present evidence for the medicalization of society; give two examples of the medicalization of deviance.

10. Illustrate how cultural factors affect the experience of illness and pain, as well as the selection of treatment.

11. Explain why the interaction between physicians and patients may be problematic.

12. Present a functionalist view of the medical institution.

13. Present Parsons's theory regarding the significance of the sick role to the individual and to society; then discuss the criticisms that the theory has raised.

14. Using a conflict perspective, analyze the strengths and weaknesses of the U.S. system of health care.

15. Identify factors that contribute to the escalation of health care costs and discuss measures to curb them.

16. Discuss the relationship among health, environment, and lifestyle.

17. Summarize sociologists' point of view regarding the most effective ways to reduce disease.

# IDENTIFYING KEY QUESTIONS AND THEMES

Good health has become a critical value in the modern world; in fact, we consider good health a basic right. Since illness affects every society, the human response to sickness is always socially organized, with specific ideas about what illness means, who treats the sick, and how and where treatment occurs. *Medicine* is the institution concerned with the maintenance of health and the treatment of disease.

The institution of medicine changes with the evolution from preindustrial to postindustrial societies. In the simplest societies, there are usually only two roles: the sick person, and the healer, often a religious figure relying on magic or rituals to treat disease. As societies become increasingly complex, the institution of medicine is based on a scientific approach, includes specialized roles, organizations, and facilities to treat the sick, and becomes much more costly. Sociologists study the relationship of the social context to how illness is understood and managed.

## Sickness and Society

*What are the social effects of disease? How do social factors inform us about who will become ill?*

Disease has many social effects, the most obvious of which is that a society is disrupted when people are too ill to function in their social roles. An *endemic disease* is one that is always present in a large part of a population. An *epidemic disease* is one that affects a significant part of a population in which it is normally uncommon. Diseases of short duration are called *acute;* diseases of long duration are called *chronic.* The effects of any disease often extend beyond the individual to the family, the community, and even the society. Epidemic diseases can have particularly far-reaching consequences: in some cases, they have destroyed entire societies. Despite remarkable medical advances, disease will always be with us, emphasizing the link between our health and the ever-changing environment.

Just as disease has a social impact, social factors influence disease. Studies of disease reveal the interplay of cultural practices and such social characteristics as age, race, social class, and gender. In every society, then, diseases tend to occur in predictable patterns.

## Epidemiology

*How does epidemiology contribute to our understanding of the origin of disease?*

*Epidemiology* is the study of the origin, distribution, and means of transmission of disease in populations. In trying to discover the crucial link between disease and its sources, epidemiologists look at whatever social and cultural characteristics the victims have in common. This approach has provided useful information about the spread and prevention of diseases such as cholera, legionnaires' disease, toxic-shock syndrome, and AIDS (acquired immune deficiency syndrome). The AIDS epidemic serves as one striking example of the mutual influence of society and disease. Many social factors are associated with the spread of the disease, including changing sexual norms, drug-abuse patterns, and global jet travel. Likewise, certain changes in behavior can reduce the incidence of diseases like AIDS.

## The Development of Medicine

*How did the Hippocratic and germ theories of disease shape the medical profession?*

The historical development of the modern medical system includes such factors as the evolution of theories of disease and its treatment, which groups claim authority to practice medicine, and what effect their practices have had on general health. The ancient Greeks favored theory over practical investigations of illness.

The Hippocratic model proposed that the health of an individual required a balance of four "humors," or body fluids. Coupled with support from the Church, this theory suppressed the development of scientific inquiry into disease for thousands of years.

The germ theory began in Europe during the Renaissance as the nonreligious roles of scientist and physician emerged. New discoveries informed doctors about the workings of the heart, the existence of microorganisms, and the importance of hygiene in controlling bacteria. Once the link between infectious organisms and disease was established, medical practice could become scientific and reliable.

Germ theory helped to launch modern medicine as we know it. Doctors focused on better and more effective ways to stop disease-causing organisms, becoming increasingly absorbed in the study of disease rather than in the care of patients. Over time, they acquired sophisticated techniques and developed a special vocabulary that patients did not understand. Physicians eventually became powerful and highly trained professionals, with the sole right to practice medicine and to direct its growth. With this power they also gained enormous social prestige and the wealth that accompanies it.

## The Medical Profession

*What is involved in the professionalization of medicine? How has the medical profession received special treatment or similar treatment by other professions? What is significant about the socialization medical students and nurses undergo? In what ways has U.S. society been medicalized?*

Because of the specialized and vital knowledge medical people possess, they tend to enjoy high social status. The unique social and historical forces within each society shape the privileges doctors receive. In societies with lower standards of health care, physicians generally have lower status than that of U.S. physicians. The rising status of doctors over the past century is due not only to advances in medical knowledge but also to concerted efforts by doctors to advance their own interests. The role of physician evolved from a job with access open to almost anyone, charlatan or not, to a regulated profession.

A *profession* is an occupation requiring extensive, systematic knowledge of, or training in, an art or science. Professionals in every field form associations to protect their interests and control access to their work. For doctors, the American Medical Association (AMA) is a powerful association that has achieved a legal monopoly over the practice of medicine in the United States. The elevated status of doctors is reflected in high salaries, prestige, and autonomy. This enviable combination has served as a model for other occupations trying to professionalize. However, current social trends may bring the status of medical professionals into line with that of other professions. Power is gradually passing from the physicians

themselves to the large bureaucratic organizations that employ them. In addition, other groups with a stake in the health care system are exerting pressure to contain costs and provide quality care.

Preliminary socialization for medicine begins early in life when tentative career choices are made. Medical students are disproportionately likely to be male, white, wealthy, and to have a close relative who is a doctor. Once engaged in the lengthy training for the profession, medical students and doctors not only learn about the science of medicine, but about the profession as well. Medical socialization includes information on medical ethics, appropriate physician-patient interaction, and the importance of maintaining some degree of emotional detachment from sickness and death. Nurses undergo a fairly similar socialization process, which results in a more realistic understanding of their role and how they can help patients. Their initial altruism may be tempered by the realities of low salaries and lack of autonomy, contributing to the high "burnout" rate among nurses.

Some sociologists suggest that the growth of a powerful high-status medical profession has resulted in a ***medicalization of society,*** a process in which the domain of medicine is extended over areas of life that were previously considered nonmedical. In the United States, evidence of this trend includes (1) the growth of the medical institution in terms of personnel, costs, and related organizations; (2) the medicalization of life events that were once considered natural and inevitable, such as childbirth; (3) the medicalization of deviance, whereby medical people claim authority over behaviors that were once regarded as sinful, criminal, or immoral and are now diagnosed as sickness; and (4) the public acceptance of medicalization as the correct way to treat a range of social problems. Despite challenges of its authority, the medical institution continues to be one of major importance to modern society.

## Health-Seeking Behavior

*How do cultural factors affect the experience of illness and pain? How do different subcultures use alternative health care systems? Why is the interaction between doctor and patient potentially problematic?*

The assumptions of our particular culture influence the

way we interpret our symptoms and what kind of treatment we seek and use when we are ill. Social definitions help us label and validate diseases. Likewise, our socialization into a particular culture or subculture influences our health-seeking behavior and shapes our responses to the experience of pain. Some ethnic Americans use their own unlicensed medical systems, such as the Chinese-Americans' use of acupuncture, the American Indians' use of natural medicines, and the Mexican-Americans' belief in folk medicine in lieu of "Anglo" doctors. However, the majority of Americans accept the medical profession's authority over disease, and consult a physician.

There are basic sociological distinctions made among the concepts of *illness,* the subjective sense that one is not well; *disease,* an objective pathology of the body, such as an infection; and *sickness,* the condition of those who are socially recognized as unwell. The presence of one condition does not imply the presence of the others. It is the interaction between doctor and patient that attempts to bring a consensus of these psychological, physiological, and sociological phenomena. A distinction is also made between signs, objective features that the physician can medically test, versus symptoms, subjective features that the physician knows indirectly through the patient's reports. Doctors are more inclined to pay attention to signs, while patients are more interested in their symptoms.

The encounter between physician and patient can be a highly complex one because the medical and lay subcultures are so different. Common understandings may be especially difficult to reach when the social, economic, and educational backgrounds of the participants differ greatly. Having more scientific knowledge, and being on familiar turf, the physician dominates the encounter. Observations of patient-physician interactions indicate that the two parties negotiate a diagnosis, blending the patient's expectations and needs with the doctor's knowledge and authority. This negotiation may even include the prescription of placebos or unnecessary medications in order to satisfy the patient's wish for "treatment."

## Medicine: A Functionalist View

*What are the features of a functionalist view of medicine? How did Parsons describe the sick role? What are the functions of the sick role for society? What are the functions of the medical institution?*

Talcott Parsons, a functionalist theorist, argued that a society can function smoothly only if most of its members are able to play their roles most of the time. Since sickness is disruptive to society, society must have a means of determining who is legitimately sick. To do so, society uses an institutionalized *sick role*—a pattern of behavior expected of someone who is ill. Parsons argues that the sick role carries special privileges and responsibilities and is crucial for the normal functioning of society. According to Parsons, (1) sickness is a form of deviance, but because it is involuntary, the person is excused; (2) sick people can claim exemption from normal social duties; (3) sick people should want to get well, otherwise they are perceived as trying to escape their responsibilities; and (4) sick people should seek technically competent help to verify the sickness and to aid in their recovery.

Although the concept of the sick role has enjoyed immense success, it has been criticized on several counts: the focus on acute rather than on chronic disease; the focus on curative as opposed to preventive medicine; the lack of attention to the variety of ways people deal with illness; and the stigma of deviance that is associated with some diseases. However, the theory does describe how illness is socially controlled (through the sick role) and is thus not a matter of individual experience alone.

The medical institution has four main functions: (1) the maintenance of health through medical care and public health measures; (2) the treatment of disease, involving a variety of roles and organizations; (3) research and innovation; and (4) social control to maintain the prevailing norms of the society.

## Medicine: A Conflict View

*What are the assumptions of the conflict view of medicine? How effective is the conflict view in explaining the American health care system?*

The conflict view of medicine assumes that good health is a highly valued resource that is unequally distributed in society; competition over this resource shapes a society's health care system. One's chances of enjoying good health are linked to socioeconomic status, which, in turn, is related to healthy living conditions and access to good health care. People in lower socioeconomic groups are likely to have limited exposure to health education, poorer sanitation, more hazardous working conditions, lower standards of nutrition, and less ready access to health care. In the United States, patterns of health and disease are closely linked to race and class. Here, as everywhere else, social and economic background literally affect one's life chances.

In most industrialized societies, health care is provided as a public service. The United States is the only modern industrialized nation without some form of national health insurance. Instead, a "medical-industrial complex" sells goods and services for profit. The strength of this capitalist arrangement is technologically advanced health care. The weakness lies in unequal access and distribution of services. Opinion polls show that most Americans would prefer a national health-insurance system, a proposal strongly opposed by the AMA. The real question is whether health care, like education and public safety, should be a tax-supported social service or whether it should remain a highly commercial enterprise.

## Health Costs in America

*What factors contribute to the escalation of health care costs? What actions are currently being taken to control these costs?*

Health care in the United States costs one-tenth of the gross national product. Several factors contribute to this expense: (1) the pressure for profits from doctors, hospitals, and insurance companies; (2) federal support of health care through Medicaid and Medicare; (3) rising hospital costs, accounting for 70 percent of health care costs; (4) "defensive medicine"—overuse of medical tests—related to fear of malpractice lawsuits; and (5) surplus doctors and redundant procedures. Some piecemeal efforts are in place to curb these costs, including the development of health maintenance organizations (HMOs), encouraging people to get second opinions before major surgery, use of generic drugs, and setting limits on the amount government will reimburse hospitals for certain treatments.

## Disease, Environment, and Lifestyle

*What is the relationship between health and environment? What do sociologists suggest is the most effective way to reduce disease?*

Modern medical techniques have had a negligible impact on the overall death rates in industrialized countries during the past century. In large part, lower death rates are attributable to higher standards of nutrition and innovations in public health. There is no sign that the overall extent of disease is decreasing, although the kinds of diseases that prevail and cause the majority of deaths are certainly changing. Because people do not succumb to infectious diseases of childhood, they live longer and face chronic diseases of middle and old age, such as cancer or heart disease. The causes of these diseases can be traced to the relationship between individuals and their natural and social environment. In other words, individuals' habits of eating, smoking, drinking, and exercise, as well as exposure to environmental hazards and pollution, are significant contributors to, or preventors of, disease. Unfortunately, these chronic conditions are very resistant to medical intervention; they require changes in lifestyle and environment. The dangers of smoking, nonuse of seatbelts, and high-cholesterol diets are well known, yet Americans continue to take health risks by not acting on this knowledge. For example, the epidemiology of cancer shows a significant correlation between smoking and the disease, especially lung cancer. Although correlation does not prove cause, no other plausible explanation has been suggested to explain the link between those who smoke and those who get cancer, a relationship tested across many samples and under many conditions. Rather than concentrating only on advances in treatment of disease, the sociological study of medicine suggests it would be cheaper and more effective to focus on prevention of injury and disease, in part by changing people's dangerous health habits.

## DEFINING CORE CONCEPTS

*After studying the chapter, write a sociological definition in your own words for the following core concepts. Then give an example from your own experience to illustrate your definition. Refer to the chapter to check your work.*

| *Core Concept* | *Sociological Definition* | *Personal Illustration* |
| --- | --- | --- |
| acute disease | | |
| chronic disease | | |
| endemic disease | | |
| epidemic disease | | |
| epidemiology | | |

| *Core Concept* | *Sociological Definition* | *Personal Illustration* |
| --- | --- | --- |
| illness/disease/sickness | | |
| medicalization of society | | |
| medicine | | |
| profession | | |
| sick role | | |

## PUTTING IDEAS TOGETHER

The medical institution, like other social institutions, is characterized by norms, values, statuses, and groups. As individuals come into contact with the medical institution, they bring their unique backgrounds into play.

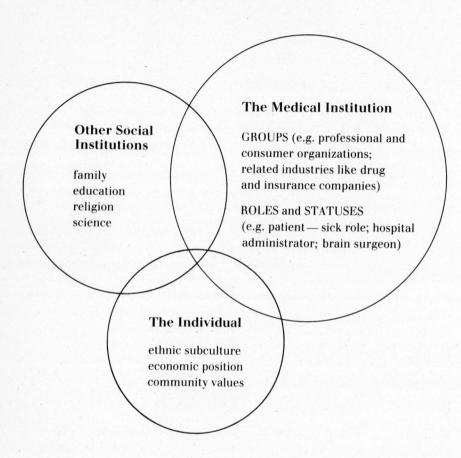

**Other Social
Institutions**

family
education
religion
science

**The Medical Institution**

GROUPS (e.g. professional and
consumer organizations;
related industries like drug
and insurance companies)

ROLES and STATUSES
(e.g. patient — sick role; hospital
administrator; brain surgeon)

**The Individual**

ethnic subculture
economic position
community values

# Testing the Concepts

## MULTIPLE-CHOICE QUESTIONS

*After studying the chapter, try to answer each of the twenty-five questions below. Mark the alternative you think is correct; then look at the correct answer and the explanation provided at the bottom of the page. Try to state why the other alternatives are incorrect, and check your understanding of the correct answer.*

1. Individuals differ in what kinds of help they seek when they're ill, how they experience pain, and which informal cures they use. Some of these individual differences are explained by the following variables. Which one is particularly important?
   a. ethnicity
   b. gender
   c. social class
   d. area of residence
   e. age

2. The institution of medicine plays a more central role in modern societies than in preindustrial societies largely due to
   a. the emergence of a sick role.
   b. the rise in the number of patients and illnesses.
   c. the separation of the medical and religious institutions.
   d. the greater faith people have in healers' ability to help them.
   e. the overlap of the medical and economic institutions.

3. What is the fundamental principle underlying epidemiology?
   a. Medical science is able to cure anything, if enough research is done.
   b. Disease does not strike at random.
   c. Acute diseases pose the greatest threat for industrialized countries.
   d. The medical institution should stick to diseases and not try to solve social problems such as alcoholism.
   e. The health care system could be decentralized to the community level.

4. Which of the following illustrates the medicalization of life events?
   a. having a baby at home using natural childbirth methods
   b. having a ruptured appendix removed in a hospital emergency room
   c. moving into a hospice to face death from terminal illness
   d. having a fat-suction operation because you feel overweight
   e. calling the pediatrician with a question about your child's chicken pox

---

1. **a.** *Sociologists have studied patterns of ethnic differences in interpretation of symptoms, response to pain, and choice of home remedies. These subcultural variations affect the kinds of treatment people seek when they are ill as well as the responses of family and friends to sickness. See pages 437–438.*

2. **e.** *Medicine has become a highly specialized profession with many occupational roles. The cost of medical care has increased dramatically, and whether medical costs are borne by individuals or their government, a substantial portion of economic activity is devoted to medicine. In the United States, one out of every ten dollars goes to health-related goods and services. See pages 425, 435–436.*

3. **b.** *Epidemiologists study diseases—who gets them, how they are transmitted, and what social and cultural factors affect those probabilities. Such research shows that disease follows certain patterns that can be predicted, not for individual people, but for communities. See pages 427–428.*

4. **d.** *The medicalization of life events refers to taking normal life events and making them medical problems or having them handled by the medical institution. Cosmetic surgery like fat-suction is an example of medical intervention on behalf of norms of beauty, not health. See page 436.*

5.  Physicians have the highest prestige ratings and the highest average incomes of any occupation. How would a sociologist explain this situation?
   a.  the dislike people have for the sick role
   b.  the successful professionalization of the medical field
   c.  the gratitude sick people feel toward those who cure them
   d.  the high incidence of illness in our society
   e.  the advanced technological state of the medical institution

6.  Becker and others have studied the socialization process for medical students. They documented a change from _____ to _____ .
   a.  doubts about medical knowledge/confidence in medical knowledge
   b.  feelings of infallibility/feelings of self-doubt
   c.  idealism about helping the sick/realism about the possibilities and limits of modern medicine
   d.  guidance by personal ethics/lack of ethical standards to follow
   e.  fear of emotional involvement with patients/caring about each patient as a person

7.  As societies move from preindustrial to industrial arrangements, what change is evidenced in the medical *institution?*
   a.  an increase in endemic diseases
   b.  a higher life expectancy for individuals with healthy diets
   c.  an increase in specialized roles
   d.  a decreased emphasis on preventive medicine
   e.  a greater overlap between illness, sickness, and disease

8.  Which of the following statements is true about epidemic disease in a modern society such as the United States?
   a.  Recent epidemics have primarily affected children.
   b.  Medical science is better able to treat endemic disease than epidemic disease.
   c.  There are periodic outbreaks of epidemic disease but they are quickly controlled.
   d.  Epidemic disease (such as the influenza outbreak in 1918) is not altogether unlikely.
   e.  For citizens living in conditions of inadequate sanitation, it is a constant condition.

---

5.  **b.** *The medical profession is strongly controlled by its members. Medical school admissions are kept low enough to create a demand for doctors. The knowledge and skill possessed by doctors is closely guarded, resulting in high esteem and high salaries in a free-market health care system. See page 434.*

6.  **c.** *Most students enter medical school with idealistic notions of helping others. As they progress through the system and encounter the pressures of a medical education, they learn the norms of that professional subculture, including distancing oneself from patients, protecting other doctors, and adhering to the AMA code of ethics. See page 435.*

7.  **c.** *The complexity of industrialized societies is mirrored in all its institutions. The medical institution* becomes more centralized, more elaborate, and includes more specialized roles. The growth of health-related work, such as medical insurance, psychological and physical therapy, and pharmaceuticals reflects the medical institution's increasing complexity. See pages 425–426.*

8.  **d.** *Epidemic disease is controlled by basic standards of sanitation and public health, a program of vaccines, and effective treatment of diseases when they occur. However, despite all the medical advances, devastating epidemics still threaten modern industrialized societies. AIDS is now reaching epidemic proportions because its cure is not known and efforts at prevention and education are just beginning to take effect. See pages 427, 429.*

9. A major health care concern in the United States is the increase of chronic diseases. Why is this a problem?
    a. The likelihood of epidemic contagion poses a serious threat.
    b. They are resistant to medical intervention.
    c. They are undetected in many cases until they have reached the terminal stage.
    d. They strike young children most frequently.
    e. Epidemiological information is not relevant to chronic diseases.

10. Sociology contributes to epidemiology by demonstrating that
    a. illness is related to cultural practices.
    b. illness increases with modernization.
    c. doctors have become more professionalized.
    d. the sick role is a deviant role.
    e. a person's family medical history is the key to predicting his or her health.

11. What is involved in the medicalization of deviance?
    a. Criminals are allowed access to the same medical care as anyone else.
    b. Taking drugs, even with a prescription, is considered deviant.
    c. The sick role is not tolerated.
    d. Society thinks of some illnesses as deviant behavior.
    e. Deviant behavior is treated as a medical problem.

12. If we were to do a comparative study of the status of doctors in various countries, perhaps the most telling information we would collect is
    a. the proportion of men and women in the field.
    b. the incidence of epidemics and whether they were eradicated.
    c. whether the country's system of medicine is socialized or capitalist.
    d. the doctors' adherence to the Hippocratic oath.
    e. the percentage of doctors working in private practice.

13. Which of the following has been most important in unraveling the mystery of AIDS
    a. the medical test that identifies those who are carriers of the virus
    b. epidemiological work on the social characteristics of victims
    c. rapid government funding for AIDS research
    d. germ theory
    e. the long incubation period of the virus

---

9. **b.** *Chronic diseases result from unhealthy environmental conditions and lifestyle choices. Although some of these diseases can be kept in check and a person's condition improved, individuals are rarely cured. Medical intervention is much more effective in treating acute disease. See page 448.*

10. **a.** *Epidemiology is the study of disease in populations. Sociologists have identified some of the social factors and cultural practices, such as diet, drinking and smoking habits, health maintenance, and stress, related to disease. See pages 427–428.*

11. **e.** *The medical institution is extremely powerful in modern societies. Many problems or behaviors that were once considered deviant are now defined as illnesses and* come under the care of the medical profession. Examples include alcoholism, mental illness, and certain types of unconventional sexual behavior. See page 436.*

12. **a.** *The high status of the physician is correlated with a high proportion of male practitioners. In countries where women dominate medicine, the status of doctors is much lower. See page 433.*

13. **b.** *Epidemiological work, in part done by sociologists, revealed the pattern of AIDS and explained the link between some social characteristics and the likelihood of getting AIDS. This allowed medical researchers to zero in on a specific population for study and to narrow down the possible causes of the disease. See pages 429–430.*

14. The unique aspect of health care in the United States that underlies many of its problems is that
   a. doctors prefer to work in large hospitals rather than in private practice.
   b. physicians' annual salaries are too high.
   c. health care is a service run for profit.
   d. medical knowledge has not kept pace with medical advances in Western European countries.
   e. insurance rates have not kept up with the actual cost of health care.

15. The most damaging legacy of the Hippocratic theory was
   a. resistance to scientific evidence.
   b. inflated incomes and prestige of physicians.
   c. lack of professional ethics.
   d. the clash between medical and religious definitions of death.
   e. hypocritical behavior by patients who say they follow doctors' advice and then do not.

16. How do physicians differ from other professionals?
   a. Because of the life-and-death nature of their work, they are more willing to be openly critical of a colleague's incompetence.
   b. They work longer hours.

   c. They have more control over their own profession.
   d. They have more than one licensing agent.
   e. Their fees are more responsive to the demands of the marketplace.

17. The textbook gives an extended example of research on smoking and disease. What general lesson for the American health care system can be drawn from it?
   a. In research, correlations are not causes; the findings of such studies are meaningless.
   b. More attention needs to be paid to prevention, not cure.
   c. Diseases occur at random; cancer can happen to anyone.
   d. Laws against unhealthy behavior are effective.
   e. The public heeds medical recommendations about their health.

18. Lawrence, a corporate lawyer, has been putting in his usual long hours at the office in spite of a serious cough that forces him to lie down and catch his breath. He says he is sick but refuses to take the time to see a doctor until a major case is settled. The negative response he receives from his colleagues is due to

---

14. **c.** *Most industrialized countries have some form of socialized or subsidized medicine, whereas the U.S. system of health care is based on the free enterprise system. Health care is extremely expensive, and people with less money often receive poorer quality care than do the rich. See pages 444–445.*

15. **a.** *The Hippocratic theory blended religious teachings and medical science, with the latter conforming to the former. Scientific evidence that differed from church doctrine met with a great deal of resistance. As a result, sound medical inquiry was suppressed until the Renaissance when the nonreligious roles of physician and scientist emerged, clearing the way for the germ theory and its emphasis on infectious microorganisms. See pages 431–432.*

16. **c.** *Physicians have considerably more control over their own working conditions, who is licensed, how medical education is handled, and how fees are set than do those in other professions. See page 434.*

17. **b.** *Smoking has been linked to a range of diseases. All of these diseases are difficult to treat once they have been diagnosed. An emphasis on prevention—in this case, not smoking at all or stopping smoking—is a much more effective way to approach the problem. See page 449.*

18. **b.** *The sick role allows people to take time off from their usual responsibilities in order to attend to their health. Part of the sick role is the expectation that medical help will be sought and doctor's orders will be followed. It is a violation of the sick role to claim illness but not seek help or drop regular duties. See page 441.*

a. their perception that he has not practiced preventive medicine.

b. his failure to conform to the sick role.

c. the high cost of his eventual medical care.

d. his overplaying the sick role.

e. Lawrence's inability to interpret his own symptoms.

19. Taking a conflict perspective, a sociologist looking at the medical institution in the United States would be most likely to investigate

a. potential abuse of the sick role.

b. uneven access to and unequal quality of health care for all Americans.

c. the effectiveness of Medicare in caring for the elderly.

d. nurses' level of satisfaction with their work.

e. patients' use of second opinions in making medical decisions.

20. The AMA describes any national health-insurance proposal as "socialized medicine." This description is

a. accurate and correctly suggests that such a plan is a step in the direction of a socialist state.

b. inaccurate and fails to admit that in other countries national health plans provide a greater abundance of health services.

c. accurate but fails to acknowledge that many services in the United State are "socialized."

d. inaccurate and fails to acknowledge that such a plan would provide greater equality in health care.

e. not relevant to the medical institution.

21. Karen frequently calls in sick, about once a month, usually on Fridays, with a migraine headache. She says she's ill but her co-workers scoff and think she wants a long weekend. Sociologists would say Karen

a. has a sickness, but not an illness or a disease.

b. has a disease, but not an illness.

c. has an illness, but not a sickness.

d. is taking the sick role too far.

e. has a disease and is deviant.

22. The United States has an extremely high rate of infant mortality compared to other technologically advanced societies. What feature of American health care would explain this problem?

a. unequal access to medical care for different social classes

b. lack of sufficient medical research

c. a shortage of pediatricians

d. patients who don't follow doctors' orders

e. more doctors who work for HMOs and corporate employers instead of in private practice

19. **b.** *Conflict theorists assume that good health care is a highly valued resource over which there is competition in a capitalist system. Such a view would lead to an investigation of the quality and equity of health care available to different social groups. See page 443.*

20. **c.** *To most Americans, the label "socialized medicine" suggests "socialism," which they regard negatively. In fact, however, many public services in the United States—from police forces to the educational system—are "socialized" because they are paid for by taxes and freely available to all. Such an approach to health care would ensure a more equal distribution of health care services. See page 445.*

21. **c.** *Sociologists distinguish between illness, disease, and sickness. Karen feels ill (a subjective judgment) and has a disease (a biological condition of recurring headaches). She is not considered sick by others, a social judgment, because she acts suspiciously in playing the sick role. See page 439.*

22. **a.** *Because medical care in the United States is a profit-making service, the ability to pay affects the quality of care received. Lower social classes have a high incidence of mental and physical illness, as well as higher rates of infant mortality, due to limited access to high-quality care. See page 444.*

23. Sociologists have identified many factors contributing to soaring health care costs in the United States. Which one of the following is *not* a factor?
    a. hospital costs
    b. HMOs
    c. Medicaid and Medicare
    d. defensive medicine
    e. surplus doctors, redundant procedures

24. Patients often complain that they do not understand their doctors and are too intimidated to ask questions. How would a sociologist explain this problem?
    a. By its very nature, most medical information defies adequate translation into everyday language.
    b. The heavy demands on doctors' time make it impossible for them to spend time answering questions that are usually based on a complete ignorance of medicine.

c. Some doctors have big egos and feel important when they toss out big words.
d. The subculture of doctors involves maintaining control of the doctor-patient interaction.
e. Part of the sick role is accepting the medical advice you have paid to receive.

25. Every society seems to have healers who enjoy relatively high social status. One reason for this is that
    a. most patient–physician encounters do not involve serious disease.
    b. the healers have an inborn talent for what they do.
    c. societies have customs that cannot be explained.
    d. sickness makes everyone desperate for help.
    e. the healers have access to and control of vital knowledge.

---

23. **b.** *For years, medical costs have risen faster than the rate of inflation — with detrimental effects on the budgets of government, employers, and families. Some steps have been taken to contain costs, including prescription of generic drugs, limits on amounts reimbursed to hospitals for particular treatments, and development of HMOs — health maintenance organizations staffed by salaried physicians and offering a full range of services to consumers who pay a (lower) fixed annual fee. See pages 445–447.*

24. **d.** *Doctors are trained in technical knowledge, not communication skills. They form a subculture that is different from that of their patients. It is important for doctors to control the interaction so that they retain the role of the expert. This behavior, sometimes unintentionally, makes communication with patients difficult. See page 439.*

25. **e.** *Sickness is part of every society, and those whose knowledge and skill enable them to relieve the pain and suffering of illness are rewarded with high social status. They carefully guard and control that position by restricting access to knowledge and skill that creates it. See pages 425, 433.*

## A CASE STUDY

NAME

COURSE/SECTION NUMBER

In 1984, the Humana Hospital in Louisville, Kentucky performed its first artificial heart transplant on William Schroeder. One of his predecessors, Barney Clark, received an artificial heart in a university research hospital, and lived for a short time. The Humana team went on to transplant three more artificial hearts within the next year, announcing each event with a great deal of fanfare. When Schroeder was able to leave the hospital on special life-support systems, a news conference called for the event got national press coverage. The doctors on the Humana team became instant celebrities, and appeared on the talk-show circuit. Stock in the profit-making hospital rose steadily.

1.   How would a conflict theorist analyze the development of artificial heart transplants?

2.    Which elements of a capitalist health care system are evident in this case?

3.    What are the strengths and weaknesses of medical breakthroughs occurring in private, profit-making settings?

# Applying the Concepts

NAME
_____

COURSE/SECTION  NUMBER

## APPLICATION EXERCISE ONE

1.    Choose an example of a social-personal problem, such as eating disorders (obesity, anorexia, bulimia), alcoholism, facial disfigurement, mental retardation, etc., and answer the following questions.

    a.  How has this problem been medicalized? How does the medical institution get involved in, take control over, and treat the problem?

    b.  How is the problem, or how was it, treated differently by other institutions, such as the criminal justice system, religion, or education?

    c.  How does the medical institution maintain social control over this problem?

2.    Take the example either of home births or home deaths (e.g., hospice care for the terminally ill). How have birth and death been medicalized? How have these movements met with resistance from the medical establishment? Why?

## APPLICATION EXERCISE TWO

1.    American television provides its viewers with many glimpses of the lives of doctors, nurses, and other medical personnel. Watch at least three episodes of a medical show, such as "General Hospital" or "St. Elsewhere." Comment on the following:

    a. evidence of a subculture of medical people

    b. social distance and communication problems between doctors and patients

    c. social stratification in medicine

    d. social control

2.    Give a sociological explanation of why there are so many television shows about doctors, and not about plumbers, teachers, secretaries, or grocery-store clerks.

NAME

COURSE/SECTION NUMBER

## APPLICATION EXERCISE THREE

This chapter described the social institution of medicine. Remember that a social institution is a patterned way for society to meet a need — in this case, health care for its members. All social institutions have roles, statuses, and involve a certain degree of stratification.

Think back to the last time you or someone you know was sick enough to require medical attention from a doctor and, possibly, hospitalization.

1.    What evidence did you see for the requirements of the sick role? What privileges were associated with the role?

2.    What were the physician's role requirements? How did the physician demonstrate the special status she or he deserved because of technical knowledge? For example, a doctor will not perform certain tasks, like changing bedpans, because they are not part of the role, and thus hinder impression management. Did you find examples of problematic communication between patient and doctor? Did you see evidence of the doctors' subculture?

3.    Particularly in the hospital setting, what evidence did you see of stratification of medical personnel? Who gave orders? Who performed which duties?

4.    Can you provide an example of how ethnic background played a part in the definition of the illness and its treatment? Does your (or the patient's) ethnic background include any home remedies or special traditions related to illness?

# CHAPTER 17

# The Economic Order

## Reviewing the Concepts

### LEARNING GOALS

*After studying this chapter, you should be able to:*

1. Discuss the economic order and the importance of economic activity.

2. Distinguish among the primary, secondary, and tertiary sectors, and the shifts in each associated with increasing industrialization.

3. Explain the idea of division of labor and the consequences of surplus wealth.

4. Compare Durkheim's concepts of mechanical and organic solidarity in terms of social cohesion.

5. Define "anomie" and describe its sources and consequences.

6. Contrast occupations and professions and explain the trend toward professionalization.

7. Present Marx's analysis of alienation and work.

8. Outline the patterns of worker satisfaction in the United States.

9. Give examples of the use of sociological ideas to improve human relations and working conditions in industrial settings.

10. State the three ways in which property is owned and discuss the social consequences of each.

11. Characterize capitalism as an ideal type and as it actually appears in countries such as the United States.

12. Characterize socialism and democratic socialism as ideal types, and give examples of each, citing the Soviet Union and other communist-ruled societies as well as the countries of Western Europe.

13. Explain convergence theory, providing evidence for and against it as an economic trend.

14. Characterize the economic system in China.

15. Present the features of a corporate economy.

16. Describe the extent of economic control exerted by large corporations, noting its social consequences.

17. Explain the increase in multinational corporations and its global consequences.

18. Discuss current concerns about unbounded economic growth and global modernization.

19. Outline the social consequences of unemployment for the individual and for society.

20. Characterize the world of work in a postindustrial economy.

## IDENTIFYING KEY QUESTIONS AND THEMES

The *economic order* is the institutionalized system for producing and distributing goods and services. Beyond providing basic necessities of food and shelter, economic activity is an important component of human culture and social structure. The principal means of production that a society uses — hunting and gathering, horticulture, pastoralism, agriculture, industrialism, or postindustrialism — strongly influences the size and complexity of the society and the character of its cultural and social life. As Marx and other theorists indicated, there is a close link among economic structures and social issues, social inequality, and social change. Of course, economic activity is also an important part of everyday life; we derive much of our personal and social identity from our work.

### The Sociology of Occupations

*How does the economy change with the process of industrialization? What is the significance of an increasingly specialized division of labor? What is involved in the process of professionalization?*

Sociologists study the way a society's occupational structure develops and changes. Any economy contains three basic sectors. The *primary sector* gathers or extracts raw materials; the *secondary sector* turns those raw materials into manufactured goods; and the *tertiary sector* provides services or information. The process of industri-

alization, in which economies move from preindustrial to postindustrial arrangements, changes the proportion of people involved in each sector. In preindustrial societies, the primary sector predominates; in industrial societies, the secondary sector; and in postindustrial societies, the tertiary sector. As industrialization takes hold, workers labor outside the home, receive wages instead of producing their own goods, and live in cities rather than in small communities. The economy of the United States is highly concentrated in the tertiary sector.

In the course of economic development, the *division of labor* — the specialization by individuals or groups in particular economic activities — becomes more complex in order to meet the highly technical demands of postindustrial work. In small hunting and gathering societies, there is little division of labor except on the basis of age and sex. As economic production evolves from pastoral and horticultural societies to agricultural societies, the division of labor increases. These societies produce *surplus wealth* — more food and other goods than is necessary to meet their producers' basic needs — that relieves some people of subsistence activities, allowing them to specialize in other roles. Industrial production depends on specialization for maximum efficiency and production.

The French sociologist Emile Durkheim tried to determine the social consequences of the division of labor in modern societies. Durkheim's main concern centered on the factors that contributed to or reduced social solidarity. He concluded that increased specialization encourages individualism at the expense of community, reducing social solidarity. Durkheim identified two bases for social solidarity.

According to Durkheim, traditional societies are held together by *mechanical solidarity,* a form of social cohesion based on the similarity of members: everyone does much the same work, holds common values, and possesses characteristics very much like those of other members of society, resulting in a "collective consciousness." Modern societies, on the other hand, are held together by *organic solidarity,* a form of social cohesion based on the differences among members, making them interdependent. These societies offer diverse economic roles, resulting in corresponding differences in values and personal characteristics. The basis of social solidarity, then, shifts from a cohesion based on the similarity of the members to one based on their differences.

In modern societies, the division of labor, with its emphases on differences among people, increases individuality, and reduces loyalty to the community and its shared sentiments, values, and beliefs. The outcome may be *anomie,* a condition of confusion that exists in both individual and society when social norms are weak, absent, or conflicting. Having little commitment to shared norms, individuals feel detached from other people and are inclined to pursue their private desires without regard for the interests of society as a whole. Social control of individual behavior becomes more difficult, and society faces possible deviance, disorganization, or even disintegration.

As Durkheim predicted, the division of labor that characterizes modern societies does seem to result in anomie. However, modern societies retain enough consensus on norms and values to guide most individual behavior and to avert the social breakdown Durkheim feared.

One effect of specialization in modern economies is the appearance of professions. A *profession* is an occupation requiring extensive, systematic knowledge of, or training in, an art or a science. Professions are generally the highest paid and most prestigious occupations, and are distinguished from other occupations by several characteristics. First, the skill of professionals is based on systematic, theoretical knowledge, not merely on training in particular techniques or procedures. Second, professionals enjoy considerable autonomy over their work

and are able to make independent judgments. Third, professionals form associations that regulate their profession's internal affairs and represent its interests to outside groups. Fourth, professionals set standards for, and regulate admission to, the profession. Fifth, all members are expected to adhere to a code of ethics established by the profession.

The trend in society is for nonprofessionals to try to "professionalize" themselves in the hope of gaining greater prestige and income. This transformation typically follows a sequence: creating a professional association and setting qualifications for membership; establishing a code of ethics; and legitimizing and enforcing occupational certification, thereby gaining control over the number of members. Attempts to professionalize jobs in the primary and secondary sectors of industry have generally met with only limited success. In the tertiary sector, however, the number of jobs with "professional" or semiprofessional status is growing rapidly.

## The Nature of Work

*What is alienation? What factors are associated with worker satisfaction in the United States? How have human relations programs in industry affected alienation?*

Work is a central part of our existence; it is the activity that occupies most of our waking adult lives. The income that work produces largely determines our social status. Work greatly affects our identity and feelings of self-worth as well. The term *alienation* refers to the situation in which people lose control over the social world they have created, with the result that they find themselves "alien" in a hostile environment. According to Marx, the extreme division of labor in modern societies is a primary source of alienation. Each worker has a limited economic role with diminished responsibility and thus a corresponding lack of satisfaction with the products of that labor. Work becomes a means to an end rather than an activity in which human capacities are challenged and expanded. In capitalist economies, the surplus profit goes to the owners rather than to the workers, further aggravating this situation.

Analyses of work in the United States have focused on the degree of worker satisfaction. Although many workers say they are satisfied with their jobs and would work even if it were not financially necessary, many doubt that they would pursue the same job if they could begin their work career again. Overall job satisfaction may come from intrinsic or extrinsic rewards. The following factors contribute to satisfaction: independence and control, financial rewards, opportunity for promotion, opportunity to use talents and to develop individual potentials, varied and interesting tasks, and job prestige. In general, worker satisfaction is higher in the tertiary economy, especially among skilled information workers.

Sociological evidence has guided efforts toward adjusting work to reduce alienation by humanizing the workplace. For instance, experiments conducted by Elton Mayo at the Hawthorne plant of the Western Electric Company highlighted the influence of peer-group norms on worker productivity. Mayo's subjects, trying to please his team of researchers, established their own norms of productivity as a group, and bettered their performance with each new change in their working conditions. This experimental response has come to be known as the "Hawthorne effect," in which the subjects' assumptions about what the researchers are trying to prove contaminate the experiment.

Mayo's findings led to a new "human relations" approach to the workplace, which has included the use of incentives, better wages and working conditions, greater human contact, profit-sharing, teamwork, job rotation, and an opportunity to participate in workplace decisions. The end result of these efforts is that today's workers have more control over and satisfaction with the workplace than was the case a few decades ago.

## Capitalism and Socialism

*What is the fundamental difference between capitalism and socialism? How is the concept of property central to distinguishing the two? What are the characteristics of a capitalist economic system? What are the characteristics of a socialist economic system? What are the distinguishing features of democratic socialism and communism as economic institutions?*

**Capitalism** and **socialism** are the two basic economic systems in the modern world. In capitalism, the means of production and distribution are privately owned; in socialism, they are publicly owned. The terms "capitalism" and "socialism" each represent an *ideal type,* an abstract description constructed from a number of real cases in order to reveal their essential features. In actual societies, there is a great deal of variation within each economic system, and no political system represents a pure example of either economic arrangement.

The key distinction between capitalism and socialism lies in the form of property ownership. *Property* is the set of rights that the owner of something has in relation to others who do not own it. Property is established in a society through social norms, often expressed in law, that define the conditions under which people may own property. The scarcity of resources results in competition among people to own them. Ownership of property may take one of three forms: (1) Communal ownership exists when property belongs to the community as a whole and may be used by any member of that community. (2) Private ownership exists when property belongs to specific persons. (3) Public ownership exists when property belongs to the state or some other political authority that claims the property on behalf of the people as a whole. As Marx and others pointed out, those who own the means of producing and distributing goods and services are potentially in a position of power over those who do not own them.

Capitalism is organized around the deliberate pursuit of personal profit and relies on market competition as the mechanism for determining what is produced, at what price, and for which consumers. In a capitalist system, the goal of profit making is seen as normal, morally acceptable, and socially desirable. Market forces of supply and demand theoretically ensure that the best possible products are available at the lowest possible price. Thus, the profit motive provides the incentive for initial production; competition among producers offers the public a range of goods and prices. For the capitalist system to work, the government would ideally adopt a policy of *laissez-faire* ("leave it alone") and not interfere with the competitive process.

Although the United States conforms most closely to the ideal model of capitalism, capitalism in its pure form has never existed. The U.S. government regulates and supervises many aspects of economic activity. For example, it influences the level of production and consumption through its budget and tax policies. It safeguards competition in the marketplace by restricting growth of a *monopoly,* a single firm that dominates an industry, or of an *oligopoly,* a group of a few firms that dominates an industry. At the same time that capitalism in the United States has been highly productive, it has resulted in marked social inequalities. Nevertheless, Americans generally endorse private ownership and the pursuit of profit.

Socialism rests on the assumption that the goal of economic activity is the fulfillment of social needs, and it holds that public ownership of the means of production is the best way to address the interests of society as a whole. This economic system, therefore, relies on centralized planning, rather than market forces, as the mechanism for determining what is produced, at what price, and for which consumers. The aims of a socialist economy are the efficient production of needed goods and services and the achievement of social equality by preventing the accumulation of private wealth. As in the case of capitalism, no actual society entirely conforms to the ideal model of socialism. In reality, two very divergent forms of socialism exist today. Many governments in Eastern Europe and Asia practice an authoritarian form of socialism known as Soviet-style socialism, whereas many Western European governments practice democratic socialism.

Soviet-style socialism exists in countries that are ruled by communist parties. These countries consider themselves to be in a stage of socialism, a preparatory step toward their true goal of *communism,* a hypothetical egalitarian political and economic system in which the means of production and distribution would be communally owned. The economy of the Soviet Union conforms to the ideal socialist model in some respects and is particularly notable for the intensity of its centralized planning. However, it seems to be a long way from its goal of communism, particularly the communism that Marx advocated.

*Democratic socialism* is a political and economic system that aims to preserve individual freedom in the context of social equality achieved through a centrally planned economy. Under such a system, the state takes ownership of strategic industries and services only, and allows competition in other areas of the economy. Very high tax rates are used to prevent excessive profits and to maintain an approximation of social equality.

The example of democratic socialism has led some scientists to propose *convergence theory,* the hypothesis that the similar problems faced by capitalist and socialist societies may influence their evolution toward a common ultimate form. Both capitalist and socialist societies are heavily industrialized, urbanized, and bureaucratized. Both have economies that must constantly grow in order to satisfy consumer demands. Both need to ensure economic opportunities and, at the same time, manage pollution and scarce natural resources. As noted previously, capitalist and socialist economies are ideal types; in reality, nations with one type of economy already incorporate elements of the other type. Thus economic convergence appears to be the trend. The question is whether more liberal economic policies will lead to political convergence as well.

The economic system of China has shifted considerably under different political regimes. With one-fifth of the world's population, this large agricultural country has operated as a communist-ruled socialist society since the revolution of 1949. During Chairman Mao's rule, communal ownership was the norm. Since Mao's death, China has adopted certain elements of a capitalist economy, allowing some private ownership of property and land. Financial incentives, consumer goods, and differentiation of jobs into grades and/or ranks are all part of the effort to modernize and industrialize the economy. However, these changes occur within the boundaries of a commitment to socialism.

## Corporate Capitalism

*What are the characteristics of corporate capitalism? What is the significance of the multinational corporation?*

The modern American economy is no longer based on the competitive efforts of individual capitalists, but is now dominated by the large *corporation,* a legally recognized organization whose existence, powers, and liabilities are separate and distinct from those of its owners or employees. The largest commercial and industrial corporations exert enormous political and economic power.

Achieving prominence only in the late nineteenth century, the corporation is a relatively new social invention. Corporations are owned by stockholders rather than by a single individual. In theory, the stockholders control the corporation by electing a board of directors and voting on company policies at annual meetings. In reality, the running of corporations is in the hands of the management, which supervises company operations and makes most major policy decisions, which in turn are approved by the board and "rubber stamped" by the stockholders. Thus, corporate structure tends to separate ownership of the firm from control of the firm.

The size and economic power of the major corporations in the United States is immense, with the top 100 corporations owning almost half the manufacturing assets in this country. Some of the major corporations, such as Exxon and General Motors, have budgets larger than those of most countries in the world. The largest corporations are linked together through *interlocking directorates,* social networks consisting of individuals who are members of several different corporate boards. This overlap puts considerable political and economic power in the hands of a few.

The domination of the American economy by corporations has several important consequences, not the least of which is that corporations are able to use considerable political leverage on national policies, pushing for their own privileges, influencing the country's tax structure, and reducing competition. Another striking feature of American corporate capitalism is the vast amount of money spent on advertising, designed, in part, to create markets by suggesting new products that consumers "need." Americans are socialized into a consumer culture in which happiness and self-fulfillment are linked to having newer, better, and more things. Corporate capitalism is also distinguished by "paper entrepreneuralism"—the pursuit of profits, not by producing goods or services, but by using clever accounting procedures, manipulating the tax laws, and buying, selling, or dismembering other corporations. Last, the American public has learned to favor spending its money on the consumption of goods and services provided by private enterprise rather than contributing to taxes for goods and services provided by public authorities. In fact, U.S. citizens actually pay lower taxes than the citizens of virtually every other industrialized society. Thus, the United States has a generally affluent private life alongside generally poor public facilities. Such an ordering of priorities would seem peculiar to socialist societies, but it is consistent with the values of the American capitalist system.

The establishment of large corporations has transcended national borders. A *multinational corporation* is a corporate enterprise which, although headquartered in one country, conducts its operations through subsidiaries that it owns or controls around the world. These wealthy multinationals account for more than a quarter of total world economic production and often have larger budgets than their host countries. Because three-fifths of the multinationals are headquartered in the United States, American influence in foreign economies is considerable. One possible consequence of this power is *neocolonialism,* the informal political and economic domination of one society over another, such that the former is able to exploit the labor and resources of the latter for its own purposes. There is substantial evidence of multinationals' interference in the affairs of foreign governments as well as of their use of illegal activities in pursuit of their own profit. On the other hand, multinational corporations encourage economic growth in foreign countries, develop local industry, and employ a large labor force, perhaps improving the quality of life of the local citizenry. Investment by multinationals has been welcomed lately as other means to economic development become problematic. Yet the motives of multinational corporations are largely commercial. When they are threatened by uneasy political alliances or when cheap labor and natural resources have been exhausted, multinationals may leave the host countries, with disastrous effects on the domestic economies. In short, the rapid growth in size and power of these multinational corporations is cause for concern: they are run for profit by a tiny elite, yet are not subject to the authority of any one nation, nor are they hampered by other social controls over their activities.

## Unemployment

*Which groups are most affected by unemployment? What are the social consequences of unemployment for the individual and society?*

The expansion of American industry since the Great Depression kept rates of unemployment fairly low in the nation until the series of recessions in the mid-1970s pushed the unemployment rate to nearly 11 percent. No society has completely full employment; in the United States, an unemployment rate of 4 percent is considered tolerable. However, the rate of unemployment in this country has gone beyond the "tolerable" level, currently fluctuating around 7 percent. Moreover, official unemployment statistics do not tell the whole story; for example, some people have simply quit looking for work, and therefore are not counted as unemployed.

The loss of a job can have a devastating effect on an individual and produce consequences that go beyond the loss of income. Even if financial concerns are temporarily alleviated by unemployment benefits, the social and psychological impact must be dealt with. Prolonged unemployment often leads to boredom, despair, family problems, and lack of self-confidence. Even those who have a job are affected by high unemployment, for they begin to fear for their own future and may work for abnormally low wages or take jobs below their level of skill rather than have no job at all.

The *general* rate of unemployment depends on factors influencing the entire economy, such as the price of oil, the number of people of working age, and economic cycles of recession and recovery. In a capitalist economy such as the United States, companies hire and fire as their needs change. Even with economic growth and new markets, there are not enough jobs for all Americans. The *specific* rate of unemployment depends on factors influencing only certain categories of the population; thus the rate varies by age, gender, education, ethnicity, etc.

In recent years, unemployment has become a severe problem in the United States for certain categories of the population. The problems of unemployment disproportionately affect more women than men, more nonwhites than whites, more blue-collar workers than white-collar workers, and more teenagers and elderly people than middle-aged adults. Many jobs are lost to automation and to cheaper foreign labor. College graduates tend to experience more underemployment than unemployment, as they find themselves in jobs demanding far less skill than their education provided. The reason for this is that the number of college students seeking work has grown more quickly than the number of jobs demanding college-level skills. Now that the baby-boom generation has completed its education, the situation should relieve itself.

## Postindustrial America

*What are the characteristics of work in a postindustrial economy? What are the implications for a global economy?*

The United States is pioneering the transition from an industrial to a postindustrial economy, in which jobs in the tertiary, or service, sector will dominate. Although in many cases this change will require educated workers who are specifically trained in relevant job technology, most new jobs will be low-skill, low-paying service positions. In all likelihood, the labor market will continue to be segmented—one group of workers in corporate career paths with good job compensation, supported by marginal workers with less job security and fewer rewards. Another trend that will continue in the postindustrial economy is the increasing interdependence of foreign economies for raw materials and manufactured goods as well as for trade. In short, the world is becoming a single marketplace.

## DEFINING CORE CONCEPTS

*After studying the chapter, write a sociological definition in your own words for the following core concepts. Then give an example from your own experience to illustrate your definition. Refer to the chapter to check your work.*

| Core Concept | Sociological Definition | Personal Illustration |
|---|---|---|
| alienation | | |

| Core Concept | Sociological Definition | Personal Illustration |
|---|---|---|
| anomie | | |
| capitalism | | |
| corporation | | |
| communism | | |
| convergence theory | | |
| democratic socialism | | |
| division of labor | | |

| *Core Concept* | *Sociological Definition* | *Personal Illustration* |
| --- | --- | --- |
| interlocking directorates | | |
| mechanical solidarity | | |
| monopoly | | |
| multinational corporation | | |
| neocolonialism | | |
| oligopoly | | |
| organic solidarity | | |

| Core Concept | Sociological Definition | Personal Illustration |
| --- | --- | --- |
| primary sector | | |
| profession | | |
| secondary sector | | |
| socialism | | |
| surplus wealth | | |
| tertiary sector | | |

## PUTTING IDEAS TOGETHER

The characteristic that distinguishes the main economic systems, as ideal types, is the ownership of property.

### The Relationship of Property Ownership, Profit, and Inequalities in Economic Systems

Pure capitalism (owned by individuals)    Corporate capitalism (owned by corporations)    Democratic socialism    Soviet-style socialism    Communism

| property privately owned | ⊢————————————————————————————————————————┤ | property publicly owned |
| profit a goal | ⊢————————————————————————————————————————┤ | fulfillment of social needs a goal |
| economic inequalities | ⊢————————————————————————————————————————┤ | few inequalities, classlessness |

Capitalism is an ideal-type economic system, never seen in its pure form in any society. The goals of capitalism are pursuit of profit within a system of free enterprise. The capitalist system of the U.S. economy has been analyzed by sociologists (and anticipated by early sociologists like Marx and Durkheim) in terms of its functions and dysfunctions. Its deviations from the ideal type have important consequences.

## Dysfunctions of American Capitalism

| Features of American Capitalism | Possible Dysfunctions |
|---|---|
| Increased division of labor and specialization | Anomie (Durkheim) Alienation (Marx) |
| Increased professionalization | Underemployment |
| Increased mechanization, computerization | Unemployment |
| Accumulation of wealth from profit | Social inequality |
| Separation of ownership of the means of production from workers | Alienation |
| Separation of ownership of the means of production from management | A noncompetitive corporate economy |
| Expansion into overseas markets | No control over multinational corporations |

There are three main sectors of economic activity within any economy: primary sector, secondary sector, and tertiary sector. The relative importance of each sector in a society is associated with other characteristics of the economic order.

## Relationships Between Economic Sectors and Economic Characteristics

|  | Primary Sector | Secondary Sector | Tertiary Sector |
|---|---|---|---|
| Level of economic development | low ⊢————————————————————————⊣ high |  |  |
| Professionalization | low ⊢————————————————————————⊣ high |  |  |
| Underemployment | low ⊢————————————————————————⊣ high |  |  |
| Unemployment | high ⊢————————————————————————⊣ low |  |  |
| Worker dissatisfaction | high ⊢————————————————————————⊣ low |  |  |

# Testing the Concepts

## MULTIPLE-CHOICE QUESTIONS

*After studying the chapter, try to answer each of the twenty-five questions below. Mark the alternative you think is correct, then look at the correct answer and the explanation provided at the bottom of the page. Try to state why the other alternatives are incorrect and check your understanding of the correct answer.*

1.  The American economic system cannot be described as pure capitalism. Which of the following examples, however, is most consistent with the ingredients of capitalism?
    a.  Churches do not have to pay property tax.
    b.  Highways receive federal funding and are publicly owned.
    c.  The President's deregulation of oil companies increases the profits from this monopoly.
    d.  American automakers ask for a trade ban with Japan to reduce competition with their compact cars.
    e.  Airline companies offer special fares to attract customers to their companies.

2.  The economic system of corporate capitalism differs significantly from which of the features of an ideal-type capitalist economic system?
    a.  Pursuit of profit is the goal.
    b.  Free competition exists among buyers and sellers.

    c.  Property is privately owned.
    d.  Economic growth is good for the society as a whole.
    e.  Economic leaders are likely to be able to influence political and social institutions.

3.  A society characterized by "mechanical solidarity" would have an economy comprised mostly of
    a.  large-scale bureaucracies.
    b.  tertiary industries.
    c.  a high degree of technological development.
    d.  extreme division of labor.
    e.  primary industries.

4.  The U.S. economy can be labeled
    a.  laissez-faire capitalism.
    b.  corporate capitalism.
    c.  democratic socialism.
    d.  pure capitalism.
    e.  democratic capitalism.

5.  According to Marx, what feature of capitalism aggravates the problem of worker alienation more than other economic systems?
    a.  Inflation rates are very high.
    b.  Work roles are concentrated in the tertiary sector.
    c.  The profit produced by the worker goes to someone else.
    d.  The standard of living of the average citizen is relatively high.
    e.  Specialized training is required for many jobs.

---

1.  **e.** *Pure capitalism is based on the pursuit of profit in a system of free enterprise. Competition is the necessary ingredient to motivate businesses to offer the best goods and services at the lowest prices. Airlines compete for passengers and offer bargain fares to attract people to their companies. See pages 462–463.*

2.  **b.** *The pure form of capitalism, whereby competition occurs in a system of free enterprise, is a thing of the past. Monopolies and oligopolies in the economic system of corporate capitalism reduce competition and result in a concentration of economic power. See pages 463, 469.*

3.  **e.** *Mechanical solidarity refers to the pattern of social organization that characterizes preindustrial*

societies. *Roles are extremely similar, since most people working as artisans or farmers use raw materials in the primary sector. See pages 454, 456.*

4.  **b.** *The economic system of the United States is capitalism. The majority of economic transactions occur between corporations rather than among small businesses and individual consumers. See pages 468–469.*

5.  **c.** *According to Marx, work in modern economies becomes a highly specialized, enforced activity—a situation that may result in feelings of alienation, or powerlessness and isolation, from the products of one's work. This feeling is intensified in a capitalist system, where the products of work are owned by capitalists rather than by the workers who create them. See page 459.*

6. Under democratic socialism
   a. no public ownership of strategic industries is allowed.
   b. the economy is regulated by the government in accordance with national priorities.
   c. private ownership of the means of producing and distributing wealth is not permitted.
   d. rates of taxation are very low in comparison to those of capitalist nations.
   e. citizens are not allowed to vote for candidates to represent them; there is only one political party and the head of it rules the country.

7. One of the dysfunctions of multinational corporations is
   a. the possibility of illegal activity to guarantee their investments.
   b. the wealth they generate for their stockholders.
   c. the wealth they generate toward economic development of poor countries.
   d. the fierce competition for the business of the average consumer.
   e. the employment opportunities for American college graduates.

8. In the United States, depending on the administration, government regulations have controlled, if not owned, such things as railways, airlines, energy resources, and other strategic industries and services. This practice is closest to which economic system?
   a. laissez-faire capitalism
   b. socialism
   c. communism
   d. democratic socialism
   e. corporate capitalism

9. In the postindustrial economy, the greatest demand for workers will be
   a. in the secondary sector.
   b. in the highly technical fields like telecommunications.
   c. in the occupations controlled by labor unions.
   d. in foreign languages.
   e. in low-paying service positions.

10. The best evidence for convergence theory is
   a. the high taxes that support the welfare state in Sweden.
   b. the close approximation of most governments to ideal types.

6. **b.** *The government controls the vital industries and services, regulating the economy in line with policies designed to distribute wealth in a socialist manner. Some free enterprise is allowed, but all strategic industries are government controlled to ensure basic standards of living for all citizens. See page 466.*

7. **a.** *Multinational corporations do not fall under the authority of any one nation. Given their vast financial holdings, they rank as large countries in economic strength and consequent political power. This influence has been used in illegal ways in the past to interfere in the affairs of foreign governments and to influence foreign policies in directions favorable to future profits. See pages 471–472.*

8. **d.** *In a system of democratic socialism, the key industries are controlled by the central government and managed according to planned national goals. Some private property is owned by individuals outside these critical industries. See page 466.*

9. **e.** *The greatest number of jobs will be in the tertiary sector, but not in positions that require high qualifications or offer high pay. Those core positions will be filled by a few employees and supplemented by technology. Most people will work on the periphery, providing support services at low wages. The result of such an economy is a segmented labor market. See page 475.*

10. **d.** *Convergence theory is the hypothesis that, in practice, governments move away from ideal-type forms of socialism and capitalism, and become more alike, each borrowing from the other. The United States has a basically capitalist economy, but often adopts socialist strategies, such as government support of private corporations. See page 466.*

c. the military's labor disputes in Poland.

d. the bailout of U.S. corporations like Chrysler, Lockheed, and Penn Central by Congress.

e. the deregulation of the airline industry in the United States.

11. The economic order refers not only to the production of goods and services but also to their distribution. What did Karl Marx mean by "surplus wealth"?

a. the wealth produced by workers to meet their basic needs

b. the wealth produced by workers in excess of their basic needs, taken as profit by the owners of production

c. the wealth or earnings industrial workers have after taxes

d. the amount of money a worker earns above the national poverty line

e. the profits of a company that are distributed to workers through profit-sharing or dividend plans

12. Which of the following prerequisites must societies meet before their division of labor becomes specialized?

a. adequate natural resources

b. democratic form of government

c. efficient production techniques

d. a concept of property

e. surplus wealth

13. Marx argued that worker alienation would be a serious problem in modern industrial economies. What policy could be adopted by industry to reduce the condition of alienation as Marx described it?

a. increased training and specialization for workers

b. higher pay

c. more efficient production techniques

d. worker participation in decision making

e. a shorter work week

14. According to Durkheim, the division of labor in modern industrialized societies results in

a. the creation of a social elite.

b. better supervision and better control of workers.

c. a state of anomie.

d. a collective consciousness.

e. loyalty to one's company rather than to a community.

---

11.  **b.** *Marx felt that society was divided according to ownership of the means of production. Owners exploited workers by taking the surplus wealth, or profit, that labor produced. Workers were unable to enjoy the fruits of their labors, while owners expanded their holdings with the profits earned for them by the workers. See pages 453, 455, 459.*

12.  **e.** *Only when a surplus is produced can members of society be freed from subsistence labor and take on other more specialized roles not related to meeting basic survival needs. The development of agriculture led to the production of a surplus, a more specialized division of labor, social classes, and urban settlements. See pages 455–456.*

13.  **d.** *Marx described alienation as a feeling of estrangement from one's work. If workers were allowed greater input in and control over decision making about the products they produced, working conditions, etc., alienation would be reduced. See pages 459, 461.*

14.  **c.** *Durkheim felt that social solidarity is maintained by common norms and values, reinforced by common work roles in small societies. As societies become larger, and the division of labor is more specialized, differences among individuals become exaggerated. A state of anomie, or normlessness, may result when there are few or conflicting norms to guide behavior. See pages 456–457.*

15. A distinction can be made between professions and other types of occupations. Which one of the following characteristics of a profession do other occupations share?

    a. sufficient income to place a person in the upper-middle or upper class

    b. carefully controlled admission based on specific credentials

    c. considerable autonomy over one's work

    d. a code of ethics that members of the occupation must adhere to

    e. access to the occupation based on mastery of systematic and theoretical knowledge

16. Which feature or trend of the U.S. economy is likely to *increase* worker alienation, according to *Marx?*

    a. professionalization

    b. division of labor

    c. human relations programs in industry

    d. democratic socialism

    e. increased participation of women in the labor force

17. The research conducted by Mayo and his associates at the Hawthorne plant of the Western Electric company led to the development of the "human relations" approach to industry. Which of the following sociological findings would be consistent with this approach?

    a. Even in big factories, workers form closeknit primary groups that add meaning to their work.

    b. The greater the income, the more satisfied the worker.

    c. As the story on the General Motors assembly line indicates, workers appreciate efficiency procedures that make their work loads lighter.

    d. Modern workers sense the improvement in their working conditions as compared to those of their predecessors.

    e. Scientific management has improved American industry to the point that it is the most efficient system in the world.

18. What change in China's economic system since Mao's death has most contributed to the country's productivity?

    a. economic aid from other countries

    b. more government-owned department stores and small businesses

    c. peasants' ownership of small plots of land

    d. new resources of coal and oil, relieving China of any energy problems

    e. workers' commitment to carrying on the teachings of Mao

---

15. **a.** *Although professions are generally the highest paid occupational roles, some occupations have been able to command high salaries without professionalizing. For example, manual work that is difficult or dangerous might pay very well, but has no body of knowledge or special association to distinguish it as a profession. See pages 456, 458.*

16. **b.** *The trend toward increased division of labor will exacerbate alienation—feelings of powerlessness, isolation, and meaninglessness about one's work. The factory system in the United States has workers assigned to a small task, unconnected to the total product, affording limited challenge or responsibility. Such tasks are external to the worker, who does not identify with his products and feels alienated from them. See page 459.*

17. **a.** *Mayo and associates found that any attention paid to the factory workers resulted in increased productivity. Informal primary groups within the factory set production norms and "humanized" the work environment. By reinforcing these primary group relationships, factory managers could increase production and maintain some level of worker satisfaction. See page 461.*

18. **c.** *Under Deng Xiaoping, peasants are allowed to own small plots of land and reap the profits from their produce. This private ownership has increased productivity and relieved the food crisis. See pages 467–468.*

19. In 1980 and 1981, the federal government made substantial loan guarantees to the Chrysler Corporation to help it cope with financial difficulties. What characteristic of the American economy does this example illustrate?
    a. a movement toward socialism
    b. the emphasis on human relations in industry
    c. the interdependence of corporate capitalism and government
    d. expansion of the tertiary sector
    e. citizens' endorsement of private affluence over public squalor

20. Which of the following statements about employment and underemployment in the United States is accurate?
    a. The United States has a lower unemployment rate than other industrialized countries.
    b. Unemployment benefits have taken care of the difficulties related to losing a job.
    c. High unemployment is associated with high underemployment.
    d. A college degree is a good way to protect oneself from unemployment or underemployment.

    e. Individual characteristics, such as lack of skill and motivation, are more explicative of unemployment than are social factors.

21. A major theme in nearly all of Durkheim's writings is
    a. the tendency for occupations to become professionalized.
    b. the alienating effect of capitalism.
    c. the importance of shared norms and values in maintaining social solidarity.
    d. the decline of individualism in modern society.
    e. the importance of work for determining social class.

22. One indication of the advanced development of industrial societies is
    a. the presence of primary and secondary industries.
    b. a majority of the work force employed in tertiary industries.
    c. a relative balance of employment in secondary and tertiary industries.
    d. the total elimination of employment in primary industries.
    e. the control of unskilled factory work by large corporations.

---

19. **c.** *The modern American economy is dominated by a few major corporations with enormous political and financial power. The troubles at Chrysler were serious because of the disastrous economic effects they could have on the (unemployed) workers, the Detroit community, related industries, and the federal government. Under a system of corporate capitalism, the government and large corporations cooperate informally in running a planned economy: Chrysler and the federal government are mutually dependent. See pages 466, 468–469.*

20. **c.** *High underemployment often accompanies unemployment as workers are willing to take jobs beneath their qualifications or work for lower wages for fear of being without a job altogether. Employers can*

*offer fewer benefits to employees and still find workers. See pages 473–474.*

21. **c.** *Durkheim was an early functionalist whose concern rested with social stability. He felt that important social norms must be shared in order for society to maintain its cohesiveness. The economy could change the way society was organized, from mechanical to organic solidarity, but social stability must be preserved. See pages 456–457.*

22. **b.** *As the economy becomes more advanced, a greater number of people will be involved in tertiary industries, such as white-collar and professional work. The jobs formerly handled by unskilled or manual laborers may be accomplished through automation. See page 454.*

23. The blue-collar worker's employment situation is most negatively affected by which pair of factors?
   a. changes in the tertiary sector; greater locus of control
   b. the global economy; extrinsic rewards
   c. intrinsic rewards; strong unions
   d. tariffs on foreign goods; low price of oil
   e. fewer young workers; quotas on foreign goods

24. Perhaps the most important effect of the modern corporation's structural development is
   a. separation of ownership from control.

b. control of corporate activities by shareholders.
c. ownership of firms by private citizens.
d. ownership of firms by foreign investors.
e. workers' involvement in decision making.

25. Which of the following is *not* part of the tertiary sector?
   a. a car rental agency
   b. a medical clinic
   c. a Coca-Cola bottling plant
   d. a hi-fi repair shop
   e. a university

---

23. **b.** *Blue-collar workers are most vulnerable to unemployment, shifts in the economy, and foreign competition. Their instrisic satisfaction with work is low, they have few marketable skills to transfer to new jobs and, therefore, work for the best wages they can get. See page 474.*

24. **a.** *Corporations have no single owner, but are collectively owned by stockholders. These stockholders indirectly hire a set of managers to run the day-to-day operations of the corporation, separating ownership from control. See page 469.*

25. **c.** *The tertiary sector involves service activities. Soft-drink bottling is part of the secondary sector, as raw materials are converted into manufactured goods. See page 454.*

## A CASE STUDY

NAME

COURSE/SECTION NUMBER

The cloud of lethal chemicals spread quickly over Bhopal, India, killing many people as they slept. Other residents ran from the city, blinded by the stinging substance in their eyes. Final tally put the death toll in the thousands and the number of injuries caused by the chemical spill at tenfold that amount. Devastation lingers as increased deaths from cancer, emphysema, and birth defects begin to show up. Union Carbide, an American company, owned the plant in Bhopal. It claimed that faulty work practices by local workers, or possibly even sabotage, caused the accident. Bhopal residents blame the company for not informing workers and the city as to the deadly nature of the chemicals being manufactured there, and for neglecting to take adequate safety precautions. Immediately after the accident, lawyers from around the world arrived in Bhopal to represent the victims in lawsuits against Union Carbide. But suits are difficult to settle, since the company is U.S. based.

A second, smaller accident occurred at the Institute, West Virginia plant of Union Carbide. That plant had better safety features so no one was injured. The residents of Institute hope the plant reopens. In the depressed economy of West Virginia, every job is important.

1.   In what ways is Union Carbide a multinational corporation?

2.   The production of chemicals is an example of which economic sector?

3.    How much responsibility should Union Carbide take for the accidents in
Bhopal and Institute?

4.    Union Carbide is an American company working within a capitalist
economic system. What elements of the capitalist system of doing business are
displayed in this case study?

# Applying the Concepts

NAME
_____

COURSE/SECTION  NUMBER

## APPLICATION EXERCISE ONE

Interview two people in two different occupations, one representing a blue-collar job, and one a professional position. Ask each person about the satisfactions and stresses associated with his or her job. Ascertain the opportunities for advancement and how an employee is rewarded for doing a good job. Lastly, ask about the informal structure in their workplace and how it supports or hinders their organization's formal goals. Use the space below to write up any conclusions you have about the different work experiences described by these people and where you suspect alienation from work might occur.

## APPLICATION EXERCISE TWO

Choose three products, which you use, that are made by three different large manufacturing firms. Your task is to play detective and find out what other products are made by that corporation or its subsidiaries. For each product, identify three or more products produced by the same parent firm, demonstrating the extent of the corporate economy in the United States. Sometimes this information is on the product label; it may also be available in the reference room of the library in business directories such as *Standard and Poor's* or *Dun and Bradstreet*. If possible obtain a conglomerate's annual report. These are available on request from many corporations or from stock brokerage firms.

Product 1 and name of firm:        Three other products from the same firm:

1.

2.

3.

Product 2 and name of firm:        Three other products from the same firm:

1.

2.

3.

Product 3 and name of firm:        Three other products from the same firm:

1.

2.

3.

NAME

COURSE/SECTION NUMBER

# APPLICATION EXERCISE THREE

Get ready to play a game of international "Price Is Right." For this variation on the television game show, you will find the price of an item in the United States and compare it to the price for that item in another country. The object of the game is to explain why there is a difference in the prices. Your explanation should be based on information in Chapter 17 about the different types of economic systems (capitalism, soviet-style socialism, and democratic socialism) and the different sectors (primary, secondary, and tertiary).

|  | *Actual U.S. Price (in Your Community)* | *Hypothetical Price in Another Country, in U.S. Dollars* |
|---|---|---|
| Product 1: a pair of men's blue jeans | | U.S.S.R. $97.50 |
| What characteristics of each economy explain the difference in price? | | |
| Product 2: a pound of white sugar | | Jamaica $3.00 |
| What characteristics of each economy explain the difference in price? | | |
| Product 3: a pound of rice | | Thailand 5¢ |
| What characteristics of each economy explain the difference in price? | | |
| Product 4: having a baby | | Great Britain free |
| What characteristics of each economy explain the difference in price? | | |

# CHAPTER 18

# The Political Order

## Reviewing the Concepts

### LEARNING GOALS

*After studying the chapter, you should be able to:*

1. Define the sociological concepts of the political order and the state.

2. Explain Weber's definitions of power, legitimacy, and coercion.

3. Distinguish among Weber's three types of legitimate authority in terms of their basis for power and their stability over time.

4. Outline the emergence of the state.

5. Characterize the state in modern industrial societies.

6. List the four functions of the state in maintaining social order; compare this with a conflict view of the state.

7. Contrast the theories of Hobbes, Rousseau, and Marx on the origin and role of the state.

8. Explain the stages through which human societies evolve, according to Marx.

9. Synthesize the views of functionalist and conflict theorists about the state.

10. Contrast the three basic forms of government.

11. List six prerequisites for democracy.

12. Discuss the ideas of liberty and equality as defined by various governments.

13. Contrast the characteristics of political parties in the United States with those in other democracies.

14. Discuss the current trend toward political realignment.

15. Describe the political behavior of interest groups, using examples.

16. Present evidence of ways in which interest groups support or interfere with democratic government.

17. Summarize Mills's view of the concentration of power in the United States.

18. Outline Reisman's perspective on the levels of power in the United States.

19. Discuss Domhoff's findings with regard to the presence of a governing class in the United States.

20. Characterize voter participation in the United States.

21. Indicate how an informal power structure can exist within a community and overlap with elected leadership, citing evidence from recent studies.

22. Discuss the significance of the military-industrial complex.

## IDENTIFYING KEY QUESTIONS AND THEMES

Politics is a universal process, taking a variety of forms in different cultures. The *political order* is the institutionalized system through which some individuals or groups acquire and exercise power over others. The highest level of power in modern society is that of the *state,* the only authority that successfully claims a monopoly on the right to use force within a given territory. While the state may delegate some of its powers to other authorities, it retains its central place in the political order. As opposed to the government, which consists of the individuals who happen to be in power at a particular time, the state is an impersonal social authority.

## Power

*What is power? How can different types of power be classified?*

Max Weber was one of the first sociologists to study political *power.* He defined it as the ability to control the behavior of others, even without their consent. Power may come from such resources as wealth, status, prestige, strength, or particular knowledge and skills. The ultimate basis of power, however, is the ability to compel obedience from others, if necessary through the threat or use of force. The exercise of power may be legitimate or illegitimate. As you may remember, *legitimacy* is the generally held belief that a political system is valid and justified. Legitimate power is based on people's recognition that those who apply it have the right to do so. Weber used the term *authority* to refer to this legitimate power. On the other hand, illegitimate power, or *coercion,* is the form of power whose legitimacy is denied by those to whom it is applied. Power based on authority is usually unquestioningly accepted by people, because obedience to it has become a social norm. Power based on coercion, on the other hand, tends to be unstable, because people obey only out of fear. This distinction between authority and coercion is an important one in that it indicates whether a political system will survive over time—an outcome that is possible only if its participants recognize its legitimacy. If the majority of citizens in any society no longer consider their political system legitimate, it is doomed, for its power can rest only on coercion, which will fail in the long run. The recurrence of revolutions throughout history documents people's unwillingness to live under coercion.

## Types of Authority

*What are the three types of legitimate authority according to Weber? What are the characteristics of each type?*

Max Weber distinguished three types of legitimate authority: traditional, legal-rational, and charismatic. Each type is legitimate because it rests on the consent of the governed and allows the exercise of power within socially defined limits. In a political system based on ***traditional authority,*** power is legitimated by ancient custom. The authority of the ruler is generally founded on unwritten laws or religious teachings, as seen in monarchies and chieftainships. Obedience to traditional authority is not questioned; the birthright of the leader guarantees the power. In a system based on ***legal-rational authority,*** power is legitimated by explicit rules and procedures that define the rights and obligations of the ruler. This form of authority is characteristic of the political systems of modern societies based on written constitutions and laws. The power of an official derives from the office that person holds, not from the leader's personal characteristics. Once a person has left or been removed from office, the power remains with the office. In a system based on ***charismatic authority,*** power is legitimated by the unique and remarkable qualities that people attribute to a particular leader. Weber called this extraordinary quality "charisma." The exceptional personal characteristics of charismatic leaders make their authority seem legitimate to their followers. Charismatic leaders are particularly influential in leading revolutions. However, charismatic authority is inherently unstable because it rests on the unique qualities of a particular individual and cannot be easily transferred to another person or retained in a given office. For this reason, political systems based on charismatic authority are usually short-lived; they either collapse or evolve into legal-rational systems. Each of these forms of authority represents an ***ideal type.*** In other words, each is an abstract description (based on a number of real cases) and in reality is only approximated to a greater or lesser degree by any given political system. In

practice, political systems and political leaders may derive their authority from more than one source.

## The Rise of the State

*What is the functionalist perspective on the role of the state? How does the conflict perspective present a different view? What are the current sociological perspectives on the state?*

Until as recently as a few centuries ago, most people lived in small groups, organized as tribes or nations, under the often informal authority of local rulers, without the influence of central political insititutions. The emergence of the state as a separate institution, then, is a relatively recent historical development closely linked to a society's level of cultural evolution and, in particular, to its means of subsistence. In hunting and gathering societies, formal political institutions are absent; in pastoral societies, where there may be a surplus of food and some individuals more wealthy and powerful than others, authority emerges in patterns of chieftanship, usually hereditary. It is in agricultural societies, characterized by a large food surplus and the first appearance of social classes, that the state emerges as a distinct social institution. In preindustrial societies, the state is typically based on a system of traditional authority. In industrial and postindustrial societies, the nature of the state shifts, as the enormous wealth generated by industrialism creates a large middle class. Mass education, mass communication, and a fairer distribution of wealth result in a more politically sophisticated population. As regimes based on traditional authority are overthrown, legal-rational authority becomes the basis of the state's power. The responsibility of the state expands enormously in order to regulate social conditions. In taking on these additional tasks, it becomes one of the most dominant institutions in a society.

## The State: A Functionalist View

*According to functionalists, what are the four functions of the state?*

From the functionalist perspective, the emergence of the state as a central institution can be explained in terms of the four functions it serves. (1) The state takes responsibility for codifying important norms in the form of laws and enforcing them through a criminal justice system.

(2) The state provides an institutionalized process for the distribution of resources: it acts as an arbitrator between conflicting interests, establishing a means of resolving disputes and determining policy, presumably for the greatest social good. (3) A complex modern society requires coordinated planning and direction: the centralized decision making of the state provides this necessary overview. (4) The state is responsible for political, economic, and military relations with other societies. It must speak on behalf of all the people in one society if these relations are to be effective. All four of these major roles reflect the functionalist emphasis on the preservation of social order.

## The State: A Conflict View

*How do conflict theorists characterize the role of the state?*

An alternative view is that the state emerged largely to safeguard the interests of the privileged. Rousseau, an early theorist, argued that in protecting the "haves" in their conflict with the "have nots," the state becomes the source of, not the solution to, social injustice. Marx, the most influential conflict theorist, felt that all societies are divided into two or more classes, one of which dominates and exploits the others. The ruling class always uses social institutions, particularly the state, to maintain the status quo and thus its privileges. Marx analyzed various societies throughout history and argued that class struggle is the dynamic force in all cases. He described several stages through which human societies evolve: primitive communism, slavery, feudalism, capitalism, socialism, and communism. Marx's collaborator, Engels, felt that the final outcome to this evolution would be a classless communist society in which the state would "wither away." However, the idea that the role of the state is significantly reduced in a classless society is perhaps the weakest element of Marx's theory. Indeed, modern countries operating under a socialist or communist system have a stronger political state than most capitalist countries. Contemporary conflict theorists have expanded on Marxian analysis, focusing on social conflict in general rather than on class conflict alone. Thus they study conflict among the many groups within a state seeking to advance their own interests.

Current thinking about the role of the state and its functions draws from each theoretical perspective. Conflict theorists stress the role of the state in protecting the interests of the dominant group(s) and serving as arbitrator among many competing groups. Functionalists emphasize that the state has many nonoppressive roles, unrelated to class conflict, aimed at maintaining social order. Whether one takes a conflict perspective, a functionalist perspective, or a synthesis of the two, the state emerges as the central authority in society.

## Forms of Government

*What are the characteristics of authoritarian and totalitarian forms of government? What are the prerequisites of a democracy? What is the relationship between liberty and equality?*

Forms of government may be classified according to the relationship between the rulers and the ruled. The three basic types of modern government are ***authoritarianism, totalitarianism,*** and ***democracy.*** Rulers in authoritarian regimes allow little or no public opposition and usually cannot be removed from office by legal means. Authoritarianism may take several forms, including monarchies, dictatorships, and juntas. Although authoritarian governments allow no challenges to their control of the political sphere, they may acknowledge and deal with other centers of influence, such as business and religion. Totalitarianism is an authoritarian form of government that aims for complete control of all aspects of social life, including the media, the military, the economy, and other social institutions. Like authoritarian governments, totalitarian governments cannot be legally removed from office; unlike authoritarian governments, they are very resistant to revolution or to change toward a more democratic form. "Democracy" comes from a Greek word meaning "rule of the people." It describes a form of government based on the participation of the people. Pure democracy as an ideal type has never existed in practice, for it is an unwieldy process for decision making. The societies we consider democratic recognize that the powers of the government derive from the consent of the governed. Thus they have institutionalized procedures for choosing officials, a system called representative democracy. This form of government is historically recent, rare, and fragile; representative democracy is found only in a handful of countries, having not yet successfully extended its reach to newly independent nations in Africa and Asia. Some countries, especially in Africa and Eastern Europe, have elements of representative democracy, but the electoral process is controlled more by the state than by the people.

Several basic conditions must exist in order for a democracy to thrive. (1) Most stable democracies are characterized by advanced economic development. An advanced economy assumes an urbanized, literate, sophisticated population that expects and demands some participation in the political process. Advanced economies also tend to be politically stable, resting on a large middle class that has a stake in society and resists massive social upheaval. (2) Democracies are strengthened when formal and informal restraints limit government power. Laws and/or a constitution restrict the power of any given office and provide means to remove ineffective or coercive leaders from office. Beyond these formal checks and balances, informal pressure from the general public and media keeps government power within socially acceptable limits. (3) Democracy is most likely to survive in a society in which there is general consensus on basic values and a widespread commitment to the existing political order. The absence of major political cleavages makes smaller compromises possible; government need not go on the defensive or become coercive to contain dissident groups. (4) Tolerance of criticism and of dissenting opinion is fundamental to democracy, allowing minority views to be expressed within the acceptable channels of democracy rather than outside them in radical tactics. (5) To make informed choices, the citizens of a democracy must have access to relevant information. Free speech, freedom of the press and other media, and honesty on the part of politicians promote an open exchange of ideas. (6) By definition, power in a democracy is diffuse. The U.S. Constitution apportions power to three branches of government, with a system of checks and balances to prevent the consolidation of power in the hands of a few. Other power bases exist in lobbying groups, political parties, local governments, labor unions, and corporations.

Liberty and equality are two concepts closely associated with democratic life; yet, in reality, it is difficult for them to coexist. Complete liberty allows people the freedom to pursue the lifestyle and individual goals they choose, unencumbered by government intervention. Equality, on the other hand, is a social goal that may require government intervention. The United States has chosen to emphasize personal liberty at the expense of social equality. Socialist societies stress social equality, with infringements on personal liberty.

## The American Political Process

*What are the distinctive characteristics of American political parties? How do interest groups contribute to political decision making in the United States?*

A *political party* is an organization whose purpose is to gain legitimate control of the government. Parties are vital to a democracy because they link the voter to the government, define policy alternatives, transmit public opinion, encourage political participation, and recruit and offer candidates for public office. American political parties have several characteristics that distinguish them from their counterparts in other industrialized societies. For one, the United States has only two major parties, the Republican and the Democratic, which are basically loose coalitions, marginally tied to socioeconomic classes or specific party platforms. Elections are decided by a simple plurality rather than on the basis of proportional representation of minority parties, a system used in many European democracies. Whereas voters in systems based on proportional representation are likely to vote for the party because of its position on specific issues, Americans are more likely to vote for the candidate, because of his or her personal characteristics.

Since World War II, American political parties have realigned themselves with various coalitions of voters. The Democratic party's historical domination of the political scene has given way to the growth of the Republican party, which currently enjoys the support of many subgroups in American society. The significance of this realignment will depend on the transition from Reagan to other Republican leadership and the maintenance of allegiances between disparate groups. The near future may see a trend toward dealignment, in which voters increasingly disregard party labels and split their tickets.

Because of the loose nature of American politics and the broad spectrum of political views within each party, virtually every issue brought before Congress is open to the influence of interest groups. An *interest group* is an organization or group that attempts to influence political decisions on specific issues that might have an impact on its members or their goals. These groups may be small or large, temporary or permanent, secretive or open. All attempt to gain access to and sway those who have power. Interest groups use a variety of tactics to achieve their goals; most groups rely heavily on *lobbying,* the tactic of directly persuading decision makers. Many large interest groups maintain professional lobbyists in Washington to attend to their causes.

The principal resource of these powerful interest groups is money. The high cost of political campaigning means that candidates depend on contributions from individuals and larger groups. Political action committees (PACs) — organizations established by interest groups for the purpose of raising and distributing campaign funds — must report their campaign contributions, and the records show heavy donations, especially to incumbents. In the past decade, the number of PACs and the amount of money they contribute to campaigns has increased tenfold. It can be assumed that the various interest groups expect and obtain some payoff in return for their financial assistance to candidates. Thus the strength and influence of these interest groups are a mixed blessing. On the one hand, these groups, working behind the scenes, are able to win favors that may not be in the public interest. On the other hand, interest groups on all sides of an issue compete with one another, thereby diffusing power and reducing the possibility of a monopoly. Interest groups also provide a means for otherwise unorganized, relatively powerless citizens to gain political influence. In any case, interest group activity and lobbying by PACs play important roles in the informal side of American political life.

## Who Rules?

*How centralized is political power in the United States? Is there a power elite or a pluralist model at work?*

In a representative democracy, power is theoretically vested in the people, who then delegate it to their representatives. However, social scientists have observed that power is actually concentrated much more in the hands of the leadership than in their constituents. Robert Michels argued that in any organization, the concentration of power (oligarchy) is essential to efficiency. Vilfredo Pareto pointed out that in all societies elites emerge and tend to dominate the group, including political ones; as long as political systems are open and new rulers replace old ones, a "circulation of elites" protects against tyranny. Gaetano Mosca insisted that every society contains a small ruling class and a larger class that is ruled.

Sociologists studying the American political scene have somewhat different views on the degree of centralization of political power in our system. C. Wright Mills argued that the United States is dominated by a small, informal group of powerful and influential individuals, called a power elite. These individuals come to power because of the importance of the positions they hold in government, large corporations, and the military. Their overlapping bases of power result in consolidation of influence among a few individuals who determine social and political policy in all these spheres. Under this *power-elite model,* there are three distinct levels of power and influence. The highest is the power elite, which operates informally and invisibly and makes all the important decisions. The middle level consists of the legislative branch of government, the various interest groups, and local opinion leaders, and makes decisions of secondary importance. At the lowest level of political influence is the mass of powerless, unorganized citizens, who have little direct influence and may not even know that the decisions are being made.

By contrast, the *pluralist model* sees many competing interest groups shaping government decisions. This viewpoint, conveyed by David Riesman, acknowledges the unequal distribution of power, but suggests it is not as concentrated as Mills indicates. Reisman believes there are two basic levels of power in the United States. The upper level consists of "veto groups," strong interest groups that compete with one another and thus cannot form a unified or coordinated power elite. Shifting coalitions emerge, depending on the particular issue at hand. These veto groups appeal to the lower level, the unorganized public, for their support.

Empirical studies of the power-elite and pluralist models have found support for both. Domhoff identified a concentration of power in the United States that bears many similarities to the "power elite" described by Mills. The wealth and high status of this small, uppermost social class provides its members with considerable power. Yet members of this elite do not necessarily work for their own advantage and may not be involved in government decision making at all. Thus the amount and use of their power is not fully determined.

At the other end of the political spectrum, the ordinary voters have an opportunity to actively participate in the political process. Yet, the turnout of voters in American elections is strikingly low; only 60 percent of the registered population votes in national elections. Political participation by voting is closely associated with social class; the lower a person's social class, the less likely that person is to register to vote or to actually vote. Surveys of nonvoters reveal feelings of political alienation and apathy.

As far as community politics are concerned, analyses of the power structure in small towns and cities validate the presence of political and economic elites here as well. Yet the identity of these elites, their level of influence, and the degree of centralization of decision making depend on the characteristics of the community itself.

Finally, much can be learned about the political process from looking at the *military-industrial complex,* a term first used by President Eisenhower to describe the informal system of mutual influence between the Pentagon and major U.S. corporations. Large armament contracts awarded by the military are sought by corporations because they are more profitable than regular competitive commercial enterprises. The volume of military business, coupled with additional revenues from cost overruns and projection errors, places the Pentagon in a position of immense importance to the U.S. economy. It is the largest single formal organization in the world, owning more property than any other organization and having economic interests in three-fourths of the nation's congressional districts. Because many large corporations derive so much of their income from large defense contracts, they constantly lobby the Pentagon and the Congress to spend ever increasing amounts of money on defense. Mills argued that "military capitalism" is at the heart of the power elite, a view that is supported by the overlapping company directorships among military and corporate leaders.

While we still lack the detailed information necessary to delineate the exact nature of the American power structure, studies of the "governing class," political participation, community politics, and the military-industrial complex indicate that most important decisions are made by a small and privileged part of the population.

## DEFINING CORE CONCEPTS

*After studying the chapter, write a sociological definition in your own words for the following core concepts. Then give an example from your own experience to illustrate your definition. Refer to the chapter to check your work.*

| *Core Concept* | *Sociological Definition* | *Personal Illustration* |
| --- | --- | --- |
| authoritarianism | | |
| charismatic authority | | |

| Core Concept | Sociological Definition | Personal Illustration |
|---|---|---|
| coercion | | |
| democracy | | |
| ideal type | | |
| interest group | | |
| legal-rational authority | | |
| legitimacy | | |
| lobbying | | |
| military-industrial complex | | |

| *Core Concept* | *Sociological Definition* | *Personal Illustration* |
|---|---|---|
| political order | | |
| political party | | |
| power | | |
| power-elite model | | |
| pluralist model | | |
| state | | |
| totalitarianism | | |
| traditional authority | | |

## PUTTING IDEAS TOGETHER

The political institution provides an orderly system for the use of legitimate power, or authority. The highest level of power is that of the state. The emergence of the state is closely related to the level of cultural evolution of a society, and in particular to its means of subsistence: the state first appears in agricultural societies and becomes a dominant institution in industrial societies.

Sociologists differ on the degree to which power in the United States is concentrated in the hands of a small elite.

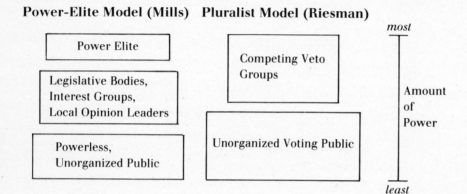

# Testing the Concepts

## MULTIPLE-CHOICE QUESTIONS

*After studying the chapter, try to answer each of the twenty-five questions below. Mark the alternative you think is correct, then look at the correct answer and the explanation provided at the bottom of the page. Try to state why the other alternatives are incorrect and check your understanding of the correct answer.*

1. From the conflict theorists' perspective, the state exists in most modern industrial nations to
    a. safeguard the interests of the subordinate masses.
    b. maintain social equality.
    c. provide government of the people, by the people, and for the people.
    d. maintain the status quo and protect the power of the ruling class.
    e. prevent internal conflicts or wars with other nations.

2. Mothers Against Drunk Driving (MADD) was started by a small group of women who had lost children in alcohol-related auto accidents. Now thousands of people have joined MADD, and attempt to pressure state, local, and federal government officials to clamp down on drunk driving. MADD is a(n)
    a. political party.
    b. interest group.

    c. primary group.
    d. power-elite group.
    e. veto group.

3. Regarding voter participation in elections, the textbook claims that in the United States, voter turnout
    a. declines beyond age thirty.
    b. is high among socially disadvantaged persons.
    c. is highest among the middle-income group.
    d. is low compared with other democratic nations.
    e. has all of these features.

4. In a political system based on charismatic authority, power is legitimized by
    a. traditional customs.
    b. the birthright of the ruler.
    c. a constitution and laws.
    d. a person with exceptional leadership qualities.
    e. a "junta" or small group of military officers.

5. C. Wright Mills and David Riesman have a difference of opinion concerning which aspect of the political process?
    a. the merits of the two-party system
    b. the legitimacy of the role played by PACs
    c. the concentration of power
    d. the growing importance of voters splitting their tickets
    e. the bases for legitimate authority among rulers

---

1. **d.** *Industrial societies are based on the ownership of private property by a class of individuals who hold the powerful positions in society. Marx believed that the ruling class always uses social institutions, particularly the state, to maintain its privileged position. See page 485.*

2. **b.** *An interest group lobbies for positions advantageous to its members. The members of MADD are concerned about drunk driving and put pressure on public officials to do something about this problem. They contribute money to campaigns, write letters, stage demonstrations, and use other techniques to make their concerns known. See page 493.*

3. **d.** *Voter turnout in the United States is relatively low; also, it is skewed by overparticipation of some*

*groups (e.g., those in higher social-class levels) and underparticipation of others (e.g., minorities, the poor, and young people). See pages 498–499.*

4. **d.** *A charismatic leader possesses special appeal and is considered legitimate by followers because of these exceptional qualities. See page 482.*

5. **c.** *C. Wright Mills described the power base of the United States as a power elite. Riesman felt that power was concentrated in the hands of a few groups but that competition among these various "veto" groups kept a reasonable balance of power. Both theorists were describing the concentration of power in American society. See page 496.*

6. A typical member of Mills's "power elite" could be
   a. an Irish immigrant in Boston who becomes a powerful cardinal of the Catholic church.
   b. an Episcopalian Harvard graduate, in a successful career in the State Department.
   c. a Texas cattleman who, despite his lack of formal education, has worked his way from rags to riches.
   d. a third-generation New York Jew who runs his father's diamond business.
   e. Congresswoman Barbara Jordan, who left Congress to teach at the University of Texas.

7. A band of guerrillas seeking to overthrow the government succeeds in almost completely disorganizing the country's political system. Weber would say their leader has _____ but not _____.
   a. power; authority
   b. tradition; charisma
   c. legal-rational authority; traditional authority
   d. monolithic power; pluralistic power
   e. coercion; power

8. Which of the following characteristics of a society is most conducive to democratic government?
   a. diffusion of power

   b. charismatic authority
   c. a power elite
   d. a single strong political party
   e. controls on dissenters with minority opinions

9. A politician argues that mass transit is important, not only for the community in which it is used, but also for the nation as a whole. Taxpayers in rural areas should contribute to mass transit in urban areas to reduce America's dependence on foreign oil. This argument is consistent with which approach to the role of the state?
   a. the conflict approach
   b. the pluralist approach
   c. the functionalist approach
   d. the legal-rational approach
   e. the interactionist approach

10. The change in leadership in Iran from the Shah to the Ayatollah Khomeini would be described by sociologists as a shift from _____ to _____.
   a. a power elite; interest groups
   b. traditional authority; charismatic authority
   c. coercive power; legal-rational authority
   d. democracy; coercion
   e. a political party; a state

---

6. **b.** *A member of the power elite, according to Mills, possesses overlapping bases of power. This hypothetical individual has an upper-class background, is likely to be Protestant and to have an Ivy League education, and will bring that power base to his prominent government job. See page 496.*

7. **a.** *The guerrilla leader has the power to achieve his objectives, but this power is not legitimate except within his group. Authority is legitimate power, according to Weber. See page 480.*

8. **a.** *If power is diffuse within a society, no group can obtain a monopoly. The power of a democratic government is limited by law and spread through branches at state and local levels. Political input comes* from many sources, making a representative democracy more likely. See page 489.

9. **c.** *The functionalist approach recognizes the importance of planning and direction by the state to maintain the necessary coordination of a complex society. In this example, the burden of transportation must be shared by all citizens if the country as a whole is to stay economically stable. The self-interest of one group (transit nonusers) must be balanced with the needs of another group through the power of the state. See pages 484–485.*

10. **b.** *The Shah represented traditional authority vested in him from his family line. The Ayatollah Khomeini was a charismatic figure capable of mobilizing enough support to lead a revolutionary overthrow of the traditional government. See pages 481–482.*

11. Which of the following statements about liberty and equality is valid?
    a. Equality is only possible under a democratic system of government.
    b. The more of one, the less of the other.
    c. Most citizens want more liberty, no matter how much they actually have.
    d. The United States emphasizes equality over liberty.
    e. Capitalism is an attempt to balance the demands of liberty and equality more evenly.

12. Compared to other societies, American political parties are unique in
    a. the number of people who are members.
    b. their ability to recruit and offer candidates for public office.
    c. the extensiveness of differences between the major parties.
    d. the lack of ties to specific social classes.
    e. their ability to transfer public opinion to official leaders.

13. Which of the following explains the strong influence of interest groups in American politics?

    a. the loose coalitions that make up our political parties
    b. the lack of legitimate authority in American politics
    c. the presence of a power elite
    d. checks and balances on the power of government officials
    e. the active participation of the American voter

14. Evidence for a major party realignment can be seen in
    a. the coalition of young voters, wealthy voters, and Christian fundamentalists.
    b. the decline in numbers of people who have either a Republican or a Democratic party affiliation.
    c. the shift of black voters from the Democratic to the Republican party.
    d. the importance of labor-union endorsements for any successful Presidential campaign.
    e. the emergence of third-party candidates such as Lyndon LaRouche.

---

11.  **b.** *Liberty and equality are difficult qualities to balance in a society. Liberty refers to the personal freedoms of the individual; these rights can result in infringements on others, denying them equality. The state is expected to balance these qualities; in the United States, liberty is emphasized over equality, while in socialist countries, the reverse is true. See page 490.*

12.  **d.** *American political parties are really loose coalitions of people with fairly general platforms and political goals. While there is some association between social-class membership and party affiliation in the United States, this correlation is not nearly as strong as in other industrialized countries, where party affiliations are much more narrowly defined and often tied to occupations. See pages 491–492.*

13.  **a.** *Interest groups are organized around a small set of specific issues they wish to endorse for the benefit of their membership. In some countries, political parties are set up this way and function as interest groups. Because political parties in the United States are loosely organized, interest groups, with their specific focus and heavy funding tend to be very influential. See pages 493–494.*

14.  **a.** *In the 1980 election of Ronald Reagan to the presidency, a new coalition of voters teamed up to give him 49 of 50 states. It included those from the conservative South and West, young people, and Christian fundamentalists, as well as traditional Republican groups, such as upper-income voters. Especially given demographic trends toward increases in the Reagan-coalition-type voters, this may signal a party realignment. See pages 492–493.*

15. The governments of Haiti and the Philippines were overthrown in 1986. The form of government instituted by their ex-rulers, Duvalier and Marcos, respectively, could be classified as
   a. a junta.
   b. authoritarian.
   c. totalitarian.
   d. a monarchy.
   e. democratic.

16. Which of the following features of charismatic authority is *not* shared with traditional and legal-rational authority?
   a. It is short-lived.
   b. It is legitimate.
   c. It is based on power.
   d. It is present in developing societies.
   e. It can exist against the will of the majority of citizens.

17. Which of the following statements about the state is valid?
   a. The emergence of the state as a separate institution is linked to the means of subsistence.

b. A state exists whenever a group has definable boundaries.
   c. States are formed by charismatic leaders.
   d. States have existed since the beginning of human civilization.
   e. Early states had more social equality than do current ones.

18. What did President Eisenhower mean by the "complex" in "military-industrial complex"?
   a. the increasing complexity of the federal government
   b. the importance of having military leaders as candidates for public office
   c. the embarrassment military leaders feel when stories come out about $300 toilet seats
   d. the substantial mutual influence of the Pentagon and U.S. corporations
   e. the size of some military bases and their importance to the local community's economy

19. Which aspect of Marx's analysis of the role of the state seems to be *incorrect* in light of modern evidence?
   a. Political and economic power resides in the same class.

---

15. **b.** *Authoritarian governments tolerate little or no public opposition. Elections, if permitted at all, provide limited opportunity for opposition-party candidates to win. Duvalier and Marcos permitted no direct challenge to their authority to rule for life—only a coup could bring about a change in leadership. See page 486.*

16. **a.** *Charismatic leadership is based on the exceptional qualities of a specific individual. If the leader dies or is overthrown, power is not easily transferred to another person. In general, charismatic leadership is short-lived, and ends with the demise of the individual or becomes routinized as legal-rational authority. See page 482.*

17. **a.** *The state emerged when the method of subsistence produced an economic surplus. The presence of a surplus*

*is the foundation for social-class differences and for a central political authority to maintain social order. See page 483.*

18. **d.** *Eisenhower warned about the mutual influence of the major U.S. corporations that manufacture weapons and the Pentagon, which purchases them. He felt this military-industrial complex was becoming a dominant feature of American economic and political life, with insufficient checks and balances to its potential power. See page 500.*

19. **d.** *Contrary to Marx's prediction, modern socialist and communist societies have greater centralization of authority than do capitalist forms of government. See pages 485–486.*

b. The state comes into existence when classes emerge in society.

c. Social institutions support the status quo.

d. The role of the state is significantly reduced in a classless society.

e. The power of the state is likely to increase in a socialist society.

20. Studies of large and small communities around the United States have produced which conclusion about who rules?

a. Most communities have elites, but their influence depends on the characteristics of the community itself.

b. The military-industrial complex describes the ruling body in most communities.

c. A common form of community rule is "machine" politics.

d. Most communities have the active involvement of voters at all social-class levels to protect against the development of an elite.

e. Members of the upper-upper class still dominate the decision-making process in major cities in the United States.

21. King Darius IV has plundered, abused, and overtaxed his people. He is deposed and exiled in a popular uprising. His next of kin is installed as Darius V. This scenario suggests a political system

a. based on legal-rational authority.

b. based on illegitimate authority.

c. based on traditional authority.

d. based on a charismatic leader.

e. based on authoritarian leadership.

22. Legal-rational authority

a. emphasizes a government of laws, not of people.

b. is seldom found in modern societies.

c. is legitimated by ancient custom.

d. has historically been the most common source of legitimation of power.

e. typically involves one leader or family who governs for an extended period of time.

23. Studies of power indicate that Richard Nixon's cover-up of Watergate

a. failed only because it became public.

b. was justified by Nixon's good intentions.

c. destroyed the authority of the presidency.

d. was exposed and investigated because of the diffusion of power in the American political system.

e. revealed the instability of charismatic authority.

---

20. **a.** *There is a general pattern of concentrated power in most communities. But studies of various large and small communities show that the members of this elite group and the type and extent of their influence varies with the characteristics of the community. See pages 499–500.*

21. **c.** *In a system based on traditional authority, power is legitimated by custom. In this case, the family line of kings determines successors to rulers who are deposed. See pages 481–482.*

22. **a.** *Legal-rational authority, exhibited in the government of the United States, grants power to persons under the law. They hold a position and are thus entitled to certain privileges. Once the person is out of office, he or she loses that power, which remains with the office. Thus the qualities of the individual do not entitle him or her to power; laws confer the power on a particular office. See page 482.*

23. **d.** *Even though there is a heavy concentration of political power among elites in the United States, the political system has enough checks and balances to prevent gross political abuses. See page 489.*

24. Research on political participation has shown that
    a. income and age are correlated.
    b. social class is probably a determining factor.
    c. social class is unrelated to voting.
    d. sex is the main variable in voting.
    e. most Americans register but do not vote.

25. In which country would you be *most likely* to find representative democracy?

    a. a country with an advanced economy
    b. a country with an undeveloped economy
    c. a country without a large middle class, the only significant exceptions being the United States and Canada
    d. a country with a tradition of democracy
    e. a traditional society with an agricultural economy

---

24. **b.** *Political participation is closely correlated with social class. The lower a person's social class, the less likely that person is to register as a voter, to vote, to belong to a political organization, or to attempt to influence the views of others. See pages 498–499.*

25. **a.** *Democracy is based on the assumption that the mass electorate is capable of exercising judgment in shaping government. An educated, literate public is a prerequisite. An advanced economy produces a large middle class possessing these qualities and a fairly stable society. See pages 483, 487–489.*

## A CASE STUDY

NAME

COURSE/SECTION NUMBER

In the 1986 elections, two more Kennedys were candidates for the House of Representatives — Joseph Kennedy and Kathleen Kennedy Townsend, both children of the late Robert F. Kennedy. Joe was elected. Their father was U.S. attorney general and a presidential candidate before his death. One uncle, Edward Kennedy, is a senator. John F. Kennedy, another uncle, was president. Other families are prominent in American politics as well: the Longs and Boggs of Louisiana, the DuPonts, the Rockefellers, the Dodds, and many others. Take a look at the U.S. Congress (a list of its current members is readily available in your library's reference room).

1.    What evidence is there for a pluralist or a power-elite model in the last national election for Congress?

2.    Give evidence for or against the text's hypothesis regarding a party realignment.

3.   Pick one member of Congress and indicate the amount of money contributed to his/her campaign by political action committees.

4.   On what committees does that member sit? Which interest groups are concerned about the actions of those committees?

5.   Do you think wealthy candidates are less tied to special interests because they are financially independent, or does wealth distort their ability to represent a nation of poor and middle-class people?

# Applying the Concepts

NAME

COURSE/SECTION NUMBER

## APPLICATION EXERCISE ONE

Review the recent copies of your local newspaper. Cut out articles about foreign news events that show leaders who possess the three types of authority distinguished by Weber. Attach the articles and respond to the following questions for each article.

1. How did the leader claim the authority?

2. How is the authority evident? What are its boundaries?

3. How stable is this type of authority?

4.    What are the characteristics of this country's economic institution and division of labor? Do the political and economic institutions support a dominant-class ideology?

5.    Analyze the news events according to a functionalist perspective.

6.    Analyze the news events according to a conflict perspective.

## APPLICATION EXERCISE TWO

When individuals are born into a society, the political order and distribution of power already exist. As a result of the process of socialization, people accept existing social institutions as good, natural, and right. Few seem to realize that these social institutions, having been created by humans, could be re-created in different and perhaps better ways.

The following is an excerpt from the U.S. Declaration of Independence. First, read it and record your own reaction to what it says. Then answer the questions below.

> We hold these Truths to be self-evident, that all Men are created equal, that they are endowed by their Creator with certain inalienable Rights, that among these are Life, Liberty, and the Pursuit of Happiness.—That to secure these Rights, Governments are instituted among Men, deriving their just Powers from the Consent of the Governed, that whenever any Form of Government becomes destructive of these Ends, it is the Right of the People to alter or to abolish it, and to institute new Government, laying its Foundation on such Principles and organizing its Powers in such Form, as to them shall seem most likely to effect their Safety and Happiness. Prudence, indeed, will dictate that Governments long established should not be changed for light and transient Causes; and accordingly all Experience hath shewn, that Mankind are more disposed to suffer, while Evils are sufferable, than to right themselves by abolishing the Forms to which they are accustomed. But when a long Train of Abuses and Usurpations, pursuing invariably the same Object, evinces of Design to reduce them under absolute Despotism, it is their Right, it is their Duty, to throw off such Government, and to provide new Guards for their future Security.

1.    How does this document support the idea that the United States is a democracy or a representative democracy?

2.    Give evidence for each of the four functions of the state according to the functionalist perspective.

3.   How would a conflict theorist describe the actual evidence of this document in our daily life?

4.   Social scientists have shown this document and the Bill of Rights to a sample of American citizens and have asked them to comment on the words. A high proportion of Americans, not recognizing the documents they are reading, express disagreement, disapproval, or qualifications about these constitutional rights. How would you explain these reactions?

5.   How is the dilemma between liberty and equality evident in this document and in the political life of the United States?

NAME

COURSE/SECTION NUMBER

# APPLICATION EXERCISE THREE

Political action committees (PACs) are organizations established by interest groups to influence political contests and legislative outcomes. This pressure is applied mostly at the federal level and largely through activities that have come to be known as "lobbying." According to national polls, the specific goals of PACs usually represent a statistical minority, rather than a majority, of public opinion. According to the Federal Election Committee (FEC), the following PACs contributed these sums to federal candidates between January 1, 1979, and November 21, 1980 (an election year):

| | |
|---|---|
| National Association of Realtors | $1,532,105.00 |
| United Auto Workers | 1,514,981.00 |
| American Medical Association | 1,348,585.00 |
| National Automobile Dealers Association | 1,034,875.00 |
| Machinists and Aerospace Workers | 836,910.00 |
| AFL-CIO | 791,092.00 |
| American Milk Producers, Inc. | 778,289.00 |
| United Transportation Union | 724,693.00 |
| National Association of Life-Underwriters | 637,192.00 |
| Carpenters and Joiners of America | 555,008.00 |

1.   What are the implications of this funding for a representative democracy like the United States?

2.   On what kind of authority does the power of PACs depend?

3.    How might functionalists analyze the relationship between interest groups and the political order, and between U.S. citizens and interest groups?

4.    How might conflict theorists analyze these relationships quite differently?

5.    Assess which power thesis, power-elite or pluralist, is most applicable in the case of interest groups?

# UNIT 5

# Social Change in the Modern World

# CHAPTER 19

# Social Change

## Reviewing the Concepts

### LEARNING GOALS

*After studying this chapter, you should be able to:*

1. Define social change.

2. Explain why social change is difficult for sociologists to study.

3. Describe how environmental factors influence social change.

4. Discuss the three sources of cultural innovation, giving examples of each.

5.  Identify demographic factors that have affected or will affect social change.

6.  Present the theory of technological determinism.

7.  Compare the roles of individual action and collective action in social change.

8.  State the position of two theorists who held a cyclical view of social change.

9.  Identify the assumptions of theorists associated with the early evolutionary theory of social change.

10. Characterize the sociocultural-evolution theory of social change.

11. Discuss the work of Talcott Parsons as an example of a functionalist theory of social change.

12. Summarize the position of Marx and later sociologists who advocate a conflict theory of social change.

13. Summarize the strengths and weaknesses of the three major theories dealing with social change — the sociocultural-evolution, functionalist, and conflict theories.

14. Distinguish the features of developed and less developed countries.

15. Outline social and economic development according to the modernization model.

16. Explain the world-system model with regard to modernization and its consequences for developed and less developed countries.

17. Identify the conditions conducive to revolutionary change.

18. Describe the role of social scientists in predicting the future.

# IDENTIFYING KEY QUESTIONS AND THEMES

*Social change* is the alteration in patterns of culture, social structure, and social behavior over time. No society can successfully prevent change, although the rate, nature, and direction of change differ greatly from one society to another. Sociologists have always been interested in social change—particularly in the shift from preindustrial to industrial societies. Because social scientists have been unable to indicate precisely how societies form as relatively stable units in the first place, theories of social change are not altogether satisfying. Social change involves a complex of interacting factors, some of which cannot be anticipated. In addition, the unique features of each society make a comprehensive theory of social change difficult; predicting the experiences of one society from the past events of another is risky. However, these problems are not insurmountable, and sociologists have achieved an understanding of the processes that social change involves.

## Some Sources of Social Change

*What factors generate changes in all societies?*

Sociologists have identified a number of sources of social change: the physical environment; cultural innovation; population; technology; and human action.

The physical environment exerts a strong influence on the culture and social structure of a society. The climate, available raw materials, geographic barriers and assets, etc. may set limits on the type of society that will develop as well as on how it will change. Additionally, humans alter their environment, sometimes depleting its resources in the process.

Cultural innovation may occur through the processes of discovery, invention, or diffusion. A *discovery* is a new perception of an aspect of reality that already exists. This discovery, if shared within the society, adds to the society's culture and store of knowledge—it becomes a source of social change, however, only when it is put to use. An *invention* is the combination or new use of existing knowledge to produce something that did not exist before. Inventions may be either material (cigarettes, microchips) or social (slavery, democratic institutions).

Since inventions are based on a culture's existing store of knowledge, the rate of inventions increases exponentially. The process of *diffusion* involves the spread of cultural elements from one society to another. Given modern communication capabilities, diffusion is a major source of social and cultural change. Diffusion may involve nonmaterial culture, such as norms and values, as well as material culture. Material culture tends to be accepted more readily than nonmaterial culture.

Any significant change in population size or growth rates may affect or disrupt social life. A large population puts heavy demands on natural resources, resulting in mass migration, social disorganization, and conflict over scarce resources, among other outcomes. The distribution of a population greatly affects social relationships, as evidenced by urbanization. Changes in a society's demographic structure in terms of age, race, or gender influence social life as well.

Another major source of social change is *technology,* the practical applications of scientific or other knowledge. Most technological innovations are based on existing scientific knowledge and technology. The more technologically advanced a society is, the more rapid the technological change and the resulting social change. A society must carefully decide how to use the technological knowledge it has created. *Technological determinism* is the view that the technology available to a society is an important determinant of its culture, social structure, and even of its history. Proponents of this theory emphasize the way in which technological innovations may result in *culture lag*—a delay between a change in material culture and the adjustment of nonmaterial culture to the change. The social impact of such innovations as the printing press, the automobile, television, etc. seems to provide support for this theory. As with other sources of change, however, technological innovations occur in relation to other influences. Therefore, their impact is best understood in the context of an interacting system.

One obvious source of social change is human action: the acts of powerful leaders and other crucially placed individuals, and the collective action of large numbers of people, are two particularly important types. Although sociologists accept the historical significance of specific individuals, they believe that the social changes these individuals appear to have created may be the product of deeper social forces. That is, the actual event, and the individual involved, may not be the decisive factors. Rather, the social system as a whole may be ripe for change, and the person or event may serve merely as the trigger. To some extent, then, the impact of historic individuals and events can be explained in terms of existing social conditions.

Groups of people change society through collective behavior and social movements. *Collective behavior,* which is relatively spontaneous action that occurs when people try to work out common responses to ambiguous situations, includes such phenomena as fads, fashions, rumors, and riots. Other social action takes a more structured form—a *social movement* is a large number of people who have joined together to bring about or resist some social or cultural change. Such movements often involve campaign slogans aimed at advancing their ideas about desirable change.

## Theories of Social Change

*How have sociologists conceptualized social change? What evidence is there for sociocultural-evolution, functionalist, and conflict theories of social change?*

Early social scientists envisioned a cyclical pattern to social change. Cyclical theories developed in response to the observation that civilizations rise and fall, experiencing growth and decay. For example, Spengler made an analogy between the life cycle of a human being and that of a civilization, citing the stages of birth, maturity, old age, and death. Drawing on historical analyses, Toynbee argued that all civilizations go through a cycle of growth and decay, but that each civilization learns from its predecessors; thus the cycles build on each other toward a higher point. While cyclical theories provide an overlay for understanding historical fact, they have not proved effective in predicting and explaining what social change will take place and which societies will pass through which cycles, with what results. More useful theories include the sociocultural-evolution, functionalist, and conflict theories.

The evolutionary approach to social change is based on the assumption that societies gradually develop from simple beginnings into increasingly complex forms. Nineteenth-century theorists advanced the position that the pattern of social change is one of unilinear evolution.

Building on the work of Darwin, these theorists applied the notion of increasing complexity to human societies, arguing that they evolve in "one line" from simple to complex. Herbert Spencer and others held a view known as "social Darwinism," a position that attributed the rapid progress associated with Western countries to the supposed superiority of those peoples. This viewpoint was used to justify, among other things, colonial expansion and slavery. One problem with unilinear evolutionary theory was that it described existing societies but did not explain why or how some societies evolved and others did not. Another weakness was the lack of ethnographic evidence to support the theory. Social scientists found that while societies develop in a general pattern toward greater complexity, they do not all pass through the same stages, in the same order, or at the same rate. By the 1920s, unilinear theory had passed out of favor for its lack of usefulness and the need for a more relativistic view of change in other cultures.

Modern evolutionary theory is based on *sociocultural evolution*—the tendency for societies' social structures and cultures to grow more complex over time. Unlike early evolutionary theorists, modern social scientists describe this process as multilinear; that is, change occurs in many different ways and does not always follow the same course, direction, or speed in every society. They no longer believe that change necessarily means progress, or that greater social complexity is necessarily desirable. One advantage of sociocultural-evolution theory is that it shows how change takes place. According to its proponents, the main source of change is a shift in a society's means of subsistence, which in turn affects its culture and roles, and is the foundation for further change. The limitation of this theory is its focus on only one aspect of change, to the exclusion of other sources of change, such as war and revolution.

Functionalist theory focuses on social order rather than on social change. Durkheim was an early functionalist who tried to identify what functions such institutions as religion and education serve in maintaining the social system as a whole. Years later, the American theorist Talcott Parsons built on Durkheim's work, using this perspective to develop a theory of social order and of social change. Parsons felt that society consists of interdependent parts, each contributing to the maintenance of the whole. Society is held together by shared norms and values within the culture. When confronted with change, a society's entrenched cultural patterns help to absorb disruptive forces and maintain social balance, or equilibrium. Parsons acknowledged that change occurs, and that society must adjust to it. But he felt that change must occur gradually in order to avoid disruption of the social system. In later years, Parsons became particularly interested in the evolutionary changes that occur in a society. He believed that as societies become more complex, a process of *differentiation* takes place. For example, new institutions may develop to take over functions that were previously served by a single institution. To avoid social disorganization, a process of *integration* must follow, in which new norms help bridge the gap between the new institutions and the ones whose functions they are taking over, reasserting a smoothly running whole. Functionalist theories are subject to criticism for taking a conservative view of society that appears to endorse the status quo and to view change as disruptive.

Karl Marx and later conflict theorists argued that change is a central dynamic in society, that conflict is a normal process; existing conditions in any society form the basis for conflict and change in the future. Marx concentrated on change caused by tensions among competing interests, particularly between the exploited and the exploiting economic classes. Modern conflict theorists focus not just on class conflict but on social conflict in general. They study tensions among many different groups—for example, those between workers and managers, conservatives and liberals, males and females, as well as conflict between different nations, different racial and ethnic groups, different age groups, etc. Conflict theory is helpful in understanding many forms of social change. Yet it cannot explain why not all social change involves direct conflict, nor why, in some cases, change does not occur where conflict is present. In fact, no single contemporary theory appears to account for all social change. Therefore, a synthesis of the sociocultural-evolution, functionalist, and conflict theories seems the most reasonable approach to a comprehensive theory of social change. Sociocultural-evolution theory is promising in that it explains how societies evolve from the simple to the complex, changing their mode of production to the most efficient subsistence strategy possible. Functionalist

theory emphasizes the fact that societies are stable, enduring systems; but, as conflict theory demonstrates, competition over values and resources leads to continuous change. Thus a combination of the three theories, whereby some common patterns are recognized but no single model is advanced, seems the most feasible solution at this time.

## Global Development and Underdevelopment

*What insights derive from a modernization model or a world-system model of development? What are the consequences of global dependency and neocolonialism?*

One of the most significant social changes is the transition from a preindustrial to an industrial type of society. Societies generally fall into one of two groups: ***developed countries,*** such as the United States and Japan, are highly industrialized and comparatively affluent societies where most people enjoy a high quality of life; ***less developed countries,*** mostly located in the "third world," are comparatively poor nations where conditions of poverty prevail.

Sociologists use two different models to understand the various patterns of modernization and economic growth in the world. One views development in terms of ***modernization,*** a process of economic, social, and cultural change that facilitates the transition from preindustrial to industrial society. Under the modernization model, countries follow a similar pattern as they become modern industrialized societies. Advocates of this theory believe that less developed countries can use developed countries as models and accelerate the modernization process by obtaining foreign aid and changing their social institutions, among other things. Some modernization theorists emphasize a change in individual psychology, claiming that people in industrial societies are more likely to have goal-oriented, ambitious outlooks. While the modernization model offers a fairly optimistic view of the world's future, it does not fully address less developed countries' history of colonial dependency nor the different environmental and economic situations they face, compared to the industrial countries they seek to imitate.

Other social scientists view development in the context of the ***world system,*** a network of unequal economic and political relationships among the developed and the less developed countries. According to these theorists, the highly industrialized "core" countries exploit the "periphery" of less developed countries. *Neocolonialism* — the informal political and economic domination of some societies by others, such that the former are able to exploit the labor and resources of the latter for their own purposes — results in a system of international stratification. This dependency relationship is strengthened by: (1) export dependency; (2) large debts; and (3) *multinational corporations* — corporate enterprises headquartered in one country but operating through subsidiaries around the world. World-system theory is strongly influenced by conflict theory, and pinpoints the fierce international competition among countries. Its weakness lies in the fact that it does not explain why some countries break out of the dependency cycle and successfully modernize.

## Revolutions

*What conditions are conducive to revolutionary change?*

A *revolution* is the violent overthrow of an existing political or social system. Revolutions challenge the legitimacy of the social order and bring about dramatic change in a short period of time. Unlike a *coup d'état,* which involves the restricted use of force to replace one set of leaders with another, a revolution generally involves mass violence and results in more substantial change. Sociologists have long been interested in conditions that give rise to revolutionary behavior. These conditions include: (1) widespread awareness of an unequal distribution of societal resources; (2) a context of rising expectations, in which people who have accepted a deprived situation in the past now feel they have a right to something better; (3)

the blockage of alternative channels to change; (4) weaknesses in existing political institutions that threaten the legitimacy of the current government; and (5) a breakdown in the military.

Revolutions are almost always led by well-educated members of the middle class, rather than by members of the oppressed class that the revolution is intended to serve. While a certain critical mass of people must be mobilized to back the revolution, the support of the majority of the people is not required. Revolutions are usually followed by periods of great uncertainty as the new regime struggles to establish its own legitimacy, negotiate with competing groups for power, and bring about improved social conditions. Often revolutions result in the creation of nondemocratic and even totalitarian political institutions in the new regime's attempts to retain control. Paradoxically, U.S. foreign policy is highly antirevolutionary, in part because of the fear that communist-led uprisings will realign the balance of power between the United States and the Soviet Union. Despite this fact, many revolutions in third-world countries are successful in overthrowing traditional and often tryrannical governments.

## Predicting the Future

*What does social science tell us about the future?*

Social scientists can make confident predictions about specific areas of society, such as population growth. However, global predictions are much more difficult. Social scientists differ on such questions as how long industrialization will continue, and whether it will bring hardship and scarcity, or enhance the quality of life on a global scale.

# DEFINING CORE CONCEPTS

*After studying the chapter, write a sociological definition in your own words for the following core concepts. Then give an example from your own experience to illustrate your definition. Refer to the chapter to check your work.*

| *Core Concept* | *Sociological Definition* | *Personal Illustration* |
| --- | --- | --- |
| collective behavior | | |
| culture lag | | |
| developed country | | |
| diffusion | | |
| discovery | | |
| invention | | |
| less developed country | | |

| *Core Concept* | *Sociological Definition* | *Personal Illustration* |
| --- | --- | --- |
| modernization | | |
| multinational corporation | | |
| neocolonialism | | |
| revolution | | |
| social change | | |
| social movement | | |
| sociocultural evolution | | |
| technological determinism | | |

| *Core Concept* | *Sociological Definition* | *Personal Illustration* |
|---|---|---|
| world system | | |

## PUTTING IDEAS TOGETHER

A sociological view of change takes into account the large-scale processes involved in social change. Functionalist theory, sociocultural-evolution theory, and conflict theory focus on different aspects of the process. It is important to remember that the particular cultural context of each society influences the sequence of change and its results.

| SOCIOCULTURAL–EVOLUTION THEORY focuses on the tendency for society to change from simple to complex forms (via a multilinear process) based on a shift in its basic means of subsistence | FUNCTIONALIST THEORY focuses on the more gradual aspects of social change and how society adjusts to these sources of change while maintaining equilibrium | CONFLICT THEORY focuses on the more abrupt aspects of social change and how society copes with the many changes caused by tensions between competing interests |
|---|---|---|

SOURCES OF SOCIAL CHANGE
physical environment
population
cultural innovation
human action
technology

→

CONSEQUENCES OF SOCIAL CHANGE ARE SEEN IN
culture, social structure, socialization, interaction, deviance, sexuality, stratification, social class, race and ethnic relations, family, education, religion, science, economics, politics, populations, urban life, collective behavior

Revolutions are substantial upheavals that radically change social and political structures. Certain characteristics make such violent action likely to occur. The ideal-type characteristics of a democracy stand in contrast to those characteristics that are conducive to revolution, explaining why revolutionary change is rare in democracies, and why evolutionary change is the rule.

| *Conditions for Revolution* | *Characteristics of an Ideal Type Democracy* |
|---|---|
| Channels for change are blocked | Tolerance for dissent |
| Awareness of unequal distribution of societal rewards resulting in widespread grievance | A large middle class and some surplus from an industrial economy |
| A context of rising expectations | Consensus on basic values and absence of major cleavages |
| Weakness in existing political institutions leading to loss of legitimacy | Checks and balances; diffuse power |
| Military breakdown | Military acts reasonably within legal limits |

# Testing the Concepts

## MULTIPLE-CHOICE QUESTIONS

*After studying the chapter, try to answer each of the twenty-five questions below. Mark the alternative you think is correct, then look at the correct answer and the explanation provided at the bottom of the page. Try to state why the other alternatives are incorrect and check your understanding of the correct answer.*

1. A basic tenet of sociocultural-evolution theory is that
   a. change is natural and moves societies in the direction of greater complexity.
   b. simple societies are superior to complex societies.
   c. change is harmful and will eventually lead a society to destroy itself.
   d. there is no real change in society; there are simply variations on a common theme.
   e. societal development consists of a series of high and low points, occurring in a cyclical pattern.

2. The term "culture lag" refers to
   a. preliterate cultures.
   b. the rigidity that sets in when a society fails to respond to change.
   c. the technology of developing nations.
   d. the inevitability of new problems growing out of solutions to old problems.
   e. the fact that material culture usually advances more quickly than nonmaterial culture.

3. What did people call the enforced spread of Western culture, which was justified as the thankless but noble task of bringing "higher" forms of civilization to "inferior" people?
   a. manifest destiny
   b. a matter of destiny
   c. the white man's burden
   d. the decline of the west
   e. cultural diffusion

4. The construction of the Aswan Dam in Egypt resulted in increased irrigation of the desert land around the Nile River. Many more people can now be fed by the agriculture made possible by the irrigation. Which of the following sources of social change would you identify as the best explanation for this new development?
   a. events
   b. collective behavior
   c. population dynamics
   d. technology
   e. physical environment

---

1. **a.** *Evolutionary theories are based on the assumption that societies gradually develop from simple beginnings and move into more complex forms. This change is gradual and is supported by historical and anthropological evidence about the development of modern industrial society. See page 517.*

2. **e.** *William Ogburn studied the connection between technological determinism and the specific social and historical events that followed. He found many cases in which a change in material culture, such as the invention of the cotton gin, took some time to be accepted and integrated into nonmaterial culture. Ogburn called this gap "culture lag." See page 512.*

3. **c.** *Cultures show varying degrees of ethnocentrism, or belief in the superiority of their own way of life. Much social change can be traced to the belief held by members of Western culture that their values, such as Christianity, were superior and must be brought to and forced on other peoples. See page 517.*

4. **d.** *The technology of dam construction transformed a desert area into an agricultural area. This change resulted in food production and human settlements that were previously impossible. See page 511.*

5. A revolution is most likely to occur when which of the following factors is present?
   a. a legitimate government is in place
   b. many people are poor or oppressed
   c. there is a context of rising expectations
   d. a majority of the people support social change
   e. most people accept their inferior status as deserved

6. Durkheim's view of social change emphasized the aspects of society, such as religion, that provide stability and continuity, and hold society together. This view of social change is consistent with
   a. unilinear evolution theories.
   b. cyclical theories.
   c. conflict theory.
   d. modernization theory.
   e. functionalist theory.

7. Discovery, invention, and diffusion are the three sources of _____ innovation.
   a. irreversible
   b. environmental
   c. cultural

d. progressive
e. industrial

8. From the text's description of revolutions, we know that they are
   a. frequent in history.
   b. usually led by well-educated members of the middle class.
   c. followed by a period of calm.
   d. generally followed by the establishment of democratic governments.
   e. begun and carried out by the masses.

9. According to the text, the best general theory of social change would merge
   a. the functionalist view of Parsons with the concept of equilibrium.
   b. unilinear and conflict perspectives.
   c. cyclical theory with social Darwinism.
   d. sociocultural-evolution theory with functionalist and conflict perspectives.
   e. the ideas of culture lag and technological determinism.

---

5. **c.** *Conditions of inequality alone are not sufficient for a revolution. The support of the majority of the people is not necessary. People must believe they have a right to something better—this context of rising expectations often leads to revolution if other legitimate channels are blocked. See page 526.*

6. **e.** *Durkheim was an early functionalist who focused on social order and stability rather than on change. He identified the components of a society that reinforce social solidarity. While change was recognized, Durkheim and other functionalists felt that maintaining social order was most important. See page 517.*

7. **c.** *These three sources of cultural innovation produce social changes in the society at large. See pages 510–511.*

8. **b.** *Revolutions are usually led not by members of the oppressed class but by well-educated members of the middle class, who have promoted an awareness of social inequalities and the lack of alternatives for redress of grievances short of revolution. See page 526.*

9. **d.** *The sociocultural-evolution view shows how societies continue to evolve into more complex forms, and recognizes the variety of directions these developments might take. Functionalist theory focuses on the importance of maintaining order and stability especially during periods of change. Conflict theory recognizes competition and tension as the main source of change. The blend of these different perspectives gives the most accurate view of social change. See page 520.*

10. According to the functionalist perspective, social change is
   a. harmful to society.
   b. the source of social statics.
   c. rare.
   d. an alteration in social equilibrium to which society must adjust.
   e. an indication of a poorly functioning society.

11. What premise do the social change theories of Spengler and Toynbee have in common?
   a. Civilization fluctuates between the modern and the traditional.
   b. Each society is better than the preceding one.
   c. The situation of each culture is so specific that change occurs in a unique fashion.
   d. Each civilization is like a biological organism.
   e. There are cycles of social change.

12. In what way is modernization as it occurs today in the less developed parts of the world different from the modernization experienced by the United States?
   a. It is unwanted.
   b. It occurs much more rapidly.
   c. It retains personal values of the culture.

   d. It removes social inequalities.
   e. It maintains religion as a central belief system.

13. Which of the features of democracy make revolution less likely to occur?
   a. tolerance of dissent
   b. presence of a power elite
   c. presence of a charismatic leader
   d. high legitimacy of the government
   e. lack of social equality

14. World-system theorists argue that neocolonialism describes the relationship between developed and developing countries. What evidence would support this view?
   a. the presence of multinational corporations
   b. the willingness of people in underdeveloped countries to defer gratification
   c. free and democratic elections
   d. the use of political and economic sanctions against South Africa
   e. the prosperity of countries with monarchs

15. Some of the earlier functions of the religious institution have been taken over by newer institutions. For example, the provision of welfare to the poor is now

---

10. **d.** *Functionalists are concerned with the stability of the social order. When one aspect of society changes, the other parts of society must also adjust to maintain a state of social equilibrium. See pages 517–518.*

11. **e.** *These theorists viewed social change as occurring in a cyclical pattern. Spengler saw civilizations as going through a life cycle; Toynbee identified a pattern of challenge and response. See page 515.*

12. **b.** *Because underdeveloped countries today are confronted with the process of modernization whether they want it or not, they face rapid social change. Most countries strive to keep up with competition in the industrialized world and seek the material benefits that come with modernization. See page 525.*

13. **a.** *A democracy is characterized by a tolerance of criticism and of dissenting opinions. This serves as an*

*escape valve for people, allowing them to express dissatisfaction and receive some redress. Revolutions typically occur when people feel that the alternative channels to change are blocked and that they are powerless to make their demands known. See pages 489; 526.*

14. **a.** *Multinational corporations are headquartered in one country but conduct their operations in many others. The host countries have minimal, if any, control over the corporation's policies and products. The domination of underdeveloped countries by developed ones is called neocolonialism. See pages 523–524.*

15. **b.** *Parsons felt that as societies become more complex, new social institutions emerge, taking on many of the functions that were previously undifferentiated and assigned to one institution. He called this process differentiation. See page 518.*

primarily a function of the state, and the explanation of
the nature of the universe is now primarily a function
of science. This tendency is an example of
   a. multilinear evolution.
   b. differentiation.
   c. integration.
   d. the growth of "bridging institutions."
   e. discovery.

16. Social movements are examples of which type of
social change?
   a. cultural innovation
   b. discovery
   c. human action
   d. population dynamics
   e. diffusion

17. As the "baby boom" generation ages, the changing
demographic structure will produce social changes.
Elderly people will increase their ranks and will require
additional social services. This is an example of which
source of social change?
   a. human action
   b. cultural innovation
   c. population dynamics

   d. physical environment
   e. technology

18. The Social Security system was begun in the 1930s
as a way of providing support for people in the
postretirement years and protecting them against
poverty. Which pair of concepts would Parsons's theory
of social change use to explain the introduction and
acceptance of the Social Security system?
   a. diffusion; population
   b. differentiation; integration
   c. equilibrium; human action
   d. cultural innovation; culture lag
   e. cyclical change; modernization

19. Which of the following criticisms of the conflict
theory of social change is *incorrect*?
   a. Conflict theory does not account for all forms of
      social change.
   b. All conflict does not have an economic base.
   c. Conflict theory has not been useful in analyzing
      historical events.
   d. Conflict theory falsely assumes there are always
      scarce resources.
   e. Conflict theory is not a comprehensive theory of
      social change.

16.  **c.** *Human action may be organized into social
movements to achieve specific social changes. The civil
rights movement is one case in which organized, joint
human action resulted in significant changes in the
United States. See page 514.*

17.  **c.** *Shifts in the population—whether in raw
numbers of people or their distribution in terms of some
characteristic, such as age—affect the society. The U.S.
population will become older in future years, a shift that
will result in social changes as the elderly work for social
benefits for themselves. See page 511.*

18.  **b.** *Parsons theorized that as societies become more
complex they undergo a process of differentiation;*

*various institutions take on the functions previously
performed by a single institution. The care of the elderly
in the United States, which used to be handled within the
family institution, now is addressed by Social Security,
nursing homes, and other services. The functions of these
various institutions must be integrated to preserve social
equilibrium. See page 518.*

19.  **c.** *Conflict theory has accurately been applied to
historical events. In almost all cases, hindsight identifies
some class conflict or general social conflict over scarce
resources. The theory is not as useful in predicting social
changes, however, or in identifying an economic base for
most conflict. See pages 519–520.*

20. The process of worldwide modernization adds credibility to which general theory of social change?
   a. cyclical theory
   b. sociocultural-evolution theory
   c. unilinear evolutionary theory
   d. culture lag theory
   e. ecological theory

21. Modernization theorists believe one key to development is _____, while world-system theorists emphasize _____.
   a. revolution; technological determinism
   b. multinational corporations; inventions
   c. a change in individual psychology; reducing international stratification
   d. neocolonialism; adherence to the model of currently developed countries
   e. large families; small families

22. An example of diffusion would be
   a. the invention of the atomic bomb.
   b. the sale of an American nuclear reactor to a less technologically developed society.
   c. the discovery of the principle of atomic fusion.
   d. the improvement in methods of generating atomic power.
   e. the construction of new nuclear power plants in the United States each year.

23. Which of the following statements about inventions is true?
   a. Inventions occur exponentially.
   b. The likelihood that a particular invention will be made depends primarily on the presence or absence of creative individuals.
   c. The term "invention" can be applied only to material products.
   d. Inventions occur gradually as cultures progress technologically.
   e. Inventions are usually based on completely new knowledge.

---

20. **b.** *Modernization is a general trend throughout the world, but the pace and form of modernization vary from culture to culture. The process is evolutionary, moving from the simple to the complex; the variety of forms requires a multilinear explanation. See page 517.*

21. **c.** *Modernization theorists emphasize a psychology of hard work and deferred gratification, a sense of individualism and personal control as the key to development. World-system theorists focus on the inequalities between nations and the need for fair allocation of resources before development can occur. See page 525.*

22. **b.** *Diffusion is the spread of cultural elements from one society to another. In this case, the technology of nuclear reactions is transmitted to a country without that technology. See pages 510–511.*

23. **a.** *All inventions are based on previous knowledge. The more objects, ideas, discoveries, and inventions in a society's knowledge base, the more rapidly future inventions can be made. See page 510.*

24. Why was unilinear evolutionary theory so widely accepted?
   a. American society was evolving rapidly at that time and the theory enhanced the national mood of optimism.
   b. It was advanced by very prominent political leaders hoping to be elected.
   c. It provided a flattering and convenient justification for colonial rule over "inferior" people.
   d. It meshed with an observed fact of history, the rise and fall of civilizations.
   e. It supported the facts drawn from ethnographic research rather than the speculations of "armchair anthropologists."

25. Which of the following examples could best be explained by conflict theory?
   a. the replacement of the feudal system with modern capitalism
   b. the rapid rate of technological change in modern societies
   c. the fact that societies tend to be stable and endure over time
   d. the changing norms of sexual morality in the United States
   e. the many lives that have been saved since the discovery of a smallpox vaccine

---

24. c. *The unilinear theory of evolution suggested that societies move in a single line of development from primitive to more civilized forms, similar to the biological evolution described by Darwin. The so-called advanced societies felt a burden to bring more primitive cultures along the evolutionary chain, thereby justifying their colonial rule. See pages 516–517.*

25. a. *Conflict theorists argue that social change results from struggles over scarce resources. In this example, the period of the Middle Ages was characterized by conflicts between landowners and peasants, and the struggle gave way to a capitalist economy. See pages 519–520.*

# A CASE STUDY

Saudi Arabia is an oil-rich desert country that has experienced a great deal of social change. Its hostile environment poses problems for food cultivation and water supply and has restricted the development of large urban populations. Yet this small nation is one of the wealthiest in the world, largely due to the world fuel crisis. In November 1973, the OPEC council met to quadruple the price of crude oil on the world market. Saudi Arabia's gross national product zoomed upward as a result of this price increase in their one export. Although the Saudis have a monarchy and traditional religious customs characteristic of developing countries, their vast wealth puts them in a position very different from that of other developing nations. The country has a captive market for its oil and more money than it can spend as long as oil prices remain strong. Conversely, when oil prices drop, the economy falls, too.

Several changes have occurred in Saudi society in the past decade. In an effort to modernize, the government has launched massive literacy efforts. All citizens are sent to school, although boys and girls are taught separately, in line with religious custom. The increased wealth has allowed the purchase of many technological innovations; Saudi Arabia may well become one of the most technologically advanced countries in the world on the basis of its international purchasing power. For example, the process of desalinization (removal of salt from water to make it drinkable) is of great importance to the Saudis; they are using all the relevant technology from around the world to accomplish this goal. The Saudis' increased wealth has brought an influx of foreign business persons and other visitors. While they do not have citizenship rights and most are not permanent settlers, their presence has affected this once isolated desert country. The internal power structure of the Saudi economy has also changed. As the oil industry has grown, more specialized jobs are required to sustain the industry. The economy has expanded to include many jobs for teachers, bankers, retailers, and other occupations that support the oil industry. The pace of social change has been unusually fast and the long-term effects are yet to be determined.

1.   What are the sources of social change in Saudi Arabia?

2.   How might the phenomenon of culture lag manifest itself in this country?

3.    Which factors press for changes in the social structure of Saudi Arabia?
How does modernization typically affect the class structure of a country?

4.    The neighboring country of Libya is also rich in oil. It has a socialist form
of government, and the pace of modernization is slower than that in Saudi
society. How does the political economy (the joint effects of the political
system and the economic system) of a country affect the modernization process?

5.    How would a functionalist analyze the changes taking place in Saudi
Arabia? How would a conflict theorist assess the situation?

6.    If you were advising Saudi Arabia as to how to spend its newfound wealth,
which three policies would you suggest in order to promote the most stable
long-term benefits of modernization?

# Applying the Concepts

NAME

COURSE/SECTION  NUMBER

## APPLICATION EXERCISE ONE

1.   Pick an example of a fairly recent revolution or coup, such as that witnessed in Iran, the Philippines, or Haiti. Describe the conditions that led to the overthrow of power.

2.   Identify the extent to which social change in this country was caused by:

   a.  the physical environment

   b.  cultural innovation

   c.  population dynamics

   d.  technology

   e.  human action

3.  To what extent is this a developed or a less developed country? Describe
the country from the perspective of:

    a.  a modernization theorist

    b.  a world-system theorist

## APPLICATION EXERCISE TWO

NAME

COURSE/SECTION NUMBER

1.   "Man cannot step twice into the same river for he is not quite the same man, nor is it quite the same river." Reflect particularly on the changes in your life since entering college. In what ways does this quotation speak to your own experiences?

2.   What influences—peers, classes, leaving home, and so on—have contributed to these changes?

3.    Can you think of ideas or events that have occurred in your lifetime that have produced social change affecting you directly?

4.    Pick one of the following examples of social change: the policies of the Reagan presidential administration; the civil rights activities in the 1960s; the passage of gay rights ordinances in certain cities, some of which have been rescinded; no-smoking laws; or seat-belt laws. What are the social consequences of the social changes? How would a conflict theorist and a functionalist explain these changes?

## APPLICATION EXERCISE THREE

NAME

COURSE/SECTION NUMBER

Look through your local newspaper and find a news clipping describing events in a developing country. You will use this to discuss the process of modernization. You might consider, for example, the countries of China, El Salvador, Cuba, or Haiti.

1.   What are the major sources of change in this country?

2.   What evidence do you see of the process of modernization?

3.   What are the social effects of modernization on this country's institutions, population, and culture?

4.    Is there any evidence of dysfunctions of social change?

5.    How has the process of modernization in this country differed from that in the United States?

6.    What evidence do you have to support a world-system view of development in this country?

# CHAPTER 20

# Collective Behavior and Social Movements

## Reviewing the Concepts

### LEARNING GOALS

*After studying this chapter, you should be able to:*

1. Define collective behavior and social movement and indicate the forms each may take.

2. Identify Smelser's six basic conditions for collective behavior; then, as the text did for the Jonestown example, show how they apply to the soccer riots in Europe, or the race riots in South Africa, or an example of your choice.

3. Identify several important characteristics of a crowd and contrast them with those of a mass.

4. Compare Le Bon's contagion theory with Turner and Killian's emergent-norms theory as explanations of crowd behavior.

5. Identify Blumer's four basic types of crowd and give your own examples of each.

6. Distinguish between mobs and riots as two forms of acting crowd.

7. Indicate the nature of, and the typical sequence of events in, a panic.

8. Explain the nature of rumors, and when and how they are likely to arise, providing examples.

9. Outline the nature and importance of urban legends.

10. Using examples, explain how mass hysteria comes about and how it subsides.

11. Distinguish between fashions and fads.

12. Present a sociological explanation of a public and list factors affecting public opinion.

13. Cite television commercials to illustrate at least three propaganda techniques.

14. Describe a social movement, generally, and the special case of millenarian movements, specifically.

15. Contrast the positions of a psychological theorist, a strain theorist, and a resource-mobilization theorist on a social movement such as gay rights.

16. Present examples of the four types of social movements.

17. Describe the range of tactics a social movement might use to reach its goals; discuss the tactic of terrorism.

18. Indicate the four stages that may be involved in a social movement and discuss the impact each stage could have on the social problem it seeks to redress.

## IDENTIFYING KEY QUESTIONS AND THEMES

Social norms guide most of our day-to-day behavior, ensuring that our interactions with other people follow a regular and predictable course. However, there are certain conditions in which norms seem unclear, or even absent, and the people involved appear to collectively improvise conduct in response to these conditions. Sociologists call this *collective behavior*—relatively spontaneous social action that occurs when people try to work out common responses to ambiguous situations. This unstructured behavior is seen in mobs, panics, rumors, urban legends, mass hysteria, fashions, fads, and public opinion. Another form of social behavior that can disturb the established patterns of social life is the *social movement*—a large number of people who have joined together to bring about or resist some social or cultural change. While some social movements are loosely structured, many hold clearly defined goals and have well-established procedures for meeting those goals.

### Collective Behavior

*How have sociologists studied collective behavior? What are the six conditions for collective behavior identified by Neil Smelser?*

By its very nature, collective behavior is difficult to study. For one thing, it is so unstructured and unpredictable that sociologists cannot easily apply their scientific methods of analysis. In addition, data may come from the recollection of untrained observers who witness the wide range of phenomena falling under this category. Yet some conclusions can be made about collective behavior.

Sociologist Neil Smelser argues that collective behavior is essentially an attempt by people to alter their environment when they are under stressful conditions of uncertainty, threat, or strain. The form that their collective behavior takes depends on how they define the problem facing them. Smelser identifies six basic conditions, all of which must be met, for collective behavior to occur. (1) Structural conduciveness refers to the surrounding conditions that make a particular form of collective behavior possible in the first place. For example, the political system of Iran under the shah made extreme revolutionary activity likely as the means for social change. (2) Structural strains, or any social condition that places pressure on people, encourages them to make a collective effort to relieve the problem. (3) People must develop some generalized belief about their situation by sizing up the problem and forming an opinion about what should be done. (4) Precipitating factors are necessary to trigger the collective behavior. (5) When a precipitating incident has taken place, people must be mobilized for action. (6) Having met the preceding five conditions, collective behavior is inevitable when there is a failure of social control to prevent the behavior from occurring. The mass suicide at the Peoples Temple in Guyana is an example of collective behavior illustrating each of Smelser's basic conditions.

### Crowds

*What have sociologists identified as the distinguishing features of a crowd and a mass? What are the two main theories of crowd behavior?*

A *crowd* is a temporary collection of people who are in close enough physical proximity to interact. On the other hand, a *mass* is a collection of people who are concerned with the same phenomenon without being in each other's presence. Not all sociologists find this distinction useful, since certain kinds of collective behavior can occur in both a crowd and a mass. In any case, some of the most striking episodes of collective behavior occur when people are close enough to interact.

Two main theories have been proposed to explain the distinction between crowd behavior and everyday group behavior. The *contagion theory,* advanced by Le Bon, argues that individuals lose much of their self-identity and even their self-control in a crowd situation. According to this theory, people become less capable of rational thought when they are caught up in the frenzy of the crowd, and a "collective mind" develops, whereby members of a crowd are dominated by a single impulse and act almost identically. While sociologists dismiss the idea of a "collective mind," there is no doubt that members of a crowd are more suggestible than they would be as individuals. Sociologist Herbert Blumer describes this phenomenon in terms of a "circular reaction," whereby members of a crowd respond to one another in an emotional, unreflecting way, creating a sort of ripple effect.

The *emergent-norms theory,* advanced by Turner and Killian, argues that crowd behavior can be analyzed in terms of ordinary social and psychological processes. Members of a crowd look to one another for cues and follow whatever norms seem to be prevailing. In particular, Turner disagrees that members of a crowd act in almost identical ways because of "contagion." Instead he argues that members of a crowd have various motives and intentions and that the unanimity of a crowd is often an illusion. According to emergent-norms theory, unified crowd behavior is simply another example of group conformity. As new norms emerge during the course of interaction, these norms clarify the ambiguous situation that exists and define appropriate behavior for the crowd.

## Mobs

*What are the four basic types of crowd? What are the characteristics of mobs and riots? How do they differ from other forms of collective behavior?*

Herbert Blumer distinguishes four basic types of crowd: (1) a casual crowd is the most loosely structured, consisting of a collection of individuals who have little or no common purpose; (2) a conventional crowd is deliberately planned and relatively structured, and follows established social norms; (3) an expressive crowd is usually organized to permit the gratification of its members; (4) an acting crowd takes some kind of action, such as fleeing or rioting. A *mob,* one type of acting crowd, is an emotionally aroused crowd bent on violent or destructive action. While mobs usually have leaders, their immediate and limited objectives make them a particularly unstable form of collective behavior; the lynch mob is one striking example. A riot—a hostile outburst aimed at the creation of disorder through attacks on property, people, or both — is an important form of mob behavior. Rioters typically lack social power and vent their feelings in this destructive way. Race riots may be especially violent.

## Panics

*What is a panic? What is the sequence of behaviors in a panic?*

A *panic* is a form of collective behavior in which a group of people, faced with an immediate threat, react in a fearful, spontaneous, and uncoordinated way. As normal cooperative relationships break down, feelings of fear and danger actually increase. The progress of a panic follows a fairly typical course. A sudden crisis arises; people suffer intense fear; normal social expectations are disrupted; each individual tries desperately to escape from the danger; mutual cooperation breaks down; and the problem escalates as a result. Panics are especially likely to occur during fires, accidents, and natural disasters. Because panic is such an extreme emotional state it cannot be sustained for long. Once the initial shock has worn off, some measure of order returns.

## Rumors

*What are the characteristics of a rumor? When and how are rumors likely to arise?*

A *rumor* is information, true or false, that is transmitted informally from anonymous sources. A rumor may, in varying degrees, approximate the truth, but because it is passed along informally, its validity is difficult to check. The spreading of a rumor is itself a form of collective behavior, and rumors may be an important element in other kinds of collective behavior as well. Rumors are especially likely to arise in situations where people are deprived of information or do not trust the official information they are given. A rumor, then, fills a void and represents a collective attempt to gain some understanding of a particular situation.

Researchers have studied the way that rumors are passed on from person to person. In general, what happens to the rumor depends on its content, the number of people involved in the chain of transmission, and the transmitters' attitudes toward the rumor. Highly volatile rumors are often reshaped as they are passed on.

Sociologists recognize that rumors are not simply the transmission and possible distortion of information. A rumor can best be seen as a form of communication in which people pool their resources to construct a meaningful interpretation of an ambiguous situation. The rumored death of Beatle Paul McCartney during the 1960s is one such example. Lacking concrete information about the whereabouts of McCartney, concerned fans used clues from their records and other sources to construct a case for the possibility of his death. Likewise, the rumor of the Satanic message in the Proctor & Gamble symbol seemed to spring from the need of certain fundamentalist Christians to find and target enemies in order to reinforce their own beliefs.

## Urban Legends

*What are urban legends? What purpose do they serve?*

**Urban legends,** a form of contemporary folklore, are realistic but untrue stories with an ironic twist concerning recent alleged events. Like rumors, they are a collective reaction to situations of ambiguity, including conditions that arise from a changing society. Urban legends must have a strong story appeal, seem believable, and teach a lesson.

## Mass Hysteria

*What is mass hysteria? How have sociologists studied this behavior?*

**Mass hysteria** is a form of collective behavior involving widespread anxiety, caused by some unfounded belief. Due to their anxiety, people behave in irrational ways in order to protect themselves. In extreme cases, mass hysteria can result in panic. The text presents three case studies of mass hysteria: the Martian invasion of earth, the Seattle windshield-pitting epidemic, and AIDS hysteria. In each of these cases, sociologists could identify an unfounded belief that produced anxiety within a community or the society as a whole. The fear resulting from this belief caused people to take extreme action in order to protect themselves. Episodes of mass hysteria are self-limiting; the absurdity of the situation becomes apparent and the anxiety dissipates.

## Fashions

*What are fashions? How are they characterized as collective behavior?*

**Fashions** are the currently valued styles of appearance and behavior. In a modern society, the importance of fashions is consistent with the orientation toward the future, rather than the past, and the desirability of new and different things. Furthermore, powerful commercial interests encourage changes in fashions because they profit from the demand for new styles. In addition, modern societies are highly competitive: status-conscious people may use fashions to indicate their social desirability to others. Fashions can arise at any level of society and may or may not achieve wide public acceptance. In general, fashions evolve; each new variation is a modification of its predecessors.

## Fads

*What is a fad? How do fads gain and lose popularity?*

A **fad** is a temporary form of conduct that is followed enthusiastically by large numbers of people. Fads differ from fashions in that they are more short-lived and are often scorned by the majority of the population. Fads provide a way of asserting personal identity and may appeal to young people in particular. Once a fad has become so widespread that it no longer offers participants a distinctive identity, it usually goes out of style.

## Public Opinion

*What is a public? What factors affect public opinion? What are some propaganda techniques used to influence public opinion?*

A public is a substantial number of people with a shared interest in some issue on which there are differing opinions. While we sometimes speak of the whole population as the "public," in fact there are many publics. The activities of a public may be more rational than those of a crowd; because members make individual decisions over time, group pressure is minimized. Although some of the interaction of a public takes place on a face-to-face basis, much of it occurs indirectly through the mass media. A public does not act together but forms common opinions about the issue on which it is founded.

**Public opinion** is the sum of the decisions of the members of a public on a particular issue. Poll results indicate that people may be quite willing to state opinions even on topics about which they have little factual knowledge. Despite such anomalies, in the United States, both government and commercial sectors invest heavily in assessing and influencing public opinion on many issues and problems. Such campaigns are forms of **propaganda**—information or viewpoints presented with the deliberate intention of persuading the audience to adopt a particular opinion. Propaganda techniques include glittering generalities, name calling, transfer, testimonial, plain folks, card stacking, and bandwagoning.

Public opinion is formed from media sources and from information received through social networks. Public opinion is also influenced by opinion leaders, people who spend time studying the controversy, forming opinions, and interpreting them for others. Sociologists note that awareness of others' views may influence public opinion as people tend to be swayed by the more popular trends. Public opinion can now be measured with a high degree of accuracy through the use of opinion polls. However, attention to correct methodological procedures, including careful sampling, is essential. The Coca-Cola Company's decision to switch to "new Coke" emphasizes the importance of conceptualizing an issue before measuring opinion.

## Social Movements

*What are the characteristics of social movements? What are the special qualities of millenarian movements?*

Compared to collective behavior, social movements are a much more deliberate and organized form of action found mainly in industrial societies that are subject to rapid change. In preindustrial societies, where the social system is taken for granted, social movements usually take the form of religious cults or sects. **Millenarian movements** prophesy cataclysmic upheavals within the immediate future, bringing changes that will reverse the social order. As such, they are often thought of as "religions of the oppressed." Believers cling to the hope that a major change here on earth will redress the injustice or deprivation plaguing them. Although events rarely come to pass as prophesied, millenarian movements often lay the foundation for the militant, politically motivated movements characteristic of modern industrialized societies. Social movements are rare in totalitarian or authoritarian regimes, which suppress such dissent; they flourish, however, in heterogeneous and generally tolerant societies. Because they deliberately intervene in history, social movements have brought about lasting cultural and social changes.

## Explaining Social Movements

*What types of theories have been developed to explain social movements?*

Psychological theories, strain theories, and resource-mobilization theory have all been advanced to explain the causes of social movements. Psychological theories have focused on the characteristics of the people who participate in social movements, for the most part leaning toward a view of the participant as somehow deficient. Such a view ignores the possibility that the deficiency may lie in society rather than in those trying to change it. For this and other reasons, sociologists have largely rejected the psychological approach.

Smelser and others suggest that the main factor behind the emergence of social movements is some form of social "strain." People become aware of a social problem and/or have feelings of deprivation; they respond by launching a movement that will improve the situation. This approach is useful in locating the source of social movements more firmly in the social world, rather than in the characteristics of particular individuals. But it does not adequately explain why some situations of social strain and deprivation have led to social movements and others have not.

Resource-mobilization theory builds on some of the social-strain arguments. It emphasizes **resource mobilization,** the ability to organize and make use of available resources, such as time, money, people, and skills. Given feelings of dissatisfaction about society, people must organize and take action, using the resources at their command. The focus of sociological attention, therefore, is on how and why people do mobilize and launch a social movement. One factor used to explain mobilization is the important role of outsiders. People who are not members of a disadvantaged group and yet are concerned with that group's progress may intervene to mobilize the group's resources or to bring new enthusiasm and resources to an existing movement. By definition, the disadvantaged often have few resources with which to change their situation; outsiders tend to have access to social privileges that enhance the success of social action. However, if people are not "ripe" for mobilization, it is unlikely that resources alone will launch a social movement. Resource-mobilization theory helps explain why movements might begin and succeed, but it has been criticized for downplaying whatever conditions of strain or dissatisfaction already exist.

## Social-Movement Characteristics

*What are four types of social movements? What are social-movement organizations? What is the range of tactics a social movement might adopt? How is terrorist activity studied and classified?*

All social movements have an *ideology,* a set of beliefs that justifies and explains an actual or potential social arrangement. This ideology provides an understanding of the existing problem, how the problem came about, why it persists, how to correct it, and how much worse the situation will become if the movement fails. Social movements can be classified into different types according to the ideology they hold and its consequences on their activities. (1) Regressive movements are those that aim to return to the conditions of a previous time. (2) Reform movements are basically satisfied with the existing social order but wish to change specific areas of society. (3) Revolutionary movements are very dissatisfied with the existing social order and seek to reorganize the society as a whole, perhaps by violent means, in line with the movement's ideology for a new society. (4) Utopian movements also seek significant social change, but have vaguer means and ends.

A social movement of any size and success often contains smaller groups, called social-movement organizations. As is the general trend in modern societies, social movements move toward rationalization and bureaucratization. They evolve, then, from transitory groups to formal organizations, and may cease to be social movements at all.

All social movements must use tactics of some sort to further their goals. One purpose of these tactics is to retain and enhance the loyalty of current members and to attract new members. Tactics are further used to persuade those who are not sympathetic to the movement's goals. The actual tactics selected correspond in some measure to the type of social movement involved. Reform movements generally use less extreme and less violent tactics than do revolutionary movements, for example. The greater the degree to which a movement becomes institutionalized, with access to the established power structure, the greater the likelihood it will use traditional channels for communicating with its members and the general public. Movements that have little access to power are more likely to create "news events" in order to gain attention for their issues. In some cases, social movements turn to violent tactics. Historical analysis of violent social movements shows that, unfortunately, the deliberate use of violence can be a successful tactic in helping a movement achieve its goals.

A few social movements resort to *terrorism,* the use of violence against civilian targets for the purpose of intimidation to achieve political ends. Most terrorist acts are either: (1) state terrorism—an authoritarian or totalitarian government's abusive actions against its own people; or (2) revolutionary terrorism—the use of violence to achieve the goal of creating a new society. Once terrorism begins, it often escalates into a vicious cycle of violence. In the United States, revolutionary terrorism attracts much more publicity than state terrorism. In fact, part of the effectiveness of revolutionary terrorism is the media attention it generates. Two factors are relevant to explaining why some groups turn to terrorism. Terrorists are convinced of the righteousness and necessity of their use of violence, and they often lack the means or patience to achieve their goals through less violent methods.

Social movements play a vital part in bringing a social problem to public attention. The degree of success of a social movement determines not only the extent to which the social problem is resolved, but also what happens to the movement itself. Sociologists have identified a "life course" for social movements, which includes four stages: (1) agitation, as members of the movement stir up public opinion in favor of their viewpoint; (2) legitimation, as the movement's objectives gain widespread support and the movement itself becomes respectable; (3) bureaucratization, as the social-movement organizations become increasingly structured and more absorbed with the administrative problems of the organization itself than with the social problems the organization was set up to solve; and (4) reemergence of the movement, as a response to the persistence of the social problem and as a gesture of discontent with the bureaucratization the movement has undergone. In this phase, members of the original movement regroup and renew their campaign or a new movement emerges. Many groups that were once social movements are now routinized and incorporated into the established American power structure.

# DEFINING CORE CONCEPTS

*After studying the chapter, write a sociological definition in your own words for the following core concepts. Then give an example from your own experience to illustrate your definition. Refer to the chapter to check your work.*

| *Core Concept* | *Sociological Definition* | *Personal Illustration* |
| --- | --- | --- |
| collective behavior | | |
| contagion theory | | |
| crowd | | |
| emergent-norms theory | | |
| fad | | |
| fashion | | |
| mass | | |

| *Core Concept* | *Sociological Definition* | *Personal Illustration* |
| --- | --- | --- |
| mass hysteria | | |
| millenarian movement | | |
| mob | | |
| panic | | |
| propaganda | | |
| public opinion | | |
| resource mobilization | | |
| rumor | | |

| Core Concept | Sociological Definition | Personal Illustration |
|---|---|---|
| social movement | | |
| terrorism | | |
| urban legend | | |

## PUTTING IDEAS TOGETHER

Collective behavior is relatively spontaneous social action that occurs when people try to work out common responses to ambiguous situations. This behavior can be categorized in terms of the usual source or impetus for collective action and the expected duration of the action.

| Type of Collective Behavior | Usual Source or Impetus | Duration or Endpoint |
|---|---|---|
| Mobs, riots | Anger | May continue until the target of the anger is addressed to the group's satisfaction |
| Panics | Sudden crisis causing fear | Short term; source of fear is removed or avoided |
| Rumors | Lack of information or suspicious information | Short term; information is received or constructed |
| Urban legends | Confusion about changing norms | Legends continue to be told as long as they are useful "warnings" |
| Mass hysteria | Unfounded belief causing anxiety | Self-limiting; information eventually reveals absurdity of the situation |
| Fashions | Public interest and commercial promotion | Gradual rise and fall of changing fashions |
| Fads | Need for self-expression | Short-lived; replaced by new fad |

A social movement—a large number of people who have joined together to bring about or resist some social or cultural change—is another form of social behavior that is substantially more organized. Most social movements follow a pattern, or a life course, from the time they form, in line with specific objectives, until the time they disband, having met those goals or having dissipated. Public opinion plays a key role in the legitimacy and longevity of a social movement.

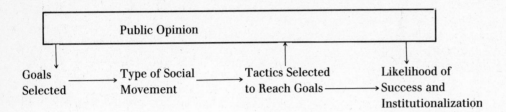

Public Opinion

Goals Selected → Type of Social Movement → Tactics Selected to Reach Goals → Likelihood of Success and Institutionalization

# Testing the Concepts

## MULTIPLE-CHOICE QUESTIONS

*After studying the chapter, try to answer each of the twenty-five questions below. Mark the alternative you think is correct; then look at the correct answer and the explanation provided at the bottom of the page. Try to state why the other alternatives are incorrect and check your understanding of the correct answer.*

1. Urban legends are important because they
   a. serve as an amusing form of entertainment.
   b. explain the current fad of science fiction.
   c. help people cope with ambiguity.
   d. promote social change.
   e. counteract rumors by providing more accurate information.

2. The rumor most likely to undergo change through transmission is the one that is
   a. deliberately created.
   b. emotionally charged.
   c. sexually oriented.
   d. more widely circulated.
   e. a falsehood.

3. The difference between state terrorism and revolutionary terrorism is that state terrorism
   a. harms fewer people
   b. gets more publicity.
   c. does not seek political ends.
   d. is a threat to other democratic societies.
   e. means the government is hurting its own people.

4. What is the essential difference between collective behavior and routine behavior in everyday life? Collective behavior is relatively more
   a. reciprocal, with members cooperating.
   b. widespread.
   c. violent.
   d. unstructured.
   e. private and intimate.

5. Smelser suggests six basic conditions for collective behavior. The emergence and passing on of an upsetting rumor might be significant in the condition called
   a. structural conduciveness.
   b. generalized belief.
   c. structural strains.
   d. failure of social control.
   e. precipitating factors.

---

1.  **c.** *Like rumors, urban legends arise in response to ambiguous situations in which proper behavior is not immediately obvious. These "legends" have a punchline, which teaches a moral lesson. See page 544.*

2.  **b.** *Rumors are an attempt to make sense of an ambiguous situation. If a rumor surrounds an emotionally charged issue, the passage of the rumor from one person to another will include subjective interpretations, distorting the original message. See page 542.*

3.  **e.** *State terrorism is the use of terror by a government against its own people as an instrument of control. As such, it does not draw the international attention that revolutionary terrorism, which thrives on*

*publicity, generates for hijackings, bombings, and the like. However, it may affect more people more severely, with less possibility of intervention from other nations. See pages 558–559.*

4.  **d.** *Collective behavior refers to relatively spontaneous and unstructured ways of thinking, feeling, and acting that occur when people try to work out common responses to ambiguous situations. See page 533.*

5.  **e.** *Rumors often serve as a catalyst to trigger collective behavior. As such, they may be precipitating events, one of the six conditions necessary for collective behavior. Rumors alone are insufficient, but in combination with the other five factors may lead to collective behavior, according to Smelser. See page 535.*

6. Only one of the following would be termed a regressive social movement. Which one?
   a. the prolife (anti-abortion) movement now gaining in strength
   b. the Jones cult, formerly in Guyana
   c. the interest in deprogramming various cult converts
   d. Mothers Against Drunk Driving
   e. the anti-nuclear peace groups in Europe

7. "Tonight Show" announcer Ed McMahon appears on a lot of television commercials, endorsing, among other things, no-wax floors and sweepstakes. His encouraging the viewers to buy these products is an example of what kind of propaganda technique?
   a. transfer
   b. bandwagon
   c. card stacking
   d. name calling
   e. glittering generalities

8. Rumors are often a result of
   a. an attempt to create order from disorder.
   b. misinformation and overindulgence in fantasy.

c. an attempt to disrupt traditional lines of communication.
d. interpersonal "blocking."
e. a desire to gossip about someone and harm his or her reputation.

9. According to emergent-norms theory
   a. a "collective mind" emerges in crowd situations.
   b. crowd behavior can be understood within the framework of existing sociological theory.
   c. crowd behavior cannot be understood within the framework of existing sociological theory.
   d. crowds are incapable of developing their own norms; the norms must be imposed by opinion leaders.
   e. most crowd behavior is characterized by panic.

10. The key feature of a millenarian movement is
   a. spontaneous, violent action.
   b. confusion about the norms of a modern society.
   c. lack of organized religious beliefs.
   d. how quickly they die out when the desired change occurs.
   e. a prophecy of the reversal of the social order.

---

6. **a.** *A regressive social movement attempts to produce social change in order to return conditions to previous times. The prolife movement seeks to revoke the Supreme Court ruling in favor of abortion and to add an amendment to the Constitution. These actions would remove rights previously granted and thus "set back the clock." See page 556.*

7. **a.** *Transfer is a method of winning approval for something by associating it with something else known to be viewed favorably. Here a television personality, perceived as fun-loving and trustworthy, is advertising products he may not even use. But the association of McMahon with the products is recommendation enough. See page 551.*

8. **a.** *Rumors typically arise when an ambiguous situation exists with incomplete or suspect information.*

*People try to put the pieces together and make sense of the situation, sometimes substituting speculation for evidence. See page 542.*

9. **b.** *Ralph Turner and Lewis Killian dispute the idea of contagion. Instead, they argue that crowd behavior is simply an example of conformity to the group. In ambiguous situations, a crowd develops norms and informally enforces them on its members. See pages 538–539.*

10. **e.** *Millenarian movements are "religions of the oppressed." People in deprived situations prophesy a better time in the future, when the social order will be reversed and those that rule them will be overthrown. These movements are typically found in traditional societies and the prophecies rarely, if ever, come true. See pages 552–553.*

11.  The president used a media campaign to promote his budget-cutting policies. The public opinion concerning these policies reflected
    a.  the importance of significant others in helping us interpret media campaigns.
    b.  the inability of researchers to poll public opinion because it shifts so quickly.
    c.  how willing people are to change their minds to agree with policies they previously opposed.
    d.  the American public's dependency on the media in forming their opinions.
    e.  the presence of a single public, representing the average view of the population.

12.  Which of the following statements describes the role of fashion in a modern society like the United States? Fashions
    a.  are matters of personal taste having no social consequences.
    b.  show no pattern, as one fashion is unrelated to the next.
    c.  reflect an orientation toward the future and the desirability of change.
    d.  are less important than they were in traditional societies.
    e.  arise in the upper class.

13.  A crowd gathers at the City Bank, having heard news reports that many banks in the region have gone broke. The bank doors are locked, although they should be open for business. For several minutes the crowd mills around in front of the bank. A few people pound on the doors; others are yelling, "Open up," or "I want my money." Suddenly one person shourts, "I know where the bank president lives! Let's go!" and he rushes down the street with the crowd following. What type of crowd is this?
    a.  a revolutionary crowd
    b.  an expressive crowd
    c.  a conventional crowd
    d.  an acting crowd
    e.  a regressive crowd

14.  In the same situation, what does the speaker's suggestion to march to the president's home represent?
    a.  the "collective mind"
    b.  a precipitating factor
    c.  social control
    d.  emergent norms
    e.  a revolution

15.  According to contemporary sociological theorists Turner and Killian, what process will occur next?
    a.  social control
    b.  group mind
    c.  contagion
    d.  emergent norms
    e.  apathy

---

11.  **a.**  *Publics are not passive to media campaigns. The many publics form their ideas based on the interpretations they make of these events and those made by significant others: friends, family members, co-workers, and opinion leaders. See page 550.*

12.  **c.**  *Fashions change rather quickly and are significant because: people are future-oriented and like to anticipate what will be in fashion; powerful commercial interests make them so; and some use them to assert an affluent status. See page 548.*

13.  **d.**  *An acting crowd expresses itself through disruptive behavior, such as shouting, rioting, or otherwise deliberately causing trouble. In this example, the crowd is angry about the bank closing and the possible financial loss to them; the crowd is ready to take hostile action to vent these feelings. See page 539.*

14.  **b.**  *The speaker provides the catalyst the crowd needs to take action on its concerns. Thus the suggestion to march to the bank president's house precipitates the crowd's collective action. See page 535.*

15.  **d.**  *In the course of the social interaction of the crowd, new norms will emerge. The first leader may suggest further action to the crowd or other leaders may come forth. The crowd will improvise norms on the spot that will determine whether their action against the bank president is violent or not. See pages 538–539.*

16. Which of the following statements is accurate about a public?
   a. A public consists of the society in general.
   b. The activities of a public are usually coordinated and irrational.
   c. A public does not act together, but does form opinions on the issues around which it is focused.
   d. The American public often has a high level of agreement on specific social issues.
   e. Like other social movements, a public depends on contagion among the participants to keep it going.

17. Which *pair* of characteristics best describes a mob, as opposed to other types of collective behavior?
   a. expressive crowd; less structured
   b. usually has a leader; immediate and limited violent objectives
   c. motivated by fear; subject to panic
   d. casual crowd; highly suggestible
   e. long-term goals for social change; unconventional crowd

18. The usual source of mass hysteria is
   a. a natural disaster.
   b. a group mobilized for social change.
   c. enactment of an unpopular law.
   d. an unfounded belief.
   e. structural strain.

19. The distinguishing features of panic behavior are that people _____ and social norms _____.
   a. experience fear; are irrelevant.
   b. are angry; change quickly.
   c. follow the lead of others; indicate fashions.
   d. feel anxiety; question traditional authorities.
   e. want change; are structurally conducive.

20. The Black Panthers, a black activist organization in the 1960s, set up a breakfast program for black children in ghetto communities. This program eventually received funding and food commodities from the federal government, as well as assistance from city governments. While the Black Panthers were pleased to receive the assistance they argued was necessary, they could see their autonomy and control had weakened. This condition is an example of which process in the life course of a social movement?
   a. structural strain
   b. legitimation
   c. agitation
   d. decentralization
   e. popularization

---

16.  **c.** *A public is a substantial number of people with a shared interest in some issue. Although some activities of a public are conducted on a face-to-face basis, a public generally interacts indirectly through the media. As such, the members do not act together, but express their opinions as individuals. See page 550.*

17.  **b.** *Mobs are a form of acting crowd characterized by their goal of violent and/or destructive action. Lynch mobs are one striking example. Mobs have a leader with a strong influence over other members of the mob, and there is pressure to adhere to the group's immediate goal of violent action. See page 539.*

18.  **d.** *Mass hysteria is a form of collective behavior involving widespread and contagious anxiety, usually caused by some unfounded belief. See page 546.*

19.  **a.** *A panic is a form of collective behavior in which people are faced with an immediate threat and have no norms to guide their response. Natural disasters often result in panic behavior, because they are unexpected and unusual. The combination of fear and the novelty of the event produces uncoordinated and irrational behavior. See page 541.*

20.  **b.** *Social movements typically pass through four stages, if they exist to complete the life course sociologists have identified. In the second stage, legitimation, the movement gains widespread support and becomes socially acceptable. The result is a loss of initiative and control on the part of the movement and intervention by outsiders. See pages 560–561.*

21. The view that the tensions generated by social movements may lead to necessary social changes is most compatible with
    a. the interactionist perspective.
    b. emergent-norms theory.
    c. the conflict perspective.
    d. contagion theory.
    e. sociocultural-evolution theory.

22. Why are fads such as punk rock, low riding in cars, or following the movie "Rocky Horror Picture Show" particularly appealing to young people?
    a. They have money to spend on fads.
    b. They want to irritate their parents.
    c. They are looking for a way to assert personal identity.
    d. They are immature and gullible.
    e. They are susceptible to the propaganda technique of glittering generalities.

23. Which of the following statements about social movements is true?
    a. There is a typical "life course" in the interplay of social movements and social problems.
    b. Social movements attempt to bring about rather than resist social change.
    c. Most people appear to join social movements in order to find an outlet for their own psychological problems.
    d. Social movements are one of the most unstructured and short-lived forms of collective behavior.
    e. The two most common types of social movements are riots and mobs.

24. Of particular importance to resource-mobilization theory is
    a. contagion.
    b. the use of violence to achieve desired goals.
    c. the role of outsiders.
    d. the amount of deprivation a group objectively experiences.
    e. the need for precipitating events.

25. The National Commission on Civil Disorders found that with regard to urban riots in the 1960s
    a. no common underlying condition or precipitating factor was present.
    b. a single incident could be identified as a precipitating factor in each event.
    c. efforts at social control tended to reduce tensions.
    d. riots were the work of a small minority of habitual "troublemakers."
    e. mass hysteria was the basis for the violence that occurred.

---

21.  c. *Conflict theorists argue that struggles over valued social rewards, the basis for many social movements, result in social change and a possible redistribution of those resources. Social movements, by definition, disrupt the status quo and require some loss of privilege by the dominant groups in a society. See pages 556–557.*

22.  c. *A fad is often a way of expressing personal identity. Before a fad becomes too popular, those taking part show their individuality by initiating a fad or participating in a fad that runs contrary to prevailing social behavior. Youth, whose identities may not be as stable as those of adults, are more likely to be attracted to fads. See page 549.*

23.  a. *Sociologists have identified four stages through which most social movements pass if they continue to exist. These stages are: agitation, legitimation, bureaucratization, and reemergence of the movement. See pages 560–561.*

24.  c. *McCarthy and Zald's theory of resource mobilization emphasizes the role of outsiders in getting a social movement off the ground. Outsiders with substantially more resources (e.g., money, power, time) can spur a disadvantaged group to take social action and achieve change. See pages 555–556.*

25.  b. *The commission found a precipitating incident, commonly a skirmish between black residents and white police officers, which aggravated a climate of discontent and lead to overt outbursts. See pages 540–541.*

## A CASE STUDY

NAME

COURSE/SECTION NUMBER

Over twenty years ago, the Surgeon General of the United States issued the first stern warning about the hazards of cigarette smoking. As a result, packages of cigarettes and all advertising were required to carry a warning message; cigarettes could not be advertised on television at all. Nevertheless, many Americans continued to smoke and certain groups in the population, such as teenage girls, actually increased their smoking.

Several groups have organized to protest the dangers smoking inflicts on nonsmokers. ASH is one such group. Through their efforts, several states have passed clean indoor air acts that prohibit smoking except in designated areas. Restaurants and airplanes now have separate smoking and nonsmoking sections.

As more and more evidence becomes available, the hazards of smoking—to smokers, to nonsmokers, to children, and to fetuses—continue to mount. Opposition to smoking has become more intense, but has met with equally strong lobbying on the part of tobacco groups. One tobacco company now publishes a magazine designed to promote smoking and to make smokers feel good about themselves.

1.    Sociologist Neil Smelser developed a theory of collective behavior to explain why people band together to reach certain goals. Run through his six conditions for collective behavior, applying them either to a pro- or anti-smoking group.

2.    How would you classify this group in terms of the various types of social movements?

3.   What sort of tactics has this social movement used to champion its cause?

4.   How has public opinion shifted as a result of this social movement?

5.   At what stage in its life course is this social movement? Where do you
predict it will go, and what will it achieve in the next decade? What specific
outcomes would constitute a success?

# Applying the Concepts

## APPLICATION EXERCISE ONE

"The passion we feel for our fads is as strong as patriotism, or mother love . . . it is an authentic feeling, a real feeling, something to be taken seriously—even though the thing itself may seem trivial" (Rolf Meyersohn and Eric Larrabee, *Mass Leisure,* 1958). Besides feelings of passion, we spend a great deal of time and money on our fads. Some fairly recent fads include the television show "Mary Hartman, Mary Hartman," Ouija boards, soap operas, King Tut jewelry, horror movies, punk rock, streaking, Monopoly, the Beatles, Cabbage Patch dolls, and Don Johnson's "five o'clock shadow." While fads may give us a feeling of being "in," they are also a part of the economic order; for example, the gross sales for skateboards in 1976 were over fifteen million dollars.

1. Survey your immediate surroundings and list evidence of five fads.

    a.

    b.

    c.

    d.

    e.

2. How much money have you spent on these fads?

3. Who has made money from these fads? Have you?

4. How much time do you spend on fads?

5. Go back and place an asterisk beside any fad for which you have strong positive feelings. Is it true that fads contribute to your sense of identity? How?

## APPLICATION EXERCISE TWO

NAME

COURSE/SECTION NUMBER

1.   Everyone has been involved in collective behavior, if not as a participant, at least as an observer. Refer to the text and cite the characteristics distinguishing each type of collective behavior. Then provide a personal example.

| *Type of Collective Behavior* | *Central Characteristics* | *Personal Example* |
| --- | --- | --- |
| Mob or Riot | | |
| Panic or Mass Hysteria | | |

2.   Now state the outcome of each example of collective behavior and whether the outcome was consistent with the results expected for that particular form of collective behavior.

| *Type of Collective Behavior* | *Expected Outcome* | *Actual Outcome* |
| --- | --- | --- |
| Mob or Riot | | |
| Panic or Mass Hysteria | | |

3.   How did information, misinformation, or lack of information play a part in the events? Was it most important before, during, or after the behavior?

| *Type of Collective Behavior* | *Description of how rumors, urban legends, and/or public opinion played a part before, during, or after behavior* |
| --- | --- |
| Mob or Riot | |
| Panic or Mass Hysteria | |

## APPLICATION EXERCISE THREE

Social behavior occurs all around you. Select an example of one basic type of crowd.

1. Describe the type of crowd that you observed (or of which you were a member) and why the crowd formed.

2. Now analyze this example according to Smelser's six conditions for collective behavior.

    a. Structural conduciveness

    b. Structural strains

    c. Generalized belief

    d. Precipitating factors

    e. Mobilization for action

    f. Failure of social control

NAME

COURSE/SECTION NUMBER

3.   Has this crowd evolved into a social movement? Use resource-mobilization theory to explain why it has or has not become such a movement. To what degree does it have the following features?

   a. Dissatisfaction

   b. Organization

   c. Resources

   d. Assistance from outsiders

4.   If this example has become a social movement, is it a regressive, reform, revolutionary, or utopian movement?

5.   What is the likely outcome of this social movement? Will social change occur? How will the movement itself change? Consider the processes of agitation, legitimation, bureaucratization, and reemergence.

# CHAPTER 21

# Population and Urbanization

## Reviewing the Concepts

### LEARNING GOALS

*After studying this chapter, you should be able to:*

1. Define the field of demography and give three examples of topics demographers study.

2. Explain how the three factors of birth rate, death rate, and rate of migration into or out of the society affect population growth or decline.

3. Discuss how population growth is measured and how populations of the same size may vary internally.

4. Evaluate Malthus's argument about population growth.

5. List some causes of rapid population growth.

6. Outline the stages of demographic transition and discuss the relevance of demographic-transition theory.

7. Identify three American demographic characteristics and explain the impact of each on the United States and the world.

8. Describe three strategies governments use to reduce population growth; assess the impact of ideological influences on social attitudes about population limitation.

9. Define urbanization and give a sociological definition of a city.

10. Characterize the historical city.

11. Characterize the contemporary city, both in less developed and developed societies, and outline its prerequisites. ·

12. Illustrate the concepts of a central city, suburb, metropolis, and megalopolis as they are used to describe different aspects of urban life.

13. Summarize the ecological approach to urban development.

14. Discuss and evaluate the three models of urban growth.

15. Distinguish between Tönnies's concepts of *Gemeinschaft* and *Gesellschaft* as they relate to the definition of a community.

16. Assess the significance of Wirth's view of the three key features of the city.

17. Present two modern views of the city.

18. Evaluate the evidence for disorganization or vitality in contemporary urban areas.

19. Indicate how the Bureau of the Census classifies data on urban concentrations.

20. List two important population trends in the United States in terms of degree of urbanization.

21. Describe the process of suburbanization.

22. Identify factors that have led to the deterioration of central cities.

23. Outline the trends in condominium and single-family home ownership, metropolitan government, and recycling of buildings, and discuss their impact on American cities.

## IDENTIFYING KEY QUESTIONS AND THEMES

Rapid population growth in a context of limited natural resources is one of the most serious social problems in the modern world. Its impact is seen most dramatically in cities, which are growing at an unprecedented rate. In their study of human population, sociologists focus on two related areas: *demography*—the study of the size, composition, distribution, and changes in human populations—and *urbanism*—the nature and meaning of city life.

### The Study of Population

*What is the science of demography? What are the dynamics of demographic change?*

The science of demography studies the interplay of population dynamics and social factors. Demographers analyze population data obtained from a census or other sources and make projections for the near and distant future. These forecasts take into account environmental, social, and cultural factors that influence population trends—for example, social values that affect family size and health conditions that affect average length of life.

Growth and decline of any society's population is affected by three factors: the birth rate, the death rate, and the rate of migration into or out of the society. The *birth rate* is the annual number of births per thousand members of a population. This basic measure indicates the society's *fertility*—the actual number of children the average woman is bearing. Fertility must be distinguished from *fecundity*, which is the potential number of children that could be born to a woman of childbearing age. Of course, the number of children women actually bear is lower than the number they biologically could have.

The *death rate* is the annual number of deaths per thousand members of a population. The death rate is related to *life expectancy,* the number of years that the average newborn in a particular population can be expected to live. Life expectancy varies greatly from one society to another, largely as a result of differences in infant mortality rates and health care. Life expectancy is distinguished from *life span,* the maximum length of life possible in a particular species.

The *migration rate* is the annual difference between the number of immigrants entering the population and the number of emigrants leaving the population per thousand members of the population. Migration rates do not increase or decrease global population, but indicate shifts from one geographic area to another due to two interacting factors. The first factor is "push," which refers to conditions that encourage people to emigrate. The second is "pull," which refers to conditions that encourage people to immigrate.

Changes in population size are measured by the *growth rate,* the difference between the number of people added to, and the number of people subtracted from, a population, expressed as an annual percentage. Even though growth percentages may seem small, their long-term impact can be staggering. This is because population growth is *exponential,* with the increase each year based not on the original figure, but on the accumulated total up to that time. A useful way to analyze the effects of exponential growth is *doubling time,* the period it takes for a population to double its number. The short doubling time in many of the world's developing countries indicates rapidly growing populations and suggests that world population will reach 8 billion by 2020. Clearly, population cannot continue to increase at this rate. It can be halted only by a sharp decrease in the birth rate, a sharp increase in the death rate, or some combination of these factors. If each set of parents produced only enough children to replace themselves, we would ultimately have *zero population growth* (ZPG), a situation in which population size would remain stable.

However, even if ZPG were the population pattern from this moment on, the world population would continue to increase for many years. The reason for this is that the large number of children already born would still grow up and reproduce. Thus a society's *age structure*—

the relative proportions of different age categories in a population—is another important demographic determinant. Developing countries have a higher percentage of people under age fifteen; consequently, these countries have a vast potential for population growth even if their birth rates decline over the next few years.

## The World Population Problem

*What are the dimensions of the world population problem? What is the Malthusian trap? What are some of the causes of rapid population growth? What is the theory of demographic transition?*

Birth rates are associated with the society's level of industrialization. In preindustrial societies, birth rates were always high because children were considered economic assets. It was not until the advent of the Industrial Revolution that the value of large families was questioned. Thomas Malthus, who lived during this period of economic change, argued that the natural tendency of population growth is to increase exponentially. However, since food supplies are limited by the amount of cultivated land, increases in agricultural production can be made only in a simple additive fashion. The Malthusian trap refers to this gap between population demands and available food. Human beings, Malthus asserted, were destined to press against the limits of the food supply, and the inevitable fate of most people would be misery, hunger, and poverty. Of course, Malthus could not have anticipated the technological advances that would increase agricultural production and improve birth control. His basic argument is difficult to refute, however; population growth cannot increase indefinitely in a world that has finite resources.

In demographic terms, the countries of the world fall into two main categories: the developed nations and the less developed nations. (In between these lies a third group of countries with intermediate birth and growth rates.) The developed countries have low birth and growth rates, while the developing countries have high birth and growth rates. Rapid population growth is, therefore, primarily a problem of the poorest nations. Although there is enough food to provide subsistence worldwide, these resources are unequally distributed. To put an end to hunger, rich nations would have to reduce their consumption as well as resolve their various sociopolitical disputes. In the meantime, the quality-of-life gap is steadily widening.

The main cause of population increases in less developed societies is that the death rate has been sharply reduced by improved health standards while the birth rate has remained very high. The resulting high rate of growth adds to an already large population base, producing a greater strain on limited natural resources. In this case, dramatically lower death rates reflect technological advances in sanitation, nutrition, and medicine (material culture), while birth rates, linked as they are to cultural attitudes that often place a high value on large families (nonmaterial culture), tend to change more slowly.

Demographers have observed an historical sequence in population change called *demographic transition* — the tendency for birth rates to drop and populations to stabilize once a society has achieved a certain level of economic development. According to demographic-transition theorists, people generally have as many children as they can support; those in urban, industrialized societies, where children are an economic burden, come to prefer small families and voluntarily limit the number of children they have. The demographic transition appears to proceed through three basic stages. (1) In the first stage, typical of traditional societies, there is a high birth rate and a high death rate, resulting in a stable population. (2) In the second stage, typical of developing societies, the birth rate remains high, but the death rate drops, and population grows rapidly in societies shifting from preindustrial to industrial modes of production. (3) In the third stage, typical of advanced industrial and postindustrial societies, the birth rate drops, as large families come to be seen as a liability, and the death rate remains low; the result is a tendency toward zero population growth. While the demographic transition is almost complete in Europe, Japan, and North America (evidence supporting demographic-transition theory), many societies in the world appear to be stuck in the second stage. If the majority of them follow the sequence, they will eventually show signs of a declining birth rate. However, demographic-transition theory assumes that birth rates will decline only when countries become economically advanced. The poorest and most populous nations are precisely those that will have difficulty reaching this level of advancement, given their precarious situation. By the time they

have reached it (if, in fact, they do), the pressure on the world's resources will be overwhelming. Developing countries seeking to match both the growth rate and the standard of living of modern industrial nations like the United States may well come up against a planet that is no longer able to support large human populations at anywhere near the level now enjoyed by advanced industrial societies.

## Population in the United States

*What are the characteristics of the American population? Do we have a population problem?*

The U.S. Bureau of the Census gathers information about American demographic characteristics. The current population of the United States exceeds 240 million, with a median age of about thirty-one years. The birth rate is low and reflects a consistent decline in fertility over the past 150 years. There are few signs of the anticipated population growth as the baby-boom generation moves through its childbearing years. The reasons are not clear; however, the low birth rate seems to be the result of such factors as employment of women outside the home, postponement of marriage, a preference for small families, improved birth-control techniques, and easier access to abortion. The death rate in the United States is also low, at 9 per thousand, with an average life expectancy of 75 years. The age structure will show an increase in the over–sixty-five group, accompanied by a corresponding increase in the death rate.

A commission on population growth in the United States recommended a national policy of zero population growth. While the current fertility rate (1.8 children) puts American women below the rate necessary to accomplish this, ZPG is not expected to be reached until well into the next century. The major concern surrounding U.S. population growth is not so much its absolute size as its impact on world resources. The lifestyle to which Americans have become accustomed is economically costly. Indeed, a new American child presents a greater threat to the ecology of the planet than fifty children in developing countries, in terms of the resources demographers predict it will use. As nations become increasingly interdependent, population growth and resource consumption in one country—particularly in the United States—must be considered in relation to the rest of the world.

## What Can Be Done?

*What strategies are used to control population?*

There are three major strategies used to reduce birth rates: family planning, antinatalism, and economic improvements. Family-planning programs have encouraged parents' use of contraceptives to limit the number of their offspring. However, no society has managed to achieve a significant drop in its birth rate by these means alone. The decision to use contraceptives resides with the couple; their attitudes about ideal family size may not coincide with the needs of society. Demographers argue that population problems are not primarily the result of unplanned children or lack of contraceptive use, but rather, arise from cultural values that place a premium on large families.

A second strategy for population control is antinatalism, which involves public policies intended to discourage births. In addition to educational programs aimed at changing social values and attitudes about family size, some countries have experimented with gifts, cash rewards, tax exemptions, and official limits on the number of children per couple.

A third approach is the promotion of economic development in recognition of the connection between economic progress and lower birth rates. Many demographers now believe that if a society's resources are fairly distributed and people are allowed to enjoy the basics of life, such as food, shelter, etc., they will feel a sense of optimism toward the future and will voluntarily limit the size of their families. In most developing countries, a tiny elite benefits disproportionately from the society's resources, while the mass of the people remain in hopeless poverty. Economic development, then, may be a long-range strategy to reduce global population growth in line with demographic transition.

Political, religious, and other ideological influences mitigate the success of efforts to limit the population. For example, religious beliefs may encourage reproduction, or prohibit birth control and abortion.

## Urbanization

*What are the characteristics of the preindustrial and the industrial city? What social changes have come about with urbanization? What is the ecological approach to urban analysis? What are three patterns of urban growth?*

***Urbanization***—the process by which population is concentrated in cities—is one of the most significant trends of the modern world. More and more of the world's residents now live in urban areas, especially in developing nations. A ***city*** is a permanent concentration of relatively large numbers of people who do not produce their own food. Large-scale urbanization has occurred only in the course of the past century, as the technology for food production improved to the point where most people were free to undertake other occupations. Additionally, urban growth depended on efficient means of food transportation and storage.

The first urban settlements appeared between 5,000 and 6,000 years ago in the Middle East and Asia. As techniques for domesticating plants and animals were developed, urban settlements began to appear elsewhere. These ancient cities were very small, possessing only limited means to produce and transport a food surplus. Large aggregations of people living under conditions of poor sanitation, leaving them vulnerable to periodic epidemics and plagues, characterized the major urban centers that developed in Europe after the fall of the Roman empire. Despite these and other problems, cities drew increasing numbers of people. Kinship networks were the basis of social organization in these historical cities. With rare exceptions, the governments were monarchies or oligarchies. There was usually no separate commercial district; instead, the city was divided into "quarters" for various occupational, religious, or other social groups.

Small (and relatively uncomfortable) as these preindustrial cities may have been, they revolutionized human social organization. Political and economic institutions became more complex. The city-state evolved as the typical political unit. Occupational specialization increased, which resulted in further division of labor. Eventually, cities became what they are today—centers for trade, communication, learning, and innovative ideas.

The rapid growth and spread of cities coincided with the advance of the Industrial Revolution. Modern cities rest, to varying degrees, on this industrial base, and rely on mechanized agriculture, sophisticated communications, improved transportation and storage facilities, and the variety of specialized, nonagricultural jobs that industrialism provides.

Two features distinguish most of the cities in less developed countries: rapid growth and extensive poverty. Displaced rural migrants flock to the cities in search of work and, instead, find unemployment and poor living conditions. City services cannot keep pace with the rapid population influx. Consequently, unemployment rates are high, wages are low, and basic facilities are inadequate. Most of these cities have a small, affluent political and commercial hub, surrounded by poor neighborhoods, and, beyond, a ring of slums and shantytowns inhabited by squatters and new arrivals.

Cities in industrialized nations, which developed much more slowly, continue to absorb a trickle of rural migrants. In general, the larger cities in the developed societies take the form of a central city, consisting of a small number of the very wealthy and a large number of the very poor, surrounded by suburbs, which are primarily residential areas that grow up around a city as the urban population expands. This combined area is called a *metropolis,* and it forms an economic and geographic unity. If these areas expand and merge with other metropolises, they form a *megalopolis.* At present, the trend is toward these virtually unbroken urban tracts consisting of two or more central cities and their surrounding suburbs, some of which may eventually cross state and even national boundaries.

Urbanization follows certain predictable patterns. Sociologists use an *ecological approach*—one that analyzes cultural elements in the context of the total environment—to study urban land use and growth. Geographic factors, such as transportation routes and natural resources, affect where cities are likely to form. Social factors also influence the appearance and development of cities. For example, a city may be built or destroyed as a result of political decisions. Land use is often planned or controlled by zoning laws. Urban residents are not randomly distributed within the city, but are located in neighborhoods with residents of similar racial and social-class characteristics. Technological inventions such as the au-

tomobile and mass transportation also influence urban patterns, in these cases, making it possible for the labor force to move away from the city's center.

Urban sociologists offer three specific models to explain the distribution patterns of people and facilities within a modern city. (1) The concentric-zone model suggests that the typical city consists of zones that radiate out in circles from a central business and administrative district. Each successive zone contains a different type of land use: the central business district is followed by a zone in transition, which includes marginal businesses and minority-group ghettos, followed by a zone consisting of working people's homes, and then the homes of the more affluent at progressively greater distances from the center. (2) A second pattern is the sector model of urban development. Hoyt suggested that cities grow outward from the center to the periphery largely in wedge-shaped sectors of different land use. As the city expands, both low- and high-rent areas move outward. Residential and industrial areas occupy their own sectors, as newly developed areas take on the character of the existing adjacent area. (3) The multiple-nuclei model suggests that a city has a series of "nuclei," or specialized areas centered on retailing, entertainment, etc., distributed throughout the city. These nuclei allow easy public access via automobiles and highways to whatever the city offers. Each of the models provides a means of analyzing urban development patterns based on case studies of American cities.

## The Nature of Urban Life

*What are the characteristics of urban life? In what ways does the urban community differ from the small rural community? How have sociologists conceptualized the transformation involved in urbanization?*

A *community* is a social group with a common territorial base and a sense of shared interests and "belonging." Tönnies was one of the first sociologists to examine the differences between urban and rural communities. He distinguished between the *Gemeinschaft* and the *Gesellschaft.* The *Gemeinschaft* is a small "community" in which most people know each other. Interpersonal relationships are the basis for social cohesion and social control and are reinforced by strong family ties. The *Gesell-schaft,* on the other hand, is an "association" that contains a large population in which most of the people are strangers to one another. Relationships are more impersonal and are based on the functional needs people have of one another rather than on emotional commitment. Formal mechanisms of social control ensure social order. Thus the process of urbanization involves a transition from the *Gemeinschaft* to the *Gesellschaft* society.

In the 1920s and 1930s, sociologists at the University of Chicago elaborated on Tönnies's analysis of urban life. Wirth emphasized three distinctive features of the city: size, population density, and social diversity. He felt that these features combine to produce a lifestyle quite different from that found in small communities. Individuals cannot know more than a small percentage of the other inhabitants and lead a relatively anonymous existence; they interact with one another on the basis of highly specialized roles, the heterogeneous mix of residents results in a greater range of viewpoints and lifestyles.

Chicago School theorists tended to be rather pessimistic about urban life. Many of these urban sociologists came from small towns, and did most of their research in Chicago at a time when it was plagued by economic recession, racial tension, and high crime rates. More recent analyses of the city have questioned some of their early work. Herbert Gans, for example, views the city as a mosaic of many thriving neighborhoods (particularly those oriented around a specific ethnic group), which he calls "urban villages." According to Gans, individual residents experience life in these smaller, more manageable environments, not in the anonymous city as a whole. Claude Fischer argues that the city contains many subcultures, giving people a sense of belonging. In his view, deviant interests are tolerated and even catered to, as most people find a niche within such subcultures.

According to the modern, as opposed to the classical, view, then, city living has its advantages and disadvantages. While there is no doubt that urbanites are exposed to more anonymity and isolation than are the residents of a traditional, rural community, large urban areas support a rich, diverse cultural life, and allow for occupational specialization as well as considerable intellectual and personal freedom.

## The American City and Its Problems

*What are the current patterns in urban living? What are the problems of America's central cities? What are the various strategies used for city planning?*

Two important demographic trends in the United States are increasing urbanization and a shift of population from the older cities of the Northeast and Midwest to the "sunbelt" cities of the South and Southwest in search of better climate and economic opportunities. This pattern of migration will be accompanied by a shift in economic and political power to these areas.

Although most Americans live in urban areas, the slight majority reside in the suburbs rather than in the central cities themselves. The Bureau of the Census recognizes that the political boundaries are less important than the social, economic, and communications networks that integrate various urban communities into one unit. The concept of a *metropolitan statistical area* (MSA) describes an area that contains a city (or a combination of a city and its surrounding suburbs) that has a total population of 50,000 or more. The bureau also takes into account populous adjacent metropolises, called megalopolises.

One of the outstanding features of urbanization in the United States is the rapid growth of the suburbs over the past twenty-five years and its consequences for the survival of the central cities. Suburban growth was facilitated by the construction of federally subsidized highways, the shortage of central-city housing, and the ability and desire of Americans to own their own homes. For many people, suburbs seemed to offer an ideal compromise between rural and urban life: they were close enough to the city to enjoy its amenities, but far enough away to avoid its inconveniences.

The demographic composition of the suburbs has shifted since the post-World War II boom period. While the original suburbs were, by and large, populated by more politically conservative and morally conventional middle-class residents, many of the newer suburbs are predominantly working class or include residents with diverse racial and ethnic backgrounds. A number of suburbanites are now employed in their own or adjacent communities due to the proliferation of factories, superhighways, and office complexes. In some suburbs, the symptoms generally associated with urban decay are already beginning to appear.

For some families, the goal of a single-family detached home is financially out of reach. Condominium ownership is rapidly becoming the norm and reflects housing shortages and demographic shifts in family size and income.

One consequence of suburban growth is the removal of the middle class and its tax money from the central cities. The cities, therefore, have had to rely for their income on a population that consists disproportionately of poor people. The situation is made worse by the fact that the costs of city services are higher per capita than those in the suburbs. Given these circumstances, it is hardly surprising that the urban environment has continued to deteriorate while the suburbs have greatly expanded. Racial and class divisions have also intensified, since suburban residents are primarily white, while the cities are becoming steadily more black.

The fragmentation of metropolitan governments poses a major obstacle to effective planning for the central city and surrounding region. Political boundaries between cities and suburbs are outdated; a more important consideration is the geographic proximity of a metropolitan area and the interdependence of the residents' taxes and services. However, proposals to integrate urban and suburban communities, because they do not appear to be in the best interest of politically more powerful suburbanites, are not likely to meet with much success.

Various efforts are underway to revitalize cities. A lesson has been learned from the "urban renewal" projects of the 1950s and 1960s that razed many city neighborhoods—including some "ethnic villages"—and replaced them with high-rise office buildings and luxury apartments, which were not only unappealing but also unaffordable to local residents. Many urban planners are now beginning to "recycle" buildings. One form of recycling is "gentrification," in which middle-class people ("gentry") buy and renovate older buildings in central-city neighborhoods, turning them into single-family homes. A second form of recycling is the renovation, through public funds, of deteriorating or abandoned central-city facilities. Many such facilities are turned into colorful market areas, bringing new life to the city.

## DEFINING CORE CONCEPTS

*After studying the chapter, write a sociological definition in your own words for the following core concepts. Then give an example from your own experience to illustrate your definition. Refer to the chapter to check your work.*

| *Core Concept* | *Sociological Definition* | *Personal Illustration* |
|---|---|---|
| age structure | | |
| birth rate | | |

| *Core Concept* | *Sociological Definition* | *Personal Illustration* |
|---|---|---|
| city | | |
| community | | |
| death rate | | |
| demographic transition | | |
| demography | | |
| doubling time | | |
| ecological approach | | |
| fecundity | | |

| Core Concept | Sociological Definition | Personal Illustration |
|---|---|---|
| fertility | | |
| Gemeinschaft/Gesellschaft | | |
| growth rate | | |
| life expectancy | | |
| life span | | |
| megalopolis | | |

| *Core Concept* | *Sociological Definition* | *Personal Illustration* |
|---|---|---|
| metropolis | | |
| Metropolitan Statistical Area (MSA) | | |
| migration rate | | |
| urbanism | | |
| urbanization | | |
| zero population growth | | |

## PUTTING IDEAS TOGETHER

Demography is the study of the size, composition, distribution, and changes in human populations. One of these changes is urbanization, the process by which population is distributed in cities. Because population pressures and problems pose a different set of challenges for developed countries, such as the United States or Japan, than for less developed countries, such as Chad, Haiti or Mexico, urbanization has different results.

| | *Pressure on Less Developed Countries* | *Pressure on Developed Countries* |
|---|---|---|
| *Demographic Transition* | Stagnation at Level 2 | Level 3 |
| *Population Dynamics* | | |
|   *Birth rate* | High; large families are highly valued. | Low; children are economic liabilities |
|   *Death rate* | Low. | Low. |
|   *Migration rate* | Rural migrants flood cities. | Large number of immigrants, including unskilled workers. |
|   *Growth rate* | High; rapid doubling time. | Stable. |
|   *Age structure* | Disproportionate number of children. | Increasing numbers of old people (over 65). |
| *General* | Unskilled workers and children put a heavy demand on limited resources. | Unskilled workers and the elderly affect distribution of resources. |
| | Low per capita income. | High rate of consumption and waste. |
| | No capital accumulation. | Excessive demands on natural resources, some of which are near depletion. |
| | Lack of resources to provide food, housing, education, jobs, and health care. | Unequal distribution of food, housing, education, jobs, and health care even though economy is strong. |
| | Widespread poverty due in part to imbalance between urban and rural populations. | Urban decay and poverty resulting from imbalance between urban and suburban areas; fragmentation of metropolitan governments; resources not pooled. |
| | People do not sense that things will get better in the future; resulting hopelessness and despair do not serve as impetus for change. | Population has become accustomed to a standard of living planet may not be able to support as more nations attempt to become developed. |

Urbanization is the process by which population is distributed in cities. The arrangement of human groups in urban areas has brought about changes in other social institutions and in social interaction itself. The evolution from historical to contemporary city included the shifts summarized in the table below.

## Comparison of Historical and Contemporary Cities

|  | *The Historical City* | *The Contemporary City* |
|---|---|---|
| *Size* | small | large |
| *Relationships with other people* | primary | secondary |
| *Form of social grouping* | Gemeinschaft | Gesellschaft |
| *Importance of kinship* | high | low |
| *Basis for stratification* | ascribed statuses | achieved statuses |
| *Commercial activity* | dispersed | centralized |

# Testing the Concepts

## MULTIPLE-CHOICE QUESTIONS

*After studying the chapter, try to answer each of the twenty-five questions below. Mark the alternative you think is correct; then look at the correct answer and the explanation provided at the bottom of the page. Try to state why the other alternatives are incorrect, and check your understanding of the correct answer.*

1. The main cause of rapid population growth in the less developed nations is
   a. rising birth rates.
   b. an increase in human fecundity.
   c. an imbalance in the ratio of births to deaths.
   d. a strengthening of the family's importance to society.
   e. people's tendency to marry at younger ages.

2. One of the unique demographic characteristics of the U.S. population is
   a. a high median age.
   b. zero population growth since 1950.
   c. large shifts in population every decade.
   d. the young age at which men and women get married.
   e. the large proportion of the population living in rural areas.

3. Demographic-transition theory holds that
   a. Europe's population growth experience can be used to predict future world trends.
   b. birth rates are the principal factor in rapid population growth.
   c. the final stage of transition ends with low population growth.
   d. a shift from agriculture to manufacturing prolongs the period of demographic change.
   e. the migration of people from one area to another is a major source of population stress.

4. Which of the following *best* addresses the question, "Does the United States have a population problem?"
   a. The population's rate of growth is creating difficulties.
   b. The main danger is the population's material lifestyle.
   c. Internal migration is as troublesome as population growth.
   d. A greater percentage of the population must be encouraged to practice birth control.
   e. Too many couples are delaying having children.

---

1. **c.** *While birth rates have remained extremely high, most population growth can be attributed to the decline in death rates (brought about by improved health standards), which formerly offset high birth rates. Since low death rates are a socially desirable goal, it is difficult to do much about this cause of population growth. See page 571.*

2. **a.** *The median age of the U.S. population is about 31 years. This figure reflects a long lifespan and a high percentage of people sixty-five and over, as well as a low birth rate. See page 573.*

3. **c.** *Demographic-transition theory holds that populations pass through three stages of growth, ending with a stage in which birth rates and death rates have both decreased and population remains stable. See pages 571–572.*

4. **b.** *The highly consumptive lifestyle of the American people is more costly in terms of natural resources than is behavior of the same number of people in other, more frugal cultures. Our contribution to the world population problem comes from our excessive use of food and energy reserves rather than from our numbers. See pages 573–574.*

5. The plight of the central cities is *primarily* a result of
   a. minorities who move to the cities to benefit from welfare.
   b. slum landlords who refuse to keep up deteriorating buildings.
   c. pollution caused by heavy industry.
   d. white flight and the resultant tax loss.
   e. corruption in city governments.

6. On a global scale, one of the most important urban trends by the year 2000 will be
   a. racial and ethnic integration within city neighborhoods.
   b. the improvement of city housing and sanitation facilities.
   c. the location of the world's largest cities in the developing countries.
   d. the development of affluent suburbs in rich and poor countries alike.
   e. the outmigration of people from the cities to the rural areas.

7. The Bureau of the Census recognizes over 280 metropolitan statistical areas (MSAs). The distinguishing feature of a MSA is
   a. its political and geographic boundaries.
   b. the concentration of people in the central cities.
   c. the ethnic diversity contained within.
   d. its social, economic, and communications network.
   e. its management by a single unit of government.

8. In country X, the doubling time is twenty-five years. What else would you predict about country X?
   a. It has more females than males.
   b. It has a small percentage of children under fifteen.
   c. It is in stage three of demographic transition.
   d. It has a high degree of technology.
   e. It has a large percentage of children under fifteen.

9. The sector model of urban growth
   a. suggests that the growth of cities takes place in wedge-shaped areas.
   b. emphasizes various specialized business areas that influence the character of the surrounding district.
   c. focuses on a series of zones radiating out from a downtown center.
   d. helps predict which part of a city will be in greatest need of urban renewal.
   e. has been shown to represent a universal pattern, at least for American cities.

5. **d.** *The growth of the suburbs has resulted in a move by much of the white middle class out of the central cities and into the suburban areas. With their departure, the taxes they contribute have also been removed, leaving the central cities with high costs, low revenues, and a majority of residents unable to contribute much to city services. See pages 586–587.*

6. **c.** *The fastest growing cities are in the developing countries. See page 579.*

7. **d.** *A MSA is any area that contains a city (or a combination of a city and its surrounding suburbs) that has a total population of 50,000 or more. In analyzing urban areas, the bureau recognizes that the political boundaries are less important than the social, economic, and communications network that integrates various urban communities into one unit. See page 585.*

8. **e.** *If a country's population doubles in as short a time as twenty-five years, we can assume that it has a bottom-heavy age pyramid, with a large number of dependent children supported by a small adult working population. See page 568.*

9. **a.** *Homer Hoyt proposed the sector model of urban growth, with wedge-shaped areas, or sectors, devoted to industrial and residential purposes extending out from the center to the periphery. Newly developed areas take on the same character as existing adjacent areas. Industrial areas may be wedge-shaped because they tend to spring up along waterways, railroads, and so on. See page 581.*

10. In Boston and other big cities, adult entertainment spots are concentrated in one neighborhood (called the combat zone), while commercial shops are in another area, and family parks and recreation areas are located in still another section of the city, away from heavy industry. This pattern of urban growth is most consistent with

    a. the sector model.
    b. metropolitan government model.
    c. the multiple-nuclei model.
    d. concentric-zone model.
    e. commercial development model.

11. If a country institutes economic reforms that more evenly distribute the country's wealth, we expect that one result of these economic reforms would be

    a. coercive state population policies such as forced sterilization.
    b. a rise in the birth rate.
    c. incentive programs to use contraceptives.
    d. citizens voluntarily limiting the size of their families.
    e. a technological fallacy about birth control use.

12. If a sociologist were using the ecological approach in explaining the growth of suburbs in the United States, one significant factor that would be mentioned is

    a. the construction of federally subsidized highways.
    b. the desire for large homes.
    c. the increasing numbers of elderly people in the population.
    d. the damage urban sprawl has done to the environment.
    e. the desire to live with people who possess few of the characteristics of central-city residents.

13. In a *Gesellschaft*, the system of social control

    a. breaks down.
    b. pushes people toward community goals.
    c. relies on kinship ties and socialization in the family.
    d. stems from tradition and custom.
    e. becomes more formal.

14. One important change in the suburbs from 1950 to today is

    a. the improvement of mass transit systems between the central city and suburbs.
    b. the shift from single-family homes to condominium ownership.

---

10. **c.** *Many big cities have specialized areas, or nuclei, devoted to specific commercial and recreational activities. Each of these nuclei shapes the character of the surrounding district. This multiple-nuclei model of urban growth takes into account the impact of automobiles and highways on modern cities. See page 581.*

11. **d.** *As economic resources are distributed more evenly throughout a population, people begin to feel optimistic about the future and want to share more fully in the material benefits of life. As a result, they tend to voluntarily limit family size. Thus, economic development coupled with fair distribution of society's resources is one key population-control strategy. See page 575.*

12. **a.** *The construction of highways connecting the central city and the suburbs has provided suburban residents with an efficient means of transportation between work and home. They can choose the suburban lifestyle in spite of employment in the city. Since highways provide access to outlying areas, they very much affect the growth and location of urban areas. See pages 580–581, 585.*

13. **e.** *In a* Gesellschaft, *there is considerable diversity among the people, who interact mainly on a temporary and impersonal basis. People are oriented toward individual rather than group goals and may not operate from the same value system. Thus, informal social control is less effective and more formal means, such as laws and police, are emphasized. See page 582.*

14. **b.** *Many young families can no longer afford a single-family detached home and are turning to condominium ownership as a way to invest in property. See page 586.*

c. the increase in factories in the suburban areas and the resulting pollution.

d. the decline of the shopping mall.

e. the contributions suburban governments make to the tax base of the central city.

15. Older buildings, especially those with easy access to the city's business and commercial districts, are often converted into single-family homes. The upgrading of the property attracts new residents and may displace former residents. What concept in urban sociology best applies to this situation?

a. metropolitan statistical area

b. urban renewal

c. community

d. *Gemeinschaft*

e. gentrification

16. Most developing countries in the early stages of industrialization can be characterized as

a. being in stage one of demographic transition.

b. using coercive or incentive methods for population control.

c. experiencing culture lag between family planning technology and values favoring large families.

d. having high death rates due to disease and malnutrition.

e. taxing the natural resources at a higher per capita rate than industrialized countries.

17. The average American woman is now bearing somewhat less children than the number required for zero population growth, yet the population is expected to increase slightly. What factor accounts for this predicted growth?

a. population increases due to immigration

b. young adults who have delayed marriage will begin to raise families

c. a continued preference for large family size

d. an increase in the death rate

e. the high rate of unwanted births

18. Herbert Gans and Claude Fischer have reassessed the work of Louis Wirth and others in the Chicago School on urbanism. In contrast to the Chicago theorists, they argue for

a. the importance of the suburbs.

b. the vitality of some central-city neighborhoods.

c. the preference for rural and small town life.

d. the infeasibility of metropolitan government.

e. the restrictions urban life places on intellectual and personal freedom.

---

15. **e.** *Gentrification involves purchasing older buildings and recycling them through renovation into desirable property. Many architecturally appealing but deteriorating apartment buildings have been converted into single-family homes and sold at premium prices to middle-class residents moving back into the city or looking for good investments. See page 587.*

16. **c.** *Family planning technology is often available before people have changed their ideas about desired family size. Moreover, people may not know about or be willing to use contraceptives even when they are available. Thus a lag exists between the material culture (in this case, contraceptives) and the ideas and values that make up nonmaterial culture. See pages 571, 574.*

17. **b.** *Our population age pyramid has a large group of "baby boomers," who are currently in their childbearing years. Even with a low number of children born per woman, the population will increase slightly because of the many people at the childbearing age and the ever-increasing life span. See pages 573–574.*

18. **b.** *Gans and Fischer found a number of vital neighborhoods within the central city and many residents residing there by choice. Ethnic neighborhoods, for example, showed considerable solidarity. The anonymity and hostility described by Wirth were not the dominant qualities of city life. See pages 583–584.*

19. Which of the features below is shared both by the preindustrial city and the cities of newly developing countries in the 1980s?
    a. the migration of people away from the farm to the city in search of specialized jobs
    b. the small size of the city population
    c. the city as a center for arts and entertainment
    d. the lack of a separate city government, in favor of national leadership
    e. the preponderance of middle-class residents

20. Which of the following trends in urban housing does the text predict by the turn of the century?
    a. Most American families will live in condominiums.
    b. Rent controls will be imposed on most apartment units.
    c. Urban renewal will remove most deteriorating buildings.
    d. Most population migration in the United States will be toward the Pacific Northwest.
    e. An even greater proportion of the population will live in urban centers as opposed to rural areas.

21. The historical preindustrial city differed from the modern industrial city in that

a. its social organization was based on the nuclear family.
b. there was rarely a separate commercial district.
c. political decisions were usually made by popular consensus.
d. there was greater social mobility.
e. there were no social classes.

22. Thomas Malthus argued that
    a. food supply increases exponentially, while population growth increases in an additive fashion.
    b. the "perfectibility of man" would be achieved once population growth was checked.
    c. misery, hunger, and poverty were the inevitable fate of the human species.
    d. technical improvements in agriculture would make possible a greatly increased yield from a fixed amount of land.
    e. contraceptives and sterilization should be mandatory after a couple's second child.

23. The Chicago sociologist Louis Wirth wrote an essay entitled "Urbanism as a Way of Life." What are the three distinctive features of cities, according to Wirth?
    a. noise, crime, high costs

---

19. **a.** *The production of a food surplus allowed some people to abandon agricultural pursuits and come to the city to specialize in other jobs. In the cities of developing countries, migrants to the city hope to find more lucrative jobs than that of farm work. See pages 577–578.*

20. **a.** *Condominium living will become a major form of home ownership for Americans as housing prices continue to rise, land becomes more scarce, older apartment buildings are renovated, and lifestyles change, resulting in a preference for smaller units with lower maintenance. See page 586.*

21. **b.** *Commercial activity in the historical city was scattered throughout the city, as artisans and traders worked out of their homes. Cities were divided into "quarters" for various social-class, religious, and/or*

*ethnic groups, and thus commercial activity occurred in all neighborhoods. See page 577.*

22. **c.** *The Malthusian trap describes the disaster inherent in the inability of food production, growing arithmetically, to keep pace with exponential population growth. As a result, Malthus predicted misery, hunger, and poverty for the majority of the human species. See page 570.*

23. **d.** *Wirth's essay contains the classic statement of the Chicago School's position. He argued that three features — size, density, and social diversity — are distinctive to the city. These features combine to form an urban lifestyle very different from that of small communities. See pages 582–583.*

b. individualism, segmented work roles, isolation

c. race riots, cultural diversity, alienation

d. size, density, social diversity

e. efficient use of space, anonymity, apathy

24. The importance of ideology is shown by the change in the U.S. position on population control. The text describes a shift from a position of _____ to one of _____.

a. financial incentives; limits on the number of children per family

b. antinatalism; economic improvements

c. free contraceptives; sterilization

d. mandatory abortions; antinatalism

e. economic improvements; free contraceptives

25. The human population, which already numbers over 4.9 billion, at current growth rates is

a. increasing and could double within four decades.

b. holding steady, with population increases in urbanized nations balancing the effects of malnutrition and starvation in poor countries.

c. decreasing because of the rapid spread of urbanization.

d. holding steady, with population decreases in urbanized nations balancing out the population increases in underdeveloped countries.

e. decreasing because of widespread use of contraceptives.

---

24. **b.** *In 1964, the United States lobbied for a global policy of antinatalism, advocating the use of birth control as the means to control population growth. However, in 1984, it reversed itself, arguing in favor of economic improvement as the way to support a growing population, a change of position reflecting the president and other leaders' opposition to abortion and mass availability of contraceptives. See pages 575–576.*

25. **a.** *Rapid population growth, particularly in developing countries, will probably result in a total world population exceeding 8 billion within the lifetime of most of today's students. See page 565.*

## A CASE STUDY

NAME

COURSE/SECTION NUMBER

The People's Republic of China has the highest population in the world. In spite of incredible increases in food production, it is almost impossible to adequately feed such a large number of people. Consequently, the government has embarked on a set of family-planning policies and incentives designed to keep the population growth rate as low as possible. There is an official limit of two children per family, and couples are strongly encouraged to have only one child. For example, the government pays for one child's schooling; if another child is born, not only must the parents bear the expense of its schooling, but they must also repay the government for the costs of the first child's schooling. Food rations and housing privileges are doled out in preference to smaller families. In addition, the legal age of marriage has been raised: the taboo against children born out of wedlock ensures that most Chinese will wait for marriage before deliberately bearing children. Sexuality is not emphasized and all sexual contact is expected to occur within the context of marriage. Thus, tangible policies are reinforced by general cultural norms. All citizens are called on to do their duty for the state and the national goals of modernization. Reducing the population is one of these goals, not just a matter of personal choice. Those couples who do have several children face strong social disapproval. This network of policies and cultural norms has led to a substantial drop in the growth rate of the population.

As the text indicates, lowering birth rates is not enough. The distribution of the population between rural and urban areas is also significant in China's efforts at successful modernization. Communal farm plans have been modified to allow peasants private ownership of small parcels of land and the opportunity to sell extra produce for their own profit. Nonetheless, many Chinese choose to migrate to the larger cities in order to gain employment in factories. Like other developing countries, China's cities are severely strained by these population shifts and the resulting demands for decent housing, sanitation, education, and jobs. However, China's citizens are not as free to move from one place to another as the citizens of some developing countries; thus its planned economy has lessened some of the effects of rural to urban migration.

1.    In what stage of demographic transition would you place China? What kinds of population-control strategies has China used? How would you evaluate the effectiveness of these measures?

2. Contrast the population characteristics of the United States with those of China. What population policies do both countries share? Which are different? Identify one approach to population that would work better in the United States than in China, and one for which the reverse would be true.

3. Based on what you have learned in this chapter, if you were hired by the Chinese government as an urban sociologist, what issues would you want to raise about urban growth, urban problems, and solutions to those problems? How does the pattern of urban growth in a developing country differ from that of the industrialized cities in the United States?

# Applying the Concepts

NAME

COURSE/SECTION NUMBER

## APPLICATION EXERCISE ONE

You have been elected to the City Council of Acme City. The council's job is to advise the mayor and the various city departments. The total population of Acme City is 260,000, distributed as follows:

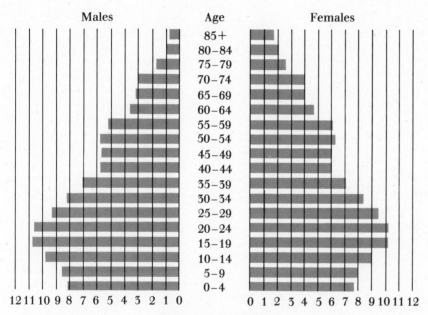

1. What are the social characteristics of this community?

2.   Assess the city's requirements for the following services:

   a. Grade schools, junior high schools, and high schools

   b. Hospitals and types of medical specialties (e.g., pediatricians, gynecologists, etc.)

   c. Housing and other services for the elderly

   d. Police and fire protection

   e. A zoo and other recreational facilities

   f. Museums and other cultural facilities

g.  A civic center

h.  Shopping malls

i.  Adult education and training center

j.  Gasoline stations

k.  Cemetaries

l.  Forms of public and private transportation

## APPLICATION EXERCISE TWO

Reread the Bureau of the Census definition of a Metropolitan Statistical Area (MSA). Choose any MSA with which you are familiar. You might consider where you grew up, went to school, worked, commuted, regularly shopped, or frequently visited, for whatever reason. Obtain a map of this metropolitan area. (Any commercial road map will do.) Be sure to attach it to this assignment.

1.    Identify the major transportation routes on your map and then comment on how the transportation corridors have affected the development and growth of the city.

2.    How did the various modes of transportation affect the development of the MSA?

waterways

horses and wagons

automobiles

trains

mass transit (buses and subways)

aircraft

NAME

COURSE/SECTION NUMBER

3.   Describe the natural geographic barriers, such as mountains, waterways, deserts, and other features of the terrain, that influenced the founding of the city.

4.   Which of the three patterns of urban growth best describes this area? On your map, mark the commercial districts, residential areas, industrial parks, and suburbs.

5.   How did this MSA become a center for trade, communications, ideas, innovation, and learning?

6.  How have recent construction of highways and buildings, urban renewal projects, and other changes affected this MSA? What is the impact on surrounding neighborhoods? What is the impact on the growth and/or deterioration of the central city?

7.  Look in an almanac (available in the reference room of the library) and provide the population figures for the MSA in 1960, 1970, and 1980. Based on these data, comment on the explanations you provided in the preceding questions for whatever changes have occurred.

NAME

_____

COURSE/SECTION NUMBER

## APPLICATION EXERCISE THREE

Until the 1930s and 1940s, retail shopping districts were concentrated in the downtown commercial areas. Small neighborhood shops supplemented these commercial centers. Highly organized, elaborate, and sprawling shopping malls, including a wide range of establishments and services, began to appear in outlying suburban areas after World War II.

Select a large shopping mall complex in your area.

1.   What factors led to the development of this mall in this particular spot? (Refer to your map and describe transportation routes, for example.)

2.   What combination of factors contributed to the shift of commercial shopping from a central business district to the suburban areas?

3.   Think about the particular shopping area you use most. What factors contribute to your continued patronage? What factors contributed to its development? What is occurring in the surrounding geographic area that will enhance or limit its commercial success in the future?

4.    Some observers suggest there is "a shopping mall society." What kinds of people patronize this mall? What are the various roles and statuses you see? Are there any "shopping mall norms" you can identify that differ from "downtown shopping norms"? How do the physical characteristics of this particular mall affect what goes on there?

5.    Downtown merchants have experienced a loss of business to the suburban malls. What other social consequences might you hypothesize have occurred because of the mass construction and use of malls by the general public?

# CHAPTER 22

# Technology and Environment

## Reviewing the Concepts

### LEARNING GOALS

*After studying this chapter, you should be able to:*

1. Define technology and its role in social change.

2. Distinguish between the goals of science and technology.

3. Trace the historical development of science, explaining the role inventions played in linking science and technology.

4. Summarize the process by which science grew into a modern social institution; describe the relationship between basic and applied research in a technological society.

5. Explain scientific innovation as one aspect of the social construction of reality.

6. Illustrate the four norms of science according to Merton and then indicate ways in which each norm can be violated.

7. List the functions and dysfunctions of competition in science; discuss the significance and pervasiveness of priority disputes.

8. Explain how paradigms guide "normal" scientific investigation; then outline the process leading to scientific revolution and paradigm change.

9. Present an example of the situation called "technological fix."

10. Discuss some of the dysfunctions of technology as well as the reasons behind the American public's disillusionment with it.

11. Illustrate the link between societal forces and technological products, using the terms "technological determinism" and "culture lag"; list three problems that might result from the lack of systematic social control over science and technological innovation, providing an example of each.

12. Outline the historical impact of the printing press and mass literacy on society; discuss some of the social consequences of twentieth-century innovations in the mass media.

13. Illustrate these three concepts pertaining to modern telecommunications: socially constructed news; the agenda-setting function of the media; participatory democracy through interactive technology.

14. Highlight some of the consequences of computer technology in terms of personal privacy and the nature of work; illustrate the link between social values and computer use by contrasting the role computers play in the United States and the U.S.S.R.

15. List some of the potential benefits and harmful consequences of genetic engineering.

16. Outline some of the dilemmas posed by biomedical technology used to prolong the life of seriously ill newborns or elderly persons; identify some of the unsettling questions raised by new pregnancy and birth technologies.

17. Define ecology and ecosystem; indicate the contribution of sociology to the understanding of each.

18. Summarize the complexity of the pollution problem.

19. List the health hazards associated with the use of pesticides and synthetic chemicals and the disposal of industrial wastes.

20. Characterize the problem of polluted rivers and lakes in relation to the supply of fresh ground water.

21. Discuss concerns about the destruction of the ozone layer, the growing problem of acid rain, the changing global climate, and the increase in space garbage.

22. Identify some of the important issues concerning the management of natural resources and nuclear power.

23. Outline the difficulties involved in the retrieval and distribution of fresh water.

24. List some of the social policies that would ward off the extinction of certain species; illustrate the precarious balance among the various parts of the ecosystem.

## IDENTIFYING KEY QUESTIONS AND THEMES

One of the distinctive features of human culture is the use of tools to act on our social and material world. All societies, no matter how simple, have *technology*—the practical applications of scientific or other knowledge. Technology is a major source of social change, with outcomes that advance human progress as well as some that cause additional problems.

### Science and Society

*What is science? How and why has science emerged as a major social institution in the modern world? What are the characteristics of the modern institution of science?*

*Science* refers to the logical, systematic methods by which knowledge is obtained, and to the actual body of knowledge produced by these methods. Science and technology are related, but technology is the much older of the two and can involve the application of any knowledge, scientific, magical, religious, or otherwise. However, because scientific understanding is necessary for an advanced technology, the link between science and technology has become closer with modernization. Science is a major social institution in modern, industrialized societies.

Science was present in a few ancient societies, such as Greece. Yet these societies had few specialized scientific roles and made little effort to link science to technology. Science was considered a philosophical and intellectual pursuit. The rebirth of learning in the sixteenth and seventeenth centuries marked the beginning of modern science, although there were still no specialized scientific roles. Many scientific discoveries were made and applied to the problems that faced society at the time, particularly warfare, navigation, and industry. Until the turn of the century, science remained a respectable leisure activity, the usefulness of which was not yet generally recognized. In this century, the relationship between science and technology has become fully recognized and exploited. American society relies on advanced technology to sustain its industrial base. The modern institution is "big science" with deep involvement in big organizations, big money, and big politics and a sizable expansion of scientific roles.

Many research scientists are employed by industry, educational institutions, and the government. In fact, the federal government provides about half the funds for scientific research. Research oriented toward increasing the sum of knowledge is called *basic research; applied research* has the aim of finding technological uses for scientific knowledge. The allocation of research money is significant in setting the research agenda.

### Scientific Innovation

*How does the social construction of reality shape scientific innovation? What are the four norms of science? How are these ideal norms modified by counternorms? What are the functions and dysfunctions of competition in science? How do paradigms guide "normal" scientific investigation? What is the process of paradigm change and scientific revolution?*

Scientific research is a form of social behavior. As such, it is one aspect of the *social construction of reality*—the process by which people create their understanding of their environment. The topics scientists study and the questions they ask are influenced by social forces. Discoveries that challenge important existing assumptions or values may provoke controversy, criticism, and resistance. Scientists such as Galileo and Darwin were denounced for their discoveries, although we take these scientific contributions for granted today.

Functionalist Robert Merton identified four norms of science that help ensure the orderly advance of scientific work. (1) Universalism is the norm that emphasizes the universal nature of science and its findings. Any particular characteristics of the individual scientists themselves are irrelevant to research findings, which must be evaluated purely in terms of their scientific merit. (2) Communalism refers to the idea that scientific knowledge should be made available to the entire scientific community and is not the property of the individual discoverer. Science grows through sharing the cumulative work of others. (3) Altruism guides scientific inquiry. Scientists should be free from self-interest in their professional work; knowledge should be produced honestly and for its own sake rather than for any reward the individual might receive. (4) Organized skepticism refers to the expectation that scientists will be skeptical and suspend judgment until all the facts are at hand; that is, scientists must constantly question theories and data and critically investigate them. This skepticism is "organized" in the sense that it is built into the scientific method itself. These four norms are sometimes violated by scientists who keep their work secret, forge data, seek fame or profit, or judge researchers by their personal characteristics. Nevertheless, the norms operate to move the scientific enterprise forward toward the development of new knowledge and the discovery of its possible technological applications.

Another important factor in scientific innovation is competition among scientists. Professional recognition is accorded to those who arrive at a discovery first and thus is very important to the scientist. The American scientific community is highly stratified, with the greatest honors going to a small number of scientists. Social mobility in the scientific community depends on the volume and recognition of an individual's publications. Due to this reward system and the importance of the publication of new discoveries, there are often intense *priority disputes* in science: scientists are worried about being scooped or anticipated by another researcher. This desire for recognition may be dysfunctional in that it encourages secrecy. Competition may have positive outcomes as well: it encourages scientists to make their findings known as soon as possible; reduces wasteful duplication of effort; and stimulates scientists to explore new specialities where they have a greater chance of making significant contributions.

Thomas Kuhn points out that there are two kinds of scientific innovations: the cumulative increase of knowledge during the "normal" process of research, and the radical change in knowledge that results from a scientific "revolution," in which scientists come to look at their subject matter in an entirely different way. Scientists use a *paradigm*—a shared set of concepts, methods, and assumptions about a scientific discipline—to determine the scope of a problem, a solution, an appropriate research method, or a discovery. Scientists then work to fit nature into the conceptualization of a current paradigm. These paradigms are useful in organizing the vast and complex world of nature and making scientific work more efficient. As research continues under a certain paradigm, new problems will be generated, some of which cannot be solved under the existing paradigm. Those that do not fit

are called anomalies. At some point, these anomalies can no longer be ignored and the paradigm must be modified to take them into account. New paradigms often meet with resistance, but eventually are adopted because they yield better results. Paradigms may be influenced by nonscientific considerations, as in the anti-Semitic response to Einstein's theory of relativity by Nazi Germany.

## Technology and Change

*What problems does technology pose for society? To what extent can and does modern society control the nature and direction of technological change?*

Many people are ambiguous about the impact of technology on society. One reason is that technology is such an important factor in social change. Often, technological changes create unanticipated problems, which in turn lead to a *technological fix*—the use of technology to solve problems, including those created by prior technology. The "fix" may result in an ever more complex cycle in which a fix leads to a problem, which provokes a further fix, which produces another problem, and so on. A second reason for public ambiguity is that technological innovation causes economic dislocation: products and even workers are made obsolete by such processes as *automation,* the replacement of workers by nonhuman means of production. A third reason is that technological disasters—particularly those involving "high tech" items such as the space shuttle—shake public faith in technology. Another source of public concern is the actual purpose of all our technological gadgetry: we have learned to associate it with the "good life," but does it really make us any happier? Some critics argue that we are becoming intoxicated with technological "hubris," the boundless arrogance that often precedes a fall. And finally, the rapid pace of technological innovation is disconcerting to many people, for their environment changes so quickly that they have little time to adjust.

Although some sociologists argue for *technological determinism*—the view that technology is an important determinant of culture, social structure, and history—most sociologists see technology as only one of several interacting factors that influence social change. Technology is neutral: its impact depends on whether and how people choose to use it. Unfortunately, modern technology has advanced so rapidly that social means of controlling it have lagged behind. This is a classic example of *culture lag,* the delay between a change in material culture and the adjustment of nonmaterial culture to the change. In practice, lack of social control over technology threatens three main problems: unforeseen and even disastrous impacts on the social and natural environments; diversion of technological resources away from desirable social goals; and the creation of an informal, behind-the-scenes *technocracy*—rule by technical experts on whom public officials rely for information and judgments. Currently, it is unclear who has, or should have, the prime responsibility for decisions about socially significant technological innovations.

## Technology and the Social Environment

*In what ways does technology influence the social environment? What are the existing and possible future implications of important technological innovations in such areas as the mass media, computers, genetic engineering, and biomedicine?*

The mass media are the various forms of communication that reach a large audience without personal contact between the senders and the receivers. The media include both print media, such as books, and electronic media, such as TV. The mass media emerged after the invention of the printing press in the fifteenth century. This highly influential innovation paved the way for the mass literacy that is now the foundation of postindustrial society. In this century, the electronic media have also had a dramatic impact on the social environment, for they have turned the planet into a "global village" in which information can be disseminated almost instantaneously to billions of people all over the world. The mass media are not simply a neutral technology, however: in each society, their form and content depends on such social factors as the degree of governmental or commercial influence over program content. In all modern societies, the media, particularly TV, have also become an important agent of socialization. Additionally, the media serve an "agenda-setting" function, particularly with regard to the way they select and present news.

Although computers are a very recent technological innovation, they already pervade everyday economic and social life. Thanks to the culture-lag phenomenon, some other aspects of culture have not yet caught up with this innovation. For example, there are still many legal uncertainties about new forms of computer crime. Computers also pose new threats to the individual's privacy, for they make it easier for outsiders to monitor and analyze the electronic trail we leave through life. In addition, computers are changing the nature of work and the workplace, particularly since they make it possible for many people to do their "office work" at home. The influence of social factors on computerization is revealed by the Soviet experience: the Soviet Union has relatively few computers, largely because the political leadership fears the free flow of information. A revolution in computer science and technology will be necessary if the Soviet Union is to become a postindustrial society, but that change may have broad and important implications for Soviet society.

Genetic engineering involves the rearrangement of genetic material within and among species, so as to create altered or even new organisms. This new technology may produce a biological revolution of profound social, economic, and ecological consequences. In agriculture, for example, the productivity of animals and plants could be enhanced; in medicine, new vaccines or drugs could be manufactured. Some critics are concerned that genetic engineers might carelessly or accidentally release dangerous new microbes or other organisms into the environment. They call for greater social control over the technology, pointing to the past effects of inadequate monitoring of the use of pesticides and other chemicals. There is also concern about the possible engineering of human genes to produce "improved" personal or physical characteristics in our own species. For some, genetic engineering offers great opportunities—but to others, it risks the "hubris" of "playing God."

While advances in biomedicine have transformed the treatment of the diseased, they have created new problems in the process, notably unprecedented ethical dilemmas. It is now possible, for example, to keep alive defective newborns and suffering or comatose patients long beyond the point at which they would normally have died. Similarly, new technologies, such as those for artificial insemination and surrogate motherhood, are affecting the process of conception and pregnancy. The result is a variety of ethical, legal, and familial dilemmas. Research is currently proceeding, too, on new biomedical technologies that could dramatically affect social life— for example, methods for preselecting the sex of children and for delaying (or even halting) the aging process. Such technologies could have major (and perhaps unwanted) social consequences.

## Technology and the Natural Environment

*What are the principles of ecology? How does pollution affect the natural environment? Are natural resources adequate to the demands we place on them? What role does our technology play in species extinction?*

***Ecology*** is the science of the relationship between living organisms and their environments. Life forms exist in ***ecosystems,*** communities of organisms within their natural environments. Ultimately, all organisms on the planet are interdependent, for they are involved in delicately balanced cycles and relationships. Traditional societies were often closely aware of this ecological balance; but in the modern world, we seem to believe that our technology has insulated us from nature—that we are somehow no longer a part of it.

Pollution of the natural environment takes several forms. Chemical pollution, much of it from synthetic pesticides and industrial wastes, now poses a long-term hazard to our environment and, in particular, to our food supplies. Water pollution is a serious problem, especially because so much of the underground water on which we depend is now chemically contaminated. Air pollution poses significant long-term threats to human and other life: it is depleting the planet's ozone layer, creating acid rain, and helping to gradually warm the Earth's climate in ways that may disrupt the planet's ecology.

Modern industrialized societies use vast amounts of resources, notably wood, minerals, fossil fuels, energy, and water. Extractable supplies of some minerals are likely to be exhausted within a century, and new synthetic substitutes, such as plastics and carbon fibers, will probably have to be found. Nuclear energy is a controversial high-technology energy resource, for many people regard the reactors as unsafe and are concerned about the disposal of radioactive waste products. Fresh water is also a problematic resource, because demands for it in the United States and elsewhere are beginning to exceed the supply. It remains to be seen whether the industrialized and industrializing world will be able to find technological solutions to such problems, or whether the effects of pollution and resource depletion will put a brake on economic growth.

Industrial technology is wreaking havoc with other species on the planet, for natural habitats are shrinking and being destroyed under the impact of economic development. Massive extinctions are taking place primarily in the tropical rain forests, where more than half of the planet's animal and plant species live. These forests are rapidly being destroyed in order to accommodate human economic ambitions and population growth. The loss of these life forms will have many practical drawbacks for humanity; for example, the forests contain many useful plants and also help to remove carbon dioxide from the atmosphere. Apart from these practical considerations, we might, out of respect for life, just let this multitude of animal and plant forms continue their existence of millions of years.

## DEFINING CORE CONCEPTS

*After studying the chapter, write a sociological definition in your own words for the following core concepts. Then give an example from your own experience to illustrate your definition. Refer to the chapter to check your work.*

| *Core Concept* | *Sociological Definition* | *Personal Illustration* |
|---|---|---|
| applied research | | |
| automation | | |
| basic research | | |
| culture lag | | |
| ecology | | |
| ecosystem | | |
| paradigm | | |
| priority dispute | | |

| Core Concept | Sociological Definition | Personal Illustration |
|---|---|---|
| science | | |
| social construction of reality | | |
| technocracy | | |
| technological determinism | | |
| technological fix | | |
| technology | | |

## PUTTING IDEAS TOGETHER

Although science and technology are closely linked in industrialized societies, they are actually quite distinct phenomena. Science refers to the logical, systematic methods by which knowledge is obtained, and to the actual body of knowledge produced by these methods. Technology, on the other hand, refers to the practical applications of scientific or other knowledge.

Unlike technology, science has appeared only rarely in human societies in the past. However, a scientific understanding of the world is necessary for an advanced technology. The diagram below summarizes some of the factors that contribute to the growth of science in a society and its institutionalization.

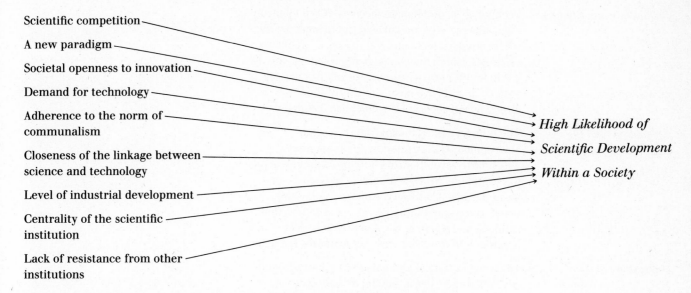

**The Growth of Science**

Scientific competition

A new paradigm

Societal openness to innovation

Demand for technology

Adherence to the norm of communalism

Closeness of the linkage between science and technology

Level of industrial development

Centrality of the scientific institution

Lack of resistance from other institutions

*High Likelihood of Scientific Development Within a Society*

Scientific innovation is a social process, for it is influenced by factors in the scientific community and in the wider society. The history of science shows resistance to innovations and an up-and-down pattern in the growth of scientific knowledge. The table below summarizes functionalist Robert Merton's assessment of the four norms that guide the scientific enterprise, as well as potential violations of those norms.

## The Social Process of Scientific Innovation

| *Norms and Ideas of Science* | *Possibly Contradictory Counternorms and Ideas* |
| --- | --- |
| Universalism | Stratification in science |
| Communalism | Priority disputes and competition |
| Altruism | Desire for professional recognition |
| Organized skepticism | Adherence to dominant paradigm |

Technological and social change are intimately connected, particularly in the modern world. Although many see advanced technology as the key to the future, others fear its potentially disruptive effects on the social and natural environments. The table below summarizes some of the achievements and problems associated with modern technology.

| | |
|---|---|
| *Technology and Change* | Technology is problematic because it is a factor in social change—particularly in the modern world, where complex technological fixes are applied to existing social and technological problems, only to produce still more problems. Society has not yet evolved an effective means of controlling the direction and content of technological change. |
| *Technology and the Social Environment* | The influence of technology on the social environment is illustrated by the mass media, which have revolutionized human communication; the computer, which is an essential element in postindustrialized society; genetic engineering, which is altering the nature of living things; and biomedicine, which now influences life, death, and pregnancy in ways that were not generally foreseen. |
| *Technology and the Natural Environment* | Advanced industrial technology can have dramatic ecological effects. It is leading to extensive pollution of air, water, and land, with disruptive effects on the health of organisms and the climate of the planet. It is also leading to the rapid depletion of resources, such as minerals and fresh water. Additionally, the combined effects of pollution and habitat destruction are causing a mass extinction of other species. |

# Testing the Concepts

## MULTIPLE-CHOICE QUESTIONS

*After studying the chapter, try to answer each of the twenty-five questions below. Mark the alternative you think is correct; then look at the correct answer and the explanation provided at the bottom of the page. Try to state why the other alternatives are incorrect, and check your understanding of the correct answer.*

1. Which of the following is an example of technology rather than science?
   a. the principle of atomic fusion
   b. a self-programmed method of studying sociology, based on educational psychology theory
   c. Einstein's theory of relativity
   d. research into the causes of divorce
   e. Durkheim's theory about mechanical and organic solidarity

2. In the scientific community, professional recognition comes from
   a. work on a longstanding research team.
   b. replication of major research studies of one's predecessors.
   c. a successful teaching career.
   d. publication of original research.
   e. interdisciplinary work.

3. To solve the problem of unwanted births, scientists invented the birth control pill. This situation is an example of
   a. an anomaly.
   b. a scientific paradigm.
   c. technological determinism.
   d. cultural lag.
   e. a technological fix.

4. The destruction of most of the world's rain forest by the end of the century, in response to population expansion, will have which of the following consequences?
   a. newly cleared land that will be fertile for agriculture
   b. a reduction in fresh ground water
   c. extinction of many species
   d. reduced use of pesticides
   e. discovery of new oil, gas, and coal reserves

---

1. **b.** *Technology is the practical application of scientific knowledge. In this example, the basic scientific research of educational psychologists has been applied to the task of teaching sociology more effectively. See page 592.*

2. **d.** *Publication of original research creates an exchange of information among scientists. Those who frequently publish significant new work are rewarded with high status within the scientific community. The world of science is stratified, with the higher statuses going to a small number of scientists who are the most published. See page 596.*

3. **e.** *The pill was a technological fix to unwanted pregnancies but led to other social problems. The sexual revolution brought more nonmarital sexual activity, and a rise in illegitimate births, followed by a rise in abortions. See page 599.*

4. **c.** *Many exotic and as yet uncatalogued species live in the world's rain forests, which are now being cleared for population settlements. The loss of these habitats will result in the extinction of many species. See page 620.*

5.  Sociologists project that computers will have which of the following effects?
  a.  Some people will work exclusively from home; but most people will want some human contact in an office.
  b.  Soviet society will never encourage use of computers as a part of a modernization campaign.
  c.  Those who work with computers will have less workplace autonomy.
  d.  Computers will not take hold in industry because machines cannot replace human workers.
  e.  Most people, given the chance, will elect to use a computer and work out of their homes.

6.  Which of the following examples illustrates culture lag in biomedicine?
  a.  People don't take advantage of available technology.
  b.  The human life span probably has an upper limit of 115 years no matter what science does to extend it.
  c.  We have no vocabulary or concepts to cover new family relationships such as surrogate parents.

  d.  Our society does not give medical technicians as much status as physicians.
  e.  New diseases, such as AIDS, are discovered just as other diseases are cured.

7.  Competition in science may be useful in promoting
  a.  disinterestedness.
  b.  communalism.
  c.  scientific innovations.
  d.  universalism.
  e.  replication of previous work.

8.  A paradigm in science is
  a.  an innovation.
  b.  a scientific revolution.
  c.  a set of assumptions.
  d.  a scientific anomaly.
  e.  a technology.

9.  The most significant result of the invention of the printing press was
  a.  mass literacy.
  b.  more employment.
  c.  fewer religious books.
  d.  better education for a ruling elite.
  e.  the growth of a large middle class.

---

5.  a.  *Computers will allow people to work from home, but many people will seek face-to-face contact with others in an office setting for at least part of their work time. See page 606.*

6.  c.  *Culture lag refers to the time gap between changes in material culture (such as birth technology) and attitudes about how to incorporate, accept, and use that culture. The new birth technologies result in family relationships for which we have no vocabulary. See page 611.*

7.  c.  *Competition among scientists may result in new scientific discoveries. Ambitious scientists explore new specialties, new theories, and test new hypotheses as well*

as challenge the assumptions and findings of other scientists. See pages 596–597.

8.  c.  *A paradigm is a set of beliefs or assumptions that guides the work of scientists. It forms a conceptual base in which a scientist poses a problem and seeks solutions in empirical evidence. See page 597.*

9.  a.  *The printing press led to the mass production of books and newspapers, allowing most people access to the printed word. The oral tradition of passing along news was supplanted by written materials, which required reading at some basic level for most of the citizenry. See pages 602–603.*

10.  Which of the following statements about the institutionalization of science is accurate?
  a.  The social institution of science was founded by the Greeks.
  b.  Modern science grew rapidly with specialized scientific roles directed toward applied problems.
  c.  There is a basic conflict between science and religion.
  d.  The most significant scientific knowledge was created in the Middle Ages.
  e.  Most scientists in the United States work in university settings.

11.  Which of the following statements about global resources and pollution is supported by the text?
  a.  Coal resources are depleted and countries are switching to oil and gas for fuel.
  b.  Wind and sun energy will be major sources of power in the next decade.
  c.  Improved methods allow the transfer of fresh water to arid areas, such as the Southwestern United States and the deserts of the Middle East.
  d.  The U.S. public approves of the construction of nuclear power plants as a safe, clean energy source.
  e.  Pollution damage is raising the temperature of the global climate.

12.  A consequence of American dominance in global communications is
  a.  cultural pollution, in the eyes of foreigners.
  b.  censored news broadcasts.
  c.  the reporting of news as it happens.
  d.  a high ratio of high culture to popular culture.
  e.  evidence of dissent about American foreign policy.

13.  Several writers have warned society about the dangers of a technocracy. Which of the following examples illustrates such a danger?
  a.  On the recommendation of military scientists and engineers, members of Congress vote for a new weapons system, even though they are not sure whether it will work.
  b.  A large corporation hires a staff of scientists to gain a technological edge over its top competitors.
  c.  Manufacturers develop an alarm clock that wakes you with a familiar voice as the latest gadget for Christmas gift-giving.
  d.  The government reduces the amount of funding for basic research.
  e.  Environmental impact statements must be filed before potentially hazardous industries can be constructed.

---

10.  **b.**  *Science emerged as a modern social institution in response to the technological needs of the society. Many specialized roles developed, and science became a highly valued, central activity rather than a distrusted, marginal activity as in the past. See pages 593–594.*

11.  **e.**  *Air pollution is creating a "greenhouse effect," which is steadily warming the global climate. See pages 616–617.*

12.  **a.**  *Many other countries fear that American print and electronic media will distort their culture, especially among young viewers, and consider the impact of American media to be "cultural pollution." See pages 603–604.*

13.  **a.**  *A technocracy describes the direct or indirect rule of a small group of experts who have gained positions of authority because of their scientific knowledge. These experts may have knowledge beyond the grasp of nonscientists and thus are asked to make judgments on behalf of the others. See pages 601–602.*

14. Which of the following statements about genetic engineering is supported in the text?
    a. Public support of genetic engineering is high.
    b. Genetic engineers are sharing their research with one another to speed up the discovery process.
    c. The push for genetic engineering comes from commercial interests.
    d. Genetic engineering research has focused primarily on rats.
    e. Genetic engineering has received the support of religious leaders who want to end people's suffering from inherited diseases.

15. Which of the following characteristics is necessary for the development of the modern institution of science?
    a. The influence of religion in a society must be minimal.
    b. Corporate industry must be willing to fund basic and applied research.
    c. Science must become a central activity for the society.
    d. Scientists must communicate their findings in an understandable way to the general public.
    e. Scientists cannot be overly rewarded for their work, or they will be motivated only by profit.

16. The United States has a remarkably high number of Nobel Prize winners, indicating significant scientific achievements. What is the main reason for this performance?
    a. heavy funding from government and industry to do research
    b. government controls on applied research
    c. scientists' desire to solve social problems
    d. the violations of the norms of science
    e. other cultures' lack of technology

17. Which of the following statements about the history of science and technology is accurate?
    a. Every society has at least a simple technology.
    b. Science has existed since the beginning of human societies.
    c. Science must develop more quickly than technology if social change is to occur.
    d. Science and technology have similar goals.
    e. The American public has steadily increased its faith in science for solving problems.

18. The shift from hunting and gathering to industrialism as the means of subsistence results in
    a. a slowdown of the rate of population growth.
    b. pollution and depletion of natural resources.
    c. an attitude shift, where people feel they are part of nature.
    d. a paradigm shift for the general public.
    e. the beginning of technology.

---

14. **c.** *Many of the experiments in genetic engineering are supported by commercial interests that seek to promote their products and services. Scientists do not share their results with others to avoid losing their competitive, and therefore financial, edge. See pages 607–608.*

15. **c.** *Science has recently become a major social institution in most industrialized societies. Specialized roles have been created and science is no longer seen as a leisure activity but rather as having a central function in society. See page 594.*

16. **a.** *The government and industrial sectors in the United States heavily fund applied research. As a result, they expect a payoff in useful knowledge and technological advances. See page 594.*

17. **a.** *Technology is the practical use of knowledge. All societies, whatever their level of development, have used their knowledge to create objects of culture to use in social life, whether they are sticks to create fire or steam engines to power locomotives. See pages 591–592.*

18. **b.** *Industrialization involves manufacturing, the use of raw materials, and the need for fuel to power machines. Pollution and the depletion of natural resources are the result. See page 614.*

19.  According to Thomas Kuhn's *The Structure of Scientific Revolutions*, dramatic breakthroughs occur in science through
   a. seeking some new paradigm to explain an apparent anomaly.
   b. the accumulation of data in different disciplines over time.
   c. the comparison of data with hypotheses.
   d. the sudden insights of individuals.
   e. extensive funding for applied research.

20.  It seems that the ancient Greeks did not develop an elaborate technology because they
   a. had no science.
   b. inherited a distaste for technology from ancient Roman culture.
   c. were an intensely practical people and had little interest in the world of ideas.
   d. valued science as an aspect of philosophy rather than for any practical value that it might have.
   e. did not have the equipment to develop it.

21.  Which of the following would be a violation of the scientific norm of organized skepticism?
   a. A sociologist refuses to consider a new theory because it conflicts with the prevailing wisdom.
   b. A college refuses to hire a professor because of his or her religious beliefs.
   c. A government laboratory "classifies" research findings so that they will be kept secret.
   d. A scientist attempts to further his or her career by fraudulent research.
   e. A researcher releases preliminary results to the press knowing they will bring him considerable personal attention.

22.  The word "hubris" refers to
   a. any intermediate species produced by gene-splicing.
   b. a cloud of airborne toxic material.
   c. the kind of pride or arrogance that comes before a fall.
   d. the ground-level flora of the tropical rainforest.
   e. a flaw or "bug" in a computer program.

23.  Which statement about American nuclear waste is *true*?
   a. Modern nuclear reactors consume their own waste as fuel.
   b. The waste is recycled to make nuclear weapons.
   c. The waste is stored in temporary containers.
   d. The waste is detoxified to minimize any risk of radiation poisoning.
   e. The waste is buried in secure, permanent dumps.

---

19.  **a.** *When the prevailing set of assumptions about a scientific phenomenon, called a paradigm, no longer explains it, a paradigm shift occurs. This significant shift in the way scientists conceptualize their theories and solutions is called a scientific revolution. See page 597.*

20.  **d.** *The Greeks took a philosophic view of science, which they considered an intellectual exercise in logic. The rigid class divisions between slaves and citizens in ancient Greece meant that the upper classes had leisure time to pursue intellectual pleasures without regard to their applied usefulness. See page 593.*

21.  **a.** *The norm of organized skepticism ensures that all research results will be considered and evaluated on scientific criteria. Scientists are expected to suspend judgment until all the facts are at hand. See pages 595–596.*

22.  **e.** *Hubris was the ancient Greeks' word for an arrogance that defies the gods. Some critics argue that the ambitions of modern technology are marked by hubris, and that we may be overreaching ourselves. See page 600.*

23.  **c.** *Nuclear waste, which is highly radioactive and dangerous, is stored in temporary containers. Permanent dumps are planned, but there are political difficulties in reaching a consensus on where to locate them. See page 619.*

24.  Which resource is plentiful in the United States?
  a. fresh water
  b. coal
  c. chromium
  d. zinc
  e. uranium

25.  A self-sustaining community of organisms within its natural environment is called
  a. ecology.
  b. an ecosphere.
  c. the biosphere.
  d. a zootropical zone.
  e. an ecosystem.

---

24.  **b.** *The United States has reserves of coal that will last for centuries—although using this resource will cause extensive air pollution. The other resources are in short supply. See pages 618–619.*

25.  **e.** *All living things exist within an ecosystem, whether the system is as large as the surface of the planet or as small as a drop of pond water. See page 614.*

# A CASE STUDY

NAME

COURSE/SECTION NUMBER

In May, 1987, two events served as grave warnings about the problem of effective garbage disposal in this and other nations. A barge loaded with tons of garbage from New York sailed down the eastern seaboard and into the Caribbean looking for a dump site. None of the states bordering the coast nor any of the Caribbean countries would take the load, which grew steadily more smelly and fly-infested with each day. Finally the captain had to turn back and appeal to the State of New York to find a dump site on Long Island. Area residents were angered to be the final resting place for such a mess.

In neighboring New Jersey, the state legislature passed a mandatory recycling law. Residents must separate their garbage into papers, cans, and bottles so that these materials can be cleaned and recycled rather than put in land fills. New Jersey is a small, densely populated state and has literally run out of room to dump its garbage. Again, residents were angry that they had to go to the extra effort of washing bottles and cans and binding up newspapers instead of putting everything in trash bags and setting it out for collection.

1.   What evidence do you see for government intervention in waste management in these scenarios and in your own community? Is this type of intervention a proper government role?

2.    Sociologists are often asked to help with environmental impact projects, in which an assessment is made, in advance, of a proposed project, such as the construction of a landfill. What questions might sociologists ask and how might the sociologists contribute to the solution of these waste disposal problems in the northeastern United States?

3.    Can you cite technological developments aimed at solving this problem? Explain. Does the solution lie primarily with science and technology or with attitude and behavior change?

# Applying the Concepts

NAME

COURSE/SECTION  NUMBER

## APPLICATION EXERCISE ONE

Sociologist Dr. Barbara Katz Rothman has written a book entitled *The Tentative Pregnancy*. It is based on her interviews with genetic counselors and couples about the experience of using new technology to test for birth defects. The term "tentative" refers to her finding that women who used amniocentesis (a test for birth defects) often waited for the results before "going public" with their pregnancy. They waited longer to wear maternity clothes and to tell their friends of the pregnancy; they also felt first fetal movement at a later date than women who did not use the test.

1.   Rothman argues that getting all of the available information about a fetus and possible abnormalities via these tests is becoming a social norm. Do you agree or disagree?

2.   Are these tests for genetic abnormalities a technological fix? Why or why not?

3.   What is the social impact of these tests?

## APPLICATION EXERCISE TWO

NAME

COURSE/SECTION NUMBER

1.   Scan your own room, and make a list of ten items it contains; for example, telephone, rug, heater, book, chair, compact disc player, computer, and so forth. For each item, decide how new technology has created or improved each item within the last ten years. Consider advanced technology such as electronics, information management, automation, and synthetic materials.

| Item | Evidence of Technology |
|------|------------------------|
| 1. | |
| 2. | |
| 3. | |
| 4. | |
| 5. | |
| 6. | |
| 7. | |
| 8. | |
| 9. | |
| 10. | |

2.   Pick *one* of these items that is important to you personally. Go to the library and look up its history of development in a current encyclopedia. Identify elements of the following:

a.  the institutionalization of science

b.  the norms of science

c. the social process of innovation

d. resistance to innovation

e. the social control of science and technology

3.    Choose a major scientific or technological innovation. Describe how your social life would be affected if this one scientific or technological innovation had not been made.

## APPLICATION EXERCISE THREE

Select a recent copy of a news magazine, such as *Time* or *Newsweek*, that reports a scientific or technological breakthrough. For example, you could select the manufacturing of synthetic fuels, experiments with "test-tube" babies, cloning of mice, the use of electronic chips for computer memory, a new theory of economics, or the space shuttle. Also read the subsequent issues (usually two or three weeks later) that carry letters to the editor on the scientific report. Summarize or attach the article.

1.   Is there evidence of resistance to this innovation? Can you anticipate resistance?

2.   Are any of the letter writers concerned about the norms of science? Do you note any evidence of norm violations?

3.   If the article does not address these issues explicitly, speculate about the following:

   a. social controls that are needed as a result of this breakthrough

   b. the phenomenon of culture lag

   c. the difference between science and technology

   d. the source of sponsorship and funding of this research and the implications of that source

   e. the next state of scientific or technological development likely to follow

# CHAPTER 23

# War and Peace

## Reviewing the Concepts

### LEARNING GOALS

*After studying this chapter, you should be able to:*

1.  Provide a sociological definition of war and peace.

2.  Explain why war is a highly structured social activity and indicate those factors that encourage war.

3.  Describe how technological advances have changed the nature of weaponry, defense systems, as well as the method, scope, and cost of making war.

4. Characterize the hostility between the United States and the Soviet Union and explain how their definitions of reality perpetuate each country's "demonization" of the other.

5. Identify factors, including the military-industrial complex, that contribute to the arms race.

6. Summarize U.S. nuclear strategy and its system of mutual deterrence.

7. Present the purpose of "star wars" technology and assess its strengths and weaknesses.

8. List conditions that increase or decrease the likelihood of nuclear war.

9. Identify the four immediate effects of a nuclear attack on populated areas.

10. Identify the long-term effects of a nuclear attack in terms of the individual's physical health and psychological well-being, as well as its effects on the social organization of society and the ecosystem.

11. Explain how and why the superpowers spar along the continuum of war and peace.

12. Evaluate the argument that nuclear weapons help to prevent war.

13. Present the conditions necessary for arms control.

14. Assess the adequacy of arms-control agreements between the United States and the Soviet Union.

15. List the factors that encourage or impede disarmament in the United States and the Soviet Union.

16. Explain the role of the United Nations and international law in promoting international peace-making efforts.

17. Discuss how collective action may offer the best prospect for peace.

# IDENTIFYING KEY QUESTIONS AND THEMES

The nuclear age dawned in 1945 when the United States exploded an experimental bomb in the New Mexico desert. Nuclear warfare began shortly thereafter with the bombing of the Japanese cities of Hiroshima and Nagasaki. Today there are more than 50,000 nuclear weapons —enough to wipe out humanity several times over. War has always been one of the most unpleasant of all human endeavors, but it now threatens unprecedented havoc and perhaps even the survival of our species. Sociologically, *war* is sustained military conflict between politically organized groups, while *peace* is sustained amicable relationships between politically organized groups. Whether the United States and the Soviet Union choose war or peace is perhaps the most vital question currently facing the future of humanity.

## War and Society

*Why do people go to war? How has warfare developed over the centuries?*

It is sometimes argued that war occurs because people have an aggressive "instinct." This simplistic view overlooks the facts—including the fact that most people and societies are at peace most of the time, and that some societies seem able to avoid war completely.

The origins of war are political, for it occurs as a result of a decision on the part of political leaders to engage in warfare rather than choose any of the other possible alternatives. Soldiers do not go to war because they "feel aggressive"; they go because a legitimate political authority orders them to do so. Many factors can influence the decision for war, including calculations (or miscalculations) about the other side's intentions, about the economic costs or benefits, or about the outcome of the conflict. Frequently, military preparations seem to cause rather than avert war; if one country seems to be preparing for conflict, its potential enemies are likely to do the same, which in turn precipitates increased militarization by the original country, and so on.

The history of war is largely the story of the development of ever more advanced weapons and means of delivering them, as well as the development of defense systems. Rapid technological innovations in warfare have made mass killing much easier and more impersonal. At one time, war meant soldiers physically attacking each other, but today it can mean a handful of people destroying a distant city merely by pressing a button. Over the centuries, the number of people involved in warfare has steadily increased, and in the nuclear age civilian populations as well as military personnel are at risk. Internationally, colossal sums of money are spent for military rather than other social purposes.

## Superpower Hostility

*How did the superpowers become hostile? What is the arms race and what propels it? What are the principles of nuclear strategy? Would a "star wars" defense be workable?*

The United States and the Soviet Union are the most powerful countries on Earth and represent quite different ways of life, for one advocates capitalism, and the other communism. As mutually hostile nations, they tend to "demonize" the other, regarding the opposing side as aggressive, unreasonable, and treacherous. Citizens of both countries know remarkably little about the other country or its way of life. Americans, for example, are generally ignorant of the catastrophic loss of life suffered by the Soviet Union when it was invaded by Nazi Germany in World War II, and of how this experience has affected the Soviet outlook. In the aftermath of World War II, the Soviet Union established communist rule in most of Eastern Europe, while Western Europe remained capitalist. The United States, Canada, and other Western European countries formed the North Atlantic Treaty Organization to oppose Soviet expansion, and the Soviet Union and the Eastern European countries formed the Warsaw Pact in response.

Since then, the superpowers have been engaged in an *arms race,* a process in which each side continuously attempts to gain or maintain superiority in weaponry. Although the United States held a lead in the race until the late 1970s, both sides are now roughly equal. The arms race is propelled not only by rivalry between the superpowers, but also by internal factors in each society. In the United States, the *military-industrial complex* is an informal system of mutual influence between the Pentagon, which buys armaments, and the major U.S. corporations that sell them. The Pentagon depends on these suppliers and, therefore, protects them from normal market forces, while the suppliers encourage the Pentagon and Congress to spend ever more money on weapons systems. These pressures maintain or even escalate the arms race, even though many of the resulting weapons systems are over-priced and defective. There are presumably parallel pressures in the Soviet Union from its own military and armaments bureaucracies.

The main focus of the arms race is nuclear weaponry. Nuclear strategy changes under the influence of technological innovations in this field. Since 1949, when the Soviet Union developed its own nuclear weapons, nuclear strategy has rested on the threat of MAD—mutually assured destruction. Under this doctrine, each country deters the other from warfare by holding its population hostage, for an attack can be expected to provoke a devastating counterattack. To ensure this counterattack, both countries maintain an immense arsenal of nuclear weapons that can be delivered through a strategic "triad" consisting of land-based missiles, submarine-based missiles, and bomber aircraft.

However, new nuclear weapons, such as small "battlefield" bombs and warheads on small cruise missiles, are designed for limited use as an adjunct to conventional warfare. Also, highly accurate intercontinental missiles can now hit the other side's land-based missiles, making possible a theoretical "first strike," in which one side would destroy much of the other's weaponry, leaving it vulnerable to further strikes if it did not surrender. Such innovations seem to be leading to a new strategy of NUTS—nuclear-use theories.

The Strategic Defense Initiative—"star wars"—is a proposed space-based antimissile system that would use elaborate new technologies to defend against Soviet intercontinental missiles. Experts generally agree that the system would not be able to adequately protect the population as a whole; thus its primary purpose would probably be to protect American missiles against a first strike. Critics have raised several objections to the project: its extraordinary cost; its use of complex and untried new technologies; the inherent unreliability of its millions of lines of computer instructions, which could never be tested in practice; and the difficulties of launching vast amounts of material into space and then constructing and

maintaining that system. Critics also point out that the Soviet Union could foil the system in various ways: by "blinding" it; by overwhelming it with cheap decoys; by attacking the system itself; by circumventing it entirely, delivering nuclear weapons from submarines or cruise missiles; or by inventing some altogether new weapon. In any case, an effective "star wars" system could increase the danger of war if it is seen as a threat by the Soviet Union. After all, how would the United States react if the Soviet Union developed a shield against American attack, while maintaining the means to destroy the United States? Like the ineffectual Maginot line that was once supposed to defend France against attack from Germany, "star wars," in the end, could become just one more obsolete element in the arms race.

## Nuclear War

*Can nuclear war happen? What might be its immediate effects and its long-term consequences?*

Nuclear war may be "unthinkable," but it is not impossible. Such a war is probably least likely to break out as a result of a deliberate surprise attack, or first strike, simply because of the risk of massive retaliation. However, nuclear war could break out during extreme tension between the superpowers. If either side suspects, rightly or wrongly, that the other is about to use its weapons, then it would make military sense to hit first—"use it or lose it." Especially in a tense international crisis, miscalculation or error could easily lead to war. The superpowers might also be drawn into conflict through involvement in conventional wars in such "hot spots" as the Middle East. The proliferation of weapons itself increases the danger of nuclear war, because the more weapons there are and the more nations that have them, the greater the risk that they will be used. This danger is enhanced if minor nations with unstable leaders get control of nuclear weapons, which then could be used anonymously from unmarked ships or planes. Terrorists, too, might eventually gain access to and even use nuclear weapons. Additionally, war could break out as a result of technological or human error—particularly when the interval between a (true or false) warning of a missile launch and its expected arrival allows too little time for rational human judgment.

The immediate effects of a nuclear attack include (1) an electromagnetic pulse, which would destroy electronic circuits; (2) a blast, crushing all objects in its path; (3) heat, which would ignite flammable materials over a wide area; and (4) radiation, which damages living cells both in the immediate area and, later, in areas where contaminated dust lands as fallout. In the longer term, any survivors would face severe problems, including psychological stress; shortages of food and water; the need for shelter from the elements and radioactive fallout; the ravages of disease; the collapse of social structure; predations of bandits; and the imperative of restarting agricultural production. It is quite possible, however, that the climatic effects of a nuclear war and its resulting clouds of smoke could bring about a prolonged "nuclear winter" in which global temperatures might plunge below freezing, causing much plant and animal life, including, perhaps, most or all of humanity, to die out.

## Prospects for Peace

*What are the prospects for peace? What steps can be taken to reduce the possibility of war and enhance the likelihood of peace?*

The immediate choice is not just an "idealistic" one between war and peace, for these conditions are merely opposite ends of a continuum. Instead, people can choose practical measures that move the world one way or another along the continuum, steadily making either war or peace more likely.

Many people hold the view that nuclear deterrence is the best way to avoid war. They point out, probably correctly, that the fear of nuclear holocaust has prevented the United States and the Soviet Union from going to war for more than forty years. However, this strategy of MAD has a crucial drawback in that it is an all-or-nothing gamble—if it fails, it fails catastrophically. Also, MAD is undermined by the arms race, which continually introduces instability into the balance of power on which MAD depends.

An alternative to MAD is **arms control,** or mutually agreed limitations on the nature, numbers, and uses of weapons and defenses. Successful arms control requires trust, which can be strengthened if there are suitable means of verifying that both sides are sticking to their agreements. However, the construction of small, mobile, and easily hidden missiles soon will make verification increasingly difficult. Several important arms-control agreements have already been reached, but further agreements depend largely on the political will of the superpower leaderships. Recently, the Reagan administration has adopted a hard line on arms control, while the Soviet Union has been more conciliatory.

Ideally, arms control would eventually lead to **disarmament,** or the steady reduction in the nature, numbers, and uses of weapons and defenses. This process would be a gradual one, probably starting with a freeze on new weapons and gradually leading to scrapping of existing ones in a series of carefully verified stages. Although the prospects of disarmament may now seem remote, both superpowers, in fact, have a great deal to gain from establishing peaceful relations and diverting their military expenditures to other more socially useful goals.

The very existence of a series of militarized and sovereign independent states creates preconditions for war. Fortunately, two international peace-keeping mechanisms are already in place, notably the United Nations and the World Court. Despite an imperfect record, these bodies have successfully ended or averted several wars. However, compliance with their resolutions is voluntary, since no independent state will yield its sovereignty to an international body. Thus the U.N. is most effective when the superpowers agree on a course of action.

Ultimately, collective action by ordinary people may offer the best prospect for peace. Throughout history, **social movements**—consisting of large numbers of people who come together to bring about or resist social or cultural change—have shaped history. At present, peace movements are largely confined to the Western world, for the Soviet people as yet do not have the freedom to develop social movements that challenge their own government—although modern Soviet society does show signs of greater openness. A good example of the crucial role a social movement may play in effecting change is the Peace Movement of the 1960s, which helped bring the Vietnam war to an end. Similarly, movements of concerned people around the world could ultimately end the nuclear menace that threatens to destroy the world as we know it.

# DEFINING CORE CONCEPTS

*After studying the chapter, write a sociological definition in your own words for the following core concepts. Then give an example from your own experience to illustrate your definition. Refer to the chapter to check your work.*

| *Core Concept* | *Sociological Definition* | *Personal Illustration* |
| --- | --- | --- |
| arms control | | |
| arms race | | |
| disarmament | | |
| military-industrial complex | | |
| peace | | |
| social movement | | |
| war | | |

## PUTTING IDEAS TOGETHER

Countries tend to spar along the continuum that runs from war to peace. The text explains pressures leading to war-like activity and counterpressures for peace. The intensity of one set of factors over another helps us understand why conflicts occur and how they can be reduced.

| *The Reality or Threat of War Increases With* | *The Reality or Likelihood of Peace Increases With* |
|---|---|
| demonizing of the other country | cultural relativism |
| military build-up | arms control |
| interlocking social institutions in support of war (e.g., military-industrial complex) | a military that is not a central social institution |
| cultural norms in support of war | cultural norms in support of peace |
| social construction of reality that war is the best alternative | perception that other alternatives are available |
| political and military elites in charge of decision making in a system with minimal checks and balances | collective actions/social movements for peace |
| political isolation or political superpower status leading a country to ignore international pressure for peace | international peace-making activities and laws |

# Testing the Concepts

## MULTIPLE-CHOICE QUESTIONS

*After studying the chapter, try to answer each of the twenty-five questions below. Mark the alternative you think is correct; then look at the correct answer and the explanation provided at the bottom of the page. Try to state why the other alternatives are incorrect, and check your understanding of the correct answer.*

1. The Warsaw Pact is
   a. a human-rights agreement between the United States and the Soviet Union.
   b. a mutual defense treaty between the Soviet Union and its East European allies.
   c. a promise by Poland to remain neutral in any superpower conflict.
   d. an international treaty restricting the spread of nuclear weapons.
   e. a pledge of mutual support on the part of several Western nations in the event of the outbreak of war.

2. The principal Western military alliance is called
   a. the North Atlantic Treaty Organization.
   b. the League of Nations.
   c. the Western Alliance.
   d. the Marshall Plan.
   e. the World Court.

3. Gold-plating refers to
   a. extravagance in weapons spending.
   b. bribery by defense contractors.
   c. expensive dinners and other means of lobbying congressional defense committees.
   d. loading weapons with electronic and other "high tech" devices.
   e. a highly advanced system of land-based shields.

4. The strategic "triad" includes
   a. land-based missiles.
   b. Great Britain.
   c. nerve gas.
   d. antimissile systems.
   e. tanks.

5. The strategy of a "first strike" is based on the idea that
   a. one country could destroy the other by striking first.
   b. one country could strike first at the other country's missiles, hoping to force a surrender.
   c. one country could strike first with "battlefield" nuclear weapons in a limited war.
   d. no second strike would be possible.
   e. one country could strike first at the other country's bombers, possibly ending the conflict right there.

---

1. **b.** *The Warsaw Pact pledges the Soviet Union and its communist-ruled allies in Eastern Europe to mutual military aid; it was their response to the creation of NATO. See page 631.*

2. **a.** *The United States, Canada, and several Western European nations formed NATO in order to halt Soviet military expansion in Europe. See page 631.*

3. **d.** *The term refers to the way weapons are made ever more expensive and complicated by being loaded with the latest high-tech gadgetry. See page 632.*

4. **a.** *The strategic triad consists of three different means of delivering nuclear weapons—land-based missiles, submarine-based missiles, and bomber aircraft. See page 634.*

5. **b.** *A "first strike" would be an attack on the other side's land-based missiles. The country under attack would then face the choice of surrendering (and saving most of its cities) or retaliating with whatever weapons it had left (and risking a second strike against its population centers). See page 635.*

6. How many times has the United States exploded a nuclear bomb on a city?
   a. once
   b. twice
   c. three times
   d. four times
   e. never

7. According to the text, the United States and the Soviet Union are in a state of
   a. peace.
   b. war.
   c. undeclared war.
   d. hostility.
   e. accord.

8. War occurs because
   a. humans are naturally aggressive.
   b. political leaders choose war rather than alternative means of settling differences.
   c. war is functional in that it revitalizes societies.
   d. militarism is present in all societies.
   e. it is the only way to solve important conflicts.

9. In the sociology of war, "demonizing" refers to
   a. reducing military expenditure.
   b. building up one's arsenal.
   c. using religion to justify conflict.
   c. techniques for demoralizing enemy forces.
   e. attributing wickedness to one's enemies.

10. Which one of the following statements is *false*?
    a. The Soviet Union and the United States were allies in World War II.
    b. The Soviet Union has been invaded three times during this century.
    c. Russians refer to World War II as "the Great Patriotic War."
    d. The United States suffered greater casualties in World War II than the Soviet Union.
    e. The United States once invaded the Soviet Union to put down its revolution.

11. The "star wars" system would be designed to
    a. protect against intercontinental ballistic missiles.
    b. retaliate against the Soviet Union in the event of nuclear attack.
    c. protect against all Soviet nuclear weapons
    d. attack Soviet installations using X-ray lasers.
    e. effectively harness the "frozen" energy in matter.

12. The Maginot line
    a. is part of the Reagan doctrine of communist containment.
    b. successfully kept Nazi forces at the outskirts of Moscow.
    c. was a notoriously unsuccessful defensive system.
    d. runs along the 38th parallel.
    e. is a line in the sky beyond which missiles could not pass.

---

6. **b.** *The United States exploded nuclear bombs on the Japanese cities of Hiroshima and Nagasaki at the end of World War II. See page 625.*

7. **d.** *The United States and the Soviet Union are in a state of hostility, a sort of limbo between the violence of war and the amicability of peace. See page 626.*

8. **b.** *War occurs as a result of a political decision. Leaders can always choose other alternatives, including negotiation or surrender. See page 627.*

9. **e.** *When two countries are in a state of hostility or at war, their peoples tend to develop negative stereotypes about the other, viewing the opposing side as wicked or demonic. See page 629.*

10. **d.** *The Soviet Union suffered by far the greatest casualties in World War II—it lost forty times as many people as the United States did. See pages 630–631.*

11. **a.** *The "star wars" system is designed to protect against intercontinental missiles that pass through space. The system would not be effective against nuclear weapons delivered from bombers, off-shore submarines, or low-flying cruise missiles. See page 637.*

12. **c.** *The Maginot line was a French defensive system that proved irrelevant under the actual conditions of German invasion in World War II. It has become the symbol of an expensive but useless defense. See page 637.*

13. Which of the following countries is *not* a nuclear power?
   a. Germany
   b. France
   c. China
   d. Great Britain
   e. United States

14. After a full-scale nuclear war,
   a. global temperatures would rise, because of the heat of the explosions.
   b. there would definitely be no human survivors, because the planet would be radioactive.
   c. electromagnetic pulses would continue for years.
   d. various "hot spots" would burn for years.
   e. global temperatures would fall, because smoke and soot would block out the sun's rays.

15. The strategy of deterrence through mutually assured destruction (MAD) works best if
   a. the contending parties are evenly balanced.
   b. the United States has the advantage.
   c. the arms race keeps up at a steady pace.
   d. one country is clearly inferior in weaponry.
   e. the United States continues to adopt a hard line on arms control.

16. According to the text, nuclear war can ultimately be prevented by
   a. the influence of the mass media.
   b. the use of nuclear deterrence.
   c. the collective action of ordinary people.
   d. social and economic reforms.
   e. full-scale dismantlement of the military-industrial complex.

17. According to the text, what process may help to encourage greater "openness" in Soviet society?
   a. a shift from an industrial to a postindustrial mode of production
   b. the rift between the Soviet Union and China
   c. the Soviet peace movement
   d. the war in Afghanistan
   e. the "star wars" defense system

18. Which of the following is a necessary condition for successful arms control?
   a. proliferation
   b. verification
   c. microwave observation satellites
   d. interdiction
   e. advanced technological research and development

---

13. **a.** *The nuclear powers are the United States, the Soviet Union, China, Great Britain, and France. See page 638.*

14. **e.** *Scientists calculate that nuclear war would produce a "nuclear winter" because immense clouds of smoke and soot would prevent the sun's rays from warming the earth. See page 644.*

15. **a.** *Mutual deterrence works best if the sides are evenly balanced, for then there is no obvious advantage to starting a war. However, if one side is superior, it may be tempted to use its superiority aggressively; and if one side is inferior, it may be tempted to strike before its position gets any worse. See pages 645–646.*

16. **c.** *The lesson of sociology is that, in the final analysis, it is the acts of countless individuals that create and shape society and history. See page 649.*

17. **a.** *A postindustrial society thrives on the free and open exchange of information. If the Soviet Union moves from a predominantly industrial to a predominantly postindustrial mode of production, some loosening of totalitarian controls seems inevitable; the Soviet people may gain a greater say in their destiny. See page 650.*

18. **b.** *Countries with a history of hostility tend to mistrust one another, and will not reduce their own weaponry unless they are sure the other side is doing the same. Thus some means of verification is necessary, so that each side can be sure the other is complying with the terms of their agreement. See page 646.*

19. The history of arms control shows that
    a. agreements between the superpowers are virtually impossible
    b. both superpowers have faithfully adhered to the terms of agreements.
    c. a number of significant arms-control treaties have been achieved.
    d. the Soviet Union will not agree to arms control.
    e. smaller nations continue to hamper efforts at disarmament.

20. The Soviet Union faces a nuclear threat from
    a. the United States only.
    b. the United States and Great Britain.
    c. the United States and China.
    d. Poland and Czechoslovakia.
    e. every other nuclear power in the world.

21. The peace-making efforts of the United Nations are hampered by the fact that
    a. compliance with U.N. resolutions is voluntary.
    b. less than half the nations of the world are members.
    c. the United States does not recognize the rulings of the World Court.
    d. communist countries are now the single largest voting bloc.
    e. such efforts did not prove effective in the past.

22. The United States did not use nuclear weapons to win the war in Vietnam because
    a. it had no nuclear weapons at that time.
    b. nuclear weapons would be useless in a civil war.
    c. American public opinion would not have tolerated such use of nuclear weapons.
    d. China would have retaliated with its own nuclear weapons.
    e. top decision-makers worried about the long-term health consequences involved in making such a decision.

23. According to the text, nations that make extensive military preparations
    a. generally manage to avoid war.
    b. always get involved in war.
    c. are likely to get involved in war.
    d. only attack nations that lack such preparations.
    e. only get involved in wars of their own choosing.

---

19. **c.** *Many arms-control agreements have already been achieved—some multilateral, involving many nations, and some bilateral, involving just the United States and the Soviet Union. See page 646.*

20. **e.** *One reason for Soviet insecurity is that, unlike the United States, it does not have only one nuclear enemy: it has four—the United States, China, France, and Great Britain. See page 648.*

21. **a.** *No country is willing to give up its sovereignty to an international body, and the United Nations has no means of enforcing its resolutions on independent states. See page 648.*

22. **c.** *American public opinion places an informal constraint on the use of the country's nuclear weapons, even though those weapons might have been effective in local conflicts in Korea, Vietnam, or elsewhere. See page 649.*

23. **c.** *Nations that make military preparations tend to provoke similar preparations in their existing or potential enemies. The result is often a cycle of mistrust and hostility that eventually leads to war. See page 627.*

24.  Which of the following effects of a nuclear explosion would be *least* likely to cause direct damage to human beings?
    a.  heat
    b.  electromagnetic pulse
    c.  direct radiation
    d.  blast
    e.  fallout radiation

25.  Lifton's study of Hiroshima survivors showed that their immediate reaction was
    a.  panic
    b.  hysteria
    c.  hatred
    d.  mental paralysis
    e.  looting

---

24.  **b.**  *Electromagnetic pulse destroys electronic circuits, but is basically harmless to human beings. The other effects can all be lethal. See page 640.*

25.  **d.**  *It seems that the "normal" human response to the destruction of one's world is apparent apathy—a shutdown of thought and emotions as protection against the horror. See page 642.*

## A CASE STUDY

NAME

COURSE/SECTION NUMBER

On the cover of a weekly news magazine, a young face stares out blankly. The young man's eyes blaze with determination and anger. In his hands he holds a high-powered rifle; a round of ammunition is wrapped across his chest. He couldn't be more than sixteen, and perhaps as young as twelve, but his expression bears none of the innocence of childhood.

This picture illustrates an article about Shiite Muslim soldiers in Lebanon; their training, their commitment, and their spiritual zeal. It isn't the first time in history that religious convictions have been evoked to justify killing and war. In this case, the young man had volunteered for military service and was being trained to die in a suicide bombing. In his equivalent of "boot camp," the young man and his peers begin the day with prayer and religious instruction. Many of the lessons focus on the glory of death in the name of their deity, and the wonders of the afterlife each young man would experience when his mission was complete. After a hard day of physical conditioning and practice drills, the young men relax over the evening meal, often returning to the topic of the afterlife, or the glorious funeral celebration that would be held in their honor.

1.   Like the Japanese kamakaze pilots, the suicide bombers in the Middle East violate a basic assumption about warfare: that each soldier wants to live. What are the cultural supports for the very different view that knowingly giving one's life is a valued act? What are the implications for warfare and weaponry if terrorists can rely on sacrificial soldiers?

2.   What are examples of collective action within the countries of the Middle East that support the state of war? How is war socially structured?

3.   These countries do not operate within a military-industrial complex. What replaces that complex as the "fuel" for war? How does a country get young men to eagerly enlist for missions that will surely result in their deaths?

# Applying the Concepts

NAME

COURSE/SECTION NUMBER

## APPLICATION EXERCISE ONE

For this exercise, identify a current (or recent) conflict or war involving two or more countries, or a civil war within a country. Examples include: Iran versus Iraq, factions in Lebanon, factions in Uganda or Mozambique, border skirmishes between North and South Korea, Israeli versus Palestinian settlements, Contra versus Sandanista forces in Nicaragua, and so forth.

1.   Discuss the history of the conflict, identifying the points of tension that precipitated the war and those that perpetuate it.

2.   Do you have evidence of propaganda that shows each side "demonizing" the other?

3.   What is the role of the superpowers in this conflict?

4.   How is this war a socially structured activity? What are the roles, rules, and relationships involved in keeping the war going?

## APPLICATION EXERCISE TWO

NAME

COURSE/SECTION NUMBER

Political and religious leaders all cry out for world peace. In this exercise, you will take a look at how political and religious groups go about the work of achieving peace. Identify a group that is much concerned with peace. Consider major religious denominations, Clergy and Laity Concerned, Scientists Against Nuclear War, or anti-nuclear and peace groups in your community.

1. Find out what statement about peace orients the group's activities. If possible, attach that statement, or paraphrase it.

2. In what ways is this group part of a social movement? What actions has the group taken to change current laws or public policies toward more peaceful ends?

3. Evaluate the extent to which this group has approached its goals of peace. How might it be more successful?

## APPLICATION EXERCISE THREE

NAME

COURSE/SECTION NUMBER

When the war in Vietnam ended over a decade ago, soldiers came home to a country in turmoil and one in which there was little appreciation for the fighting they had done. A cohort of young men (and women) were caught up in that war, as soldiers, as draftees or draft resisters, as conscientious objectors, as protestors, or as friends and family. For many people, the war in Vietnam was a failure: some see it as a conflict that the United States should have never entered; some see it as a war that could have been won if U.S. military power had been put to full use. In the years since the war, books and movies have reinterpreted that painful time in Vietnam and here in the United States.

1.   Review a movie such as "The Killing Fields," "The Deerhunter," or "Platoon." How has the image of the war and those who fought in it shifted from 1973 to the year in which this film was made?

2.   What is the current image of the Vietnam war as reflected in print media—magazines, novels, non-fiction?

3.    Why did it take a decade for Americans to build a memorial to the 35,000 people who died in Vietnam?

4.    How do you think the Vietnam war will be presented in history books for students both in the United States and Vietnam who were not born when the war ended?